About the Author

Alexandra McRobert is a 500-hour registered yoga teacher educator, certified life coach, and holds a Bachelor of Arts and a Bachelor of Education from Queen's University in Canada. She has lived overseas since she was twenty-three in Kuwait, Abu Dhabi and Bali, Indonesia. Alex founded The Mindful Life Practice, a worldwide community for those seeking connection and spirituality on a recovery journey – whether that is recovery from alcohol addiction or something else. Alex teaches yoga online and in-person in Bali, and she leads retreats in Bali and around the world. She also runs 200-hour and 300-hour yoga teacher trainings. Alex is the host of the *Sober Yoga Girl Podcast*. In her free time, she writes, plays guitar, and likes to spend time with her cat, Princess.

Sober Yoga Girl

ALEXANDRA MCROBERT

First published in 2024 by Fuzzy Flamingo

ISBN: 978-1-7390943-7-9

Editing and design by Fuzzy Flamingo
www.fuzzyflamingo.co.uk

A catalogue for this book is available from the British Library.

This book is dedicated to anyone who is suffering and searching for a solution. May this book be a lighthouse to help you find your way back to the shore.

Contents

"Once we have spoken our saddest story,
we can be free of it."
– Taylor Swift

Introduction

It was in July 2020 when the idea for *Sober Yoga Girl* came to me. I don't really remember where I was or how it came about; I just remember that I began. Once I started writing, I couldn't stop. It was like I was digging myself out of a deep, dark, hole with every word I put on the page.

On the 8th of August 2020, I wrote the following post on *Facebook*:

> *About 14 days and 83,895 words later, I finally got to the happy ending of my first draft of my memoir.*
>
> *I have no idea what I'll do with this book. But I have to say, now I understand why Augusten Burrows said he wrote his way out of addiction (qtd in Felsenthal). If you haven't tried writing yet, I highly recommend it. Even if it's just for you.*

I thought this was the ending, but it was actually the beginning. I spent the following year, until June 2021, working with my first editor, Saloni Lakhia. We met every week for a few hours and dissected, reorganized and simplified the book's content. It is thanks to her that this story got its seven-*chakra* structure, and I was able to release the least important parts of the story and lean into the most important parts.

I found this writing, editing and revising process more beneficial than therapy. In being forced to make sense of and organize the story of my book, I made sense of and organized the story of my life. Thank you, Saloni, for guiding me through that process.

The book stayed on my hard drive for a few years when I pitched my book to traditional publishers (and got rejected). I wondered if it would ever go anywhere. During that time, my international yoga business grew, I was able to quit my full-time job as a school teacher, and I moved from Abu Dhabi to Bali, Indonesia. I began traveling around the world running yoga retreats and yoga teacher trainings. Several painful events I wrote about in the original book came full circle: I had an opportunity to resolve conflicts, heal wounds and move forward. The book continued to evolve and change. And as I thought more and more about self-publishing, I decided to do it, because nothing about my career has been traditional: from choosing sobriety in my late twenties, to launching a *Zoom* sober yoga community, to running a business where I can work remotely and travel around the world. So, why start doing things traditionally now?

I decided to work with Jen Parker on a second edit, and this edit was a process of once again revising, rewriting and really reflecting on what mattered to me, more than three years after I wrote the book. I was able to witness my own personal growth and evolution during that time, and how the world has changed, too. I spent the year of 2023 working with her.

In early 2024, some of my friends, former colleagues, and yoga students read the book and gave me feedback. This is when the book finally came to life. Thank you to the handful of people involved in this phase, including the characters in the book (who go by different names in real life) Atif, Saad, and friends Fran and Yasmine, for taking the time to read this book and give me feedback.

I also want to give a very special thanks to Sarah Millman, my third editor, who is also one of my yoga students, retreat guests and Yoga Teacher Training graduates. Sarah thoroughly edited this book for a third and final time, focusing on continuity and sentence structure. Sarah played such a massive role in the final edition, which Jen Parker also supported in typesetting and bringing through to publishing in the end.

During this time, we worked on an extensive works cited list for the book. Every effort has been made to acknowledge the original teachers, writers and leaders who have inspired me.

I also visited both Saloni Lakhia, my first editor, and Anvita Dixit, my yoga philosophy teacher, in person in Mumbai, India in early 2024. Anvita gifted me a copy of *Pātañjala Yoga Sūtra: Sanskṛta Sūtras* authored by Dr P.V. Karambelkar, published by the yoga institution where she grew up, Kaivalyadhama. It is one of the oldest yoga institutions in the world. It is 100 years old. I want to thank Anvita for educating me on the authentic teachings of yoga from India, which I have done my best to incorporate into this book, using her teachings and this reference as a guide.

My 200-hour yoga teacher training manual had the following words written on the inside of the cover: "Ong Namo Guru Dev Namo". The translation of this phrase is, "I recognize and bow to the teachers and teachings that carry us from darkness into light". In 2019, when I traveled to Massachusetts to train with my teacher Rolf Gates, he taught me that yoga doesn't belong to anyone. He said, "It's been passed from heart to heart, through thousands of years." I want to acknowledge all of the teachers who passed this wisdom to me, including:

- Rolf Gates, who was my teacher long before I met him in 2019. His book, *Meditations from the Mat,* is what lit the spark of inspiration to follow this path. Thank you, Rolf.
- All of my teachers at Samatva Yoga in Kingston, Ontario, Canada, who were my very first teachers from 2010-2015.
- All of the educators in Baja California, Mexico, where I graduated from my 200-hour yoga teacher training in 2014.
- All of the teachers in Bali, Indonesia, where I graduated from my 300-hour yoga teacher training in 2017.

- Tommy Rosen, with whom I had the gift of attending a Recovery 2.0 retreat in India in 2024.
- The many teachers I have been blessed to be guided by along the way around the world, particularly in Kuwait, Abu Dhabi and Bali, who are too many to mention.

This book would never have been written if it weren't for Dan Kumar. Dan, my psychic healer, transformed the entire course of my life in May 2019 and is still to this day one of my biggest cheerleaders and supports. If I had never met him, all of this would still be a dream. Dan was the catalyst for me manifesting this reality. Through believing in my potential, Dan helped me believe in myself. Thank you, Dan.

When I finally decided to move forward with the book in 2024, I was glad that I'd waited so long for it to be published. I had so many years to sit and reflect on the true purpose of this story, and how I can move forward with it, with three yogic philosophies in mind: 1) *ahiṃsā*: causing as little harm as possible; 2) *satya*: telling the truth as I personally recall it; and 3) following my *dharma*, including my experiences in the story only if they serve a purpose: both the book's purpose and my life's purpose.

The disclaimer is: In this book, other than my family, none of the characters really exist. They're a combination of many people I met along the way in Canada, Kuwait, Abu Dhabi and now Bali, with made-up names and character traits. There's no hero or villain in the story – because there is good and bad in all of us. As well, some of the locations and timelines have been changed. But everything that I've written about in *Sober Yoga Girl* did happen, in my recollection and opinion.

My story is unique because I traveled and lived around the world and had different experiences in each place during my twenties. I want to be clear that no place is good or bad and none of the stories are reflections themselves of the countries in which they occur. Every experience is based on me and who I was at the time I experienced it – more so than the location in which I found myself.

I want to give thanks and gratitude to my parents, my sister and, by extension, the rest of my family, for giving me the freedom and space to share my truth, even if at times it has been painful.

And finally, to my Santiago, though he goes by a different name in real life. Elizabeth Gilbert wrote in *Eat, Pray, Love*:

> *People think a soul mate is your perfect fit, and that's what everyone wants. But a true soul mate [*sic.*] is a mirror, the person who shows you everything that is holding you back, the person who brings you to your own attention so you can change your life. A true soul mate is probably the most important person you'll ever meet, because they tear down your walls and smack you awake … Soul mates, they come into your life just to reveal another layer of yourself to you, and then they leave … [A soul mate's] purpose was to shake you up … tear apart your ego a little bit, show you your obstacles and addictions, break your heart open so new light could get in, make you so desperate and out of control that you had to transform your life, then introduce you to your spiritual master…* [*sic.*] (246)

If this definition is true, then I suppose I married my soulmate after all.

The biggest thanks goes to Santiago – for not only playing this role in my life, but for giving me the permission, support and encouragement to publish this story, even if our story didn't end with a 'happily ever after'. Thank you, Santiago. Your support of this book, *Sober Yoga Girl,* means the world to me.

Brené Brown wrote, "One day you will tell your story of how you overcame what you went through and it will be someone else's survival guide." (Halpert 1)

It is my hope that this book can become someone's survival guide.

With love,

Alex

PART ONE

Root *Chakra* – I Am Grounded

The first *chakra* is the root *chakra*. It is the color red and is located at the base of the spine. The Sanskrit term for this *chakra* is *muladhara*, which means 'root support'. The root *chakra* forms our foundation. It is about our home, finances, and grounding. It's related to our survival instincts. If we have any feelings of insecurity, abandonment or a lack of self-confidence, that might mean our root *chakra* is imbalanced (Judith 34).

ROOT *CHAKRA* YOGA CLASS SERIES:

In times of uncertainty, chaos, and stress, we need our mindfulness practices more than ever, which is why I've created for you a special series called "Grounded".

"Grounded" is for absolute beginners, but students of any level can enjoy it.

By the end of the eight classes, you will know all the foundational poses of yoga, and different breath practices to bring you into balance.

Join me for "Grounded" to cultivate inner peace – and learn how to use that inner peace to help those around you.

https://bit.ly/TheMindfulLifePractice_Grounded

ROOT *CHAKRA* PHOTO LIBRARY:

On The Mindful Life Practice blog, you can check out photos from my childhood and young adulthood, written about in The Root *Chakra* section of the book, here: https://www.themindfullifepractice.com/post/childhood-memories

CHAPTER 1

THE ENDING

I was twenty-five years old when I came closest to dying by suicide.

"Ashhadu an la ilaha illa Allah…"

3:19am. I was half sleeping, anyway, but any part of me that was asleep rolled over and woke up to the haunting call to prayer echoing through my apartment. I'd lived in Mahboula, Kuwait for two years, a few feet away from a mosque – and it had become familiar to hear this call every morning.

In most parts of the world, the darkest and quietest part of the night is right before dawn. Not in Mahboula. By four in the morning, water trucks were backing up, street dogs were barking, and hundreds of workers were beginning their day. They were waking up in their dorm rooms, descending from their apartments and forming lines on the road below. Crowded shuttle buses would take them to their construction sites to start their workdays. It was close to fifty degrees Celsius outside, and I could imagine salty sweat was already dripping off these men's foreheads as they stood outside waiting for their buses.

I lay in bed hearing the chaos that I'd lived amongst for two years, but my mind was disassociated from the present moment. Mentally, I had left the here and now. I was floating far above my body, viewing it from overhead. I could see myself curled up in a fetal position on the mattress. My imagination took me further – up the elevator, to the top floor of the building, the thirteenth floor. I'd ascended the staircase to the roof. I'd had to climb over water tanks to get to the ledge. The orange sun would soon be beginning to rise over the neighborhood. I'd feel the hot, sticky, dusty wind on my skin. The sounds from the road below would get quieter and eerier. I'd look beyond the ledge, seeing the tiny workers, the water trucks, the buses, the sand, the dust and the sky. I imagined jumping into the air and feeling nothing as I fell through the sky for ten seconds. My fall would be broken only by the concrete below, blood splattering and limbs flattening. And it finally would be over.

Four hours before, I had experienced a heartbreaking ending. I had returned to Kuwait at midnight to meet my husband after a trip to Canada, for a short stopover before we took the next flight to Bali for our honeymoon. After he left, I planned to stay longer in Ubud for my 300-hour advanced yoga teacher training. I'd been looking forward to this trip since I'd booked it a year earlier, before I'd even met him. But now, I no longer wanted to go to Bali at all.

"*Chaparrita*," he greeted me as he wrapped me in a hug after getting out of the airport taxi in Mahboula. *Chaparrita* was the nickname I'd come to love from him, which he told me meant 'cute girl' in Spanish. He helped me carry my heavy duffle bag through the dusty, dreary courtyard, into the dull metal elevators upstairs to our new apartment, which we'd moved into only ten days before. He wanted to show me what he'd been working on while I was away.

He'd built a wooden kitchen island for our pots and pans, refitted our makeshift bathtub to have proper plumbing, and even hung a sign that said 'Santiago and Alex' on the refrigerator door. He'd picked up hummus and pita from the grocery store because he knew it was my favorite snack. I tried to force myself to eat it while I watched him open the gift I'd bought in Canada;

two Canadian T-shirt souvenirs. I picked the salt and pepper red T-shirt because I liked it, and the geometric blue T-shirt because I knew he'd like it. I sat down on the bed and looked at him. I hadn't planned what to say or prepared for this moment. My mind drew a blank. The silence was deafening while I tried to gather up the courage to speak. "I stopped wearing the diamond ring," I whispered.

"What?" he asked me.

I cleared my throat. "I'm not wearing the ring anymore."

He looked at me, confused. "Why not?"

"I can't wear it anymore. I love you, but I'm not in love with you."

CHAPTER 2

THE TRUTH

For years I lied about what really happened, telling different versions of this story to different people, keeping secrets and living in shame. Some of my best friends messaged me immediately after the engagement announcement, and I responded saying, "Don't tell anyone, but we're actually married… and I'm kind of freaking out about it." A few of my closest relatives still think I was only engaged to this man from Mexico who was part of my life for a short period of time in my early twenties. When I was living in Abu Dhabi, many of my colleagues didn't even know that this part of my life existed at all, and they thought that I was always the happy-go-lucky girl that they got to know in November of 2017.

This is the truth of what really happened: When I was twenty-four, I met Santiago, a man from Mexico living in Kuwait. In Kuwait, living with a partner outside of marriage is *haram*, or forbidden. So, less than eight months later, due to circumstances that seemed right at the time, we decided to get married. We read online that getting married in Kuwait was time-consuming and was only possible if both expats held valid residence visas, which Santiago didn't as he was between jobs. So, due to Santiago's lack of documentation, we didn't qualify to get married in the country in which we lived. The marriage felt urgent: we were living together out of wedlock and needed a marriage certificate to legally do so. We'd faced threats from security guards where he previously lived. We were moving apartments and didn't know if we'd be able to live in our new place together, being unmarried. We didn't have the time to travel to Canada or Mexico for a wedding, so we chose to elope.

Both of us knew couples who had eloped in Cyprus to make their lives easier in the Middle East. Whether they were pregnant out of wedlock or needed the paperwork to live together, Cyprus was known as the Las Vegas of the region for last minute, spontaneous weddings.

We could arrange the paperwork on Sunday, fly on Thursday, get married on Friday, and return as newlyweds on Saturday, giving the appearance on social media as if it were any other long weekend trip. We had one long weekend in April and were set to move into a new apartment in June. So that was how we ended up leaving Kuwait one day in late April as boyfriend and girlfriend and returning seventy-two hours later as husband and wife.

We were legally married before we were even engaged. After getting married at 9:30am on a Friday, popping bottles of champagne and shotgunning cans of beer all morning and afternoon, Santiago 'proposed' to me around twelve hours later, by getting down on one knee and revealing a diamond ring in a small, black box on a pitch-black, starry, empty beach. "Marriage is an army of two," was one of the beautiful phrases he said to me in his proposal. That's all I could remember, partially because I was numb from drinking all day, and partially because I was already panicking inside. *How do I say "no" when I've already said "yes"?* I disassociated from the moment. We stumbled down the beach for a few rounds of shots before eventually making it back to our hotel room. Hungover and running on a few hours of sleep, we caught an early flight back to Kuwait the next morning.

The next evening, doom was already dawning on me. This person, who I barely knew, was now my husband. By midnight we were already back in Kuwait, and influenced by his excitement, we announced to the world on *Facebook* and *Instagram* that we were engaged, when we'd actually already signed the papers and made the marriage official twenty-four hours before. Minor details. As the weeks went on, we started planning a wedding at a remote, countryside castle in Mexico for the following year, leading everyone to believe we weren't married yet – when we actually were.

When I gave him back the diamond ring, all of this flashed before me. It wasn't as simple as handing it back and saying goodbye. We'd legally and verbally agreed to be an 'army of two'. Now, I wasn't even an 'army of one'. I was defeated. And it wasn't over.

CHAPTER 3

THE VILLAIN IN THE STORY

What followed that moment in Mahboula between Santiago and I, when I gave him back the diamond ring and told him I was not in love with him? It's hard for me to say because I can't recall the words, moments, or specifics. It's all a dusty orange apocalyptic haze, like the streets in the Middle East when there is a sandstorm. Not just because it's years later, but because even as it happened, I was disconnected from the moment. I was separated from reality and operating on autopilot (as I had been throughout the entire time we were married). I just remember him leaving me by sunrise, announcing he was off to the Cyprus embassy to get us divorced (as if a divorce were as simple as one person in a marriage popping down to the embassy and requesting it). I lay in bed, curled in a fetal position, convinced I was an awful, selfish, narcissistic person. I am not sure if he said those words to me, or if I said them to myself. I know that I was planning over and over again to ride up the dingy, steel elevator to the thirteenth floor on the top of the building, to jump off the roof to my death.

Over and over again, the words played on a loop in my brain: "I am a terrible person." I was the villain in the story. I had decided that I didn't deserve to live anymore. I decided I had done something unforgivable. How could I be such a complete narcissist that I married someone and, eight weeks later, said "see you later"? How could I put him through the embarrassment, the shame, the sadness and the heartbreak? The guilt felt insurmountable, and

I couldn't see him ever forgiving me, nor me forgiving myself. The best solution seemed to be to end my life. In this moment of despair, jumping off a building seemed to be the only way out.

How had I ended up here? In Mahboula, about to be divorced, visualizing standing on the roof of a building, at age twenty-five? At that moment, I didn't really know the answer to that question. It felt like my life had spun so out of control in the previous months that it has taken years of self-reflection to even trace the steps backwards to tell you the story. I knew this: that despite ninety-five percent of me thinking I didn't deserve to live, there was a small force within me that was fighting it. As bad as things were, there was some force, deep down within me, that kept me safe. There was a part of me that didn't want to give up. And as I repeatedly imagined, over and over again, riding up that elevator to the thirteenth floor of the tower and jumping off the roof, that force helped me to see that I actually didn't need to get on that ledge. What I needed was to get on another flight back home. I needed to go to Canada, where I'd come from only a day before. Or it would be the end of my life.

CHAPTER 4

THE UNIVERSAL LESSON

I read a post once on Gabby Bernstein's *Instagram* that said, "You'll continue to attract the same person in different bodies until you show up for the universal lesson."

When I originally wrote this book in 2020, I started a chapter with the following sentence: "My childhood was not unlike any other childhood from the era, culture and society in which I was raised." Up until very recently, I would have described myself as having a 'normal' childhood. From my perception, I grew up in a middle-class home in a privileged part of Toronto with my mom, dad and sister.

My childhood was not what I would define as 'traumatic' up until recently. There was always food on the table, my physical needs were always met, and every problem was swept under the rug and not discussed. I was kept sheltered from the generational trauma that was part of both sides of my family.

It took me almost thirty years to realize a few things:

First of all, every single person has experienced trauma in their life. Trauma is part of life, and it's unavoidable. When we are able to heal from our trauma, then we are okay. It is unhealed trauma that manifests issues in the mind, body and soul.

And second, just because what I perceived to be a major trauma did not happen to me as a child doesn't mean that my childhood wasn't traumatic.

I originally wrote this book in 2020 with no references to my childhood story. The reason I made this choice was because

I found it difficult to discuss my story in a balanced way. I also avoided mentioning many of my relatives in the book because I wanted to honor and respect my family's story. A family story does not just belong to one person – it belongs to every family member. Unlike most of the stories in this book, with people from my past where names can be changed, altered and made anonymous, my relatives will always be my relatives.

In 2022, when undergoing my own healing journey, I made the decision to add in a chapter about my family story. I felt writing about my family story was necessary for a few reasons: 1) the readers could understand where I came from and why I was the way I was and 2) expressing my truth about my family was essential for my own recovery journey. The chapter was forty-five pages long. I sat with the story.

Upon later reflection, in 2023, I made a decision to once again remove this chapter from the book. When we practice the *yama(s)* of yoga, we practice both *ahiṃsā* – loving kindness – and *satya* – truth. Yes, my childhood story is my truth – however, *ahiṃsā* must always be applied to determine if a truth should be spoken. If someone may be needlessly harmed by truth, then silence may be a more skillful choice. We have to consider what we say, how we say it, and the way in which it will affect others.

In writing the story, I processed the trauma, and I let it go. I made peace with it, and I found closure. And so, I decided when it came time to publish the book that my family story doesn't need to be a chapter in it.

What I will say is whether consciously or not, parts of both of my parents' childhoods were replicated in my childhood and had an impact on me. These inherited dynamics are a normal part of everyone's childhood experience. That being said, I have the deepest compassion for my parents and all the adults who raised me. They were all doing the best they could with what they were given. When I was on a Recovery 2.0 retreat in India in 2024, Tommy Rosen said something like, "I had a tough childhood.

But I wouldn't trade that for my mom's childhood or my dad's childhood, because their childhoods were tougher." And just because my parents didn't heal all of the generational trauma that they inherited doesn't mean they didn't heal some of it.

Nicole La Pera, The Holistic Psychologist on *Instagram*, wrote, "We're subconsciously attracted to partners who have the same traits as a parent we had a conflicted relationship with. This is the subconscious mind attempting to repair our original wound."

To my relatives who I am disconnected from – I love you, from a distance.

CHAPTER 5

THE ROOT OF THE PROBLEM

Up until very recently, I accepted the western medical model of mental health. I believed that I was genetically born with bipolar disorder. I believed that there was a chemical imbalance in my brain, and nothing would make it better except pills.

I now have a completely different view of mental health. At one point in my life, a Western diagnosis and medication were lifesaving, and I recognize that for many people, medications are crucial for their well-being. But I personally no longer believe I have a chemical imbalance in my brain, nor do I believe that medication is required to "fix" me. I believe that given the trauma I went through and experienced as a child and teenager, and the lack of support and coping skills with which I was equipped, it is absolutely normal that my brain would be functioning in the way it was. Like most children from my generation, and the generations before, I was given no education on nutrition and exercise and how it impacts mental health, no therapy, no coaching, no sharing circles, no yoga and no meditation. According to the mental health statistics that were provided by John Hopkins Hospital in 2024, "1 in 4 adults suffer from a diagnosable mental health disorder" ("Mental health disorder statistics"). Moreover, every year, more than 40,000 Americans die from suicide ("Suicide and Self-Harm Injury").

When you visit a Western medical doctor for illness, you'll be tested, given prescription drugs, and sent on your way. The Western medical model tends to view each organ and system of the body as separate. Eastern medicine, in contrast, looks at everything as interrelated and connected: our body, mind and soul. There are a few models within yoga philosophy that look at this interconnectedness, one of which being the *chakra* system (Judith 25).

The *chakra* system refers to energy centers in the body. There are several *chakra* models, however the most widely accepted model is the seven *chakras* which run along the spine. The *chakras* start at the root of the spine and move all the way up to the crown. When the *chakras* are open, balanced and healed, so are we: open, balanced and healed (Judith 25).

I got accepted to university in Canada for the Concurrent Education program – the most competitive program in the province. This acceptance meant that, instead of applying to a Bachelor of Education degree post-undergrad, I could complete my Bachelor of Arts alongside my Bachelor of Education at the same time. Entrance into this program meant I didn't need to worry about my grades during my time in undergrad because, as long as I maintained a minimum average of around seventy percent, I'd be automatically accepted into the faculty of education in my fifth year at the school.

As a teenager in high school, I was a contradiction. I spent every weekend lying to my parents and sneaking off to house parties, yet I maintained a high-grade average. I was the editor-in-chief of the high school newspaper. I sang in the choir and organized events like Charity Week, fundraising car washes and leadership weekends. I was given the most prestigious award for graduates upon commencement.

At age eighteen, I always needed control, always needed a plan, always needed to know what the next step in life was. I couldn't just go with the flow and see how things unfolded for me. (Note: when one of my Yoga Teacher Training graduates, Sarah, was reading this book and editing it prior to publication, she commented, "You have changed a lot!" And she's right. I am much more comfortable with change and uncertainty ten years later.) This discomfort with spontaneity is why Concurrent Education appealed. It had a clear professional goal at the end, unlike a more generalized degree. There were only a couple of universities offering this degree within driving distance of the city of Toronto, so I accepted the offer.

What I remember about my childhood was that when I was happy, I beamed, and when I was sad, I broke. I lived my life in two extremes: there was no in between. I was a bright, bubbly, blonde girl, taking center stage in musical theater performances, yet I was also known to be overdramatic and to overexaggerate. From age nine or ten, sometimes one comment would send me over the edge, and I would cry uncontrollably, endlessly, seemingly for no reason. I wrote my first suicide note at age twelve. When my sister came upon this note when reading my diary and told my mom about it in tears, my mom asked me, "You weren't really planning to kill yourself, were you?" I passed it off as a creative writing exercise, and we never spoke of it again.

Looking back on my teenage years, I can pinpoint what I think was the first time I experienced not just mood swings, but a mild depressive episode over a long period of time. When I was in ninth grade, in high school, I wasn't very popular. In this era, we were in the early days of *Facebook*, and all of my classmates were documenting and posting about all of the parties I wasn't invited to. I spent hours each day signed in to *Facebook*, looking at other people's albums and uploads, feeling like a huge loser.

Everything changed when I met an older boy, in grade twelve, who asked me out on a date. He quickly became my boyfriend, and I suddenly went from being a nobody to being cool. Only two things in my life had changed: I had a boyfriend, and I'd started going to parties. From then on, I had a subconscious association that partying and having a boyfriend would make me popular.

After a year of being together, he broke up with me when he moved to university. At the same time, my sister went away to school, and my parents had begun dealing with legal battles unfolding within my dad's family. I felt very alone and, at times, I also felt invisible to my parents, as they whispered when I was out of the room in anxious tones about what was going on. My mom also frequently started traveling for business during this time, and my dad stayed at work late at night, so often I would find myself alone at home, which I didn't mind – it was better than the alternative.

My depression and partying accelerated. I'd get drunk, looking for boys at parties to hook up with, desperate to find a boyfriend to fill the void my ex left and distract me from how invisible I felt to my parents, both of whom were caught up in their own story. I was looking for the light. I was unaware that the light wasn't something I needed to find in the outside world – the light was something I needed to find within myself. The light would come from an *internal* healing journey, not an external one.

What I was going through was hard, but it wasn't enough to debilitate me. I managed it, somehow. My community at high school and my extracurricular activities gave me a sense of purpose and grounded me throughout this experience. I had teachers who were anchors. I kept myself busy – volunteering for every position, every job, every opportunity possible – to get me out of the house. My first real depressive episode came two years later, at age eighteen, when I went away to university.

The university I chose was one of the oldest universities in Canada, and it's known for its fairy tale cobblestone roads and limestone buildings. I had been looking forward to going away to study all throughout high school. For the first time in my life, I would have 'my own place' – a big residence room. I had full control of my life and my decisions. I was away from my parents, who were very difficult to be around at this point. They were on the brink of divorce, and I could feel the tension of that impending separation whenever I was home. University was going to be my getaway. Yet university didn't solve my problems like I thought it would. As the leaves fell, the days got shorter and the sky got darker, I got more and more down about everything.

It wasn't that I wasn't making friends or meeting people – I had a few close friends from high school that came with me to university. I also made good friends with my neighbor in residence, Nick, on the first day I moved in. After moving all my things into my dorm room and getting me set up, somehow my parents and I met and started talking to him. He was likable and friendly. Feeling happy I'd made a friend so quickly, my parents drove off, back to Toronto, leaving me hanging out in Nick's dorm room with his roommate, Zach. Nick was also from Toronto and had a great sense of humor. We immediately connected.

I wasn't alone, but what was challenging was that I was suddenly a small fish in a big pond. I had been a ten out of ten student all my life, but it seemed like at the university I went to everyone else was too. Most of my classes had over five hundred participants. Getting accepted into academic faculties and extracurricular positions were both extremely competitive. I gave one hundred percent, but it was never enough. I tried to find a place for myself but faced rejection after rejection from committees, teams and clubs. I eventually lost confidence, feeling like I wasn't worthy of these things, and I shrank back into my shell. I was simply another white blonde girl in a sea of white blonde girls at university.

I grew up in the nineties, when fast food and microwaved meals were the norm. By the time I got to university, education on how nutritious food and exercise would keep your body healthy was becoming mainstream. But I lacked awareness on how deeply these things would keep my mind healthy, as well. I didn't realize that what I ate, how I slept and how much exercise I got could have a trickle effect on my mood. I had no resources for mindfulness or mental health and no vocabulary to describe what was going on within me.

Everything was slipping away from me, except for the party scene – that was the one place where I fit in. I held onto it like somebody who is shipwrecked holds onto a plank of wood. I spent most nights having cheap vodka shots in dorm rooms and skipped a lot of Orientation Week because I was too exhausted for the morning events. As the fall semester carried on, I got more and more into partying, and it became harder and harder for me to get out of bed in the morning and make it to class on time.

I knew that the university I went to offered four free mental health counseling sessions a year for students, but I was too afraid or ashamed to go. I spent most of my time that fall in my residence room, crying.

Depression was manageable for me because I never lost control. I was the only person who was affected by my sadness and feelings of hopelessness. My suicidal thoughts didn't hurt anyone else. It was the mania that really was a problem because, when I was manic, I'd lose control. When I was manic, I'd make decisions that lacked good judgment. Mania can leave a trail of regret behind you. Hurt feelings, poor judgment and mistakes that you later have to clean up. I always felt like my depression did not impact others around me. But it was the mania that sent me to seek help.

In my second year of university, I was in distress. This was just prior to my parents' decision to get a divorce, and tension was high at their house. I avoided visiting them in Toronto as much as I could.

I had the least healthy habits at this point. I was partying a few nights a week, chasing relationships with men, and feeling heartbroken and distraught when they broke up with me. One night I had friends over for a dinner party, which led to the bar, which led to Nick coming back to my house. "Ever since I met you, I always knew we had a special connection," he said to me. Our relationship escalated, and we started spending more and more time together over the next three or four months.

After so many failed relationships, building a relationship with someone I had been close friends with felt different. It felt hopeful. But one day, I was standing in the reception of the yoga studio, operating the front desk, when I got a text from him out of nowhere. "I'm really busy with schoolwork, and it isn't the right time for a girlfriend." I was confused by this message. Where did this come from? What happened to our special connection?

I could not stop crying, and nothing made it stop. I called my parents, but they had difficulty understanding it. To the outsider, it didn't make sense. It was just a boy, right? Why couldn't I just get over it? Why couldn't I let it go?

Many years later, I am now able to understand that every time I had a breakdown, it was never about the boyfriend who broke my heart. In reality, eighteen years of unhealed wounds and trauma was spilling out of me.

I'd created a story in my head that my entire self-worth was based on whether or not I had a boyfriend, and since boyfriends were continuously breaking my heart, I believed I was unlovable. Everyone else seemed to be capable of handling life's stressors except me. Every failure – in particular, every failed relationship – defined me.

When I spoke on the phone to my sister, she provided me with the empathetic listening ear that I needed and, after gently allowing me to vent for over an hour, she suggested: "Alex, you should go to the university counseling office."

So, I called the counseling office, and I decided I'd go. Walking there felt like I was walking through a tunnel. Everyone around me was blurry and sounds were incoherent. I walked straight through the busy campus and up the stairs into the office without processing the classmates and friends I'd passed along the way. The hour was over in the blink of an eye. I can't remember it being in any way successful: sixty minutes later, I was just as depressed, lost and distressed as I had been an hour before. But I now know that mental health issues, like physical health issues, take time to heal. They're sometimes unsolvable in an hour. But the one suggestion that the counselor had for me was: you should try yoga.

CHAPTER 6

THE PULL TO PRACTICE YOGA

Yoga wasn't a brand-new concept to me – I had been innately drawn to it when I was ten years old, and it was offered at my school as a Yoga for Kids extracurricular. I remember flipping through the pamphlet of 'After Four' activities offered and being so excited when I came across yoga. I called my best childhood friends at the time – Charlotte and Olivia – and convinced them to sign up with me.

I don't remember most of the *āsana(s)* (postures) themselves – but the one that I do remember was *savāsana* (corpse pose). At the end of the class, I remember that we laid down on our backs, the room became dark, we closed our eyes, and the yoga teacher led us to imagine floating on clouds. It felt serene and peaceful.

What I loved about it was that, while practicing, my turbulent brain felt calm and still, for the first time ever. At that point in time, I also loved to write, and I would publish my own newspaper called *The Family Times* on A4 paper that I would mail out to my nana and grandad and my uncle Rick each month. Years later, my sister found an article from this time in my nana's closet that read, "BREAKING NEWS: ALEX WANTS TO BECOME A YOGA TEACHER WHEN SHE GROWS UP!" In hindsight, it was clear that I felt yoga was my purpose from very early on.

After the Yoga for Kids class ended, I begged my mom to allow me to continue with classes, and when I was thirteen, she took me to a beginners' yoga class for adults. My mom chose that class because it was the only yoga studio in walking distance from our house. We didn't know that there were hundreds of different modern styles of *āsana* practices and that one class could be vastly different from the next. I didn't enjoy this class as much. On the first day, when I arrived, the yoga teacher told me I'd worn the wrong pants for yoga. It was ironic because I'd worn Lululemon bell bottoms, which were the new yoga pants on the market at the time, and all the affluent moms and their daughters in my neighborhood were wearing them. I had chosen these pants specifically because that's what they were called: yoga pants. The teacher told me not to wear them again because she wouldn't be able to see and correct my postures properly. I shrank back, feeling small.

According to this teacher and this style of practice, there was a "right" and "wrong" way to do everything. The teacher picked apart every pose by having one individual demonstrate, while all the students gathered around and watched. She spent large chunks of time critiquing everyone's alignment, trying to conform our bodies to the perfect warrior one or two. Every week, I feared and dreaded she would pick me to be in the spotlight, and I'd end up on display for everyone to pick me apart. Luckily, I can't remember that ever happening – maybe she decided to skip me, sensing how insecure I was.

At that time in my life, I was just beginning to experience anxiety. I wasn't aware of it at the time, but it meant that I was constantly, profusely sweaty – particularly in my armpits and on the palms of my hands. It meant that I couldn't hold a downward facing dog without slipping right off the mat. I learned by the second class that I should bring a towel with me to lay over my mat – this helped keep my hands in place and my body upright, so I wasn't panicking as much about falling or sliding off the mat during the pose. I laid out my towel and, mid-class, the teacher announced in a poetic, overexaggerated, flowery voice, "For anyone using a towel, you need to learn how to correctly press through your finger pads and engage through the whole circumference of the palm of your hands. You don't need a towel; you just aren't engaging your hands properly."

I was mortified because, obviously, I was the only person in the room using a towel, and that comment was directed at me. I'm sure that everyone could see that. In my head, I thought that all of the people around me were thinking, "What a stupid girl who brought a towel to yoga. Everyone knows you don't need a towel for yoga!" This negative self-talk probably made me increasingly more anxious. Twenty years later, I know that we create a narrative in our own heads that shapes our experience. I bet in reality most of them were thinking, "That poor girl. She looks so anxious."

I didn't want to explain to the teacher why I needed it. If I didn't have the towel, I could not physically hold the pose. That's how sweaty and anxious I was. Without the towel, I'd slide straight off the mat and fall on my face. When I returned to yoga years later, there was a moment of looking back and remembering how anxious that one teacher made me. I prepped up by finding a yoga mat that was sticky enough and a towel that was grippy to bring with me so that I wouldn't have to worry about my sweaty hands. This preparation made me feel more at ease walking into the experience.

When I started yoga as a teenager, I never imagined that, years later, I'd be on the other side of the room, leading people through yoga classes. I learned throughout my twenties that the more uncomfortable a situation is, the more that we learn from it. Through discomfort, we gain wisdom. My young experiences in yoga shaped me. Now, as a yoga teacher, I'm mindful to never call out beginners and put them on the spot, publicly call out misalignment in their poses, or tell them that any props they have in place, such as a towel, are not allowed. My mission is to make my yoga class as safe as possible.

Years after finding and leaving yoga, after the counselor's recommendation in my second year of university, I went for my first hot yoga session. It was at a yoga studio in downtown Kingston. The studio was tiny, and when I pushed open the door, I was met with rows of shoes in the hall. There were scattered buddhas, small figurines, and racks of yoga clothes and books for sale. Incense was burning in the main room.

After checking in and taking off my shoes, I walked to the small room at the back of the studio. It was dark, candlelit and forty degrees Celsius. It had a giant stainless-steel letter on the wall, which I learned later was the '*Om*' sign. What I liked about it immediately was that it felt anonymous – it was so dark that no one would notice my mistakes. Because the room was so hot, everyone in the class had a towel, or they'd slip right off the mat – so I no longer felt like the overly sweaty, anxious one who the teacher would ask to put the towel away. I felt like I mixed in amongst the crowd.

I felt a twinge of separation anxiety when the teacher told me I had to leave my phone outside the yoga studio room – but soon the seventy-five minutes away from my BlackBerry Messenger notifications became revered. Immediately I was hooked – just like I was when I first tried yoga as a kid. It felt like the four corners of my yoga mat were the walls of a lifeboat.

When you're a beginner at yoga, everything is complicated and confusing. All of the poses were unfamiliar to me. Plus, it was a dark room, and all of my excess sweat from being in a heated room was dripping down my forehead and into my eyes. I had to continue to keep up in my head with all of the movements and poses that were brand new to me, while also stopping to wipe my sweat and guzzle water. The teacher was speaking in Sanskrit at points, a language I'd never heard before. Where was I supposed to put my hand? Where was I supposed to put my foot? I looked around the room, trying to copy what everyone else was doing. I was so distracted by trying to keep up with everything that I didn't have much time to think about anything else other than the present moment.

Towards the end of the class, we dropped into what is called pigeon pose, a deep hip opening shape. Instantly, tears were pouring out of me. I didn't feel self-conscious about it. The teacher didn't interrupt me; she just gave me the space to feel and cry. I didn't know why I was crying – I just cried. We rested in *savāsana* at the end, and just like in the kids' yoga class all those years before, I felt like I was floating on a cloud.

Walking out of the room, I mindfully moved, step by step, foot by foot, down the narrow, long hallway. I was a different person than I was seventy-five minutes before. Physically, my body felt spacious and lighter, but also mentally, I felt different. Up until that moment, I had lived my life walking with clouds of anxiety and depression always surrounding me. Now, for the first time in my life, I walked with neither around me. I didn't know what it was; I just knew that it was different. On the way out of the studio, I saw a sign advertising a thirty-day yoga challenge starting a few days later. Without a second thought, I signed up. I went to the yoga studio every single day. And I started to experience a bit of calm, a bit of balance and a bit of bliss.

Yoga became my haven. Whenever I felt like I was sliding into a space of anxiety, or slipping into depression, or my mind was beginning to race, the studio was where I went. That year, I went there every day, sometimes multiple times a day, so it was only natural that not long after, I began to work at the yoga studio. I was first offered a job cleaning the studio, which seems hilarious in retrospect as I didn't even know how to use a mop or clean a toilet when I got hired. I think I made the studio messier if anything. Not long after, I got promoted to a front desk job, managing the daily check-ins and sales. I loved everything about it – primarily the yoga classes, but also speaking to customers, running operations, and engrossing myself in books about yoga philosophy. It often felt like working at the yoga studio was my full-time job – and going to lectures and writing papers for my degrees were just hobbies that I did on the side. Yoga was becoming my way of life. My dream was to be able to make yoga my life one day. All I wanted was to become a full-time yoga teacher and start my own yoga retreat center, helping others find the joy and peace that I'd found in this practice.

"Alex, if you want to learn more about yoga, you should read *Meditations from the Mat* by Rolf Gates." This was a book recommendation from the owner of the yoga studio where I worked. I found it on the shelves of the studio and started reading it during my shifts at the front desk when the studio was empty and quiet. Immediately, it became my bible. Rolf Gates takes apart the ancient wisdom of the *Yoga Sūtra* and breaks it down into stories from his modern-day life, to make the philosophy of yoga more relatable to the modern student of yoga.

I learned 'yoga' in itself means 'union', or 'to yoke' in Sanskrit. It's not just about poses, which are called *āsana*. The very idea of practicing yoga is to be able to come to a state of union, or integration of the mind, body and soul, to find peace inwardly, and share peace outwardly, with our world.

I began to learn about the philosophy of yoga in much more depth. At that time, some yoga teachers would reference the most basic of yoga philosophy in classes. But when I picked up his book, I started to learn beyond the periphery. Rolf weaves in wisdom from the struggles throughout his life including having served in the military, and being in recovery from addiction to show how he used the framework of the *Yoga Sūtra* to find inner peace. I found his stories incredibly inspiring, relatable, funny and memorable. I began to make connections to how yoga philosophy could shape and impact who I was.

What yoga did was allow me to lean inwards. While I was

leaning inward, my mind was going silent – in a good way. The more inwards I went, the more I realized that yoga was not just fueling me now – it was going to fuel me for the rest of my life.

CHAPTER 7

MOM, YOGA IS MY DHARMA

After completing my Bachelor of Arts, and before carrying on with the Concurrent Education degree by completing the final year of my Bachelor of Education, at age twenty-two I had saved up all my money to travel to Baja California, Mexico for a month and become a yoga teacher. My parents didn't want me to go. They were disappointed that I would miss my undergraduate graduation to go on my yoga teacher training. "I skipped my undergraduate degree ceremony, and I regretted it for the rest of my life," my mom told me. "Don't you think skipping your undergrad graduation is something you're going to later regret too?"

Without question, I said, "Mom, my *dharma* in life is to be a yoga teacher."

My mom asked, "What does *dharma* mean?"

My understanding of *dharma* was that it was my life purpose. *Dharma* was what I was meant to do. It was what I was put on this planet for. I felt aware of my purpose, finally – and every day I was not showing up for my *dharma*, I felt in conflict with it.

Despite my parents' disappointment that I'd be missing my undergraduate graduation for a yoga teacher training, I went to Mexico. I spent a long time researching training locations and ended up choosing this particular yoga school because a favorite yoga teacher of mine had studied there.

When I landed in San José del Cabo airport, my flight had been delayed, and my luggage was lost. I was fighting back tears as I approached the counter and tried to discuss this with the woman at the desk.

I was traveling to an isolated, oceanside property in the desert, which was a few hours away from the airport. What would I do without my luggage? How would I get my luggage back? But I stopped myself. I knew the fifth *yama* of yoga was *aparigraha* – non-hoarding. Being able to let go. I remember saying in my head, *I need to be calm because everyone will think I'm not a serious student of yoga if I show up at teacher training, and I'm upset about this. I need to be calm.* I wouldn't cry or complain or tell anyone my luggage was lost. On the inside, I was panicking.

I was obsessed with this idea that real students of yoga were a certain way – and in order to demonstrate this, I needed to embody the *yama(s)* perfectly. What I realize now is that by obsessing over how good I was at practicing the philosophy of yoga, I was judging myself. I had taken all the ways in which I had judged myself and others previously and not erased these judgments, but simply applied them to myself and my perceived inability to embody yoga philosophy. Years later, I've learned that you don't need to be perfect at embodying the *yama(s)* of the *Yoga Sūtra(s)*. There is no 'yoga police' dropping in to check to see if you're doing them perfectly or not. The *Yoga Sūtra(s)* are a framework, or guidance, for the way in which we move through life. Succeeding at the *yama(s)* is not important. What's important is looking at your life through the lens of the *Yoga Sūtra(s)* and simply trying. The whole point of the *yama(s)* and other elements of yoga philosophy is to help you to cultivate inner peace.

By the time I'd waited for my lost luggage and made it out of the airport and into the shuttle bus, it was much later than I was meant to arrive in Mexico. We drove through the desert beside giant green, spiky cactuses taller than the car. I'd never been to the desert before. We eventually pulled through a tiny gate onto the beach. I could smell the salt water and feel the breeze off the sea.

The teacher welcoming me told me that everyone had already eaten dinner and headed up for the first group meeting. The orange sun was setting. I put my small carry-on luggage into my tent on the beach, and I walked up the steps to the yoga *shala* (Sanksrit for 'home'), which was on stilts. It overlooked the palm trees, mountains, white sand, blue skies and the sunset. With a smile on her face, my yoga teacher Emily, a woman with long gray hair down to her hips who looked like she was in her fifties or sixties, said, "Welcome! You made it just in time. We're about to meditate."

My heart started to race. While everyone around me calmly closed their eyes, stacked their vertebra one at a time, and sat serenely on their meditation cushions, I had one eye open looking around the *shala* in a panic, thinking, *Does everyone else know how to do this but me? I don't belong here. I'm not good enough to be here.* I spent the entire thirty minutes as everyone meditated around me panicking. I went back to my tent on the beach and sobbed. I felt so inferior. What I realize now, in retrospect, is that I wasn't able to meditate because I was worrying about not being able to meditate. There is no right or wrong way to meditate. Much like how to practice yoga philosophy, the only way to practice meditation wrong is if you are sitting there judging yourself for being terrible at meditation the whole time.

I've learned from various teachers of yoga philosophy as I've gotten deeper into my studies that these thought spirals, which all human beings experience, are referred to in yoga philosophy as our *vṛtti*. *Yoga Sūtra* 1.2 is "*yogaścittavṛittinirodhah*" which translates to, "Yoga (is) bringing to complete cessation the functional modifications of the citta (mind)" (Karambelkar 5). Our *vṛtti* help to shape our *sanskāra(s)* (Karambelkar 558). The *sanskāra(s)* are impressions on the brain that eventually affect our *vāsanā* or our larger personality traits, which, in turn, can impact our entire experience of the world (Karambelkar 518 – 521). These *sanskāra(s)* create *kleśa(s)* or causes of human suffering. The goal of our yoga and meditation practice is to shine a light on all of these habits of the human mind. Once we become aware of these tendencies of the mind that run on autopilot within us, we can consciously begin to change the pattern (Karambelkar 5).

The second day, in the same yoga *shala*, the twenty-two of us sat in a circle. Every day for that month we'd practice *Satya Circles*, or truth circles. We were asked to stand up and introduce ourselves, one at a time. As the people before me took their turns, I could barely hear their words because I was panicking about what I would say when the time came. When it was my turn, I rushed to stand, quickly blurting out, "Hi! I'm Alex, and I'm happy to be here!" I quickly sat down as soon as I stood up, praying it would be over.

But it wasn't over. Emily gently said to me, in front of everyone, "Stand up. Take a deep breath, and then do it all over again." She smiled and watched. After I did, she said, "There. Much better." I've remembered that moment for the rest of my life. Whenever I'm overwhelmed, I just need to take a deep breath and start again.

One of the fundamental practices in yoga is *prāṇāyāma*, or breathwork. Many modern yoga studios in the Western World gloss over this essential element of our practice. Most people think that they know how to naturally breathe, but we've actually lost this ability through nervous system dysregulation, the prevalence of stress, and restricted breathing patterns. Natural breathing includes breathing through the nose, if it's possible, allowing the belly to swell with the in-breath, feeling the ribs and torso expand, and allowing the breath to be effortless. *Yoga Sūtra(s)* 2.49 – 2.53 explain the practice of *prāṇāyāma* (Karambelkar 298 – 333). According to *Sūtra* 2.53, once you have mastered your *prāṇāyāma* practice, your mind can become steady, and you are able to choose focus, concentrate on your priorities, experience fewer distractions, neutralize any distractions that do arise, and obtain a calmer, more focused mind (Alderman). This moment in which I learned from my teacher Emily to take a deep breath was the embodiment of this philosophy.

The first two of the *kleśa(s)*, or causes of human suffering, are *avidyā* and *asmita (*Karambelkar 177). The simplest way to explain *avidyā* is that "we have forgotten who we are." It's a lack of spiritual practice. We are no longer connecting to why we're here, our purpose or a higher power. This absence of a spiritual practice directly causes the second *kleśa*, *asmitā*, which is the ego. The ego can move in two ways: we can have a big ego or a small ego. When our ego is too big, we think we're too powerful. When our ego is too small, we play ourselves too small. And I was playing myself too small here. I'd forgotten my spiritual practice. And because of that, I'd lost sight of my purpose and the gifts that I had to offer the world.

By the end of this first 200-hour yoga teacher training, I remembered who I was. The daily practice of yoga had transformed me. We were all asked to co-teach a five-minute segment of a yoga class to the whole group. I was no longer terrified of using my voice in front of a group of adults. I was excited. I confidently stepped up to teach a short segment of a crescent lunge to warrior three transition. The cues came out of my mouth effortlessly and seamlessly. No nerves, no anxiety, no fear. Another teacher leading the yoga teacher training, when giving me feedback, said, "You've clearly taught yoga before, right?"

"Never," I told her.

"Really?" she asked me. "You seem so confident and sure of yourself. This is what you were born to do." I was so proud of myself in that moment. Earlier in the year, I told my mom that yoga was my *dharma*. Now, my teacher said it too, confirming what I believed about myself.

These two moments for me, from the first to the last day of the yoga teacher training, are like data points on a map – showing who I became over the course of that month. This transformation was thanks to the *āsana*, *prāṇāyāma*, and meditation practices, and the yoga philosophy I studied, which helped me open my heart, among many other practices like physical exercise, reduction of sugar and caffeine, a healthier diet and time spent grounding in nature. All of these practices changed who I was on a profound level. Once I witnessed the power of this transformation in myself, I knew that this was what I wanted to do professionally – to help hold space for this transformation in others.

I have learned through my yoga philosophy classes with my teacher Anvita in Mumbai about the stages that make up our preparation towards deep concentration, for *samādhi*. In *Yoga Sūtra* 1.17, Pātañjali explains that our journey towards *samādhi*, or consciousness, will pass through four stages of *samprājnata*. Later in the *sūtras*, Pātañjali introduces the three stages of *samādhi*, in *sūtra* 1.46 (*sabija samādhi*), *sūtra* 1.51 (*nirbija samādhi*), and finally *sūtra* 4.29 (*dharma-megha samādhi*). I have often heard *sūtra* 1.17 referred to as the four stages of lower *samādhi* and *sūtras* 1.46, 1.51 and 4.29 referred to as the three stages of higher *samādhi*, however Anvita corrected me that these are the four stages of *samprājnata*, preparation towards concentration, followed by the three stages of *samādhi*, or consciousness. The first phase of *samprājnata* is referred to as *vitarka*, or thought and reasoning (Karambelkar 38 – 51). In my experience, this stage occurs when we first approach yoga philosophy through books, quotes and exposure to our teachers. This initial exploration of yoga might occur in the early days of our studies of yoga, when we attend lectures, read books and participate in classes. For me, this phase took place when I first discovered yoga at university and read Rolf Gates' book, *Meditations from the Mat*. The second phase of *samprājnata* is called *nirvicāra* (Karambelkar 38 – 51). This is the emotional response, or the moment when the teachings begin to touch our hearts. I remember this moment for me – it happened when I was attending a *Kirtan*, or *bhakti* yoga chanting session on my yoga teacher training in Mexico. Being hugged and embraced by my classmates, I was in tears. This was what it felt like – when the teachings were stepping out of the text and into my heart. The third phase of *samprājnata* is called *ananda* (Karambelkar 38 – 51), or causeless bliss. Our happiness is always there, but in the modern world, we've lost it. We have to come home to this contentment: first through knowledge and second through the emotional response to this knowledge. When we come home to this internal contentment, it's called *ananda*. And finally, the fourth phase of *samprājnata* is *asmitā* (Karambelkar 55 – 59). If the pure bliss becomes continuous, then our knowledge travels to the deepest part of our consciousness. It is in this moment when we begin to live yoga.

When I got back from Mexico, I went back for my final year of school. I had graduated from the Bachelor of Arts portion of my Concurrent Education degree in June, but I still had one more year left to complete before I was a certified teacher. This was the Bachelor of Education focus year. So, after returning from Mexico, I had to go back to school for eight more months. I'd spend the bulk of this year in my Bachelor of Education courses and on practicum – long-term placements for two months at a time in classrooms, where I'd be teaching children the majority of the time. But I already felt confident and assured that teaching yoga was the path for me – the Bachelor of Education was just something I had to do along the way.

My boss at the yoga studio, Jess, could see that I had evolved over the summer since I'd been away. She immediately added me to the schedule and gave me a hot power yoga class to teach. It felt so good to know she believed in me. After that first class went well, I was soon teaching five, six classes a week – every time a class opened up on the schedule, it felt like Jess offered it to me. I began to see how, the moment I stepped into my *dharma*, things just began to fall into place. I was keen to get the experience, so sometimes I taught more like ten or twelve classes in a week, subbing in for other teachers at the studio. I naturally stepped into teaching all kinds of *āsana* classes, not just what I was trained for.

Halfway into the year, I told my parents, "I'm just going to stay here in Canada, at this yoga studio, and teach yoga." This delighted them! Just kidding. This was not what they wanted for me. They wanted me to get a 'real job'. One that was stable and secure. One that would provide me benefits and financial security. I also felt societal pressure from my classmates, the rest of my family and the world around me to step into the job that I had studied towards. It felt like rather than 'follow my heart' I should 'follow my logic' and become a professional educator.

If you had a look at my university transcript, you wouldn't believe I was the same girl from high school. High school Alex had straight A's and finished every course she started. University Alex' transcript included a full column of all the times that she changed majors, as well as a column with failed courses, near fails and dropped courses. This was mostly due to my mental health and drinking problems.

I ended up in primary-junior education, working with children aged four to twelve, not because I chose it, but because it was the only age group I was qualified to teach. I wanted to teach high school English or social sciences but being a Gender Studies major meant I didn't have the university credits to do so. I heard that teaching secondary education was something I could later qualify for, which ended up being easier said than done, so I settled on working with the little ones.

Over the five years in Concurrent Education, I didn't like what

I saw. Teachers were passionate about working with children and loved education, but unfortunately, the problems went beyond that. There didn't seem to be a lot of respect for teachers from anyone: parents, the system, the students. Teachers were overworked and underpaid. They were highly stressed and unhappy. There was no calm in the career. The classroom in general didn't seem like a conducive space for me and my mental well-being.

On top of this, there weren't any teaching jobs in Canada at the time that I graduated. Teachers had to be on the substitute teacher list for years before getting a permanent job and a classroom. Too many provinces were graduating teachers faster than demand. And five or ten years on the substitute teacher list didn't feel worth it to me – to fight for a career I'd never really wanted anyway. The effort didn't seem worth the results; I knew I'd later end up unhappy, just like many of the teachers I'd met along the way.

On the flip side, I found solace and peace teaching yoga classes in the yoga studio. My yoga students respected me and wanted to be there. Planning for my yoga classes was a joy and not a chore. I always left the classes feeling calmer, grounded and at peace. But I was paid per yoga class, and the money felt inconsistent and unpredictable.

Working for a yoga studio full time meant that my salary was out of my control and in the control of the yoga studio owner. There was no contract signed in advance about hours, pay or class allocations. The classes I was scheduled for would sometimes suddenly change, which, years later, as a yoga community founder myself, I understood. When managing a team of people, I was constantly trying to manage the cash flow with memberships and classes so that we break even as a community. But back then, as an employee in this circumstance, the unpredictability felt unstable. I began to see how financially stressful being a yoga teacher could be, in a different way from being a schoolteacher. Even though the work of teaching in a school itself didn't appeal to me, the financial security did. I began to wonder if maybe my parents were right.

CHAPTER 8

A PIZZA SHOP IN GIZA

"This is the wildest thing," my mentor educator David said as he stood at the front of the classroom of grade four and five students. This placement was the last of my many student teacher placements before I completed my Bachelor of Education degree, and I was placed as a student teacher in David's room for two months. "There is a pizza shop across the street from the pyramids of Giza. Can you believe that?"

"Woahhhh!" all the grade four and five students said.

David was reading a picture book aloud about Ancient Egypt to his class. David, as a teacher, inspired me. He was calm, cool, happy and loved his job. He respected the students, and they respected him.

David had taught abroad for two years in Egypt at the start of his career, and he spoke highly of it as the best two years of his life. He made lifelong friends, and he traveled the world while he was there. When eating lunch or having coffee with him on our breaks, I complained about the state of employment for teachers in Ontario, the struggles of working full time as a yoga teacher, and the stress about how I'd make a living post-university. He told me, "Alex, you should just go abroad and teach. Even if you hate it and decide to come home after a month or two, go abroad. It'll be a great adventure. It'll change the way you see the world completely."

His stories about living in Egypt intrigued me. As a five-year-old, my parents sent me to Saturday Morning Club at a museum in Toronto, and they had an exhibit on the mummies of Ancient Egypt. One morning, I got lost in my own imagination, staring at all the jewels and ornaments of one exhibit. When I looked up, I realized I'd gotten separated from my group.

The pyramids of Giza always felt so far away, like something larger than life, on another planet, that I'd never see in this lifetime. As a child and teenager, my family took holidays to all-inclusive resorts in the Caribbean. But to Egypt?! The Middle East felt way too foreign and far. I couldn't imagine ever being able to afford to travel there in this lifetime.

There had been an Educators Abroad recruitment fair at university a few months earlier for my cohort to get jobs overseas, but I hadn't paid much attention. I was interested in doing my yoga thing and didn't bother putting in the effort. But I watched my classmates excitedly planning their futures in Mexico, Dubai or England. I was learning from them that there was a large network of international teachers working in schools everywhere. There were also many benefits of teaching abroad. International Educators got free accommodation in most places and the opportunity to travel the world.

After meeting David and hearing about his experiences in Egypt, I started to wonder – *maybe this is what I should do. Get a job, move abroad, travel the world, have fun for a few years, and then figure things out.* But while I liked the idea of visiting Egypt, living in the Middle East did not feel right to me because of stereotypes I had in my head about the region. When my friend Claire signed for a job in Dubai, I said to her, in a very uninformed, biased and judgmental way, "I can't believe you want to work in Dubai. Women get so mistreated there." The irony being that, a few weeks later, I ended up signing a contract in an even more conservative location than the UAE (United Arab Emirates).

When thinking about where I wanted to go in the world, it was pretty simple: I've never liked being cold. Winter was never easy for me – winter wonderland never evoked a sense of comfort and coziness the way it did for so many. I wanted to be on the beaches. But the Middle East didn't come to mind. What came to mind was the Caribbean and Central and South America – probably because that is largely where I'd had my childhood traveling experiences.

I put together my resume, references and job applications, and I sent them out into the world. When I think of this time, the *Skype* jingle automatically comes to mind. I interviewed for jobs in Mexico, Venezuela and Suriname. While some of the principals that I met were incredible, none of the places or people exactly resonated. In many situations, I had to compromise on benefits – they were offering shared accommodation, and I didn't want a roommate, or they weren't offering a return flight home each summer (something I knew to expect as a benefit.) Many schools in South and Central America were offering me low salaries on the premise that the cost of living was cheap there.

I realized I was going to have to broaden my options, as South America didn't seem promising to me at that point, so I decided to open up my locations to anywhere. I paid for the upgrade to the service, which I often describe as the '*Facebook* poke' upgrade. Do you remember when people used to *Facebook* Poke? For $25, I could essentially 'poke' schools all over the world indicating my interest. So, I scrolled down the list, hitting 'send notification of interest' to every single one of them. And I started getting emails and scheduling *Skype* interviews with principals everywhere. Bangladesh. Nepal. Morocco.

I'd seen a world map thousands of times before, but I never really examined one in detail prior to this point. I started learning which countries were landlocked, which countries were on which continents, and which countries had warm and cool climates. I would watch YouTube videos about what life was like living in places like Casablanca and Suriname. I was learning more about the world than I ever learned in school.

Every morning when I came in to speak with my mentor David, I'd tell him where I'd had an interview and, each day, we'd put a bullet point on the map hanging on the chalkboard in his classroom. We'd discuss the pros and cons of each place.

I got a job interview for a teaching position in the Marshall Islands, which seemed incredibly exciting and exotic. I remember David saying, "Pros: you live on a tropical island. Cons: not a lot of places to travel to on vacation." He was right; when we looked at the map, it was literally in the middle of nowhere in the ocean. I'd be marooned on a tropical island like on the TV show *Survivor*. Not the place for me.

It hit the point where I didn't even have the time and energy to do a bit of research before the call. That's how many interviews I was doing each day. One morning, I got an email from a school director in Kuwait. I didn't even know where in the world Kuwait was, let alone that it was between Saudi Arabia and Iraq. Kuwait had an eight-hour time difference from Toronto, so I scheduled an interview with him for six in the morning.

At 5:55am, I rolled out of bed and had a few minutes to scroll around on the school website. Okay, at least it had a nice website – that was a good sign. Some international schools that I interviewed with at that time didn't even have a website – that, to me, was always a red flag. I scanned the website quickly to try and find something to mention that indicated that I had done some research on the school. The one thing I saw that stood out to me was that the school had a staff book club.

I got on *Skype* with the school director, William. He asked me, "Why do you want to come to our school?"

I said, "It seems you really care about the staff's well-being. I noticed you have a few different programs for the staff like a book club."

"A book club?!" he asked. He had no idea what I was talking about. The irony, as I later found out when I moved to Kuwait, is that the school never had a staff book club, and staff well-being wasn't the top priority of the administration.

But there was something about this school director that

resonated with me. I felt drawn to him, the school and the country – for reasons I couldn't explain. This was the right job for me.

I went into school the next morning with a big grin on my face and announced to my mentor, David, that while I hadn't had a job offer yet, I thought I was going to move to Kuwait.

"Kuwait?! All my friends from Egypt are in Kuwait."

"Really?"

"Yeah – they all moved there after Egypt. They've been living there for nine years. Let me put you in touch with them; it's probably not the same school, but at least they can give you an idea of what life is like over there."

David gave me the email address of one friend in particular, Rebecca, and I sent her an email. We quickly clicked and were sending email after email, then we switched to *WhatsApp* after *WhatsApp*. The one clear question I remember asking her was, "I know alcohol is illegal, but can you get it?"

She reassured me, "Yes, you can get alcohol here. It's illegal but not impossible to find for expats. You can also learn how to make it." And that was all I needed to hear. I was moving to Kuwait.

CHAPTER 9

TRAUMA IS THE GATEWAY DRUG

Whenever I told someone I was moving to Kuwait, their first response was often, "Where is that?"

Kuwait is mostly desert, a tiny, oil-rich country sandwiched between Saudi Arabia and Iraq. In 2015, when I was moving there, it didn't make the news often in North America. But it did in the 1990s, when Iraq invaded. That war occurred just before I was born. So, like me, many of my friends who were my same age hadn't even heard of the country before I decided to move there.

After that question, the quiz would continue from my friends, family, and acquaintances. "Is it safe there?" or, "Isn't that a war-torn country?"

"Yes, it is safe, and no, it isn't war-torn."

The last war in Kuwait was in 1991, before I was born. Unfortunately, people tend to confuse a continent with a country frequently – they hear about violence in the Middle East from the media and think that the whole of the Middle East is violent. It's not. Kuwait is actually extremely safe.

"Do they have air conditioning?"

"Yes. They definitely do."

Kuwait is a developed country, and temperatures in the summer skyrocket to over fifty degrees Celsius. Kuwait definitely has air conditioning.

"Why would you want to move to a country where women are treated so badly?"

“It’s not that bad! I don’t have to wear a hijab. I just cover my elbows and knees.”

“Alex, every time I’ve seen you, you’ve had the largest bottle of liquor in your hands, and you’re making out with some guy. You’re gonna get arrested.”

Crickets

“I’ll be fine…” (In my head: *Yep. You’re probably right.*)

One of the biggest concerns for me about Kuwait was that alcohol was illegal. There are one hundred and ninety-five countries in the world, and alcohol is illegal to consume in ten of them (“Countries Where Alcohol Is Illegal in 2024”). In retrospect, the fact that, when moving abroad at age twenty-three, I chose one of those ten countries with prohibition to move to perplexes me. I hadn’t gone a week without at least one drink of alcohol since I was a teenager.

How did I think I would survive? And why was it that I was so dependent on alcohol already at that age?

There were various factors that influenced why I began drinking in the first place, and it would be naïve to blame any one reason or cause. Growing up, I had issues in my family home that caused me unhealed trauma, and I was searching for a way to cope with it. Beyond this, I saw my parents drink alcohol regularly, and my grandparents, too. In Toronto in the 1990s, drinking alcohol seemed synonymous with stress relief and celebrations. This culture around alcohol was not unique to my family; it was woven into the culture of most families in Canada, not just mine.

When speaking about the five causes of human suffering, or the *kleśa(s)*, my teacher Rolf says that all addiction falls into the third and fourth *kleśa(s)*: *rāga* (desire) and *dveṣa* (avoidance) (“Break the Cycle: How Yoga and Meditation Can Help Heal Addiction”). In my case, when I first began drinking alcohol, I was drinking it out of desire. I desired to have fun. I desired to release stress. I desired to let loose. This is *rāga.* Once I started drinking heavily, I realized drinking alcohol was also a good way to avoid my suffering. Avoid my trauma, Avoid tough conversations. This is *dveṣa*. When we look at addiction from the Western perspective, we often see someone with addiction as having something wrong with them, or we view them as being different. "We lack compassion for the addict precisely because we are addicted ourselves in ways we don't want to accept and because we lack self-compassion" (Mate qtd. in Garrett). But when we examine dependence on any substance from the Eastern perspective, we see addiction as landing on this scale of *rāga* and *dveṣa*. When we look at struggling with drinking or any other substance in this manner, we can start to see addiction as an extreme example of a very normal human experience.

I had my first drink when I was fourteen years old, when I stole alcohol from my parents and snuck out to a park party. That night ended up in a disaster, carrying one of my childhood friends out of the park, on my shoulders. Charlotte was completely unconscious – limbs limp like spaghetti, neck weak like a rag doll, head hanging heavy. I got separated from her at the beginning of the night and later found her with an older boy in this state. I never knew what happened to her that night, but I can only guess. I think that night changed the entire trajectory of her life. I know, for me, it set me on a path of self-destruction.

Whilst most of my friends ran away from the park, I attempted to carry Charlotte home. I made it about half a block down the street, until a woman came out of her house and called the police. A police cruiser arrived shortly after, flashing red and blue lights. The two police officers asked me to call my parents. What I remember is that my parents were furious at me that night – for lying, for sneaking out, for stealing alcohol. In hindsight, with several years of maturity later, I think they missed a key point: that when everyone else left, I stayed with Charlotte. I didn't leave her alone in the park – I made sure she was safe. And I told the truth to them and the police about what happened. The practice of love and the practice of truth – *ahiṃsā* and *satya* – the first two *yama(s)* of yoga. That, I think, should have been acknowledged.

I didn't drink again for about six months, until I started dating someone older than me. But, around that time, I became obsessed with partying. I don't know whether I was addicted to alcohol yet or just suffering from major FOMO (fear of missing out). Whatever it was, I had to go to a party both nights of every weekend and couldn't see the cause and effect: how all the drama, all the chaos, all the dangerous situations and all the gossip of my teenage years were fueled by my drinking. I didn't understand that my depression and anxiety were caused by my drinking. And, if I just cut the alcohol entirely, my life would be a whole lot happier and simpler.

When I took first year psychology, I read in a textbook about bipolar disorder, and that was when I decided: *This is what is going on with me.* Bipolar wasn't a brand-new concept to me at this point – I had heard of it before, but I didn't know much about it. Growing up, I knew that bipolar ran in my dad's family. The existence of mood disorders within my family was something no one ever talked about. Also, Charlotte, the same friend I'd carried out of the park at age fourteen, had bipolar disorder. She eventually transferred to a different high school because her struggles were interfering with her academics so much.

When I found this diagnosis, the idea of it brought me comfort. I wanted a conclusion so I could have an explanation, clarity and a reason why I was the way I was. Nowadays, in 2023, I no longer identify with this diagnosis whatsoever, but in 2010 it really resonated with me.

According to the DSM (the *Diagnostic and Statistical Manual of Mental Disorders*), bipolar disorder is characterized by mood swings

– depression and hopelessness, followed by periods of being manic with high energy and irritability (qtd. in "Bipolar Disorder"). While I may not have struggled as much as Charlotte did in high school, or some of my relatives, I felt I had some form of it. I felt certain that, finally, I understood myself.

One thing that I want to share around bipolar disorder is a conversation that I had with a friend recently. When she was reading my book, she asked me, "Is there a reason why you say 'have/had' bipolar instead of 'am/was' bipolar?" I realized that the language choice that I made in this book might not be widely understood, which is why I want to explain it here. The choice to describe bipolar disorder this way is a decision to use what is called "person-first language" (Marschall). Most commonly, in our society, there is a tendency to refer to an individual with bipolar disorder by stating "He or she is bipolar." This language can be stigmatizing and make people feel labelled, abnormal, or separate from society. When I became aware of my language and made shifts towards person-first language, I found that it made a huge difference to me. In my opinion, this person-first language (e.g. "she has schizophrenia" versus "she is schizophrenic") is less stigmatizing and more inclusive (Marschall). However, not everyone likes person-first language when describing their conditions. For example, within the autistic community, there tends to be a preference towards describing an individual as an "autistic person" as opposed to a "person with autism" (Marschall). The best practice is to ask individuals or groups which language they prefer when describing themselves and then utilize the same language.

I now identify the moods that I experienced as simply extreme manifestations of the *guṇa*. The *guṇa* refer to three states explained in the *Sūtras*: *tamas* (inactivity, slowness or lethargy), *rajas* (anxiety, stress, or sympathetic nervous system arousal) and *sattva* (equilibrium) (Karambelkar 35). The nature of everything in the material world (*prakṛti*), including human beings, is change (Karambelkar 35). We move through these states. We just need to identify when we're in a state that's not *sattvic* – *rajasic* (anxious/stressed/manic) or *tamasic* (slow/depressed/low) – and constantly cultivate practices to bring ourselves back to *sattvic*, back to balance, and back to peace (Sparrowe 4). When viewed from the Eastern perspective, mental imbalances are not necessarily indicative of a mental illness – they are simply an extreme manifestation of normal emotions. Our goal as humans is to constantly try to come back, by cultivating mindfulness around the things that knock us out of balance, and implementing practices to return to center (Sparrowe 4).

At the time that I had diagnosed myself with bipolar disorder, I was twenty-two years old, had just recently started yoga, and I lacked the spiritual awareness and understanding that I have now. So a diagnosis and medication were all I wanted. I was unaware that there were other holistic alternatives that I now, ten years later, know about, and western medicine seemed to be the only solution. But I think what I really wanted was for someone to recognize my struggles, validate my experience for me, and help me feel seen. I wanted someone to see my suffering and hold space for my healing journey. I wanted to experience the world in a manageable way, the way I thought my friends and classmates did. I didn't want every day to be a fight for my life.

CHAPTER 10

IS THIS AN EMERGENCY?

At the time I was beginning to question whether I had a mood disorder, at age eighteen, my parents had a tense relationship and were on the brink of divorce. The anchor I had in my sister was not very present, as we were leading different lives. We were very far apart physically at this point – she was at university in Guelph, which was an hour west of the city of Toronto, and I was in Kingston, which was three hours east of Toronto.

My parents were both still based in Toronto, living together in the house I grew up in, and I traveled back often to visit them. During the fall and winter, I was always quite depressed and couldn't stop crying. I thought I was crying because I was homesick, and if I went home, it would make it better. But when I got home, it was always worse.

On one occasion, when I got on the train to go back to Toronto for the weekend, the train crashed into a truck, and a man died. We ended up being stuck on the train for about ten hours as the coroner came, declared the man dead, moved him, and transferred us passengers to a bus to complete the journey. I was in shock, and my way of coping was to joke about it. I posted a joke on *Facebook* making light of the incident, and one of my *Facebook* friends messaged me to tell me that they thought it was insensitive. I interpreted this as a character flaw. I had a panic attack and was in a destructive thought spiral, or *vṛtti*. By the time I was home, I could not stop hyperventilating or crying, thinking that all 1,000 of my *Facebook* friends hated me, and I was a bad person.

I sat down on the couch in tears with my mom. Telling anyone I thought I had bipolar was terrifying, let alone someone in my family. We as a family did not talk about our feelings very often. This avoidance of emotions was not something unique to my parents – it was part of their generation and their culture. Mental health was widely stigmatized, misunderstood and swept under the rug. I was so used to being shut down and invalidated that I didn't even share about the accident or the joke I made on *Facebook* about the death of the man – which was really what was upsetting me so much. I was convinced I was a bad person. As we sat on the couch, me choking back tears, I finally found the courage to tell my mom, "You know how bipolar disorder is in Dad's family? I think I have it too."

My mom said, "Honey, just because bipolar disorder runs in your family, doesn't mean you have it as well." That was the end of that conversation. I understand now that my mom was doing the best she could to support me, with no communication or coaching training on how to do that. But rather than validating my emotions or concerns, she swept them away. She never asked me why I was worried about having bipolar. I do have compassion for my mom in these moments, and I do think that she was doing the best that she could to support me.

At that point in life, I saw every misstep I made as a character flaw. My ego was unable to own up to my mistakes. I didn't understand that if I made a mistake like writing an insensitive *Facebook* post, it didn't mean that I was a bad person. I am a human being, and human beings make mistakes. I just had to make peace with my mistake and consider how I'd do better in the future. But no one had shown me how to do this.

The problem in the public Canadian medical system is that, while it is excellent public healthcare that is universally provided to all, there are long waitlists, and you must have a referral from a general practitioner to see a specialist for anything. Waiting for weeks or months to see a doctor is a common experience in the Canadian healthcare system, as reported by the Fraser Institute, who documented that wait times in 2018 could be as long as forty weeks in Prince Edward Island, and as short as sixteen weeks in Ontario (5).

The system is so bureaucratic. If I had done something dangerous, like jump off a building, then I'd be taken to the emergency room and seen immediately by someone in the psychiatry system without having to go through the process. But in this in-between, high functioning but struggling state, I had to leap through several hoops to get there.

At this point, I didn't see any other solution than to see a psychiatrist. But I needed someone to attest to that need by giving me a referral. And so, when I was in my second year at university and beginning to question if I had bipolar disorder, I thought the right person to give me a referral would be a counselor at the university mental health clinic. Since the university strongly articulated and emphasized that students should go to the mental health clinic for mental health concerns and the medical services clinic for physical health concerns, I became stuck in the mindset that mental health and physical health were two separate, unrelated issues. Consequently, when I went in for annual check-ups and told my physician that I was feeling anxious and depressed, and she suggested solutions like going for walks and eating healthier, it led me to believe that she wasn't the person to go to for mental health concerns, and that the mental health clinic was where I should go. I didn't see how interrelated, connected and holistic mental and physical health are, the way that I recognize them to be now. I also didn't understand that I needed to undergo trauma healing and make necessary holistic lifestyle changes necessary beyond western medication. My problem was my mental health, so I thought the right place to go was the mental health clinic.

I see now that the mental health clinic really wasn't the place I should have gone. Ten years later, when I visit the website, the mental health clinic is clearly described as offering a short-term mental health model, geared towards dealing with personal difficulties and daily stressors, and it is noted that more severe cases are dealt with by physicians and psychiatrists. That distinction was not communicated to me in 2011, when I was in the system.

I thought that the counselors at the mental health clinic would be trained to identify illnesses such as bipolar disorder. However, after going there to present my symptoms and receive a diagnosis, I eventually learned that this assumption was incorrect. After several sessions in my second, third and fourth years, with various counselors, one counselor in that department finally explained to me that she and her colleagues were not trained to recognize conditions like bipolar disorder, and they didn't have the authority to grant the referral I needed. She explained to me that the right person to give me a referral was a general physician in the medical services clinic. That same counselor, years later, would eventually direct me to a physician, who referred me to a psychiatrist, and changed my life. But in the beginning, I didn't know all of this. It caused me years of pain and struggle.

And because they weren't trained to diagnose or treat mental illness, it felt as though counselors were constantly downplaying and disregarding my mental health symptoms. This treatment led to me questioning the validity of my symptoms after every session. Was I just being overdramatic and overreacting? Was I actually normal and healthier than I thought I was? Sometimes it felt that way. The way the system failed me was not purposeful, by any means. I simply was in the wrong place for the support that I needed.

On top of all this, because of the high demand on the university counseling system at the time, students were rationed to four counseling sessions per year. That meant I could see a counselor for talk therapy for one session once every three months, if I was trying to evenly space the sessions out. That was not nearly enough sessions to give me the tools that I needed. Additionally, unless I described it as an 'emergency', there was a two-week wait time, minimum, to see a counselor at all. Now, ten years later, when looking at the website, I see they've solved this issue and now do a same-day appointment for students. But at the time I was there, in 2011-2015, this was not the case. If I could go back in time, google it, go straight to a physician and ask to be referred to a psychiatrist, I truly think I would have had a different experience.

Making the decision to go to a counseling office for the first time at age nineteen was terrifying. But I had to do it. I couldn't survive any longer without help. I had been waiting for someone to see my suffering and take me to a counselor. I eventually realized that I would have to be brave enough to go by myself. I finally got the courage to call the university mental health services in the midst of a breakdown in the fall of my second year. They asked me on the phone, "Is this an emergency?"

What was a mental health emergency? I didn't know. When I grew up, I was taught that the word 'emergency' was only used for calling 911. My mom and nanny continuously ingrained in my head, "Do not call 911 unless it's an emergency. Never, ever call 911 unless it's an emergency." Emergencies are for when your house is on fire, or someone has broken into your house. Neither of those things had happened to me, so I said "no." I didn't want to be the girl who cried wolf and said something was an emergency when it wasn't.

"Okay, it'll be a two-week waiting time then."

When I finally got to my appointment that I'd waited fourteen days for, whatever was urgently on my mind from two weeks before had already passed. But I didn't want to give up my spot on the list. So, the day came, and I walked across the campus to the clinic.

Walking in the door and up the stairs for the first time was anxiety inducing. I didn't want to see anyone I knew, and due to that, of course, I ran into a childhood friend from summer camp. "Alex!" she said with a big hug and a smile. "It's so nice to see you! I'm having trouble sleeping, so I came to see a counselor. Why are you here?" I was completely mortified and taken aback by how openly she was talking about her mental health struggles and asking about mine. I couldn't imagine telling her the truth, so I said nothing.

Several years later, I don't remember the experience of my first counseling session at all. While I'm sure it was helpful in some regard, in reality, an hour-long counseling session probably wouldn't do much in the long run. I needed much more support than could be given in a sixty-minute window.

I didn't want to use up my limit of four sessions from the university counseling services all at once, so after the first session, I waited a few weeks to book another. By then, I was at the back of a waitlist again, and it was a brand-new counselor who spoke to me. I never saw the same counselor more than once – they scheduled me with whomever had room on their schedule. Every time I went to a session, I had to spend the whole hour acquainting the counselor with my life story, giving each counselor no opportunity to follow my progress.

The pattern was ongoing like this: see a new counselor every few months, tell her my struggles, and then never see her again. It felt like the university was failing me, over and over. I look back and, knowing what I know now about mental health, it is unsurprising to me that the services I was receiving failed. I wasn't given any holistic living advice, and I wasn't seeing one counselor consistently. I needed long-term work with one individual counselor, not one-off sessions here and there. I also needed holistic lifestyle changes – shifts in my diet and my sleep. I needed to be removed from stressful environments to heal my nervous system. I needed space to heal my trauma. And I needed to quit drinking alcohol. Instead, it was just an ongoing loop of counselors seeing me on occasion and putting Band-Aids over problems without treating the gaping wounds unresolved beneath it all.

I also did a disservice to myself with the way that I downplayed my issues to the counselors. I believe this came out of fear. I didn't want to admit how much chaos was happening inside my brain. I didn't want to tell them it was an emergency. I didn't want them to know how much I was suffering because there was stigma around it. There was also a part of me that was scared to face it. What if I did finally get a referral to a psychiatrist, and it came true? What if I did have bipolar? Then what? Would I be unemployable? Would anyone ever want to date me? Chaos in my life had become the norm, and I was used to living my life this way. I couldn't imagine life any differently.

YOGA SERIES: YOGA FOR BIPOLAR DISORDER

As a child, teenager and young adult, I experienced symptoms of a mood disorder, anxiety and chronic stress. I lacked holistic solutions for my mental health struggles, so I managed them with alcohol and yoga. I began teaching yoga at age twenty-one, and although I knew it was my life purpose, my self-doubt and my drinking problems held me back.

Once I got sober, I no longer had booze to help me regulate my nervous system – leading me to get more and more passionate, serious about mindfulness, yoga and meditation to manage my moods. And this is why I've created these three yoga practices for those of you who are struggling with your mental health. They are perfect for you if you are experiencing extreme mind-body states and need to anchor, reconnect and regulate yourself.

https://bit.ly/TMLP_YogaforBipolarDisorder

CHAPTER 11

THE PERFECT STORM

One Saturday, at the start of the fall semester of the third year of university, my parents called me on *Skype*. I was exhausted after a weekend of partying at Homecoming and knew it was strange that they wanted to *Skype* with me. I don't think I'd ever *Skyped* with either of them – together or apart – before. Immediately, when they got on the call, they shared the news: they were getting a divorce. I burst into tears. My mom said, "Aww, she's crying because she's so sad." I couldn't tell them the truth, which was that I wasn't crying because I was sad. I was crying because I was happy. I was so relieved. For as long as I could remember, I thought that they would be much happier separated rather than together.

That day, seeing me crying and thinking it was because of their divorce, my mom suggested I use her employee benefits to see a counselor. I didn't even know that she had employee benefits that entitled me to free counseling before that moment. I was so surprised that it was even an option.

"Your work gives you and your children free counseling? What?!" I asked her. "Yes, I do want to use it."

From her point of view, there was a perfect storm of things happening in my life to need counseling. I was twenty-one years old, my grandfather was in the hospital, slowly dying of cancer; my cat, Atticus, who I had gotten as a present for my thirteenth birthday, was sick and was about to be put down; and my parents were divorcing. But for me, counseling wasn't about this current chaos in my life. It was about the ongoing chaos – the ever-present chaos that was always there. I hadn't felt happy, grounded, or well for as long as I could remember. My questions were "Do I have bipolar? Is that the reason I don't feel well?" I called the employee benefits line, and they set me up with a counselor in Kingston.

I walked through the drizzling rain to the downtown limestone city counselor's office. It was unmarked, without a sign on the front, so it took me a few looks around to find it. The counselor had gray hair, a beard and glasses. The one thing I remember telling him was, "Many relatives of mine have bipolar disorder, and I think I have it too."

He said to me, "'Bipolar disorder' is a code word for 'I can't handle my emotions'." At the time, I was stunned by this. I didn't want to go back.

I asked my mom for another referral, and I called the employee benefits line again. This time, I saw a woman who had a small counseling practice in the basement of her home in the west-end of Kingston, the suburban area. She was lovely to chat with and helped me feel seen and heard. Our eight sessions together were grounding and therapeutic for me. But at the end, the same problem was there – she was someone to provide talk therapy, not someone to diagnose me or provide tangible tools. And it wasn't going to be affordable, long-term support. So, at the end of my eight sessions, I walked away, defeated, not finding the answer I needed.

After my off-campus sessions through my mom's employee benefits were finished, I went back to the university counseling department. I told the counselor, "I think I have bipolar disorder." The more frequently I said this, the less scary it became.

This counselor told me, "I have to refer you out as this is beyond my scope of qualifications." She referred me to a doctor in the north area of Kingston, near the train station. I rode my bike to this office and got lost along the way. I ended up biking way beyond the doctor's office. This was a rough part of town that I had never been in before, and I was alone. This was before the days of smartphones and *Google Maps*, and I was completely lost. I got off my bike, sat down at the side of the road and started sobbing. Why was this so goddamn hard? I'd been to so many counselors and specialists at this point that I'd lost count. Why couldn't anyone help me? Why did I feel so alone?

When I finally found the office that day, it wasn't even what I was looking for. Somehow, I'd gotten referred to a neuroimaging clinic that was going to hook my brain up to wires to do a scan of my brainwaves. Why was I here? How did I end up with this referral? I just wanted to talk to a doctor who could diagnose me.

But because I didn't know how to advocate for myself, and because I was desperate for help, I went along with it. Maybe this was how they diagnosed people with mood disorders? I told the doctor I suspected I had bipolar disorder. The doctor hooked me up to the computer, and I had several wires extending from my head attached to the screen. I watched the brainwaves on the TV lighting up and squiggling in different colors and shapes. I actually kind of enjoyed this – it felt like meditation. At the end of the session, the doctor said to me, "Your brain is in much better shape than most clients I see!"

"Really?" I asked him.

He said, "Normally, my clients have a lot of abnormal brainwaves. Yours look relatively normal."

I said to him, "Well… I do a lot of yoga… so, maybe that's why?"

Again, I was sent on my way, defeated and still not finding the answer I was looking for.

CHAPTER 12

THIS IS AN EMERGENCY

Nick and I had maintained our friendship all throughout university. My housemates knew him as my friend for years, coming round whenever I had parties. In my fourth year, I don't remember how or why, but suddenly, the dynamic changed again. One night, he had come over for dinner with a group and ended up staying the night. And just like that, he started coming over every few days. My housemates began to see him as my partner.

This time, things were different between Nick and me. In our second year of school, our relationship had been quite casual and short. But in my fourth year, this time, he was more attentive. He delivered me thoughtful gifts and confided in me that he always thought I was the one. We were regularly sleeping over at each other's houses and bringing takeaway meals for dinner.

Nick said he had to work at the campus pub on Valentine's Day, so instead, he came over a few nights before. I made him a pop-up card, with accordion-style folding and a pun about him being my 'love bug'. We were still dating a month later when it was St Patrick's Day weekend, a huge holiday in the Canadian university scene – it is one of the few days of the year when it's socially acceptable to drink from ten in the morning. We called them 'pancake keggers' because we'd eat pancakes and drink beer. I was at his house on Saturday night of that weekend because we were planning how to celebrate St Patrick's Day on the Monday. He told me he loved me. I went home from his house floating on cloud nine, so giddy and joyful. After so many short-term, quick relationships, building a relationship like this with a long-time friend finally felt like I was building something serious.

Nick had a long-term ex-girlfriend named Claire who he'd told me he'd broken up with in the first year of university. She was also in the Bachelor of Education program with me, studying to be an educator. Because I would hang around with him and his roommate Zach, it often felt like I was 'one of the boys'. When he confided in me about his problems with Claire, he said she was 'crazy', 'psycho', 'addicted to cocaine' and 'stalking him'. Claire was very skinny and looked like she was struggling, so his stories were believable. I bought into his narrative of her being unstable. Why was she so obsessed with Nick and constantly getting in the way of my relationship with him? Why couldn't she just let him go? According to Nick, they broke up years before, but she kept turning up at his house. Why was she doing that? He clearly liked me, not her.

Throughout the entire four years of school, Claire and I had a lot of university classes together, but while we had many mutual friends, we never spoke during classes. If we found ourselves at the same table amongst friends in a class, sometimes we wouldn't even make eye contact or smile at each other. I didn't like her because she was causing Nick so many problems. I assumed she didn't like me because I was so close with her ex. He said I should keep it a secret that he and I had this special connection and were romantic together, or it would break her. Since Nick had already said that Claire was unstable, I went along with his suggestion.

On St Patrick's Day, Nick had a shift at the campus pub in the morning and afternoon, but we planned to see each other in the evening. By four in the afternoon, I was already drunk, sitting in a bar with the rest of our friends. We'd been texting back and forth all day, but he was slow to respond with vague answers. I was wondering why he wasn't replying but hoping it meant nothing. That's when Zach turned to me. "Hey Alex – there's Nick!" We watched him walk into the bar – but he was holding hands with another girl. He had told me he was going to be at work at that time, but he wasn't. He was with a third girl – not me, and not Claire – someone with whom I didn't even know he had a relationship. Tori. But she wasn't a stranger. I knew her from a volunteer program I'd done the year before.

Because Nick had told me to keep our relationship a secret, no one knew we were dating – so to everyone else, it just seemed like I was emotionally unstable or super drunk when my eyes began brimming with tears. I watched across the bar and saw Nick and Tori holding hands and then saw them lean in for a kiss. It wasn't a random kiss – from the way they looked at each other, I could tell that they had an intimate connection. Was he dating her as well?

I was so confused. I got up from the table and quickly strode out of the bar, thinking Nick would follow me. But he didn't. It was like he pretended he didn't see me. But we locked eyes as I passed him, and I know he did.

When I look back now, I wonder why I didn't confront him in the moment. It was probably a combination of things – I was in shock, I was drunk, and I didn't feel confident enough to speak up for myself. I headed back to my house, sobbing for the rest of the night. I was so confused. How could he do this to me? How could he lay in bed telling me I was his soulmate, and he always knew I was the one, and then less than forty-eight hours later be with another girl?

By the next morning, I was spiraling out of control. Knowing what I now know about hangovers inducing panic attacks, I am sure the alcohol did not help. I couldn't eat and couldn't stop crying. I was just confused. Who was Nick? He wasn't the person I knew anymore. Why would he want to hurt me so badly? The way he'd betrayed me romantically was hurtful, but what was most hurtful was the friendship he'd thrown away. He wasn't some random boy – he was Nick. Why would all of this be worth ruining our friendship? I was upset but also consumed with worry about what everyone else would think. I was worried that everyone on campus knew, and that I was the laughingstock of my classmates.

Again, I'd been triggered into an out of body experience from heartbreak, but this one was different. This wasn't just heartbreak – this was confusion and chaos too. I had an essay due for a history class that week, but no part of me could sit down and start writing without hyperventilating and crying. I went straight to calling my sister. After holding space for me for over an hour, she said, "Alex, I'm worried about you. You should go to counseling."

"I don't want to, Em! What if I have a bigger breakdown later on, and I need another session, but I've already used all of mine up? Then what?"

"Alex. Talk to them. See if they can make an exception and give you more sessions. You need to go there."

I called the university mental health office and when they asked me the question "Is this an emergency?" I burst into tears, saying it for the first time: "This is an emergency."

Because I said it was an emergency, I got to see a counselor that day, instead of managing it on my own and waiting on a waitlist. The main campus mental health office was fully booked (as usual), and so the university sent me to take a taxi out to the west campus where the Bachelor of Education faculty was located. This was the only space where they had an available counselor. Her name was Sarah. This was the woman who changed my life.

West campus was empty. The main building had a long, vacant, wide hallway, with big floor-to-ceiling glass windows. The combination of dark wood with bright vinyl orange furniture and design seemed like it came out of the 1960s. The faculty of education was very small, and all of the students were off campus at the time on their practicums. Because of this, Sarah had a large window of free time to be able to see me, unlike all of the previous counselors who were so time-crunched. From the minute I walked through the door, I felt like I was her number one priority. It felt like I mattered to her. She seemed less overworked and overwhelmed and more available to give me the tools and resources that I needed to succeed.

She sat me down, and she stayed with me for over an hour and a half – long after her workday was over. She stayed with me until she felt confident that I was okay. It felt like there were so many things going wrong that I couldn't keep them clear in my head and jumped from one thing to the other. She pulled out a piece of paper and put it in front of me. Together, we wrote a list of the main issues I was facing and narrowed it down to four. One was definitely Nick. What was going on? What had happened? And how would I process this? The second issue was that I was struggling to scrounge up the cash to pay for my yoga teacher training. My dad had stopped working five years earlier. My mom was financially supporting my sister, me and my dad – even though they were separated – on her own. I felt guilty asking my mom for money for anything. Also, I knew my mom didn't value spending money on yoga. My mom would pay for formal education at university, but not for an education in yoga, and I was scrambling to come up with the money on my own to get myself there. The third issue was my academics. In the chaos of all of my partying, I couldn't remember the last deadline I'd met on time, and my grades were plummeting because of it. The last pressing concern was my ongoing conviction that I was suffering from undiagnosed bipolar disorder – something that no counselor had been able to address. I was constantly being referred to the wrong people, who weren't helping. I just needed to see the right physician or psychiatrist to diagnose me. I needed a proper referral.

The impact of this session was that I felt seen, I felt heard and I felt organized. Seeing all my problems written out on paper and numbered made them so much less overwhelming. No one had ever done this for me before. She'd given me tangible strategies. With her help, all my problems were broken up, bit by bit. Together, we'd tackle them, as a team. She also said that she could make an exception to the rule of four sessions a year per student, since I was so distressed, and she saw me every week until I got better.

Sarah helped me sort out myself by giving me a letter to provide to my professors to get extensions on my academic deadlines. She coached me through advocating for myself and made sure it went well. She helped me find a scholarship to pay for my yoga teacher training, sorting out my money issues. And finally, she was confident enough to say as a counselor, "I am not qualified as a doctor to diagnose you with bipolar, but I will send you to someone at the university medical clinic, who will." This was the first time I'd heard this. I was in the wrong place all along. I shouldn't have been going to counselors. I should have been going to a physician at the medical clinic. Because putting people on medications for mental health is delicate and they need to be observed, we postponed the process until after the summer.

Nick did eventually text me. I was sitting in the library working on an essay when my phone lit up and buzzed on the table in front of me. "Hey Alex, I think it's best if we just stay friends for now." I read that message over and over again, with a fire in my gut. Friends? Are you kidding me? Was he pretending he didn't know I saw him with Tori? I never responded.

I continued to see Sarah weekly, and she helped me talk through all the chaos, all the confusion, and all the drama. I was slowly coming to terms with the realization that Nick was gone.

I didn't even think to message Claire – this scenario felt somewhat unrelated to her. After all, she'd broken up with him four years before, and we were never friends anyway. One day, I got a *Facebook* message from her – Nick's ex-girlfriend whom I'd hated, blamed and talked badly about for years. Gossip travels fast, and I am sure by then she'd heard about what happened between us. "Hey Alex," she wrote, "I know we haven't been on the best of terms all this time – but I want you to know I'm here if you need me. I can help explain some things to you."

Because I had nothing to lose, I thought, *Why not go for coffee with her?* I was anxious walking up the stairs to the campus coffee shop, as she and I had never really spoken before. I sat down on the orange vinyl cushion and smiled nervously. "Hi, how are you?"

She skipped the small talk and dove right into it. "I think there is something wrong with Nick," she told me. "I heard that he hurt you pretty badly, and that you're not in a good state. He hurt me a lot as well. Alex, he's a narcissist."

As I sat looking at her, my heart began to soften. No matter what she'd done to Nick, she was just a human being, who wanted to be happy, just like me. I could feel myself warming up to her with each sip of my coffee.

"What happened between you?" she asked me. I told her the brief version: we'd dated for a while in second year, and then again this past year. I walked in on him with Tori.

She looked at me, stunned, and then asked, "Did you know that I was dating him up until the third year of university?"

"What?" I asked her. "He told me you broke up in first year!" There was no way that they could have been dating all that time. But then I remembered the time I'd asked him why, if they'd broken up, was she in his profile picture on *Facebook*? He'd said it was because he felt bad for her, and she still wanted to be friends. I can't believe that I believed him when he told me that. In hindsight, it was such an obvious red flag.

"Oh my God. He told you that?! No, we were dating until about a year ago. Until me and Chelsea connected."

"Until a year ago? I was with him in second year. That can't be true... he told me he was single. And who's Chelsea?" I asked her.

"You didn't know he had another girlfriend for the past year? Chelsea. He told us lies about each other and made us hate each other for a year – but he was sleeping with her at the same time as me. And probably you, too."

I found this hard to believe. He'd told me all along that Claire was a 'psycho'. I had this idea in my head that she was his crazy ex-girlfriend for years. Could I really trust her on this? Part of me was in shock and having difficulty processing what she was telling me.

"We only figured it out one day when one of her friends saw me and him out at a party. She reached out to me because she was really struggling. We started to connect the dots and put two and two together."

"Wait," I asked her, "how is this possible?"

"We heard he'd started dating Tori, probably at the same time as us, and probably you, too. There are many other girls, too." She started naming other women from our classes who she'd heard rumors about with Nick. "Alex, he is manipulative and a pathological liar. When I heard what happened to you, it started to occur to me – I've been hating and blaming you all this time, when really none of it is your fault. He is the problem, not you."

My stomach sank. I didn't know what she was going to say to me during our coffee date, but I never could have predicted this. Obviously, Nick was dating Tori at the same time as me. That much was obvious. But Chelsea and Claire too? How could that be possible? How could one guy date so many women at once on the same university campus, pretend to be monogamous with all of them, and keep everyone around him in the dark?

I sat there with my jaw dropped, barely processing the words that I was hearing. I'd been what I'd thought of as 'close' friends with this guy for four years and in an on and off romantic relationship during that time. He seemed to be such a good guy.

"I know it seems hard to believe. There are probably many more girls that we don't even know about. I've struggled with anorexia for years, and I think a lot of it was impacted by the way he name-called me 'fat' and body-shamed me often. I was in the hospital and spent many years in therapy to recover from this."

I suddenly realized – that must have been why she was so skinny. Nick had told me it was because she was addicted to cocaine. "Claire, I have something weird to ask you – and please don't judge me. Do you have a problem with cocaine?"

Claire looked confused. "I've never tried it."

"Seriously?" I asked her.

"Yeah – why?"

"Nick told me you were addicted to cocaine."

Claire started laughing hysterically now. "Alex... this guy is more messed up than I thought."

It all just sounded too unbelievable to be true. The story I was fed for so many years was that Claire was a 'psycho'. But I had seen Nick with Tori in the bar – that I knew for sure. And why would he have done that to me, if there wasn't some truth to what Claire was saying? Had I not seen him and her with my own eyes, I truly think I wouldn't have believed Claire in that moment because what she was telling me was so far-fetched. It was just too hard to swallow. But I couldn't deny the truth of what I saw and how it lined up with Claire's story, not Nick's.

Claire invited Chelsea to come down and meet us at the coffee shop. We started going through our text messages and lining up dates. Chelsea showed me a text between the two of them, when he had gone to her house one morning for brunch a few months before. I realized by looking at the date on the text that he had slept at my house the night before. So, he'd probably left my house that morning and walked straight to hers. That was when I knew it had to be true. There was no way she'd created that text message in that moment. It had to be real.

I went to work later that afternoon and operated the front desk of the yoga studio as if nothing was happening. Meanwhile, I couldn't think straight.

After the shock wore off, the stories Claire and Chelsea had were comforting. The three of us, all having experienced Nick's abuse, had a special connection that no one else could understand. He had successfully lied to us, abused us, and manipulated us into villainizing each other – when, really, this was no one's fault but his. Nick was the only villain here. Chelsea said to me once, "Trust me, it's easier to be mad than sad." And she was right. Once

I knew what he'd done, I couldn't be sad about it. I was just angry. Anger was easier to hold.

I started to open up about my experience with my friends. When she heard what happened, one of my friends was so mad that she threw a vodka cranberry at him in a nightclub (something I did not encourage or condone – but thought was very funny at the time). He furiously texted me later that night. "Alex, I'd appreciate if you stopped talking badly about me to your friends."

I texted him back, "I told them the truth, and I can say what I want, and they can react however they want to." He didn't reply.

The movie *The Other Woman* came out about a month later, and Chelsea, Claire and I went to see it together. We'd always joked that it was based on our lives. We tried to reach out to Tori, the girl I'd seen in the bar with him, tell her the story and save her from all of this – but she was in denial. Of course, he was a master at manipulating, and our messages to her added to the story he probably told her – that we were all 'crazy' and 'obsessed with him'. The story he told us as well. And who could blame her? We'd all fallen under his spell at some point, so we understood it. She was in love with him – and when you're in love, as the rest of us knew, you can be blinded from reality.

With that girl alliance and that strong bond, I felt better. That changed everything. Up until that point, I'd thought there was something wrong with me. I'd internalized this idea that I was unstable or crazy. But having not just one, but two other women to confirm that I hadn't completely lost my mind made all the difference. When you're going through narcissistic abuse alone, you feel isolated, confused and devastated. Especially since, to the outside world, your abuser is seen as a good person, and the abuse therefore seems unbelievable. But when other people validate your experience, things change.

Since our first session, I'd told my counselor, Sarah, the 'Nick and Tori' story. We'd been over it several times already. After connecting with Claire and Chelsea, I was looking forward to seeing her again, and walking in with sadness still, but also a new clarity, confidence and understanding. My counselor Sarah agreed and affirmed my reaction, which strengthened me even more. She shared resources with me on narcissistic abuse. This ultimately helped me to stop being so hard on myself and blaming myself. She helped me realize that it was not my fault.

I debated whether to include or omit the word narcissist in this book when I told this story. As part of my practice of *ahimsa* (non-violence), I try to avoid name-calling in general as often as possible. As well, I don't want to contribute to the generalization of the word narcissist and its inappropriate use. According to Farah Therapy and Trauma Center, using the word narcissist "has become a casual and trendy buzzword." However, in the case of the word "narcissist" in this particular moment, I chose to leave it in the book because it does not come with the intention of name calling. It comes with the intention of helping other victims of narcissistic abuse recognize, process and heal from the complex trauma they may have experienced.

All humans have narcissistic traits. Sometimes, people experience momentary lapses of judgment, when they behave more narcissistically and hurt others. When someone who has behaved narcissistically feels empathy, then they are not a narcissist. In contrast, according to Preston Ni M.S.B.A. in *Psychology Today*, "a pathological narcissist will routinely use destructive narcissistic tactics in order to gain false superiority and exploit relationships."

According to Claire Jack Ph.D in *Psychology Today*, "Narcissistic Abuse is defined as emotionally abusive behaviour." She further explains, when someone has experienced narcissistic abuse, "it can take a long time to figure out that there was anything wrong with the way they were treated, especially when the perpetrator was charming, manipulative and the picture of a wonderful parent, partner, boss, or friend to the outside world."

By Claire explaining to me that Nick was a narcissist, and giving me awareness around what I experienced, she was not trying to call Nick names. She was trying to educate me on what I'd experienced, and give me the words and understanding for things I'd experienced. She taught me about manipulation tactics like gaslighting, which is when narcissists lead you to "doubt your memories, thoughts and understanding." (Taylor Counselling Group). Another thing I'd experienced is love bombing – when Nick showered me with compliments and affection to help me trust him (Taylor Counselling Group). Triangulation is another strategy of those who manipulate others in this way, which "is a technique that involves creating tension or conflicts between people and groups" (Taylor Counselling Group) to help the narcissist feel superior. This is what Nick had done by manipulating Claire and me to dislike one another, so we didn't become friends and realize what he was doing.

A common technique of narcissists is called "hoovering", which is an attempt by the narcissist to bring the victim back into their control, after the victim has set boundaries (Taylor Counselling Group). This is why education is so important on narcissism because, otherwise, victims can believe that their abuser has changed, when they haven't, and get drawn into the abuse cycle again.

Often, when victims repeatedly enter narcissistic relationships throughout their lives, there might be issues that they need to resolve within themselves. For example, according to Claire Jack Ph.D in *Psychology Today*, victims might have experienced narcissistic abuse as a child, have low self-esteem, have codependent tendencies, or be naive. Education and awareness around narcissistic abuse, then, is key, to start to look inwards and understand what is happening within you, to begin to heal and attract healthier relationships.

Once victims become educated about narcissistic abuse and

become aware that they've experienced it, they understand it and are empowered to spot the manipulation, set boundaries and limit contact with their abusers. So that is why I made a choice to utilize the word narcissist in this book. It's in no way to call Nick names because I hold no resentment to him for what happened to me so long ago. I use the word to help educate other victims of this, shine light on the issue, and empower other victims to heal. Additionally, I debated whether to include the words "crazy" and "psycho" in this chapter, too, because I do not use those words to describe people. However, I felt it was necessary to include them, to demonstrate how narcissists can use such name calling to make individuals lose trust in one another.

I carried anger and resentment towards Nick for a long time. In *Sūtra* 1.33, Pātañjali identifies the feeling of animosity as *apuṇya* (Karambelkar 98). He explains that none of our meditation practices will work to calm and clear the mind unless we heal our animosity, and he lists four practices for us to do so. The first is friendliness towards those who are happy, or *maitrī* (98 – 103). The second is compassion towards those who are suffering, or *karuna*. The third is goodwill towards those who are successful, or *muditā*. The last is indifference to those who have harmed us, or *upekṣā*. In other words, we have to eliminate jealousy, envy, judgment and hate. We have to decide that there are no villains in our story and just be neutral *(upekshā)* or even compassionate *(karunā)* to those who have hurt us (Karambelkar 98). I wasn't able to forgive Nick at this point yet, but I was able to befriend Claire and Chelsea. This decision was my first opportunity to put this important element of yoga philosophy into practice.

When I attended a Recovery 2.0 Retreat with Tommy Rosen in India in 2024, he shared that there are no bad people – just people that aren't yet conscious. When people become conscious, their behavior rises to meet their energy. When looking back on this moment, I can appreciate that Nick was not yet conscious. He might never be in this lifetime. And I have to make peace with that reality and focus on fostering consciousness within myself.

A few months later, I went away to the yoga teacher training in Mexico – and this was a cornerstone of my healing process. During the *Satya Circles* each day, we had an opportunity for sharing in a safe, non-judgmental space. Our teachers believed that we had to begin to heal our own trauma before we held the container or space in a yoga studio to help heal others. I was still not ready to tell anyone what happened with Nick, as I doubted whether they'd believe me. At times, I didn't even believe myself. I also couldn't tell them that I thought I had bipolar, as I was still living in shame and stigma. I did bring up the mental health disorders in my family and my fear that, if I ever shared my struggles with the world, I'd be stigmatized by others. It was terrifying being so vulnerable in front of a group, but also healing, as well.

CHAPTER 13

FAITH

"What is faith?" my Qur'an teacher recently asked me. Inspired by the devotion to religion that I have seen during my time in the Middle East, I decided to study the Qur'an three times a week with a teacher in Egypt. My teacher Shaima explained to me that *eman* is the Arabic word for faith. I didn't know the answer to her question, "What is faith?" so she explained to me that faith is simply believing. Whether we believe in Allah, Buddha, God, human potential, or something else entirely – she said that we all must have faith. Faith is referred to as *ishvara* in the *Yoga Sūtra(s)* and the fifth of the *niyama(s)* is *Īśvarapraṇidhāna*, or devotion.

After my yoga teacher training, I went back to university for my fifth and final year. Things there felt different this year – because I finally had faith. Of all the things to be excited about, I was mostly excited to finally see a doctor about my mental health. Fall was always a season I associated with a depressive episode, as everything was getting dark and cold, but this year was going to be different. As the season was going to change, there was going to be a sense of change within me too. I was going to see a psychiatrist. I was going to be put on medication. I also felt very connected and committed to my practice and excited to begin to teach. I finally had faith, or *eman*, or *Śraddhā*, that everything was going to get better.

This year was going to be special, too, as I was moving in with roommates that I had a strong connection with all throughout university. Nick and I no longer spoke, but his roommate Zach from first year was still a close friend of mine. Zach, my housemates and I would spend time cooking together, pouring glasses of red wine and playing our favorite board games. Claire and I became close friends at this point, too. We were both in the Bachelor of Education degree program, so we took all the same classes. We also spent our weekend nights going out together. Once, when we left the bar after a night out and went for pizza, we ran into Nick. We could not stop laughing. All these years he'd wanted us to hate and blame each other, and we'd done the opposite of that. We'd become close friends and each other's supports. We thought this was so funny. Claire later signed for a job in Dubai a few months before I signed for the job in Kuwait – and we were excited about the possibility of remaining close in the Middle East (even though we'd be a plane ride apart).

I was practicing and teaching yoga regularly, and on the whole, doing so much better, but I still struggled with my mental health from time to time. It was an unresolved question to which I needed an answer. Did I have bipolar? And how could I deal with it? My counselor from a few months before, Sarah, assured me that this question would be solved – and finally, after five years, someone in the counselor's office at my university didn't let me down. For this referral, I went to the same building that housed the mental health counselors on the university campus, but this time, instead of the mental health counseling office on the second floor, I was referred to the physicians, on the first floor. Finally, I saw a doctor. After five years of going to counselor after counselor, that doctor referred me to the campus psychiatrist. At the time, I was so relieved.

I will never ever forget driving over to Providence Care – formerly known as Rockwood Asylum for the Insane – established in 1862 on the shores of Lake Ontario in Kingston. It was a four-story limestone building, built using convict labor from the Kingston Penitentiary. It felt like a spooky, old, scary building. The people I passed on the way in were of lower socio-economic status and seemed to be presenting with more severe symptoms than me.

I felt very out of place. I walked in in my Ugg boots, my shiny Lululemon leggings and my Canada Goose, down-filled jacket, which had a fur-lined trim. As a blonde university student, I was so clearly coming from a place of privilege that was not comparable to the people around me. No one else looked like me.

Did I belong here? I was scared at this point. It was frightening to accept that this was where I needed to be. At the same time, I had wanted this moment since I was eighteen years old and read that psychology textbook, so I wasn't going to turn around now.

I walked in the wide and large doorway to the facility, which was clearly under construction. I went up to a woman sitting at a desk behind a glass wall and told her I was there to see Doctor Johns. I remember her giving me several instructions – go down the hall, take the first left, walk up the stairs, turn on your right, go through the door, go past the cafeteria, go downstairs… there were so many directions. I forgot them before I even took the first turn.

Old buildings in Canada are like this; my high school and the buildings on our university campus being similar. They were built hundreds of years ago, with renovations and extensions creating nooks and crannies. My high school even had a 'stairway to nowhere', which ascended to the third floor but didn't connect to the third floor itself. Old buildings in Canada are endless mazes. There were no maps helping individuals find their way around, and they were not the most user friendly. I was terrified. I nodded and tried to force back tears as I started on my way.

By the time I was midway down the first hallway, I was weeping. I carried on, walking alone, and I came across a construction worker in big, dusty boots, gloves and a hard hat. "Are you okay?" he asked me.

Through choked-back tears, I could barely say, "I'm looking for Dr Johns." He stopped what he was doing and started to walk alongside me, asking people along the way where the office was and escorting me there. I'll never forget the kindness of this stranger in that moment. All he did was walk beside me, but sometimes all you need is someone to walk beside you. It made me feel much less alone.

When I arrived at Dr Johns' office, I told him my story. He listened, patiently, while I cried and shared with him all the issues that I had experienced, most of which I've forgotten now. At the end, when I was done, he told me what I'd been so desperate to hear for so many years. "You're in a depressive episode. We will give you mood stabilizers. It's likely that you could have bipolar. Putting someone who has bipolar on antidepressants is very dangerous, as it can trigger mania. I can't confirm you have bipolar as I've never seen you in a manic episode, so the smartest thing for me to do is to give you mood stabilizers."

He put me on 12.5mgs (a very, very small dose) and had me follow up a week later. A week later, my mood was normal. I was smiling, laughing and feeling optimistic about everything. Dr Johns said that I most likely had bipolar disorder. As he explained, most bipolar patients react very positively to Seroquel, whereas patients with major depressive disorders take longer to recover. We increased another small amount to 25mgs and, because he had seen such a positive recovery in such a short period of time, we left it at that.

Having a diagnosis was a relief and, being on medication, I started to feel okay again. My case was transferred to physicians who continued to prescribe my medication, and I never saw the psychiatrist again. I continued to take the medication and thought my problem was solved.

I presume, looking back, that the university I went to was overwhelmed with many students struggling with their mental health, and at the time that I saw that particular doctor, I was a milder case than most. During my first year at university, in 2010, a few students died by suicide, and mental health amongst students was a growing concern. Given the long waitlists and the number of students struggling, there wasn't a necessity to keep seeing me, which is why I was transferred back to the physicians and never saw the psychiatrist again. I seemed healthy enough, and the medicine seemed to work. Neither me nor the psychiatrist followed up.

There are many things that I wish had been done differently. I wish instead of being placed on medication at such a young age, I was first educated on the importance of the food and drink that I was putting into my body. I wish I was taught some practical coping skills such as journaling, meditation, and sharing circles, for my stressors and struggles. I also wish that I had been more honest with the doctor about how much I had been drinking alcohol.

I did a disservice to myself by downplaying what an unhealthy lifestyle I was living. At that point, I was happy and bubbly and showed immediate change, and the fact that I was practicing and teaching yoga probably made the doctor think that I was on the path to recovery. I was probably one of the most proactive patients he'd ever had – getting on medication when I was still highly functioning before I hit a severe downward spiral. I projected that I was a yoga teacher, and I was struggling with a hereditary mental illness, and to a doctor, it seemed like putting me on a small dose of mood stabilizers and sending me on my way would be fine. The reality was that I was struggling with alcohol consumption and binging on sugar regularly. I lived across the street from a beer store. My three roommates were often out of the city of Kingston for long stretches of eight weeks at a time, doing placements in the city of Toronto, leaving me home alone to drink. On the weekends, with my friends, I'd binge even more. To me, drinking was normal, so I didn't see it as a problem or a red flag.

The same day that I got prescribed the medicine, my roommates and I hosted a party at my apartment. Everyone was there – Claire, Zach, and all of our other friends. I started off the night by saying, "I'm only going to have one drink…" This lasted thirty minutes. Before long, I was the drunkest girl at the party, once again.

One of my idols at the time was a yoga teacher that I often quoted in my yoga classes. She would post on *Instagram* that balance was all about having tequila shots by night and practicing yoga by morning. Drink wine, but don't forget your green juice. Walk in stilettos by night and barefoot on the beach by day. I still love this teacher very much, but I used this attitude as an excuse. I was the 'balanced yoga teacher', the one who told everyone to be zen by day and blacked out by night. 'Moderation'.

It is accurate that there is an element of yoga philosophy that speaks to moderation called *brahmacharya*. More traditional schools of thought consider this *yama* abstinence. This is the fourth *yama* in the *Pātañjalayogasūtra* text. Many people use this nod to moderation as a free ticket to continue to engage with substances and behaviors that are destructive for them. I know I have my whole life: from consuming too much fast food, to drinking alcohol, to my addictive relationship with social media. Only you can look inwards and identify if the relationship you have with a person or substance or behavior is getting in the way of who you want to be. Sometimes abstinence is a more healthy choice if moderation isn't a possibility.

At that point in my life, I thought I was acing the moderation game. I thought I was done. I thought my mental health was managed, and I could handle Kuwait. I thought I was ready for the move, but I later realized that no, I was not as ready for it as I thought I was. This wasn't like a move to the UK or the United States with similar cultural norms and values. This was Kuwait. This was a culture, history, climate and society that was completely foreign to anything I'd ever known. I wasn't aware that the next two years would become both the most challenging and the best years of my life. And so, when I got on the plane to Jeddah, Saudi Arabia a few months later, I had no idea what I was in store for.

PART TWO

Sacral *Chakra* – I Go with the Flow

The sacral *chakra*, according to yoga philosophy, is located in the abdomen, lower back and sexual organs. The Sanskrit term for it is *svadhisthana*, which means 'one's own place'. It's related to emotions, sexuality, and it is connected to the element of water. This energy center connects to our ability to live fluidly, experience depth of feelings, and embrace change (Judith 34).

SACRAL *CHAKRA* YOGA SERIES:

As human beings, it is our tendency to want to hold on – to relationships, people, places. But when we finally let go, what we receive can be beautiful – if we take the risk and are open to it.

"Release" is eight classes of a flow and let go practice – half *vinyasa*, half *yin*. We'll release the tension stored in our bodies – especially the shoulders and the hips – and discover what we need to let go of to find freedom.

Join me for "Release" – finally let go – and receive.

https://bit.ly/TheMindfulLifePractice_ReleaseBeginners

SACRAL *CHAKRA* PHOTO LIBRARY: YEAR ONE IN KUWAIT

In this blog post on my website, I share memories from my first year living in Kuwait:

https://bit.ly/KuwaitMemories

CHAPTER 14

THE BEGINNING

"I love you so much," my mom said as she hugged me hard. "Don't forget to text me when you get there."

At age twenty-three, I flew by myself from Toronto to Frankfurt, wearing my grandfather's special knitted white sweater. He'd worn that sweater to the hospital where cancer slowly killed him within two months. As he took his last breaths, I remember nervously asking my nana: "Is it okay with you if I have that white sweater?" I was afraid she'd be offended, but she was actually delighted, and it became something special that I always wore when I flew. Maybe it gave my nana comfort to imagine my grandad's arms around me, protecting me, as I traveled towards foreign lands.

When I landed in Frankfurt, I went straight to the gate for my flight to Kuwait, even though I had a six-hour layover and had plenty of time to spare. I was not an experienced independent flyer – every time I'd been in an airport, I'd been with my family or a group facilitator. This was the first time I was leading myself through an international airport and traveling through dramatic time zone changes. I was scared I'd miss the flight. The first thing I noticed was that the flight's destination was not Kuwait. It was Jeddah, Saudi Arabia. I began to panic. Was I actually moving to Saudi by mistake?

There were no flight attendants in sight to ask, so I found a plug and set up watching *The Fosters* on my MacBook. I knew that I wouldn't have internet access when I first moved to Kuwait, so I had downloaded all five seasons of *The Fosters* to watch on my MacBook throughout the flight and once I'd moved into my apartment. *The Fosters* was a popular American television drama at the time that featured a blended family and touched on LGBT issues. When I started to watch the show in the Frankfurt airport, I also started to worry – what if my colleagues looked at my computer and saw that there were two women kissing on the screen? I assumed that these people were conservative individuals because they had chosen to move to Kuwait. The irony in this was that I had also chosen Kuwait, and I was not conservative. It turned out that many of the colleagues I later met were some of the most open-minded individuals I knew. Their international exposure made them much more open-minded rather than closed.

Gradually, the crew of schoolteachers started assembling to board the flight. They didn't know me, and no one said "hello", but I recognized many faces from email exchanges we'd shared. I saw my team leader, principals and vice principals. Seeing them, even if we didn't converse, reassured me that yes, I was in the right place. I learned that the destination of the flight was Jeddah because they merged the flights that were traveling to Jeddah and Kuwait. They did that often – since neither of these locations were tourist destinations, they had to consolidate the flights.

On the plane, for the first time in my life, I saw some men wearing traditional Kuwaiti dress, which I later learned was called a *dishdasha*. A *dishdasha* was a white robe with a long, white headscarf – a *ghutrah* – and a black rope around the crown of their heads, called an *agal.* Many of the men wore leather sandals and brand-name sunglasses. They had sound canceling headphones attached to their iPhone 8s – the newest model at the time. There were Kuwaiti families on board too, with some of the women wearing *abaya* – a black dress – and hijab, a head covering.

The call to prayer echoed through the airplane televisions as we took off, which was the first time I'd ever heard it. Flights going to the Middle East from international airlines allowed alcohol on board, thankfully, so I was able to order my final beers.

Eight hours later, the flight landed in Kuwait International Airport and everyone rushed to get off the plane. I got onto the shuttle bus and then moved out into the airport. The airport swarmed with people moving in every direction. At the luggage carousel, both my suitcases came through on schedule. Helpers picked up the bags for us, and men from India hoisted them onto carts and pushed them beside us. I'd never had a person push my luggage through an airport before – I was twenty-three years old and was definitely capable of doing it myself. In fact, all my life I'd done it myself. But one of the principals, who had been on the flight with us, came around and told us, "Don't worry about it. We'll pay for the luggage carts."

The other teachers and I joined another long line, which led towards a group of men who would inspect our bags. Alcohol, pork, drugs, porn and sex toys are all *haram* – strictly forbidden – when entering Kuwait. I had a small feeling of panic, though I knew I didn't have any of these things in my bag. Would my mood stabilizers count as drugs? I didn't have to worry. It didn't seem to be any problem.

We walked through the gates. The arrivals at the Kuwait airport were unlike anything I'd seen before. So many arrivals seemed to involve a fanfare of the entire extended family holding massive confetti machines, bouquets of flowers and signs to greet their loved ones. I was amazed at how some families went above and beyond to celebrate their loved ones – my family never greeted me like this. Waiting for us, just beyond the gates, were all the people I'd seen on the school website. The principals of the high school, middle school and elementary school and even William, the man who'd hired me on *Skype*, were there to greet us.

In exchange for our passports to complete the visa process, the administration gave us an envelope with a very small amount of cash, which was meant to sustain us for a month, until our first pay cheque.

We walked outside, and that's when the heat and humidity hit me: it was like I was walking through a hairdryer. The luggage helpers put our bags on the back of a pickup truck. The other new teachers and I sat ourselves in a small, gray minivan with broken seatbelts, faded curtains and multicolor stripes across the seats. The front windows had beads, dusty curtains and small figurines. We waited for the remaining new teachers to get their luggage and to load on the bus before driving off to our new homes. The aisle filled up with jump seats pulled down to fit everyone.

Everything was foreign to me but exciting: the language, the smell, the heat and even the humidity, the way the roads all had a boulevard down the middle and U-turns were the norm. Traffic was bursting over the boulevards. It was an army of honks and beeps and horns.

We traveled for about an hour before pulling up to what seemed like a beautiful hedged archway, lined with twinkly Christmas lights. Before arriving in Kuwait, we had been given our apartment assignments via email, and so I knew I was living in the 'Addition' – a small building adjacent to the gated community where most teachers would be living.

William announced, "Addition people, come with me." Everyone assigned to the gated community – most of the group and seemingly all of the women except me – went through the hedge archway. They went into an enclosed compound called 'The Oasis'. The rest of us turned right and walked along the busy, hectic dirt road.

We came to a building with a gate. William reached through the gate, opening the latch without a key, and we followed him through the ground floor to a metal elevator and rode it up to the fourth floor. I was in apartment A-19.

I couldn't figure out how to turn on any of the lights or the power, not knowing that all power outlets in this part of the world had a little switch that needed to be turned on. When I finally figured out how to turn on the lights, I saw the place. The apartment had a long hallway, which led to a small room with a washer. There was a tiny room that was the kitchen, which was smaller than the walk-in closets in the apartment I'd lived in at university. It had a small amount of counter space, large enough to fit a microwave, but not enough to actually prepare meals. I had two bedrooms and some furniture that was falling apart. At that point in the journey, I don't even think I noticed these details – I was just beyond proud to have my own apartment for the first time in my life, which I'd gotten with my first job. I didn't care that the drawers broke when I tried to pull them open, or the bed collapsed under my weight when I sat on it. I was so excited.

The school had said they'd provide bedding, so no need to pack it, but really what they'd provided was cheap, colorful pieces of fabric that had been left folded on the mattress. Because it didn't have the elastic band of a fitted sheet, it couldn't be tucked around the mattress properly. Nevertheless, determined to be optimistic, I rolled the fabric out over the mattress, and I went to sleep.

The bright orange sun was rising over the Persian Gulf and streaming through cracks in the window curtain when I woke up around six in the morning. I pulled open the curtains fully and saw the sea, the dust and the workers in their gray and brown jumpsuits, sprawling all over the roads. I heard the honks and beeps and saw the water trucks backing up. I could feel the desert heat radiating through the window. I remember thinking, *So this is the Middle East.*

I pulled the curtains shut again – it was too hot to leave them open. I opened my suitcase and unpacked the few things I'd brought. One of the cupboards in the spare bedroom became the pharmacy of the apartment. Before moving to Kuwait, I'd heard that some shampoos, deodorants and tampons were hard to find, so I'd stocked up on them before I left. I'd excessively brought ten boxes of tampons with me.

The irony of this investment was that I went on to not have a period for the entire time I lived in Kuwait, for the first time in my life since I was thirteen years old, so I didn't even need this massive tampon supply whatsoever. I think that my period stopping was due to two reasons: first, chronic stress, and second, my intra-uterine device (IUD) being inserted, which provided hormones that reduced the likelihood of getting a period. When I accepted the job in Kuwait, something I was massively panicked about was starting a relationship with someone, having premarital sex, becoming pregnant and getting arrested. In some countries all around the world, including Kuwait, and Indonesia, where I presently live, premarital sex is illegal, as are abortions. There were stories of women going to jail over this. When I planned to move to Kuwait, due to this, a Canadian physician encouraged me to get an IUD. The device was 99.9% effective at birth control, and it was the best method of preventing pregnancy on the market (Santos-Longhurst). Moreover, once the IUD was inserted, you never had to think about it again. At the time, the benefits of the IUD sounded good to me. On reflection, I find it interesting that so little education was given to me about the IUD's side effects. That's because little research is done. One side effect I've learned now, after joining a *Facebook* support group so many years after having it inserted and removed, is that the IUD can lead women to have suicidal thoughts. In a review that summarizes the results of twenty-two studies conducted on IUD usage, Taylor and Francis Online concluded that many studies report the association between psychiatric symptoms and IUDs (Elsayed et al.). The review recommended that all doctors be aware of these risks, especially depressive symptoms and suicidality – and that counseling patients about these risks should be mandatory (Elsayed et al.).

Like my relationship with alcohol, there are many factors that caused my mental health downward spiral, and it would be both difficult and naïve to identify and blame just one. But the IUD was certainly a contributing factor. I don't think it's any doctor's fault that I ended up suicidal; I just think there was little research and awareness out there of how much hormonal IUDs can impact women's mental health. As a member of an IUD *Facebook* support group, years later, I frequently send messages of hope and support to other women experiencing depressive episodes and suicidal thoughts like I did when I was using an IUD – that once they get the device removed, it will get better.

But I'm jumping ahead. We're still in the beginning: before all of that. The first few months in Kuwait. I was in the hyper-stress, culture-shock mode of go-go-go – accomplish this, make a good impression, be the best teacher I could be. It was the 'honeymoon' phase of culture shock. I was the young, bright-eyed twenty-three-year-old, determined to have a positive impact and make a difference. And determined to prove that, despite how young I was, I deserved to be there.

CHAPTER 15

HONEYMOON

One of the best things about living in Kuwait was the beautiful sunrises and sunsets. They are brilliant burnt-orange and illuminating purples, fire reds and cotton candy pink. I think these colorful horizons are either created by the dust or the pollution in the air. In any case, I loved them. While riding the minibus down Highway Thirty to and from Mahboula in the morning and the evening, I was amazed.

In the early stages, everything about Kuwait was exciting: the sunrise, the sunset and the haunting call to prayer echoing through my apartment. I immediately felt at home within this complicated continent. Since I was a child, I had wanted to move to a continent that was hot. And I got what I'd always dreamed of – blazing heat, hot sand and palm trees. I was so happy and at home in the heat.

At the time I moved to Kuwait, I was still addicted to coffee (and have gone on-and-off with that addiction for many years afterwards), but for some reason, in the beginning, I didn't want to invest in a proper coffee machine, and so I'd drink my instant coffee as Mahboula was waking up. I think in retrospect that shows how the situation felt very temporary to me. It hadn't yet sunk in that I'd be there for over seven hundred days, so it was probably the right time to get a proper coffee machine. By my second month in the country, my colleague Connor came into my classroom one day and asked in a loving, joking tone, "Are you seriously drinking instant coffee right now? What are you doing? Get a real coffee machine!" Despite being a takeaway coffee snob all my life, getting a proper coffee machine honestly hadn't occurred to me until that moment. I think, in my mind, I was on a temporary vacation – not committing to living in Kuwait for two years.

With a travel mug filled with instant coffee in hand, I'd ride the elevator down to catch the 4:45am bus to school. I'd see the sliver of the moon hanging just beyond the mosque as I waited for my ride. Teachers would fill the lined seats with their sleepy faces – an eclectic group, including my colleague Richard, a mindfulness guru from the Southern States; Bryan, a surfer dude from New Zealand with a man bun; and Laurie, a frazzled American in her late fifties, who looked lost and ready to retire any day. Getting up that early was exciting, not exhausting.

Kuwait was so unbelievably different from anything I'd ever known. It is authentically Arabic – something so unique to this particular country in a globalized, modern, westernized world. Its uniqueness was something I only became aware of when I later saw Abu Dhabi and Dubai and could compare them. While Abu Dhabi and Dubai look so spotless they could be staged, with neatly manicured AstroTurf, rows of palm trees, glitz and glam, Kuwait remained untouched by tourism. Why was this? Some people said Kuwait never recovered from the Iraq invasion of 1991. Others thought it was consciously choosing to remain traditional, in contrast to its neighbors, the UAE. Just north of Mahboula, towards the airport, all I'd see around me was sand, with no trees or other vegetation, and sometimes it felt like I'd moved to a colony on Mars.

I had never seen a group of people stop everything and start reciting prayers in the middle of the road before. I was raised without religious practices – I never went to church, and I hadn't been directly exposed to any religions throughout my childhood like Islam. In Canada, we had a church just ten houses away from mine, but religion could have been happening inside of it and I'd have no idea – I'd walk right past it. In Kuwait, religion was an essential part of the day for many people.

At 11:00am on Fridays, when the largest prayer time would occur, I'd watch out the window of my apartment as hundreds of men bowed together, synchronized in the same postures. I wondered out loud, "Why are they all outside instead of inside?" My new friend Rebecca, who I had been connected to by David, explained that they'd already filled up the inside of the mosque, and the men outside were the overflow. They faced a direction that seemed random to me, but I learned afterwards that it was the direction of Mecca, the holy spot in Saudi Arabia where Muslims traveled for their pilgrimage.

During Friday prayers, the energy on the street changed instantly – what was chaotic Mahboula suddenly flipped a switch and became overwhelmingly calm, as the neighborhood let go of movement and received stillness. Everything shut down – stores, music, activity. Even if we weren't participating in prayer as individuals, we were participating in the action of prayer. Mahboula became deeply focused, as its residents individually and collectively spent time in the energy of reverence and acknowledgment of their culture. From my eyes, this was magical.

The only other place I had felt this energy before was within the yoga studio when the room filled up with the crowded mats of students of yoga who were all there for the same purpose. Whether we found meaning in worshipping God, Allah, Buddha, or anything else, it didn't matter – we were devoting our practice to something meaningful to us. This is what Pātañjali identified as *Īśvarapraṇidhāna*, or the practice of devotion to a higher power, which is the fifth *niyama* of yoga. I hadn't thought of or considered the parallels between my yoga practice and prayer until I saw prayer for the first time in Kuwait.

During culture shock, people often go through a few phases: the honeymoon phase being the first of them ("Culture shock part 1: the four stages"). This is the phase in which travelers become infatuated with everything – the language, people and food – in their new surroundings ("Culture shock part 1: the four stages"). I was no different. It was the first time in my life I'd been away from Canada for more than a month at a time, and the first time I'd been integrated into a culture so different from my own. It was the first time I'd lived somewhere foreign and had to adapt to a new way of being and thinking. Every single thing was exciting and moving to Kuwait was "The best decision I ever made!"

Things were so different, yet the same. Something I knew before I moved was that the workweek would be different. It was Sunday to Thursday, instead of Monday to Friday. That was because the holy day in Islam is Friday. Also, the schedules for the children at school included Arabic lessons, instead of French, like in Canada. The children who were Muslim also took Islamic studies classes at school, which were government mandated. The children who were not Muslim instead studied Spanish during that time. Religious studies were something we didn't offer at public school in Canada.

But there were also distinct similarities between Kuwait and Canada, too. Just like it was memorable to David that there was a pizza shop across the street from the pyramids of Giza, I was entertained by the fact that the school ordered a familiar pizza brand for delivery for the teachers during our first week there. The branded pizza boxes looked exactly the same as they did in Canada, except for the Arabic lettering on the logo. Within the first day or two, the school took us to the grocery store, where I could find some variation of just about everything I ate at home, except my favorite brand of nacho chips. They also took us on a trip to Avenues

Mall, which I'd heard was the second largest mall in the world, had all of the well-known Western restaurants and shops that I loved. While my apartment came furnished, I quickly sped through my small allowance provided to me by the school and cleaned out the furniture store with Rebecca for extra things to outfit my apartment – coat hangers, shower curtains, proper bedding and bathmats.

We got picked up in a taxi. On the way, the driver had to stop to fill the car with petrol (what we call gas in Canada). I remember being completely shocked that the driver left the engine running while an attendant filled the tank. First, in Canada, I'd never had an attendant fill my tank with gas – they had attendants at some stations, but my mom always said it was too expensive. We always used the self-serve pumps. But in Kuwait (and the rest of the countries in Asia I've lived in, both the United Arab Emirates and Indonesia) there was no such thing as self-serve, only full-service stations. And second, I'd never seen someone leave their engine running while gas was being filled. My mom had told me we always turn off the ignition while filling the car with gas, or it might explode. "Isn't this dangerous?" I asked Rebecca.

She shrugged. "If they turned off the ignition, the air conditioning would turn off, and it would be way too hot!" That explanation made sense to me. "Besides," she added, "I've lived here for ten years, and they do it all the time. And I've survived."

When my students were dropped off on the first day of school, the reality sank in that I was responsible for keeping twenty-six seven and eight-year-old children safe, all on my own, and that no amount of education had prepared me for it. I was twenty-three years old – I could barely even take care of myself. How was I going to take care of children? I had been a summer camp counselor before, and a babysitter, but for some reason, this felt different.

The first time I saw a list of Arabic names, I found it challenging to differentiate between them because of how similar they sounded to me. There were many Abdullahs, Mohameds and Ahmeds on every class list.

I realize in retrospect that if a Kuwaiti teacher came to Canada and taught my high school class, he'd probably say the same thing about my group of friends growing up: Emily, Emma, Amy, Alex, Ali, Becca, Becky… to native English speakers, the differences in our names were crystal clear, but to a non-native speaker, those names could all seem pretty similar, right? The same was how I, as an outsider, experienced my Arabic class list.

Balinese names, where I live now, are even more similar than Arabic ones. In Balinese culture, children are named based on their order of birth. The children that are first born are either named Wayan or Putu, the children that are second born are named Kadek or Made, the children that are third born are either Komang or Nyomang, and the children that are fourth born are named Ketut.

When I was new to Kuwait, I found myself judging the similarity of names in Arab culture. Now I realize I just didn't understand that there are different methods of naming children around the world, with no one way being superior to another.

During my final year of my Bachelor of Education, I'd done a project on names – I invited all my classmates to research the history and meaning of their names and share what they'd learned in a book that I put together. In my neighborhood in Canada, most individuals had names that had a familial significance – they may have been named after a parent, grandparent, or great-grandparent, and my classmates wrote about this in their books. My professor Shelly said to me, when giving me feedback, "I love this project because names are so important." I've thought about that a lot when learning how to pronounce names in different cultures. Names are important. So, I took the time to carefully learn them all, even if it took a while and was extremely confusing for me.

In Arab culture, people and places are often named after things. For example, *Noor* means 'light', and *Reem* means 'gazelle', and they are both common names. This was different from my experience and understanding of most of my friends' names in Canada.

Also, the same person could have three different spellings of their name on three different ID cards. This was because they were phonetically sounding out the letters from Arabic into English letters. Each Arabic letter did not have a direct match for English. In Canada, it would be considered rude if someone spelled my name with an I, like 'Alix' instead of 'Alex'. But in Kuwait, no one was offended if you wrote their name 'Nour', or 'Noor', – to them, these were the same thing.

The children brought their own school supplies with them on the first day of school. There was no storage in the classroom, and so they dropped their gigantic shopping bags on the floor, and highlighters, notebooks, zipper plastic folders and erasers spilled everywhere. I asked the children to label their notebooks, and then I stood back and looked around at this chaotic scene, overwhelmed. Most of the children were not labeling their books as I'd instructed – they were sticking labels on the backs of their books or upside down, or not at all. I didn't realize at that point that, as a teacher for children (of any nationality around the world), you must give every individual instruction as slowly and simply as possible for the children to follow along. An instruction such as, "Label all five of your books with your name and write 'Science', 'Social Studies', 'Math', 'Reading' and 'Writing' on each one," was far too complex for an eight-year-old to handle on their own. You have to give each instruction step by step. Instruction one would be: "First, take out your top book. Flip it so that it opens to the left." Then, stop and make sure each child has done that before moving on to step two. I had a lot to learn.

After we organized our supplies, I asked the children to write a story on the first day of school and watched as they began to work on it, amazed. Only half of them were writing in the books from left to right – half were opening their books backwards and writing right to left. When I was in teacher's college in Canada, I'd been taught that if children wrote in their books from right to left, instead of left to right, it was possible that they had dyslexia. I looked around the room, mystified by it.

While I knew that Arabic, unlike English, was written from right to left, I didn't connect the dots on how this difference would impact how Arabic speaking children would read and engage with English. Not only would it be totally normal for them to be confused about how to label and open their books, but even grammatical differences and letter differences would confuse them much more than a native English-speaking child. Learning two completely different languages simultaneously is very challenging. At the end of my teaching career, I understood that, as a teacher, I had to frequently remind and re-teach the children how to label, open, hold, read and write within a book – but as a first-year teacher in Kuwait, I didn't get this.

No one introduced us and educated us on these aspects of the local culture. After living in the Middle East for more than six years, it made perfect sense to me, but in the beginning, it was a culture shock. Although there was a brief cultural lesson provided by the school during my first week in the country, there was so much to learn about how this culture diverged from the North American way of living, that minute details such as grammar and language readability were overlooked. We were coached in larger cultural differences, such as to not outstretch our hands to the opposite gender for a handshake, as some traditional Kuwaiti men and women did not touch, but these smaller details seemed to be forgotten, even though they were significant.

After two days of teaching, suddenly it was the Eid al-Adha holidays, and we had a full week off school. I learned that the

Eid holidays are two of the most important dates on the Islamic calendar. Eid al-Fitr is at the end of Ramadan and marks the first day that religious practitioners can eat between dawn and dusk after a month of daytime fasting ("Eid Al-Fitr"). Eid al-Adha is linked to the story of Prophet Ibrahim in the Qur'an (Hassan). In the story, Allah asks Ibrahim to sacrifice his son, and he plans to obey this command. At the last moment, Allah gives Ibrahim a ram to sacrifice instead. Eid al-Adha is celebrated on the last day of the Hajj, which is the pilgrimage to Mecca, Saudi Arabia, that Muslims take once in their lifetime, as dictated in the Five Pillars of Islam. Even when Muslims aren't taking the pilgrimage to Mecca, it's still one of the most important religious periods each year for Muslims.

Many of my colleagues were grumbling about the timing of this very early ten-day Eid holiday because all of the new teachers were stuck in the country, as our visas weren't processed yet, and we didn't have our passports. They wanted to travel. But I didn't understand. Why would I want to leave? I just got here! I loved Kuwait, and I was so excited to have ten days of free time to explore.

At the start of the week off, I went with some colleagues down to Souq Mubarikya. I loved the souq because it contrasted the Avenues Mall, where I got to experience the modern lifestyle that was so similar to North America. The souq was an opportunity for me to learn about the history and traditions of this new country I was going to call my home. It was a maze of alleyways, with small shops selling spices, olive oil, carpets and bags made of camel skin. Silks, spears and toy Bedouin guns hung on the walls. Before the discovery of oil, Kuwait's economy was based on pearl diving, maritime trade and construction of wooden ships, so miniature figurine ships – relics of this time – were for sale everywhere.

A few days later, I was at a party within my compound, and I met a teacher named Ali, who had lived in Kuwait all his life. After speaking with me, he said, "I've never met someone so excited to be in Kuwait!" One day over Eid, he took me to visit the main tourist sites in the country. We visited the Kuwait Towers, which were under renovation (and had been for the last seven years). The towers had large blue balls on top of them, which had been observation towers at one point before the renovations began. He also took me to The Scientific Center to see a small aquarium. The last place he took me was to visit the Al-Hashemi-II – the largest dhow ever built and the one world record Kuwait held. It was a stunning, large wooden boat on the shoreline near the city. In the center was a large eye. I asked him, "What's that eye? I've seen it everywhere."

He explained to me the meaning of the evil eye. In traditional Arab culture, some believe that when anyone compliments you on your beauty or success, their jealousy could curse you. This is called the evil eye. To ward off the evil eye, Arabic speakers say *Mashallah*, which means 'God has willed it'. I had heard this expression several times since I'd moved there but didn't know the context. People hung the evil eye as a decoration on their walls or on jewelry to protect themselves.

Mashallah wasn't the only Arabic word I learned. I quickly picked up other Arabic terms because it was the language I heard spoken all around me, every day. I had never heard Arabic spoken before moving to Kuwait. People spoke Arabic passionately – but because I didn't understand what they were saying, I thought they were having arguments, when really, they were just having ordinary conversations.

I learned phrases like *Salam Alakom* (peace be upon you), *Kefek* (how are you?), *Yani* (I mean) and *Habibi* (my love). I learned *Inshallah*, which was the answer to almost every question I asked. You never got a "yes" or a "no", just an *Inshallah.* I learned it means 'God willing'. It is basically 'maybe', but over time has evolved into a softer way to say no. Even after moving away from the Middle East, years later, I still sometimes answer *Inshallah* when asked questions.

There was one Kuwaiti family that invited me into their home right away. Their son Ahmed was in my class, and after teaching him for a week, his mom Salama had added me as a *Facebook* friend. I was somewhat spooked by this – in university in Canada, I was taught to keep a clear professional boundary between parents of students and their teachers. But here, in Kuwait, we were encouraged by the school leadership to accept invitations to our students' homes for dinner to experience the local culture.

I decided shortly after meeting them to accept their dinner invitation, and I quickly fell in love with their Arab hospitality. This family took me in as if I was their daughter, inviting me over for meals weekly with them.

Hospitality is deeply ingrained into the Kuwaiti and Arab tradition, and like Salama, many of the families at the school welcomed me into their homes after one or two meetings. When I spoke about this kind-hearted practice with one of my Lebanese friends years later, she explained to me, "It is written in the Qur'an that we must welcome strangers." She told me that there is a very famous Arabic quote that states, "The stranger is blind even if he has eyes." This saying illustrates how vulnerable it feels to be an immigrant or an expat in a strange land. The stranger needs help and guidance, and that's why Arab people tend to be so welcoming to newcomers.

In 2024, I started attending thrice weekly Qur'an classes online with a teacher in Egypt. She taught me that since Allah is all loving, we must also love everyone. Muslim people believe they also must love everyone, even those who are not Muslim. This practice of hospitality was so touching to me and completely different from the way my family was at home in Canada. I grew up in downtown Toronto, and we had an independent, western city mindset – every man for himself. But in Kuwait, even though I was a stranger, everyone wanted to include me in their lives, their traditions and their culture. It was so different from anything I'd ever known. Anthony Bourdain said, "You learn a lot about someone when you share a meal together." (qtd. In Thompson.) In Kuwait, I found this to be true.

When I went for dinner at Salama and Ahmed's house, they sent one of their drivers to pick me up. Once I arrived at their home, I sat at a table with flowered centerpieces flown in from out of the country. The air was scented with warm, earthy, woody oud: which I came to realize was the unofficial scent of the Middle East. Every surface was shimmering with golden tones. I was served plate after plate of food, brought in on gold trays, served by helpers. It was a good thing I wasn't vegetarian during my time in Kuwait because every dish included lamb, chicken or beef upon rice. After stuffing my face with food, Salama would always say, "You didn't eat!" I found it confusing at first. "But I ate so much!" I soon realized that it was considered part of the Kuwaiti culture for hosts to expect their guests to eat a lot of food – and feel offended or worried if they ate very little. They were worried I would go home hungry. After every meal, they would say, "You didn't eat!" but what they meant was, "Are you finished your meal?" or, "Are you sure you're not still hungry?"

Being invited into Kuwaiti homes was always exciting. Some of the homes were quite glamorous. They had large *Diwaniyas*, which are Kuwaiti seating areas, filled with over-sized, gold-plated furniture imported from Europe. From the towering ceilings hung glittery chandeliers and majestic decorations. The sitting rooms alone could accommodate at least fifty people. The taps on the sinks were made of gold. We had rounds of Arabic coffee, tea and sweets until late into the night. At a time when I was separated from my family and homesick, this meant a lot.

In Salama and Ahmed's home, I got to ask questions about arranged marriages, rules of the *hijab* and local customs. They asked me questions too, about my life growing up in Canada. "Why did you come to Kuwait? What does your family think about it back home? What did you know about Kuwait before coming here?" I was really scared in the beginning that I might offend them by speaking about my open-minded upbringing, so I was cautious about what I said or did. For instance, later on, I didn't want them to know I had a boyfriend because I thought they'd be offended by me dating before marriage. But Ahmed's father would bring up the conversation himself by asking me about my new boyfriend when I came over for dinner, making it feel okay for me to discuss. I realize now that it was an assumption I'd made that, just because they lived in a conservative country, they would be conservative individuals. The irony was that I had chosen to move to this country, and while I respected the culture, I didn't necessarily agree with all aspects of it. Just because I was living in a conservative country did not mean that I was conservative. I realize now that there are liberal and conservative people everywhere – and we should never assume that people are one way or another based on their context. Where we are is not who we are.

In October, Salama invited me to her brother's wedding – my first Kuwaiti wedding. It was so different than any wedding I'd ever attended. Traditionally, Kuwaiti weddings are segregated by gender. However, some younger, more modern couples that I met in Kuwait choose to forego this tradition and have mixed gender weddings. This wedding held only the women in one hall and the men in another. I should have been excited about this, but I was mostly nervous about it because I would have to go to this event sober. How would I have fun without alcohol? This was the first wedding I'd attended in my life without drinking.

Because I knew the event was alcohol free, I was expecting it to be boring. But what I discovered was that the women were having just as much fun, laughing, dancing, and singing as we do at a wedding with alcohol in Canada.

During the wedding, I asked Salama if the bride was also from Kuwait, and she told me she was not – she was from Palestine.

"Where's that?" I asked her, confused. I had never heard the word before.

Salama explained to me that Palestine was a country that had existed in the Levant many years ago, before Israel occupied the land in 1948. Of course, my next question was, "What's the Levant?"

She told me that the Levant is the side of the Middle East that borders the Mediterranean Sea, whereas the Gulf is the opposite side of the Middle East. The Gulf includes the Arab states with which I was most familiar, including the United Arab Emirates, Kuwait, and Saudi Arabia. The Levant includes countries such as Syria, Lebanon and Jordan.

When Israel occupied the land that formerly belonged to Palestine, the displacement of the Palestinians from their homeland was referred to as the *Nakba*, which in Arabic means 'catastrophe'. During the *Nakba*, many Palestinians were evicted from their homes. Many were killed. Palestinians who survived fled to neighboring countries around the Levant, including Lebanon, and the Gulf, including Kuwait and the United Arab Emirates. Nowadays, there are millions of Palestinians living throughout the Middle East and the rest of the world, displaced from their homeland, which is now occupied by Israel.

Growing up in Canada, I'd heard a lot about Israel. But up until that moment, I'd genuinely never even heard mention of Palestine before, let alone the conflict between Israel and Palestine.

Salama explained to me that the bride's family actually couldn't come to the wedding because they were stuck in Gaza. They had limited freedom to travel and limited access to their passports. The officials in Israel would approve or deny their travel requests, and if they didn't have connections to someone high up in the government, then they were out of luck. So most of the guests at this wedding were friends and family of the groom – people who lived in Kuwait and could attend.

Honestly, there were a few things that were hard to accept and believe in my brain. 1) I couldn't comprehend why my Canadian education had never covered the history between Israel and Palestine, and 2) I couldn't believe that individuals were still living in these conditions today. These revelations were so shocking that I think my brain couldn't process or accept what she was telling me.

I nodded my head and listened, watching the pain in her eyes, with my hand to my heart. I couldn't imagine what living in these circumstances was like. There were no words I could say.

Pātañjali refers to suffering as *duḥkha*, and in *Sūtra* 2.15 he explains that suffering is unavoidable (Karambelkar 199 – 204). He writes that wise people realize that everything is suffering. All humans experience suffering – and everything in life will bring us pain (Karambelkar 199 – 204). A large amount of the *Pātañjalayogasūtra* focuses on how to make peace with that pain. When we achieve a state of wisdom and knowledge around life, through our mindfulness practices, we start to understand that pain is a part of the experience of being human. When we achieve that state, we can start to sit with pain and suffering – and be present with it – both our own, and others'. Sitting in the present with pain and suffering is the only way that it will eventually come to pass.

I was alone for most of the night because Salama and her son Ahmed were part of the wedding party. I stood out as the only white, blonde, blue-eyed woman at the occasion. At one point, a Kuwaiti woman with blue hair came over to talk to me. Blue hair, hiding underneath a *hijab*! A year before, I'd dyed the ends of my hair pink, but I didn't think it would suit the culture in the Middle East. I would have never predicted that a Kuwaiti woman would have also colored her hair in vibrant colors. I started to see that maybe we were more similar than we were different.

She pulled me by the arm and dragged me to the dance floor to participate in line dancing to Arabic songs. At first, I felt uncomfortable doing this sober, but I quickly forgot about my discomfort and started laughing and joking with her. After dancing, we sat down to drink Arabic coffee and eat Medjool dates. She asked me, "Why did you move to Kuwait?" I told her the story of meeting my mentor, David, and him inspiring me to move to the Middle East. The next thing she asked was, "Where do you live?"

"Mahboula," I told her.

She looked horrified. "Why do you live in Mahboula? That is not a nice place to live. No one wants to live there. What about Salmiya or Salwa? Those neighborhoods are so much better!"

"Mahboula is just where the school houses us," I explained.

"I can't believe the school has you living there… that is not a good part of Kuwait. There are much nicer neighborhoods that would be better for you to live in to have a better experience of our country." I didn't know what to say to her, so I said nothing. A moment later, she asked, "Do you know what Mahboula means in Arabic?"

"No," I said.

"Crazy lady."

"Crazy lady?"

"Yes. A long time ago, there was a mad woman who lived there. She scared everybody, so no one wanted to go. So, we called it *Mahboula* so no one would go there." I'm not sure if this story was true, or folklore, but it's what she told me that night.

Mahboula: Mad Woman. That's where I was living.

It became normal for me to feel embarrassed whenever someone asked me where I lived, and I told them Mahboula. No one wanted to live there. But I kind of liked the name Mahboula. It had a ring to it. Now, looking back on Kuwait, I like it even more. It has a special significance. Mahboula – 'Mad Woman' – that's what I would become.

CHAPTER 16

MAHBOULA: MAD WOMAN

My yoga philosophy teacher, Anvita, in Mumbai, India recently explained to me some of the basics of *Sāṃkhya* philosophy, from which yoga is derived. There are two main elements of *Sāṃkhya* philosophy: *puruṣa* (the universal soul) and *prakṛti* (the material world). These concepts are referred to as *drashta* (the witness – a synonym for *puruṣa*) and *drshya* (the seen – a synonym for *prakriti*) in the *Pātañjala Yoga Sūtra*, but they are the same thing (Karambelkar 214 – 217). *Prakṛti* can take on many forms – it has twenty-three manifestations, including the elements, the senses, actions, the mind, and the *guṇa* (Karambelkar 211). Anvita explained to me that it's as if our soul, our *puruṣa*, has gone to the theatre to watch a play. As our soul watches the play, the performers are telling a story – changing outfits and scenes. The soul, *puruṣa*, is witnessing *prakṛti* change and evolve. This everchanging 'performance' that *puruṣa* is witnessing is all of the chaos, all of the drama, all of the happenings of our everyday life. According to Yoga *Sūtra* 2.15, everything we experience in life is pain (Karambelkar 199 – 204) and it all exists for the sole purpose to lead us towards *samādhi*, or consciousness. Contrary to what many of us feel, there are not events in our lives that are working against us. If we aren't careful, and we aren't committed to our practice, we can get sucked into the performance. But if we are engaging with our spiritual practice, then at some point, eventually, the curtains fall, and we realize that we are watching a show. When we become aware of the fact that we are watching a show, we are then able to step out of the cycle of suffering and instead witness the world as it is.

At the stage in my life when I was living in Kuwait, I wasn't deep enough into my spiritual practice to understand any of this philosophy. I didn't see it at the time, but I see it now: everything that I experienced in my twenties served a purpose, and it led me, many years later, to a state of joy and liberation.

Life for the wealthy students I worked for, essentially, was like a show, in the same way life for me in Lawrence Park, Toronto, was a show. And what's behind every show? A backstage cast and crew. AKA, Mahboula.

Kuwait is a unique country because expatriates account for seventy percent of its population. From grocery store staff, to gas station attendants, to restaurant waiting staff, to doctors: people come to Kuwait from all around the world to perform the jobs necessary to keep the country operating. Most of the poor expatriate laborers lived in Mahboula, with me, and rode buses into the city every day, working twelve-hour shifts, sometimes six days a week, to send home a couple hundred US dollars a month.

All my life, I'd lived in North Toronto, which is, without a doubt, the wealthiest and most privileged neighborhood in the city. I'd heard about neighborhoods like Mahboula in Toronto, such as Regent Park or Jane and Finch, but I'd never been to them. In Kuwait, my living situation was reversed. As a teacher in Kuwait, I worked for the wealthiest children in the country, and I rode the bus home at night to live amongst the poorest. I speak often in my yoga classes about 'clarity in contrast'. For the first time, in Kuwait, I saw clarity in contrast. I lived clarity in contrast. Moment by moment. Breath by breath. Being exposed to poverty each day first-hand was an intense experience, and I learned just how much the family, country, religion and race you are born into shapes your destiny.

After a long and tiring day at work, our minibus pulled off Highway Thirty at sunset each night to see the harsh realities of life for all of the workers in the country. Our bus of teachers would be held up behind a long line of buses full of migrant workers on their way home from work, too. Every few minutes, our bus would come to a halt as another bus in front of us stopped and unloaded. The men in the surrounding apartments lived several men to one shower, and as I watched them race across the road, I imagined they were racing to be first to line up.

From my apartment, I could look out of the windows and see men lying on their dorm room bunk beds across the road – ten men to a bedroom. They'd be hanging out the window, trying to get cell service to speak to their wives and children at home in India, Pakistan or Sri Lanka. They might climb up to the rooftop to sit and get some alone time, away from their nine roommates. They hung their laundry on the rooftops. They were saving as much money as they could of their two hundred dollars a month salary to send home to their wives and children, some of whom they hadn't seen in years.

How did all of the teachers end up living in Mahboula? The story goes that the owner of the school, a Kuwaiti man, built this apartment tower, The Oasis, about seven years prior to me moving there. People said that when our teachers' housing complex opened, it literally lived up to its name, as it was a tower built on sand drifts, an 'oasis in the desert'. You would turn off the highway and drive straight over the sand dunes and pull up to the front gate of the compound. From your apartment window, you could gaze out and look straight over the sandbanks into the Gulf. Originally, it took only a twenty or thirty minute drive from the school to the apartment complex.

That was in 2008. In a very short period of time, Kuwait exploded. Mahboula became a crowded, urban desert, with buildings built quickly, yet seemed to be already falling apart. What was once idealized as an 'oasis' away from the city had its own little city built up around it. It became a chaotic, bustling, urban setting in its own way – 'Mad Woman'. The fact that our compound was still called The Oasis was ironic to me.

Most of the teachers lived inside a walled compound with play areas, barbeques and a mossy green pool (which was later closed due to rumored hand, foot, and mouth disease being transmitted, and it never reopened). They also had a family of security guards, all five of whom were named Mohamed, who manned a security desk twenty-four-seven and carefully prevented visitors from entering if they were not accompanied by a resident. However, the overflow building that I was living in, the Addition, had no such security.

At fifty degrees Celsius, it was way too hot for a security guard to stand or sit by the gate all day without a proper office. That meant that the security guard of my building spent more time in his own apartment watching movies than anything else. He had no idea who was coming in and out each day. When you unlocked the fence by reaching your hand through, you'd see his toes poking out from underneath the partially opened apartment door, as he lay on his mattress on the floor. That's how you'd know he was there.

Because of all of the safety concerns, instead of investing in proper security for the building, the school had made a concentrated effort to hire more male teachers to house in the Addition. This made me one of the only women living there.

There were twenty-two apartments in the Addition and every single one housed a single man except for the top apartments. It was as if they put us women at the top to distance us as far as possible from the neighborhood below, with a bunch of men in the apartments in between to keep us safe. Jokingly, I referred to myself as the 'Queen of the Addition'. My humor was a strategy to make myself feel better about the situation.

Rebecca was more in the loop with gossip at the school than I was and told me that a few teachers hadn't returned to school after the summer holidays, and so there were some empty apartments in The Oasis. These teachers who fled early were called 'runners'. It was most common for teachers to leave at Christmas, when the honeymoon phase of culture shock wore off, so they were sometimes called 'Christmas runners'. But teachers left in any season – Christmas, spring break or summer vacation.

So, thanks to runners over the summer holidays, there were some empty apartments within the compound. Rebecca helped me get put on the waiting list – maybe if I was on their radar, then they'd put me on the top of the list to move into The Oasis apartments when one opened up, as it inevitably did. I emailed William, the school director, asking: "Would it be possible for me to move out of the Addition apartment and into The Oasis compound, if an apartment becomes available?"

Not long after, I got what I'd wished for – William called me into his office and told me they had an apartment inside the compound for me. It was a family-sized apartment, which typically weren't given to single teachers – they were reserved for teaching couples with children. But, because it was vacant, and he knew that I wanted to move, he decided to offer it to me on one condition: I had to agree that I'd move out into a single apartment in the compound in June of the following year. I was so happy.

Moving out the following June didn't sound too bad – at least I'd have the place for almost eight months. I visited the apartment on a Thursday night after work and unlocked the door to a huge seventy-foot living room. There were three bedrooms and three bathrooms, and there was a large, sweeping kitchen. But what was most important to me was not the size of the apartment – it was that I was going to be within the gated community. I bounced into Rebecca's classroom, delighted to share the news.

By noon, all of my colleagues knew that I'd been offered the family-sized apartment because The Oasis was like an episode of an afternoon soap opera. We all lived in a very small bubble, within which gossip was a favorite activity. People were upset. Apparently, back in June, before I'd arrived, they'd had families and couples move out of these apartments because they didn't have enough apartments to go around. Instead of offering the newly available family apartment to one of those couples or families, they offered it to me, a single teacher, for no reason. People made inappropriate jokes about what I'd done to get the apartment. These comments made me anxious and upset. I worried so much about what everyone said behind my back. But a part of me was so excited that I just tried to ignore them. I packed up all my things, and on the first day of Eid holidays, I spent the morning moving into my new place.

Not long after I moved in, it became evident: like many of the units in the tower, the air conditioning was broken, and the apartment was crawling with cockroaches. But I was okay with both things – I could wait it out a few days with no air conditioning in such extreme heat until they got around to fixing it. The responsibility was on me to find a way to exterminate the cockroaches, but I optimistically said that I could live with them. "It's a family-sized apartment, after all – the cockroaches could be my family!" I was just so thrilled to be moving out of the Addition and into the main compound. After all, I felt much safer, and now I had a place in this community I so desperately wanted to join.

Once I settled into my new place, I'd get up every morning to ride the bus into work. By this point, I'd sleep in and catch the later ride at six in the morning instead of at four forty-five. Driving down the roads, the bus would pass farmers with herds of camels walking in front of the orange and red desert sunrise. The cars would dart in and around each other, racing at one hundred and forty kilometers an hour. The eight-hour time difference between Kuwait and Toronto seemed to call even more attention to just how different my life had become from my friends. Every Sunday morning at 6am, I'd be on my way into work when it was 9pm on Saturday night, Toronto time. I'd refresh my *Instagram* feed and see pictures of my friends from high school and university at nightclubs in downtown Toronto, big pints of beer in hand. I'd wonder: *Why did I choose this life when I could have been there instead?*

But there was something about the fact that I'd made this choice. I wasn't forced to come to the Middle East. I chose it, or it chose me. I didn't want to admit that I'd been wrong – that this would be harder than I thought. So, my *Instagram* became a feed of epic international experiences, giving the appearance that I was having the time of my life when that was hardly the reality. I was moving into a depressive slump. But I didn't want to go home after telling everyone that I was moving overseas for two years. I was determined to survive it.

CHAPTER 17

NO MATTER HOW FAR YOU GO, YOUR PROBLEMS FOLLOW YOU

Something I learned after moving across the world is that, as it turns out, no matter how far across the globe you go, your problems will follow you there. You cannot run away from your beliefs, your patterns and your self-destruction. In *Pātañjalayogasūtra*, these behavioral patterns are referred to as *vāsanā(s)* – the greater cumulation of our *sanskāra(s)*, or life experiences, that shape our personalities (Karambelkar 519 – 521). Your problems will persist until you take the time to sit down with them, and ask, "Why are we this way?" and "What can we do about it?"

Many of us think that our personalities are fixed. I personally thought that living with bipolar disorder was something I inherited. It was just who I was. With this stance, there was only a problem and no solution. Through a deep spiritual practice, I've come to see that all mental health maintenance, diagnosis or not, involves active work on the individual's part to stay well. It is a process of figuring out what you need to thrive: for me, I have found that my mental health flourishes when I am practicing yoga every morning when I wake up, feeling a sense of purpose through teaching yoga, getting good sleep, eating well, reducing my stress as much as possible, and having a like-minded community to help me feel grounded. Nowadays, I no longer take medication for my mental health, and I entirely manage it on a gluten-reduced, dairy-reduced, caffeine-reduced, sugar-reduced diet (which sounds as if it's high maintenance, but it's actually quite easy – I just make sure all my plates have mostly fruits and vegetables and protein sources like meats and alternatives).

When I moved to Kuwait, however, I wasn't aware that I needed to put in so much work to stay on top of my mental health. In fact, it wasn't until every single one of the strategies and structures that I had put into place had been knocked out from underneath me, that I fully realized how much effort was needed to stay afloat. It was like I was back down at the bottom of the ocean again, struggling to swim my way to the top.

When I arrived in Kuwait, I learned that, unlike the transportation system in Toronto and Kingston, which provided freedom, structure, simplicity and predictability, transportation in my new country was limited. In Toronto, I could walk ten minutes to the subway and then take the train to meet a friend anywhere in the city. In Kuwait in 2015 (similar to Bali up until recently), there were few public transport options, and so everyone either drove, took a taxi, or had their own private driver. Due to the congestion on the roads, transportation time estimations on *Google Maps* had to be tripled… and that was on a good day!

The taxi system seemed unregulated in Kuwait – another aspect of Kuwaiti transit that was completely different from anything I'd ever known. I left Toronto before the days of *Uber*, but from the street that I grew up on, you could easily walk two minutes onto Yonge Street, stick your thumb out in the air, and get into a taxi with recognizable branding. There were three major taxi companies – Beck, Royal and Diamond – and they all protected their passengers by installing meters and cameras in each of the cars and requiring that drivers' ID cards were made easily visible. The taxi system in Kuwait, on the other hand, was completely different. All of the taxis were owned by individual Kuwaitis and driven by migrant worker drivers from neighboring countries like India. Many drivers didn't speak English and didn't turn on their meters. As a young woman who was traveling alone, it was very intimidating to try to advocate and communicate for myself when I was placed in such situations.

The school recommended one taxi driver in particular to us, Raghu. He was reliable, dependable, fair with his fares and kind. Raghu drove a car called 'Taxi Easy', and most teachers at the school used his services until they got licenses and drove their own cars.

The first time that I got into his taxi, and I mispronounced his name, Raghu looked at me directly in the rear-view mirror and said, "My name is Rag-oo – like the pasta sauce." He looked serious for a moment and then broke out into a laugh. I never mispronounced it again. Names are important.

I spent a lot of time in the backseat of his car in the early days of my time in Kuwait. Raghu spoke impeccable English, along with Arabic and Hindi, making him the ideal driver. He could ask for and understand directions from anyone he came across. He rarely had to ask for directions, though; he knew the roads of Kuwait as if he had grown up in this neighborhood – an impressive feat considering how confusing the roads were to me as a foreigner. He was also respectful, kind and compassionate.

Stuck sitting in traffic with him many days a week, I'd ask him about his life and his stories. I learned that Raghu had moved to Kuwait at the age of eighteen from India. He left his wife and his son behind to make a living, and he sent them money every month. Every few years, if he saved up enough money, he'd travel back to India for a thirty-day holiday to see them.

For the first eighteen years that he lived in Kuwait, Raghu was the driver for a Kuwaiti family. Kuwaiti families often had several drivers – one for the father, one for the mother and one for the children. He was specifically the driver for two young Kuwaiti boys. He took those boys all over the country, every single day – to school, to football (soccer) matches, to playdates – and raised them as if they were his own children. After they grew up and moved away to America for university, the family no longer needed so many drivers, and he switched his work to being a taxi driver.

I came from the land of instant and the world of on demand and, to me, the name 'Taxi Easy' was a misnomer. Raghu was one man who was on call twenty-four hours a day, seven days a week, but once you called him, you had to wait until he drove across the country to wherever you were. You couldn't get a ride in the middle of the night without advance notice, or he'd be asleep when you called. You'd have to book his services a day ahead of time if you wanted a ride anywhere. Raghu drove many of the teachers from my school – and if he happened to have someone else in the car or another ride booked when you called, he couldn't get you. From very early on, I would get so unbelievably frustrated by all of the steps involved in getting from point A to point B. Having to wait for a taxi to get anywhere bothered me because it was something I'd never had to do before. Having to plan bothered me. I wanted the freedom of being able to decide on a whim what I wanted to do during the day and be able to do so independently – I'd had that freedom all my life in Toronto and Kingston. Pātañjali says that the third cause of human suffering, or *kleśa(s)*, is *rāga*, desire (Karambelkar 187). I desired freedom – something I felt I no longer had. This caused me suffering.

For the first time in my life, I had to plan, and I had to notify Raghu over a day in advance if I wanted to go anywhere. I lacked perspective in being able to see his side – and being in my yoga practice would have been the solution to start to see this. But I wasn't practicing, so I couldn't imagine what it would be like driving all over the country, navigating the chaos of Kuwaiti traffic, trying to fit in all of his customers and keeping everyone happy. I could only see things from my perspective. I was the girl who came from the land of on demand, and I expected everything instantly.

Before I signed my contract to move overseas, I searched online for a yoga studio in Kuwait. I discovered there was only one, and it was a twenty-five-minute drive away from my apartment. Only having access to one yoga studio was so different from Toronto, which had hundreds of yoga studios when I left in 2015, including three that were walking distance from my house. The website of the one yoga studio in Kuwait looked beautiful and boasted a team of experienced, full-time yoga teachers. Some of the teachers were hired from abroad, and some of the teachers were Arab. Many had over ten years' teaching experience with top name yoga teacher trainers. Teaching yoga there full time would be my dream, but I was intimidated when I read the online bios of the teaching staff. Who was I to think that I could even get a part-time job there? I was just a twenty-three-year-old yoga teacher, who went to a random little yoga teacher training center in Mexico and had one year's teaching experience at a tiny yoga studio no one had ever heard of, in Kingston, Canada. I also had imposter syndrome and self-doubt – could I really be a yoga teacher, teaching these methods of calming and silencing the mind, when I was so troubled by my own brain?

I weighed the cost and time involved with going to the yoga studio and decided that it wasn't worth it. If I wanted to go to the yoga studio in the city, it would take me around an hour to get there – one way – and since I didn't have a driver's license yet and couldn't drive, I had to pay for a taxi each time I wanted to go. The yoga classes alone were at least double the cost of the classes in Canada. It was not a habit that my teacher's salary could afford. So, I didn't even bother going. In the meantime, I had found somewhere else interesting to teach yoga.

During my first week in the country, the school took us to a well-known hotel chain resort, known internationally, which was a five-minute drive from our accommodation. I learned that in the Middle East, it was super common for expatriates to get memberships to or even live at these beach resorts. These seaside retreats provided a little bit of a haven, where expats were free to show their shoulders, wear their bikinis and socialize. The hotel had its own spa, gym, two-kilometer stretch of beach, and group fitness classes. Luckily for me, their yoga teacher had recently left the country, and they were looking for someone. Typically, expatriates are not allowed to have additional jobs without the permission of their visa sponsor, so I asked William's permission. He encouraged me to take the position, explaining that I'd have many more friends and be happier in the country if I found hobbies outside of my job as a teacher, and he was right. I was hired and put on the schedule right away.

I was so grateful to have somewhere to teach yoga. Unfortunately for me, they wouldn't work with me in terms of timing and wanted yoga to be scheduled at the end of the night. The hotel had one multipurpose group fitness room, and their classes included Zumba, Pump, Pilates and Kids' Karate. In the manager's mind, the best timing for yoga was 7pm. Due to the unpredictability of the traffic and having to wait for Raghu to pick me up, I'd often get home at 9pm from the resort. I had to get up at 5am to catch the bus to school, leaving me perpetually exhausted. But teaching yoga was so important to me that I let my sleep be sacrificed.

Being the only yoga teacher at the hotel was exciting at first but, over time, it became difficult. In Canada, I had always relied on my yoga teacher community for both inspiration and support. However, at the resort, I didn't have that resource – I alone was the yoga teacher community. My role as the sole yoga teacher also meant I couldn't attend classes as a student – something that I needed deeply to keep me grounded and committed to my own yoga practice, separate from my teaching. For me, participating in yoga classes as a student and connecting with others in a yoga community are essential in helping me stay on the path. This is referred to as your *sangha*, or community. It's said that the Buddha was asked, "What's the most important part of spiritual practice?" (Bodhi). "Spiritual friendship" was what he said. In my first year in Kuwait, I didn't have "spiritual friendship" (Bodhi). Without classes to attend and other yoga teachers to inspire me, I struggled.

Moving to Kuwait meant that I had lost yoga, I had lost my like-minded community of friends, and I'd somehow lost myself in the process. I became like a chameleon, suddenly going to sporting events because my friends liked sports, or going to the mall because my friends liked to shop. These were things I never liked before Kuwait.

One new friend introduced me to the party scene and brought me to an 'around the world' party in which people were dressing up in costumes that represented different countries. These types of costume parties happened in Canada, too, but I steered clear of them during my undergrad each year. My degree was in Gender Studies, so I was well aware of the harm that cultural appropriation causes, and it was against my values to participate in it. But, in Kuwait, I was so desperate to make friends and form bonds that I went to this party and participated. I wore a T-shirt from a local Toronto baseball team to avoid offending anyone. But I still attended the party and turned a blind eye to what was happening in the room. Who was I becoming? It was like I'd lost all personal values and ethics. I could hardly recognize myself anymore.

One of my biggest problems, since I was a teenager, was that I was convinced that the solution to my depression and sadness was to find a boyfriend. After all, that's how every Disney movie ends: a beautiful princess who is trapped in a palace cries for help, and a handsome prince comes to save her and win her love. Now the princess is complete, and the couple gets married and lives happily ever after. As a society, we are trained to think that our worth as women is defined by our relationship status – and I know this belief is not unique to me. I was convinced, whether conscious of it or not, that finding a boyfriend would solve my problems.

So, not long after I arrived in Kuwait, I began dating again. I ended up in a relationship quickly with an Australian guy, Dave, who I met at the 'around the world' party. He was the center of attention. He wanted to go to a party every night and be the last one to clear out as the sun rose. I quickly became his chameleon girlfriend, and I tolerated him picking me up and speaking on the phone with his friends while I sat in the passenger seat, silently. He'd smoke in the car and flirt with other girls in my presence. In Canada, I would never sit in a car with a driver who was smoking – here, I did so willingly. I was engulfed by him. I was convinced that a boyfriend, no matter how mismatched, would be the key to my happiness.

CHAPTER 18

FRUSTRATION

In *Yoga Sūtra* 2.15, Pātañjali describes human suffering as *duḥkha*, which is anything that causes discomfort and uneasiness (Karambelkar 199 – 204). If you think about a time when you were upset and what it felt like in your heart, this is *duḥkha*. There are four causes of *duḥkha*, outlined by Pātañjali:

1. Change (*parināma*): You suffer when circumstances suddenly change, and they affect your life (Holcombe 3). For example, when the Covid lockdown occurred in 2020, everyone's life flipped upside down suddenly.
2. Longing (*tāpa*): You suffer when you desire something that you are lacking (Holcombe 3). It can be longing for anything – for example, an event that you missed while in the Covid lockdown.
3. Habit (*sanskāra*): The third is a habit or *sanskāra*. This aspect of pain occurs when you repeatedly cause yourself suffering with a habit that harms you (Holcombe 3). Some examples of *sanskāra(s)* would be addiction to alcohol, drugs, or junk food.
4. Imbalance (*guṇa*): The fourth cause occurs when you're imbalanced – when you haven't slept well, or you're jet-lagged, or you have lost your regular practices of eating healthy and exercising (Holocombe 3).

When looking back on my first few months in Kuwait, I see that I was experiencing all of these causes of *duhkha*, or suffering, at once. Circumstances were constantly changing in my world. I was longing for my previous life. I had habits that were detrimental to my well-being. And I was out of balance. I wasn't eating well, sleeping well, or taking care of myself.

When learning about the phases of culture shock, I've read that individuals can remain in the honeymoon phase of culture shock for as long as five months before they enter a stage of frustration ("Culture shock part 1: the four stages"). It is surprising to me, therefore, that my feelings of frustration began so quickly. Towards the end of October of my first year in Kuwait is when I really began to experience *duḥkha*, or suffering.

I was still dating Dave, whom I'd met in September. He couldn't spend a night with me unless we went to a party and stayed until the end of it. I was exhausted. While I loved to socialize, I couldn't do it five nights a week with such little sleep. It was one late night after another, followed by early mornings for work.

We were arguing all the time. I'd spend the night at his house and fall asleep by eleven, while he stayed up smoking with his friends. He'd offer to drive me to work in the morning, and then when the morning came, he'd get mad about me waking him up so early. When I wanted him to drop me at work by 6:15am so that I would have time to set up before I greeted the students at 6:45am, he'd tell me that I was crazy, and I didn't need to be there that early. Exasperated, I'd tell him, "Ya, 'cause you know so much about teaching." He worked in construction management.

Our relationship was clearly toxic for me, yet I was clinging onto it for dear life. I wanted and needed to have a boyfriend, and I didn't care how disrespectful he was to me. He was filling a void within me. I was always searching for something in the outside world to make me complete, whether it was a boyfriend, alcohol, food, or anything else. I was looking for the light, unaware that

I needed to *be* the light and *bring* the light – not find the light elsewhere.

In mid-October, it was Islamic New Year, and I'd get four days off. My work visa was still being processed, which meant that my passport was still not in my hands. In September, when we had our Eid holiday and were stuck in the country, I didn't mind because I was excited to explore. But by the time it came to October, for our second holiday, I was desperate to leave. I wanted to visit Claire in Dubai. I missed her. We texted back and forth regularly about our experiences, but it felt like forever since we had seen each other in person. And I was desperate to have a cold, foamy beer. And eat some bacon.

Everyone with whom I spoke said that it was unheard of for a visa to take more than three months to process, and it had already been two and a half, so I booked a flight from Kuwait to Dubai for the long weekend. Claire and I began planning our weekend together. She was going to take me to brunch, which was apparently a thing in Dubai and in Abu Dhabi: expats started drinking at noon on a Friday and didn't stop until after midnight. Sign me up for that!

Of course, due to Murphy's law, my visa did not come through on time, meaning that my passport was not back in my hands, and again, I was stuck in Kuwait. I let this delay roll off my back; however, it was the first of many difficulties that would eventually lead me to break.

There was stressor after stressor, with no outlet to process them. I would find myself reaching my breaking point daily. One day, when I was riding the bus home to Mahboula, my eyes began to well up with tears. My friend Connor, noticing my distress, told me something that, as a first year teacher, I'd never forget. He said, "Alex, as a teacher, it is impossible to do everything well.

It's impossible. Give up. Just pick two or three things, and forget about everything else. Do those two or three things well, and forget about the rest." That advice changed me because it was permission to let go. It was permission to accept that I'd never be perfect as a teacher, and that everyone else felt the same way as I did. Everyone else felt overwhelmed. His advice made me realize that it was okay to stop trying so hard and just do the best that I could. The best would be good enough. And so, taking his advice, I chose three areas of focus for my classroom.

First, I decided that my students would learn to be great writers because I loved to write and teach writing. Second, I wanted my students to enjoy social studies, because I equally loved history, geography and culture. Third, it was my goal that one particular child that I had a soft spot for didn't get expelled or suspended from school that year. (That is another story for another book!)

Being a first-year teacher – especially a first-year elementary school teacher – anywhere in the world is difficult. You learn very quickly that the things taught to you at university about being a teacher are pretty much irrelevant without the skills to manage a class. In teacher's college, I took courses where I learned about math strategies, word walls and science experiments. In reality, those are not the most important things you need to know as a teacher.

When working with students who are so young, the content that you teach isn't all that important. In actuality, teachers need to focus on implementing classroom management strategies, fostering positive relationships with students, and creating a safe community with respect, rules and logical consequences – skills that weren't covered in our education program at university. At times, throughout my teaching career, it felt like I was a third parent for some of these kids – homeroom teachers for students aged six to twelve often spend more time with the children each day than their parents do. I dealt with things like searching for lost sweaters and water bottles, memorizing twenty-six children's schedules and making sure the students got on the right bus at home time with all of their things. I was responsible for preventing and following up on bullying. It was my job to make sure that they brought their money in for pizza day or field trips. If you can't effectively manage a classroom and take care of all of these details, it doesn't matter how competent a subject teacher you are because all of the content gets lost in the chaos.

As a first-year teacher, you aren't given any strategies, and you are left to figure everything out on your own. It's like swimming in a shark tank. What added an additional layer of frustration for me was that I just didn't understand the children in my class. We came from wildly different childhoods, cultures and experiences. What was entertaining in the first few weeks in the country became exasperating and frustrating by November.

Yoga Sūtra 4.15 says that the same thing perceived by different minds will have different appearances. *Vastusāmye vitta-bhedāt-tayorvibhaktaḥ-panthāḥ* (Karambelkar 538 – 540). This concept is something that I learned during my time in Kuwait. My childhood experiences meant that I viewed the world one way. The childhood experiences of my Kuwaiti students and their parents meant that they viewed the world in a completely different way. I wanted my students and their families to change, but in reality, I was a guest in their country. It was my job to change and understand that the way they were seeing things was different than me.

Some of the parents of the local children were removed from the classroom and school life. Drivers and nannies would pick up and drop off the kids each day. Where I was raised in Toronto, the moms of the neighborhood were helicopter parents – always present in the classroom and always eager to volunteer and be fully engaged in their children's education. As a child, I felt like the odd one out because my mom worked full time and, as a result of that, couldn't be as involved as my friends' moms. I didn't understand that in lots of Middle Eastern countries, the parents are less involved in school life, and that's seen as a good thing. They tend to implement a policy of non-interference when it comes to their parenting. The parents are fostering independence and teaching their children to solve problems on their own.

If a local parent showed up to complain about bullying, they would often say something like, "I didn't want to come, but it's the fourth time that this has happened, and I want Ahmed to deal with it on his own, but..." in contrast with North American parents who often might want to arrange a meeting immediately after the slightest sign of bullying. It's simply a different culture and way of dealing with things. I constantly interpreted the Kuwaiti parents' lack of engagement and involvement in their children's education as undervaluing education. I see now that we came from different experiences and held different values and beliefs, and we were interpreting the same thing differently.

School started at 6:45am – over two hours earlier than it did for me in Canada when I was their age. The children were late for school every day – something I interpreted as disrespectful.

In Canada, the schools were zoned, and I grew up in a city where everyone attended a school that was within a five-to-ten-minute walking distance. Everyone in my neighborhood walked or rode their bikes to school, and there was never traffic, so it was expected that everyone would show up to school on time, every day. I didn't understand the multiple factors that impacted the Kuwaitis' lack of punctuality – the traffic, for example, was terrible. Children traveled from all over the country to come to different private schools in the downtown area. Kuwaiti traditions also impacted the children's punctuality. Some Arab families, for instance, socialize late into the night – often having dinner at 10pm. Also, the children were often playing in the playgrounds until late in the evening – and this had to do with the climate more than anything else. When it was over forty degrees Celsius during the daytime, of course the parents wouldn't want their kids playing outside at two in the afternoon, as they'd get dehydrated. Social life just tended to occur later than in North America. And starting school that early in the morning simply wasn't appropriate for the local culture.

In Canada, when a child fell asleep at school, it was seen as rude. In Kuwait, some kids were falling asleep on the table regularly – but it was because they simply weren't getting enough sleep each night. While I expected the parents to put their kids to bed earlier, I see now that there was a culture clash between the east and the west. The Arab families shouldn't have been expected to modify their own culture and traditions to suit the North American school schedule that we were imposing on them.

Some of the children in my class spoke fluent English, but a large percentage of my students were from Kuwaiti, Lebanese, Palestinian, Egyptian and other Arab families where they grew up speaking Arabic. Their parents had sent them to an international school with the idea that they would learn English. However, the curriculum wasn't designed with them in mind. We taught an English language curriculum program from the United States, but it came with no supplementary resources on how to teach non-native speakers the English language. I had no training in this area. A lot of the children were misbehaving, and a lot of teachers interpreted this as a sign of disrespect. In reality, our school was failing them – we didn't have the resources or tools to support their needs, and we didn't have the cultural understanding either. It wasn't that they were trying to misbehave – for example, as previously mentioned, the kids were exhausted – but we as an academic institution could have considered changing our school hours to match the local culture, or consulting with local people and asking what they thought would be a good solution to this problem. We could have considered starting school at least two or three hours later to accommodate for their traditions and customs. We were two cultures that were not seeing eye to eye. And if we as international educators are going to go into other countries and operate schools there, we need to work together collaboratively. It's not the teachers, it's not the kids, and it's not the families – the whole system was failing all of the parties involved, and a better approach could have been designed.

We were told that the children weren't allowed to speak Arabic in the classroom, and exasperated, I found myself snapping at them every day, "*La teckalem Arabia*!" (Stop talking in Arabic!) I was trying to follow the school rules, but in retrospect, I hate that I did that. I feel like I was trying to unfairly stomp out their mother tongue. If they weren't speaking Arabic while they were in the process of learning English, how were they meant to socialize with their friends or understand my instructions? Over the years, I shifted my opinion on this language policy while working in an international school. Towards the end of my teaching career, hearing my students speak in their home language was something that I encouraged and celebrated – not shut down. When students asked me if it was okay if they spoke to their parents in their home language during student-led conferences or other special events, I always said yes. I let them read books to the class in their home language and teach their classmates words from their mother tongue. The diversity of working at an international school should be celebrated, not eliminated.

I hit a point where I was exhausted. I wanted to accomplish everything perfectly and be like Superwoman, and it just wasn't possible. Lesson planning, grading, preparing, designing my classroom, having meetings after school with the parents of the children misbehaving – I was at the end of my rope. I was failing miserably, and despite lying and insisting that I wasn't a brand-new teacher, the children sensed my weakness and inexperience and took advantage of it. This is something that most children would do, regardless of nationality. They were constantly crossing boundaries, acting out and pushing the limits. I'd had enough, and I wanted to go home to Canada. I couldn't imagine doing this for a whole year – let alone two.

CHAPTER 19

WANTING TO LEAVE IS ENOUGH

Y*oga Sūtra* 1.4 is a warning of what will happen to you if you aren't regularly practicing yoga. *Vṛtti Sāyrūpyam Itaratra* (Karambelkar 12 – 13). When we're not regularly returning to the present moment, to study ourselves, we get lost in our thoughts. We get sucked into the external world. Our thoughts, our words and our emotions become our identity. According to Pātañjali, this attachment to our thoughts is the root of all suffering. When we aren't practicing yoga, we can't separate ourselves from the chaos around us. We become this chaos. And that's what happened to me.

I was gradually becoming the chaos over a period of time – but the breaking point for me occurred one day in October, when I walked in on a colleague stealing from me. Because I didn't have a lockable cabinet in my classroom, I'd tended to leave my bag on a shelf, trusting that the people around me would do the right thing. However, I soon discovered that my trust was misplaced when I entered my classroom on that fateful day, and I found my colleague standing behind the front door with my purse in his hands, money on the top. I reported the incident to William, who didn't believe that it had happened at all, and claimed there were no security cameras to check. This blatant dismissal of my experience both upset and also infuriated me.

When I recounted this story to my other colleagues, everyone seemed to shrug their shoulders. It turned out that theft was a normal part of life in our particular workplace, where it felt to me like consequences were not enforced. Many colleagues even recounted stories of their valuables being stolen right out of their locked apartments by school maintenance staff. One person's cat had even gone missing out of her apartment one day while she was at work – unaware that anyone would be entering the apartment as she hadn't been notified of any scheduled maintenance. "Get used to it," was the attitude.

I want to be clear that this issue with theft was not a problem throughout Kuwait – because Kuwait, and the Middle East in general, is an exceptionally safe place. Theft was not normal in the public realm – in malls, resorts and public spaces, you could leave your things everywhere, and they'd be safe. The normalization of theft and misbehavior was an issue at my specific workplace. Stealing had become commonplace as a result of theft reports not being followed up within the school.

For a long time, I harbored resentment towards the administrative team at this school at the time that I worked there. It was almost as if I thought that all of these leaders were intentionally trying to harm us teachers, students and parents by not caring about our daily experiences there. I recently realized that they too were probably doing the best they could in the circumstances, just like I was. Human beings make decisions based on our situation more often than our disposition. The leadership team were probably under-resourced, under-staffed and struggling to solve problems that they didn't have solutions for. It wasn't that they didn't care that people were reporting theft to them – it was likely that they just didn't have a way to solve the issue, so it was easier to sweep under the rug.

For instance, the administrative team said they didn't have working security cameras in the school to check what happened in my classroom that day. This was probably true – but it was not the administrators' fault. They weren't the owners of the school or the people in charge of buying and installing security cameras. I do know that the staff were very underpaid too, so they probably feared firing the person I'd caught stealing from me, and not knowing where they could find an adequate replacement who would accept the job conditions. The administrative team was not responsible for any of these larger scale, school-wide issues. They were simply the people who were hired to run the school. They were not bad people. They were just doing the best they could in the circumstances in which they found themselves. This does not negate what happened or how it made me and other teachers feel, but it has helped me make peace with the story.

I have many, many friends who have accepted jobs around the world as international educators. From Vietnam, to Honduras, to Suriname, to Mexico, to Jordan, to China, to Indonesia, some of these teachers had incredible experiences at their schools, and some of them experienced similar issues to me. I've come to realize that these mixed experiences had little to do with the countries where people relocated, and more to do with the individual work environments of each teacher. I know people who stayed in Kuwait for over a decade and had a wonderful time there at the school where they worked! Similarly, although I speak very highly of my time in Abu Dhabi, where I later stayed for four years, I also know people who stayed in Abu Dhabi for a few months and had a negative experience. I emphasize the vastness of these experiences because I want to be clear – the problems that I faced at my school were not because of the country of Kuwait itself. The problems stemmed from the for-profit international teaching system and the particular school where I was working. Due to the fact that there are no unions to protect teachers, many of the for-profit international schools are cutting corners and profiting large amounts of money off tuition instead of investing some of their earnings into resources, facilities and staffing. Your employer is also your landlord. Your public life and private life become mixed in an unhealthy way. You lose all of your support systems. What I've concluded is that the individual experiences of teachers who work overseas have less to do with what country they choose to work in, and more to do with what school they accept a job offer at, and who is in leadership at the time at the school where they teach. Additionally, how resilient they are at the time they accept the job makes a difference, too. I say this because I want to be clear that the issues at my workplace are not reflective of Kuwait as a country on the whole, or my former workplace on the whole.

Looking back at this stealing incident with hindsight, I now recognize how easily our communities can modify and normalize codes of behavior that aren't normal elsewhere. "Buy a lockable cabinet," was the response from everyone with whom I worked. "You don't have any *wasta*." I quickly learned that one of the most important things that you needed in Kuwait was *wasta* – meaning 'power' or 'connections' in Arabic. It's like the white privilege of the Middle East. And teachers did not have it.

I walked into my colleague Connor's classroom, sobbing. He sat down on a desk, looked at me, and asked with sincerity, "Alex… are you going to make it until the end of the year? Or are you going to be a Christmas runner?"

Between sobs, I said to him, "I have to… (sob)… stay until March… (sob)… because my mom's already… (sob)… booked her flight here!"

I knew that there were lots of runners. They existed and, technically, I could leave if I wanted to, too. No one was holding a gun to my head and saying that I had to stay. But I felt like I couldn't leave. I felt like I could never bring myself to be one of them.

There were rumors around the school about what would happen to runners. We were told that teachers who quit their jobs before the school year ended would be banned from teaching recruitment websites, and that they wouldn't get another job after they quit. I was young and naïve, and it was my first job – I didn't understand that there was no way any of that could be true. In reality, it was tremendously difficult to recruit teachers to come to Kuwait, so they did everything they could to keep us there once we'd arrived. I realize now that quitting, leaving and making career path changes are a normal part of lots of people's lives, but I believed "the runner rumors", and I didn't want my career to be ruined.

To me, quitting was not an option. In the 1990s, I was raised with the slogan 'Quitters never win, and winners never quit'. Women especially are taught to stay and to stick everything out, no matter how hard things are. I thought that it would be shameful to leave, and I cared too much about what other people would think. Instead of looking inwards and saying, "Does being here make me happy?" I looked outwards and said: "What would people think of me if I leave?"

Years later, after having to muster the courage to quit my relationship, resign from my job, and leave an entire life that I'd created for myself, I realized that I had to unlearn this philosophy that I'd inherited during my childhood. It is okay to quit. It's okay to leave.

After two and a half months in the Gulf, I really wanted to leave. At the time, I wasn't conscious of just how many difficulties I had endured during such a short time frame. The school had let me down on so many promises. I'd caught a teacher stealing from me, and management didn't believe me. I felt alone. I was separated from my family and friends. I was struggling with my mental health and had no tools or resources.

On top of all this, I'd moved into an apartment that was more like a dungeon, as the 'Queen of the Addition', and then been upgraded to a family-sized apartment full of cockroaches: an 'improvement' that many of my colleagues found unfair. I was struggling with the overall behavior of the children in my classroom. I was in a toxic relationship, which was going nowhere. I couldn't leave the country and visit my friends in Dubai because my passport was still in the school's possession. And I felt like I didn't have a home in the country.

It didn't occur to me that I had a very long list of valid reasons as to why it would be okay to quit my job at that point. I blamed everything on myself, as if there was something wrong with me or something lacking within me to not be able to survive the circumstances. In reality, it would have been okay to leave. Connor said to me at the end of the year, "If I could give an award to someone who I thought would have been a Christmas runner but stayed, it would have been you because so many challenging things happened to you, yet you somehow found the resilience to stay." I hadn't looked at it that way, but he was right.

Everything was stacked against me, and everything was going wrong. I wanted to leave. But I couldn't bring myself to understand that if I quit my job, it wouldn't be over. When I finally quit two years later, opportunities were arising all over the world almost every day. But I couldn't see this. I was convinced that I had to stay. I couldn't bring myself to realize that I didn't have to stay, just because I'd signed paper saying that I would. It didn't matter what paper I'd signed. If you want to leave somewhere, then leave. You don't need a long list of reasons why. As Cheryl Strayed wrote in a poem that I love, "Wanting to leave is enough" (qtd. in McKenzie).

A few days after the stealing incident, I got another email from William. He asked me to come to his office on Thursday afternoon. Apparently, there'd already been a Christmas runner in October. A 'turkey ditch' would probably be a more appropriate name because it was right around Canadian Thanksgiving. She was a middle school English teacher. She hadn't lasted at our school for more than a month before she quit. She was there for such a short period of time that I'd never even met her. She'd lived in a single apartment inside The Oasis. After she quit, they quickly found a replacement for her within the country, but the new teacher had a family, and the only extra family-sized apartment was the one in which I was living. So, when William started our conversation with, "Alex, you're going to have to move apartments," and I learned that I would be moving for the third time since I'd arrived in the country a few months earlier, I felt even more overwhelmed than I had before.

"Back to the Addition?" I asked. I desperately did not want to end up back there. William reassured me that no, I wasn't moving back to the Addition. He was giving me the runner's apartment, which was in the Singles Building, inside The Oasis compound. By the end of my first term there, I'd probably be the only staff member in the history of teachers to live in all three of the apartment towers that were provided for us: the Addition, The Family Building and the Singles Building. A fact I'd laugh (but also cry) about.

The school gave me twenty-four hours to move, but they'd promised to send me some movers to help. "Eight to ten men," was specifically what William said. I called Dave, who I was still dating at the time, and asked him to come help me move, but it was Thursday night, and he had a party he wanted to go to instead. I asked my teacher friends to come over, but no one was available to help. Once again, I would pack up and move on my own. I tried to go with the flow as I took on such a big change with so little support, but all that changed when I saw the new apartment where I was moving. No wonder this woman had lasted such a short period of time at the school.

I opened the door, and there was garbage strewn throughout the apartment. The kitchen had lime green paint, with holes in the cracked walls that were stuccoed over with white adhesive. The living room walls were a shade of brown, along with hues of bright orange and baby blue. The kitchen had beads hanging across the doorway, as if it were an episode of *That '70s Show*. How could they make me move without even bothering to clean the inside of my new apartment? I could tell just by smelling inside of the apartment that a smoker had lived there previously.

I left and walked back to my family apartment to continue to pack up my things, and at this point, I truly could not stop crying. Tears were uncontrollably pouring out of me. As I threw my belongings into suitcases, I didn't know how to make the tears stop. I was in what I now know was a state of depression. I decided that I needed to take a break from packing, so I got changed into gym clothes, called Raghu and asked him to take me to the hotel for a spinning class. Maybe some endorphins would help.

As I walked through the courtyard to get into his taxi, I ran into a group of my friends returning from dinner, whom Raghu was dropping off. It was too late for them to help me with packing at that point. "Are you okay?" they asked me.

I couldn't stop my sobs as I said, "Yes… I'm fine… I just need to go to spinning."

The following morning, the 'eight to ten men' that William had promised would help me move did not show up. Again, I was on my own. I called William, furious about the situation, demanding that the school fix all the issues with the apartment that week. He strolled in hours later with his takeaway coffee and announced, "It's not that bad…" while attempting to rip off the beads from the doorway. He tried to pull them off several times before giving up. "Yeah… I'll have to get maintenance to deal with that."

He cracked open the window to air out the smell of smoke and trash, and as the apartment heated up, I said, "Oh my God, you have to be kidding me. Is the air conditioning broken in this apartment too?" Fortunately, it was not. When I asked for the walls to be painted, he said that it wouldn't be possible in a week, and I'd have to live with these colors for the rest of the year until the summer. He tried to convince me that the apartment was livable, and that I was overreacting. I demanded that the school, at the minimum, repaint the apartment within the next week, and William finally agreed.

When I told Connor about this later on, he smirked and tried to stop himself from laughing. "Alex… do you really think the school's gonna paint the apartment for you?"

"They promised they would," I said to him. "And they've let

me down so much that they can't let me down again this time."

"I'm just saying, Alex, do not get your hopes up."

While William sat at my dining room table that morning sipping his takeaway coffee, I paced back and forth in front of him, crying. I can't remember much of what I said, except the following line: "You're lucky that the school still hasn't given me back my passport from the visa process. If I had it, I'd be on the NEXT FLIGHT HOME!"

At this point, William wasn't even listening: he was typing on his iPhone underneath the table, as if I couldn't see him. I've always joked that he was online, posting 'Job Available for a Grade Three Teacher at an International School in Kuwait'.

Not long after, an anonymous review was posted about the school online. As a result of this post, I learned that there was an online database of international school reviews, and my school had over fifty reviews that I probably should have read before I'd moved there. We all speculated that the review was from the runner whose apartment I'd moved into. At the end of her write-up about the school, which covered her one month of employment there, she warned, "If you do come to this school, keep your thoughts to yourself and pray a lot so you can get through it."

At the time, my friends and I all gossiped about this woman behind her back. We thought she was overreacting. "I can't believe she quit! I can't believe she had the audacity to write this about a school she only stayed at for a month!"

Looking back now, when I read this post, I can't help but think, *all power to this woman.* She was not a bad person for leaving – she was a brave person. She wanted to leave, and so she left. She didn't stay 'just because'. She didn't care what other people would say about her behind her back for quitting. She just left. *Santosa* is the second *Niyama* in the *Pātañjalayogasūtra* text and refers to the practice of contentment. The intention is to find contentment wherever you are. However, I teach my students this topic with a caveat. The caveat is: even though our culture will want to convince us otherwise, knowing when to quit, changing direction, leaving a toxic situation, walking away and moving on are all signs of courage and wisdom. Being able to quit is a sign of a winner. If a situation constantly feels misaligned, and your happiness there is rare, then leave. Seek contentment elsewhere.

I didn't understand all of this at the time, but I see it now. I thought the most courageous thing was to stay, but leaving is an act of courage, too.

You don't need a long list of reasons to give you permission to leave. Wanting to leave is enough.

CHAPTER 20

CHANGE IS THE ONLY CONSTANT

Hercalitus, the Greek Philosopher, said that "Change is the only constant in life" (King). I have always struggled with change – and the ending of my relationship with Dave was no different. It was clear that he wasn't used to dating a woman who challenged him at every moment, and he wasn't as invested in this relationship as I was. Whereas I considered him a lifeline in Kuwait, it was evident that Dave viewed me as 'just another girl he'd met at a party'. As he faded out of my life, his project also ended, and he ended up leaving Kuwait shortly afterwards.

When he ended our relationship, I was devastated. It was as if I'd just lost the love of my life. Since my time in Kuwait, I have learned a lot about emotions. Dr Jill Bolte Taylor, a brain scientist I often reference when teaching meditation and mindfulness, teaches that an emotion takes only ninety seconds to rise and fall (qtd. in Robinson). If our emotional experience is extending longer than ninety seconds, then what is elongating it is our *vṛtti* – our thought patterns that worsen the experience. One of the *vṛtti* is *vikalpa*, or imagination (Karambelkar 16). When I imagined that this relationship with Dave was crucial to my happiness, and that I couldn't let it go – this was the elongated cause of my suffering. Not the relationship ending itself.

Now, when I look back on our relationship, I can step outside the narratives and see the relationship for what it was – leading more to my suffering than anything. I realized on a Recovery

2.0 retreat with Tommy Rosen in 2024 that my addiction to seeking happiness in the outside world was a manifestation of codependency. According to Tommy, codependency is the root of all addiction. He said during our retreat that all addiction comes from the same thing – it's an identity crisis. We look to the outside world instead of looking within. Through developing a deep spiritual practice, nowadays, I truly don't feel the desire or need to constantly be in a relationship – if a relationship doesn't bring me joy or add to my life, then I'm wasting my and the other person's time. But back then, I could not let it or him go.

Nevertheless, there was one thing that was able to lift me out of the funk that I was falling into, at least momentarily: my work visa finally came through at the start of November. I had my passport back. I could finally leave the country! I got on a plane the first weekend that I could and left Kuwait for the first time since August. I decided to take that trip to Dubai that I'd planned over a month earlier. As the plane began its ascent into the air, the flight attendant came around with a drinks cart, and I ordered my first beer in four months. I barely had time to drink it before the plane was going down again – it was landing, around ninety minutes later, in Dubai.

After months of seeing only strangers, being greeted by Claire's big smile and familiar face at the arrivals gate, so far away from home, was so comforting to me. As we drove along, talking and laughing nonstop, I noticed that in Dubai, the roads were fast moving, safe and clean. There was a system to them. We drove through the city, which was spotless – like the set of a movie – and I saw the Burj Khalifa for the first time, a building I'd only heard about and seen pictures of on the internet. I never thought that I'd see the Burj Khalifa in this lifetime.

She took me to her apartment to drop off my things before taking me out to the nightclubs. We had another friend from university, Louise, who'd also come to the Middle East at the same time. She lived in the same building as Claire, and they both worked at the same school. She came upstairs to Claire's apartment when I arrived and greeted me with a smile and a hug. Finally, it felt like home again. They gave me a tour of their apartments. I was immediately envious. Although Claire and Louise also had culture shock as a result of moving from North America to the Middle East, as well as having to acclimate to teaching for the first time in schools that were vastly different from the schools that they had attended in Canada, it was clear that their school was investing in the well-being of their teachers in a way that my school was not. Instead of offering 'furnished apartments' like my school did, their school provided its teachers with a sum of money that was to be used as a furniture allowance. Giving their teachers a set amount of money for home décor made a tremendous difference, as their apartments felt a lot more like home. Instead of the broken bits and bobs and run-down furnishings that I had at my apartment, they had nice IKEA couches and beds that they had chosen themselves. While their apartment building was also far away from the city center, it wasn't in a neighborhood like Mahboula. And they hadn't had the same security issues that I'd had – their school didn't give all of the apartment keys to their maintenance staff the way that my school did.

Their school's housing had a rooftop pool, which was clean and maintained, unlike the one in my building. When floating in the pool, we could see the Burj Khalifa. And their apartment building had working gym facilities.

But what I was most jealous of was that they could go to a bar and order a beer. We went to brunch – the brunches that I'd heard so much about – and I couldn't get over the fact that we were still in the same region. Dubai was a one-hour flight away from Kuwait, but it was worlds apart. Brunches were a haven for an expat like me. We started drinking beer at noon and were up on our feet singing 'Sweet Caroline' with our arms around other expats' backs by three in the afternoon. Whenever we got drunk, Claire and I would laugh and say, "Thank you, Nick, for bringing us together."

Why did I choose one of the few countries in the Middle East where alcohol was completely banned, when I could have chosen somewhere to live like Dubai? Ironically, now that I am completely sober, I don't even think about access to alcohol at all. If I moved to Kuwait now, I am sure I'd have a very different experience than I did in 2015.

This weekend trip to Dubai was the start of a troubling mentality around alcohol for me – living in a country where I couldn't have it meant that I would binge to excess as soon as I landed in a country where it was allowed. I developed 'destination addiction' – an obsession with the idea that I would find happiness wherever I next traveled, as alcohol would be legal there. Once I arrived, I'd drink from the moment the plane landed until the moment that I got on the plane at the end of a holiday. Each time a plane headed towards my home, I dreaded my return to a dry country.

Looking back, I see the red flags myself – but at the time, I don't think anyone else saw them. Consumption around alcohol is so normalized – not just in the Dubai expat culture to which we belonged, but also Canadian and western culture in general – that I don't even think that Claire thought my drinking was something to be alarmed about. In Dubai and Abu Dhabi, it is totally normal for expats to be chanting "Flip cup!" in a restaurant at two in the afternoon on a Friday. It was a holiday destination. But binge drinking is a global pattern, particularly in the West, and it is not unique to expat life.

I was convinced that alcohol was the problem and that if I moved to a country where alcohol was legal, I would somehow have fewer problems or be happier. I was unaware that until I stopped romanticizing or idealizing the future, I'd never find happiness in the now.

CHAPTER 21

CHRISTMAS

A Christmas wreath with evergreen foliage and red ribbons was hanging on the door when I arrived home in Kuwait. Rebecca had made the wreath herself and had left it for me when I was away on that weekend trip to Dubai. Inspired by her festive spirit, I called up Raghu and asked him to take me to the grocery store to get a Christmas tree. It would be the first Christmas tree I'd ever bought for myself. As we loaded the tree into the trunk of his car, he asked me, "Alex, are you traveling for Christmas?"

"Yup!"

"When do you leave?"

"December twelfth."

He turned to me and said, "Alex, there are only nine days until you leave for Christmas. Was it really necessary to spend all that money on a tree if you're not even going to be here for the holidays?"

I laughed. Raghu was slowly becoming a good friend more than anything else, and I loved how he said exactly what he was thinking, with no filter. "I needed something to cheer up my spirits," I told him.

For Christmas, I was traveling across the world. In one day, I'd fly from Kuwait to Frankfurt, Frankfurt to Florida, and Florida to Montego Bay, Jamaica, to meet my family at an all-inclusive resort. Breakfast, lunch and dinner on three different continents. It felt absurd. But extremely necessary.

It was a family tradition to spend Christmas in Jamaica. After my grandad died when I was twenty-one, my nana planned the trip each year. I think it helped her as a widow to have something to look forward to. I'd traveled to countries like Cuba, the Dominican Republic and Mexico with my parents, but with nana, it always had to be Jamaica.

Looking forward to this holiday was what got me through the first few months in Kuwait. It was so comforting to reconnect with my family. But once I arrived there, I began to see that I was slowly changing from my family. None of my relatives had ever traveled to the Middle East or Asia – and they hadn't spent a lot of time outside of Canada and the United States, other than resorts in the Caribbean. I tried to explain what an intense switch it was for me, to go from Mahboula, Kuwait, to Montego Bay, Jamaica, but they couldn't relate. After several drinks, my sister and I got into a fight on the first night, and she called me a brat (deservedly so – I hadn't paid her back some money I owed her). To her, it appeared that I was living the dream – receiving a tax-free salary and spending my time on the beaches, abroad. She had clearly based her interpretation of my life on the highlights reel of my *Instagram*. She didn't understand the reality of just how much culture shock had impacted me. But how could she know how hard this transition was on me if I wasn't really showing it?

And so, here I was, starting to feel like I was both too foreign for the Gulf and too foreign for my family. Where did I belong?

For those ten days in Jamaica, I drank alcohol every day as soon as it was socially acceptable – starting around noon, or earlier. I constantly used the excuse of: "Alcohol is illegal in Kuwait, so I have to drink while I can!" Whether I accepted it or not, the truth was that I was becoming increasingly dependent on having a drink.

CHAPTER 22

CHRISTMAS RETURNER

Much to everyone's surprise, I was not a Christmas runner – I was a Christmas returner. I somehow made it back to Kuwait in January of 2016, and Raghu welcomed me home by picking me up at the airport and driving me back to Mahboula. "Alex, you're back!" I remember him saying as he put my duffle bag into his trunk, as if he was surprised by this fact.

In moving abroad, I had become like a snow globe, all shaken up – and suddenly, the snow was beginning to settle, and the water was starting to clear. (This simile is something that was taught to me by my yoga teacher Rolf Gates, and I use this phrase often in my *āsana* classes to help my students visualize their nervous system switching from the sympathetic state to the parasympathetic state, or from chronic stress to rest and digest.) I was shifting from the frustration phase of culture shock to the acceptance phase of culture shock ("Culture shock part 1: the four stages"). While I didn't necessarily agree with every aspect of my new culture, I was accepting of it.

I had my passport in my possession now, which made things a lot easier for me, and I began planning trips. Having trips out of the country gave me something to look forward to and helped the time pass. The first trip was shortly after my return – a weekend getaway to Manama, Bahrain, where I met Claire and Louise. Bahrain, a tiny island country off the coast of Saudi Arabia, has the reputation of being the expat getaway for residents in Saudi for a weekend of wild. In Saudi, like Kuwait, alcohol was illegal, but in Bahrain it was legal. There was a short bridge linking the two countries, and expats located in Saudi could travel to Bahrain in under an hour using that road. Bahrain was another country, like Kuwait, that I'd never heard of before moving to the Middle East in 2015.

After we landed, we went straight to the pub, followed by a small strip of nightclubs. I drank so many beers that the next morning, hungover, I threw up during the drive to the one and only tourist site in the country: the Tree of Life. I joked about drinking to the point where I made myself sick, but in reality I felt awful. Even still, I drank again that night. In spite of the fact that I was brutally hungover, I knew that I wouldn't be able to drink once I got back to Kuwait, so I felt as if I had to make use of the opportunity.

Having the ability to travel started to make the time in Kuwait feel worth it. It was like a trade-off – my neighborhood and my job weren't the best places in the world to be, but I got to see a variety of once-in-a-lifetime places in exchange for that.

Something that was extremely common in Kuwait was having domestic helpers – drivers, cleaners and nannies. It felt ridiculous to hire a cleaner for my apartment, as a single twenty-three-year-old – in the same way it felt ridiculous to have a helper push my luggage cart in the airport upon arrival or to have a taxi driver take me everywhere. I was a little bit embarrassed about the idea of hiring one – but part of the acceptance stage of culture shock was settling into the norms of my new society ("Culture shock part 1: the four stages").

There were several nannies who lived in my building who were looking for extra money cleaning part time. They hung around in the courtyard watching the teachers' children play, and like the nannies who worked at the school in the washrooms, they often shrank into the shadows, taking up as little space as possible, making as little noise as possible. They wouldn't speak to the teachers, but we knew that they wanted work because, every so often, someone would post about their nanny on The Oasis *Facebook* group.

Rebecca introduced me to her maid, Ife, who was a nanny for a family in our building. Immediately, when I met Ife, I knew that I wanted to hire her. If there is such a thing as angels on Earth, Ife is one of them. She was born in Ethiopia. She wore a scarf over her head and long skirts. She asked me what year I was born in, and when I said 1992, we had an instant connection. Her face lit up, and she said, "*Mashallah*," (which means in Arabic, 'what God has willed has happened') "you were born the same year as my son!"

Ife could not read or write English, so all of our communication was over *WhatsApp* voice notes. Ife sang while she worked, and she regularly helped herself to my coffee, tea and food, as well as the yoga mat that I had in my spare bedroom, which she would often kneel upon to recite her prayers. The first morning that she came to my house, I was lying in bed hungover and was half asleep. I woke up to her tucking me in and stroking my hair, the way a mother comforts a sick child.

What I instantly noticed about her was that she took up space. When I'd visited friends' apartments in Kuwait, I'd noticed that their cleaners and nannies hid in the spare bedroom and shrank into silence, only speaking when addressed and never daring to sit on the furniture. But not Ife. From the first day that we met, she strolled straight into my apartment and collapsed on the couch, throwing down her things as if she was getting home from a long day of work – as if she lived there, too. I loved this about her.

Most workers referred to all adults in Kuwait as 'Ma'am-Sir'. It felt ridiculous to be referred to in this way, considering I was twenty-three years old and most of them were older than me. I'd insist otherwise. "Please just call me Alex." But they wouldn't budge. Ife, in contrast, called me 'Sugar' or 'Precious'. She loved to talk, and her smile was bright and luminescent. She'd mop the floor and tell me her life story, simultaneously. Like Raghu, she'd come to Kuwait as a very young woman. She had a son when she was young, and she left him in Ethiopia with his father to come and work in Kuwait. She hadn't seen her son in twenty-three years, since she'd left him, all those years ago. All the money she made was sent back to the father of her son for school fees and books, and she later found out he was spending that money on himself and his girlfriend, instead of her son. As she told me these stories about how hard her life had been, I would sit on the couch, with my jaw dropped. How could someone, who'd been through so much pain and suffering, be so happy, whilst someone like me, who'd had a relatively easy life, be so sad?

I asked her one day, "Ife, how are you so happy? Your life has been so hard."

And she said to me, "Sugar, the world is a sad place. You can let that make you resentful and angry about life. You can be that way, or you can just accept it. This is the way it is. You can participate in the world the way it is and choose to make the most of it. You just have to decide."

What Ife was teaching me is essentially one of the core teachings of yoga – that life is characterized by *duḥkha*, or suffering. This same lesson is taught over and over again in all of the key yoga philosophy texts that are thousands of years old. It's taught to Arjuna by Krishna in the *Bhavagad Gita*. It's the Buddha's first noble truth. It's also referenced in the *Pātañjalayogasūtra* text. This is the essence of yoga: opening up to suffering so that we can feel the pain of ourselves and others, without adding more pain to the world.

I was beginning to find friends in unlikely places – friends that I never would have made if I had stayed in my home country. Friends of all ages, nationalities, walks of life and all ways of being. Not long after my return to the country, I made another friend. An older, thin man, nearing his seventies with gray hair walked into the yoga room at the hotel one night after my yoga class. "Are you Alexandra?" he asked me.

He introduced himself as Atif and asked me if I could come to his villa to teach him private yoga classes. He had seen my name on the bulletin board as the yoga teacher at the hotel. He lived at the resort in a villa on the beach and was willing to pay me a large amount of money for the personal classes. "I'm almost seventy, and I can't bend over without sitting on a chair. My doctors say I need to do yoga, but I'm afraid to injure myself in a group class."

This was the first time that anyone had ever asked me to teach private yoga classes. I was immediately uncomfortable with the idea. There was a part of me that felt like an imposter – I didn't feel qualified enough to do it or worthy of payment for it. Money to Atif wasn't an issue, though – paying for a private session was like going to the *Bakala* – a convenience store – and buying a pack of gum. There was also a part of me that felt a little uncomfortable with this arrangement – I was twenty-three years old, and an older man wanted me to come to his home, alone? I was worried about something inappropriate happening.

He gave me his number, and I proceeded to not text him – at which point, he gave his number to the front reception of the hotel, in case I'd lost it or written it down incorrectly. When the receptionist stopped me on my way in to pass me his number again a week later, I reconsidered. It seemed as though this guy really wanted classes – and having a little bit of extra pocket cash wouldn't be the worst thing in the world, would it? I'd give it a shot, and if it felt weird, I didn't have to go back.

I went to his villa and taught him a class as the sun was setting. The sliding glass doors to the beach were open, and we could hear the rhythm of the waves. The wind from the ocean was blowing the curtains. I was so jealous – the view from Atif's villa went to the vast seaside. Instead of the chaos of Mahboula, Fintas was calm. *Kuwait would be so much nicer if I got to live here instead of Mahboula*, I thought. During the class, I was scared I'd injure him – he was strong, yet fragile. Like any good Arab host, he invited me to stay after the class for coffee, tea and dates that had been stuffed with pistachio and coated in a rich chocolate.

On the first day at his villa, I asked him the same question that I asked all of the expats I met. "Where are you from?"

"I'm from Jerusalem," he told me.

"Where's that?" I asked.

"I was born in Palestine in 1947," he explained. Exactly one year after Atif was born, in 1948, the *Nakba*, or catastrophe, began, and Israel invaded Palestine. His parents were forced out of their home. They fled the country with their one-year-old baby on their shoulders – this now sixty-nine-year-old man sitting across the table from me. Atif. They settled in Kuwait, where Atif spent the early years of his life. They then moved to Egypt, where he spent the rest of his childhood.

Atif settled with his wife and children in the United Kingdom (UK). Then he got a job in Kuwait and started working there, whilst his wife raised his daughters back in the UK. He still had a home in Egypt, near to the Pyramids of Giza, and he dreamed of building a home in the Mediterranean when he retired.

"So, I am from Jeruselem, but I am really from everywhere," he concluded. "Everywhere, and nowhere. I don't have a homeland anymore. The world is my home."

I nodded and saw the sadness in his eyes. How must it feel to never be able to return to the place where you were born? How must it feel to not really have an answer to the simple question, "Where are you from?" How must it feel to say that you're from everywhere and nowhere, because the country you were born in no longer exists?

I can still vividly recall all of the stories that were recounted to me by my many Palestinian friends over the course of the seven years that I lived in the Middle East. Yet, somehow, their pain couldn't process and register within me. It was like it was too difficult to comprehend. Their stories contradicted everything I knew about world history up until that point. The pain was also unfathomable – to have lived through such suffering and to not even have it be acknowledged by world history.

I started teaching private yoga to Atif every week, and coffee and tea evolved into dinner and desserts. I'd sometimes go to teach a class at 7pm and leave at midnight because we enjoyed speaking to each other so much. Atif pleasantly surprised me. All he truly wanted was to learn yoga from me – there was nothing inappropriate about the relationship at all. In fact, he began to feel like a father to me more than anything else. He had a grounded, unbroken presence in every conversation, and he made me feel heard. He never had his phone out in my presence. Atif wanted to be able to learn from me and to share with me. At a time when I didn't feel like I had many friends in the country, this meant a lot. Four hours would suddenly pass by in a flash. The name Atif means 'the kind one' in Arabic – and this name could not be more appropriate for him.

In the *Pātañjalayogasūtra* text, *Sūtra* 1.19 refers to those individuals who are seemingly born into the world enlightened, like Buddha or Krishna. *Bhava-pratyayo videha-prakrti-layānām* (Karambelkar 54 – 59). My teacher Anvita recently explained to me that these individuals are believed to have spent one or more previous lifetimes working towards consciousness, or *samadhi*, by practicing yoga and bringing their karmas back to zero. They got close, but they didn't quite make it to *samadhi*. If they did make it to *samadhi*, they would be liberated from the death and rebirth cycle. But because they didn't make it, they were reborn. Nevertheless, all of that work doesn't go to waste each lifetime. As they are reborn, their soul carries the work that they did previously into this new lifetime and, consequently, the individuals seem to have been born enlightened. I always thought that Atif fit into this category. I realize now with years of life experience, greater understanding of history and spiritual practice, that Atif was likely this way due to the suffering he'd experienced in his lifetime and the generational suffering of his lineage. Kino Macgregor, an *Ashtanga* yoga teacher, recently said on an episode of her podcast *Yoga Inspiration*, "Suffering is the window that cracks open your heart and pulls you into the practice." The generational trauma that Atif carried probably led him to become the kind-hearted, loving and gentle soul that I knew him to be.

I often wondered if forming a father-like relationship with me was meaningful for him because of the fact that he had been away from his daughters for so many years. He told me stories of when he showed up to Kuwait twenty years earlier, in the late nineties, and confirmed that the only thing between Kuwait City and the hotel where I taught yoga and he now lived was sand and Bedouin tents. "Rome wasn't built in a day, but Kuwait was."

He showed me pictures of his wife, daughters and grandchildren – it was clear he missed them a lot. He'd left his kids when they were five and seven.

"That must have been so hard for you, being away from your kids all these years!" He shrugged his shoulders – this was just normal for him. I'd noticed that leaving behind their families to come to work in another country was a sacrifice that a lot of parents in this region made. While Atif came from a vastly different background than Raghu and Ife, their parenting experiences hadn't been so different. Raghu had left his son and wife behind in India, and Ife had left her son behind in Ethiopia.

This was so strange to me. During my childhood in downtown Toronto, I only ever saw nuclear families, where both parents lived in the same home. It was quite unusual for parents in my neighborhood to be divorced, too – all of my friends' parents from childhood were married. One parent living in an entirely different country for work – whether married or separated – was unheard of. But here, it was totally normal.

Although I really liked Raghu and enjoyed the time that I spent in the back of his car, I was also dying for independence and freedom. Now that I had a visa, I could take my driver's test and get a license. While the roads in Kuwait were perilous, and I was already an anxious driver, I decided that I had to be brave. I needed the independence that having a car would bring.

Raghu took me one morning for my test. He waited for me in the office of the driver's license center, while I took the test alone. The exam was so different from the tests that I had taken previously. In Canada, our tests were done on the road, with an examiner in the passenger seat of the car – and I had failed a few of them because I hadn't been able to parallel park correctly. I am a cautious, slow, careful driver – but parallel parking has always been my downfall. For some reason, gauging the distance of the car from the sidewalk and reversing the car at the correct angle, has always felt impossible.

Here, in Kuwait, the driving test was completely different from Canada. While Raghu waited, I drove on a simulated course, alone in a car, which seemed much like a *Mario Kart* route. I had been told when I started the test, at seven in the morning, that I should pull over and stop when I saw a policeman and wait for directions. As I drove along the *Mario Kart* route, I never saw one, so I kept driving. I completely ran the simulated 'red light' by mistake and hit several pylon walls on the course while attempting to parallel park. While I was epically failing at parking, a policeman ran out from a small shelter, waving his arms and shouting, "*KHALAS!!* (Stop!) *Shino Hatha?* (What is this)?" I froze, mid-pylon demolition, saying, "The guy said to stop when I saw a policeman. I didn't see a policeman, so I just kept going!"

He looked confused for a moment, and then said, "Wait here." He walked back to the shelter to check on something. He came back. "Oh, the policeman was just having his breakfast. Turn around and go back to the stop sign and wait."

Confused, I turned around, drove back, found the stop sign and waited. At this point, several cars began to line up behind me. By the time it was my turn to go to the parallel parking spot, there were over twenty cars. Again, I parked as if it were bumper cars, but this time, there was one policeman evaluating over twenty cars as they moved back and forth to park. There was no way that he could accurately supervise and record who was succeeding and who was failing.

After monumentally struggling to follow the rules and parallel park, I was sure that I had failed the test. I walked back into the office, glumly. Raghu was sitting, right ankle crossed over his left thigh, reading the newspaper. "What's wrong?" he asked.

"I'm sure I failed," I told him. "I broke all of the rules, a policeman had to yell at me to stop, and I hit a bunch of pylon walls on the course while trying to parallel park."

Raghu was trying to be a supportive listener, but I could see the corner of his lip slowly started to turn up into a smile. He started laughing, and I started laughing too. I sat down beside him, and he picked up his paper again and continued to read. We awaited this announcement. Unlike in Canada, where results were given privately in the car with a one-on-one with the examiner, in Kuwait, they were announced over the loudspeaker, in front of everyone.

"Alexandra Humphrey McRobert – passed." I turned to Raghu, eyes wide, and we both burst out laughing and smiled. Decisions seemed to be made so randomly and arbitrarily, and I don't deny that my whiteness likely gave me an advantage in this case. While I was grateful to have passed and received a license, I also didn't think I deserved it, at all.

Green, white, black and red balloon-filled archways lined the pathways that led up to the school for Kuwait National Day: a time when the whole school campus transformed overnight. There were pop-up restaurants serving *shawarma* – marinated meat that had been seasoned with cumin, turmeric and paprika before it was placed onto a large, rotating cone. There were vanilla sugar cookies shaped like flags and delicately iced with the country's colors. There were dancers on campus dancing the *Dabke*, or a Levantine dance that includes elements of both circle dancing and line dancing. If there is any country in the world that knows how to throw a party, it's Kuwait.

Kuwait National Day weekend was equivalent to the Canada Day long weekend that I celebrated growing up. It was a time to celebrate the culture and traditions of the country. There were live camels and falcons on campus, which shocked me. There were women drawing beautiful, intricate, detailed henna tattoos on students' hands. I was overwhelmed by this, thinking, "I can't get over how much money these parents are spending on this party! We never had stuff like this in Canada!"

But the truth was, we had parties like this at my school and in my neighborhood growing up – I just failed to see the parallel. Every year, we had a fun fair where we'd have sugary treats, bouncy castles and ice cream trucks brought into the school. Every street also had a street party where the neighbors would shut down the road and turn it into a private event with live music, food, petting zoos and ice cream trucks. I'm sure teachers from less privileged neighborhoods thought the same thing about our parties, too.

Prior to the event, I was stuck in an internal debate. *Would it be appropriate to wear an abaya for this occasion?* I'd been taught in Canada that cultural appropriation was wearing other people's cultures as a costume. Would this be considered cultural appropriation? My colleagues didn't seem to think so, and everyone was talking about the Kuwaiti national dress that they'd be wearing, so I went to get an *abaya*. When I wore it to work, it was like I was a celebrity. A North

American woman in an *abaya* with jewels, gems and Kuwaiti colors? Arab mothers were delighted by my attire, and they kept stopping me on the school campus and asking if I could be in their Snapchat videos with them. They spoke into their cameras in Arabic as if they were news reporters. I had no idea what they were saying, but I imagined it was, "I'm standing here with a Canadian woman in an *abaya*!!" They seemed so happy to see me embracing their culture.

I started to understand what the difference was between cultural appropriation and cultural appreciation. When I joined my community in celebrating their special occasion by wearing their national dress with them, that was cultural appreciation. But if I wore their traditional dress as a costume to a dress-up party, to make fun of them without understanding anything about their culture, who they were, and why they dressed that way, that was cultural appropriation. That distinction was beginning to make sense for me.

We got five days off school for the National Day long weekend, and I got invited by Atif to visit Egypt with him. At this point in my time in Kuwait, Atif was much more than a yoga student of mine – he had grown into my family. He was three times my age and was old enough to be my father or grandfather. We were both so alone in Kuwait that we began to rely on each other for support. So, it only seemed natural that I would visit with his family, and he would visit with mine.

When he told me that he had a home in Egypt when I first met him, I gushed about my childhood memories of learning about Egypt and imagining that I'd never see the pyramids in this lifetime. "Alex, I must take you there – you have to see them! Come stay with my family. Bring a friend and come for the weekend." I decided to invite Claire.

Atif traveled to Egypt a few days before me, so when Claire and I landed in Cairo, Atif had his family driver pick us up at the airport and take us to his villa. Claire and I were staying together in a guest bedroom. His villa was very near to the pyramids. I remember when we opened the balcony doors of our room and

I'll never forget that moment – we could see the pyramids of Giza from our window, far in the distance. I thought back to that time when I was just a four-year-old girl visiting a museum and looking at the mummies in the display case. Four-year-old Alex would have never dared to dream that she would make it to Egypt in this lifetime. *How did this girl from Yonge and Eglinton, Toronto ever end up here?* I wondered. And yet here I was. This first year in Kuwait was becoming both the most challenging and the best year of my life.

While traveling to Egypt was something that I'd dreamed of all my life, and I was thrilled to be there, I had also been slowly entering an internal state of alarm. On the first morning, I noticed I had a lump on my neck that was slowly becoming red, inflamed and sore. It was low enough that I could wear a scarf and cover it up from Atif and his family, but each day it was getting bigger and bigger, and redder and redder. I tried to avoid talking about it with Claire, but I'm sure that she could see that I was entering an overwhelming state of worry.

I was invited to join Atif and his family for dinner in the revolving Cairo Tower, visit the Egyptian Museum, tour the pyramids of Giza, and go diving in Sharm El Sheikh. But while these were once-in-a-lifetime, exciting experiences, in the back of my mind, my feelings of panic and worry were rising, and I had an impending sense of doom that would not go away.

As any logical person would, I googled lumps on the neck and read all of the causes of such an illness. Cause number fifty-four on the list was HIV/AIDS. I skipped all the other fifty-three illnesses and decided, *Yup – this is what I have*.

When expats arrived in Kuwait, the government screened them for three illnesses, and one of those illnesses was HIV/AIDS. If you had either, you were not allowed to enter the country and work as an expat. I was panicking, but the thought didn't even cross my mind to see a doctor in Egypt – I would deal with this situation back in Kuwait. I didn't want to trouble Atif and his family by telling them about any of this. I didn't want them to know that I was breaking local customs and dating, and I legitimately feared that I could potentially have HIV/AIDS. My mind wandered to the worst-case scenario – I was going to get deported back to Canada, and from there, I'd receive treatment and make a career as an HIV/AIDS activist. Obviously, none of this ended up happening, and it was just an infected cyst, but this was the level of paranoia and anxiety that I was experiencing.

I said nothing. I tried as best as I could to pretend to enjoy the holiday – but instead of enjoying it and appreciating the once-in-a-lifetime experiences, whenever I separated from the family I was in a constant state of tears and panic.

At the time, I believed my tendencies for my thoughts to spiral in such a way were evidence of my mental illness. Now, I understand that having these thought patterns is not evidence of a mental illness. They are evidence that I am human. Having spiraling thoughts is a very normal human experience. Our *vṛtti* are our thoughts. A *vṛtti* is a one-time experience. In the *Pātañjalayogasūtra* text, there are five types of thoughts listed, which I teach in depth in my Yoga *Sūtra* Study program. When we allow our thoughts to take us from a) I have a lump on my neck all the way to z) I am now an unemployed HIV activist – then our mind simply is not in a skillful state. Nowadays, when I witness my thoughts spiraling, I try to figure out what caused them. Did I start the day with sugar and caffeine? Is there an unresolved conflict in my life that is making me anxious? Am I really tired? When I am teaching my students, I use a few different metaphors, one being, "The mind is the sky that holds the weather." This metaphor was taught to me by my teacher Rolf Gates. Our *citta* is our brain, or the sky. The thoughts will pass through our brain like the weather passes through the sky. The key is to have enough awareness to notice whether these passing thoughts are true or untrue, and then we should let them go. We can use two key tools from our spiritual practice to facilitate this process: *abhyāsa*, which literally means practice, and *vairāgya*, which is renunciation or being detached from the outcome (Karambelkar

27 – 28). These two tools are identified in *Yoga Sūtra* 1.12. But back then, I didn't have the awareness to return to my practice, my tools and my study. I let the storm pull me inside of it instead of standing on the outside and watching the storm from afar.

When I returned from the weekend in Egypt, I immediately wanted to go to the hospital. But none of my friends were available to go with me that day. I called Raghu. I remember sobbing as he drove me there. I was terrified. He looked at me in the rear-view mirror and said to me, "Alex, only white people cry over things like this."

That sentence makes me laugh nowadays, years later, but at the time, I was furious with him. He asked me when he should pick me up, and I said in frustration, "I don't know!" and slammed the door, going into the hospital. When I came out later that night, there he was, sitting in the waiting room, right ankle crossed over the left thigh, reading the newspaper. Raghu. He had parked the car and sat inside waiting for me. It was one of the nicest things someone's ever done for me.

I was scheduled for early morning surgery the very next day. There was a suspicion that I had a thyroglossal duct birth defect and needed immediate surgery. This was the first time in my life that I would be put under anesthesia for a surgery, and it was in a foreign country, alone, with the doctors only speaking Arabic. I had no idea what was happening. I felt so alone, so scared, and I could not stop crying. I was rolled into a surgical theater on a gurney, I gazed at the bright lights above me. Losing consciousness, I feared that I'd never wake up. None of my friends were able to come. But Raghu was there with me. He was the one who showed up.

I believe that nothing in life is a coincidence. Years later, when writing this book, I happened to be on *Facebook* one day, when out of the blue, I received this message: "Hi Alex, do you remember me?"

I said to him, "Raghu – I will never forget you."

CHAPTER 23

MOM IN THE MIDDLE EAST

By the time my mom arrived in the Middle East in March, I was excited to show her around. I'd been living in this country for eight months, and pretty much everyone in the whole country knew that my mom was coming to visit me – I brought it up in every conversation. I was so excited.

Connor, my colleague, said, "Kuwait is so small. What will you do with your mom while she's here?"

I said to him, "What I'm excited to show her is the life that I have created here. My apartment, my job, my friends, my car… all of this I've created from scratch. I'm proud of that. I want to show her."

My car: I'd finally gotten a car! I felt like I needed one for her visit, so I could take her around, and so before she arrived, I had done some car shopping. I ended up with pretty much the coolest car in the world, in my opinion – a hatchback that I dubbed the 'Desert Girl Cruiser'. It was big, white, clunky, and exactly what I had pictured when I had imagined myself driving past camels, cruising over sand dunes and riding off into the sunset.

There were a few places in the country that I was too afraid to drive to on my own because the traffic was hectic. The airport was one of them, so Raghu took me to the airport and picked up my mom. Like me, she could not stop asking Raghu questions in the car about his life, his story and how he ended up in Kuwait away from his family in India.

We arrived at my apartment in Mahboula – while I'd been

out picking up my mom, Ife had been there cleaning. When we walked in, she gave my mom a huge hug. "*Mashallah*, you are precious' mom! I am so happy to meet you!"

My mom was surprised by this affectionate greeting. She is a very private person, and it wouldn't be natural for her to embrace someone in a hug on the first meeting. But she quickly hugged Ife back. "We are connected because I have a son who was born in 1992, too," Ife said as she hugged my mom. "*Mashallah*." She pulled a chocolate cake out of the oven. "It's your 'welcome to Kuwait' cake!" My mom has never liked cake, since she is more of a chips and pretzels kind of person. But she ate the cake anyway, telling Ife it was delicious.

We only stayed at the apartment in Mahboula for a few hours before I told Mom, "I have a surprise for you. We're not staying here this week – we're staying at a beach villa at the resort!"

Atif had also surprised me and my mom. When he'd heard that she was coming to see me, he rearranged his work schedule so that he would be on holidays during the week of her visit. That way, Atif could travel to Egypt to see his family while we stayed at his villa on the beach. "Your mom shouldn't have to stay in Mahboula," he said. After his week in Egypt, he planned to come back to Kuwait and have my mom and I over for dinner. I think she was impressed at how I had made so many deep and significant connections so quickly in the country.

During the week of my mom's visit, Salama had invited us to come for lunch at her family house, too. When her father picked us up in his car, my mom immediately outstretched her hand to shake his. He quickly pulled back his hand and placed it over his heart and bowed, to demonstrate in a respectful way that he wouldn't touch her hand. "Mom," I whispered, "stop!!" I was mortified. I thought to myself, *Didn't she know that, as a woman, she shouldn't reach out to touch a Kuwaiti man? Everyone knows that!* Some of the more liberal or younger Kuwaitis that I knew did touch the opposite gender, but it was always best to be on the safe side when meeting a new Kuwaiti because you never knew how traditional they were. In retrospect, I realize my expectation that my mom would know this was being pretty harsh on her, because I hadn't educated her about this aspect of the culture. How would she know since I hadn't told her? When I first arrived in Kuwait, I didn't know this either. Details such as this one seemed so strange to me six months earlier, but now I'd adapted and gotten so used to my new culture that I'd forgotten that we didn't have these same social customs in Canada.

After a week in Kuwait, we traveled to Jordan. Our first stop on the trip was the desert of Wadi Rum, the 'Valley of the Moon'. The sand is red, which made it feel like we had landed on another planet. *Wadi* is the Arabic word for valleys that are formed by rivers. These valleys remain dry other than during the rainy season. In the Valley of the Moon, the wadi is the size of New York City geographically, but vastly empty and home to a small Bedouin population.

We had spent the day hiking through the red desert. We arrived at the desert camp of Sheikh Zayed, who was both a king and a judge for his tribe of seven hundred and fifty Bedouins in Wadi Rum. Upon arrival, he offered us Arabic tea and sweets, and he showed us how Bedouins cooked their traditional meals. They buried them, before lighting a fire on top, and cooking them in the ground.

After dinner, we hiked to the top of a mountain and, from there, we watched the sunset peek through the rock formations. I took a picture of my mom, and as I contemplated how small she looked in comparison to the vast Earth below, I had an epiphany. In the isolation of the desert, away from my iPhone and all the distractions that came with it, I had time for the internal sand to settle and the water to clear. I had a moment to experience *samyama*, which is the cumulative experience of *dharana*, concentration, *dhyana*, meditation, and *samādhi*, integration. In moments of *samyama*, we receive flashes of intuitive wisdom, or *rtambhara prajna* (Karambelkar 161 – 163). Maybe all of the struggles that I'd had in Kuwait were pretty tiny in the grand scheme of things. As we watched, the sky changed from royal blue to faded blue, to subtle pink, to brilliant, fiery orange, and finally pitch black, with brilliant bright yellow stars shining. This truly was the Mars of planet Earth.

We went to bed that night and, as we lay on cots in small tents with Disney cartoon bedding on them, I asked, "Mom, did you ever think that when I was born twenty-four years ago, we would spend my birthday in the Middle East?"

"Never," she said, while looking up at an open flap towards the stars of the desert sky. "How did we end up here?"

CHAPTER 24

HEROES RIDE BIKES

The rest of my first year in Kuwait flew by. The country was becoming familiar, navigation had become easier, and accepting things for what they were became less challenging. However, while I accepted my new country, I was still convinced that happiness was somewhere else: specifically, somewhere else with a drink in my hand.

I visited Claire in Dubai a few more times, and she came to visit me in Kuwait. We also met up in Oman. I lived for these weekends away – not only for the familiarity of seeing a friend from home, but also for the alcohol. By the end of the year, I was counting down the days to escape dry Kuwait. We had three months of summer holiday, and I had planned a trip to Spain and Germany, before returning to Canada. I couldn't wait for the culture, the architecture and the nightlife of Europe, as well as reconnecting with my friends and family at home. I'd only been to Europe twice before: I traveled to Greece when I was twenty-two years old, and I'd traveled to Italy when I was sixteen. For me, Europe had always been synonymous with alcohol.

While most of my trip I'd be on my own, I'd also planned to meet Zach, my friend from the first year of university, for a few nights in Barcelona. From there, I'd travel through Spain, spend some time in Germany, and then go to Canada. Zach was working in a hostel as a program leader in Barcelona. We'd both graduated at the same time and moved overseas. I imagine that he'd had a completely different year abroad than me – less money but plenty of partying, socializing and late nights.

The rainbow flags, women kissing women on the street, live music and short shorts immediately set me into reverse culture shock as soon as I landed in Spain. Fluorescent graffiti on the walls, artists on the busy streets, small open-faced sandwiches called pintxos and tapas. You could buy vanilla and chocolate ice cream everywhere and walk down the cobblestone alleys with a pint of beer or a glass of wine in your hand. Barcelona had a heartbeat. The energy was vibrant and filled with passion. The sound of live music filled the streets, and drunk people were spilling out of bars and nightclubs onto the pavement. It was such an extreme contrast.

I decided not to stay in Zach's hostel, so I booked my own hotel room. I rode the subway to meet him at night. He noticed right away how different I looked from when I'd last seen him – my blonde hair was now brown, and when meeting up to go out to a bar, I didn't wear a tube top and jeans, like I would have in Canada – I wore a maxi dress, a long-sleeved shirt and a covering that almost looked like an *abaya*. I hadn't noticed how much I'd changed in a year, but he saw it right away in me. Everything about my appearance was different. "You're so conservative now! Did you dye your hair brown because you stood out too much being blonde in the Middle East?"

I wasn't sure. I hadn't thought about it.

On the first night in Barcelona, we drank glass after glass of wine, and pitcher after pitcher of sangria. I got so out of control that I decided I'd pull my usual move. I would sneak out, leave Zach dancing, and make my way back to my hotel, on my own. I stumbled out of the bar and opened the door of the first car that I saw, getting into the back seat. The problem was, I didn't have a working cell phone, and I couldn't show my taxi driver where the hotel was that I needed to go to on *Google Maps*. I asked him if he knew where the hotel was, and he said no. When I suggested that we stop and ask someone for directions, he laughed and sped the car up. Frantic, I began to ask him, "Pull over the car! I'm going to get out and get in a taxi with someone else who knows where it is. Stop the car! Now!"

As the taxi driver began to speed up his car, and a language barrier clearly existed, I got more and more anxious and concerned that I hadn't gotten into a taxi after all, and that I'd ended up in a vehicle with someone who was not a safe person. I had a gut feeling that this guy was going to take advantage of my incoherent state and do something terrible to me. I had been in thousands of taxis before, alone at night, in Canada, in Kuwait, in Oman, in Egypt, in the UAE... but I had never experienced this feeling in a taxi before this moment. My instincts told me that something was very wrong. When I asked him to stop the car, he laughed and pushed the accelerator. I weighed my options – I could stay in this taxi and go with this man wherever he was taking me, or I could jump out of it.

And so, I made the decision. I grabbed hold of the door handle.

Three, two, one...

I jumped out of the car. While it was moving.

I rolled across the pavement, immediately ripped my clothes and was bleeding everywhere: my elbows, my knees, my shoulders. He stopped the car. He tried to approach me, but I was in fight or flight mode. Police officers happened to be up the street, saw the whole thing happen and approached. "Get away from me!" I screamed, and I ran.

I had been sexually assaulted while alone at night in Toronto when I was eighteen, and going to the police ended up being a traumatic, drawn-out four months of repeating myself to white male police officers when they asked me what I was wearing, how much I had drunk and where I'd been. In the end, I wasn't able to identify his face from a lineup of photos. The police officer shared with me that none of the other victims could identify him either, so unfortunately no charges were placed upon my assailant, and the whole ordeal ended up feeling like a big waste of time. In this moment, as I frantically stumbled to get away from the taxi driver, I knew that the reaction to my story would be no different. Just like the reaction had been no different in Kuwait when I caught my colleague stealing from me. No one was going to believe me based on a 'feeling' I had that the driver was a bad guy. So, while the cops wanted to talk to me, I just wanted to get away from them and get back to my hotel.

I finally made it into another cab where I felt safe, and the driver took me to my hotel. As I entered the building and walked up the stairs to my room, tears were streaming down my face as I thought about how this night had unfolded. The irony of the whole night is that all year, I'd romanticized the idea of drinking alcohol in Europe. I thought alcohol would make everything better. But was alcohol making everything better? In retrospect, it looked like it was making things worse.

If that hadn't been enough of a terrible first experience, the next day in Barcelona got worse. I was exhausted, but I couldn't miss a night of partying. I went downtown again to meet Zach. When he saw my bandages and wounds, he was shocked. "Alex, what happened to you?"

When I told him what had happened the night before, he laughed. "Alex, you were so drunk last night. I can't believe you jumped out of a car."

I shrank back, feeling small. Any woman who has been alone at night knows how scary it can be. And I will always know that I hadn't jumped from the car because I was drunk. I jumped because I was extremely terrified that I would be raped or robbed. The driver of the car was not listening to my request to stop. But if one of my closest and most empathetic male friends seemed unable to grasp the severity of the situation, how would other men react when they heard the story?

Later that night, we went out to another bar. It was swarming and packed full of people, moving in all directions. Everyone was ordering shot after shot, chanting and singing. This was not Mahboula. I pulled my purse to the front of my chest to order another drink, and that's when I saw that my wallet had been stolen while my purse had been slung over my shoulder. I burst into tears; my debit cards, credit cards and all of my money was gone. Why were so many bad things happening to me this year? It constantly felt like the world was stacked against me. Thankfully, my iPhone hadn't been taken, and my passport was back at the hotel. I was sobbing, uncontrollably, and Zach took me outside the bar to walk around and look for my wallet. I think he was mostly trying to get me out of the bar and away from his guests at the hostel, to stop me from causing a scene.

He sent me back to my hotel in a taxi and lent me ten euros to get there. When I woke up in my hotel room on my third day in Spain, my wounds were infected, I was hungover and my whole body was swollen and hurt. Zach had to work that day – he had to entertain hostel guests all day and night. In the hotel lobby, I met some American men who looked at my wounds and asked me, "What happened to you?"

When I told them the truth about jumping out of a taxi, they laughed. "What, are you James Bond? Are you afraid of moving trains too? Don't jump out of the subway car on the way to the police station – the subway driver knows where he's going!" Feeling belittled and doubted felt awful. That was only the beginning of it – every traveler I would meet would ask me the same question, and most of the male travelers responded the same way. It was only female travelers who understood what it was like to be a woman alone at night (and even then, some questioned and doubted me).

Finding my way to the police station, alone, to report my stolen wallet, communicating with my mom to get money wired to me, and getting myself into the hospital without proof of insurance caused further stress.

After I'd gotten all cleaned up and sorted out, I desperately wanted to fly home to Toronto. I just didn't want to be in Spain anymore. I wanted to go home. But I felt like I couldn't leave. I had to finish my trip, even though I didn't want to because, in my head, wanting to leave wasn't a good enough reason to leave somewhere.

There were two ironies about this trip for me, in retrospect. The first is that the whole year I'd been in Kuwait, I'd been wishing that I was living in a country where alcohol was legal. I couldn't wait to fly out and land in a destination where I could have a drink. I thought that alcohol was the solution to my unhappiness and my problems. Ultimately, I was romanticizing the drink, and I'd created this notion in my head. In reality, alcohol had created most of my problems, rather than solve them.

The second irony of my trip to Spain was how I experienced the city of Barcelona as a young woman in contrast to Kuwait. When I had announced that I was going by myself, as a single woman, to Kuwait, everyone around me questioned my safety. In contrast, no one had said anything about me traveling to Spain alone as a woman. There is a projection that women will not be safe in the Middle East, for some reason, and will be safer in Europe. But the reality was, I was safer in my entire year alone in the Middle East than I was in two nights in Europe.

Just a week or two before this trip to Spain, I was touched by Chanel Miller's victim impact statement in a sexual assault case in the United States. She articulated that there are heroes in the midst of trauma. Her heroes were two men on bikes who rescued her from being raped. She wrote, "I sleep with two bicycles that I drew taped above my bed to remind myself there are heroes in [every] story. That we are looking out for one another." Bikes had become a symbol for her to always look for heroes in every tragedy (Miller).

Less than a week after reading and being impacted by this

statement, I had two very traumatic evenings in Barcelona. With no ID, no cash, no credit cards, and several wounds on my body, I had one euro in my pocket and needed help. I didn't speak the language, and I was new to the country. Fortunately, there were so many heroes that came to my rescue after this distressing series of events: strangers who overheard me in the police station and bought me lunch; strangers who walked me around to several electronic funds transfer services looking for one that was open to receive cash; and hospital employees who allowed me to receive treatment with no proof of insurance, no ID and no money. I was so grateful. After being the recipient of so many acts of kindness, I noticed something remarkable when my doctor was cleaning my wounds – he had a bike tattoo on his right elbow. In this moment, I knew that this tattoo was a sign. Chanel Miller had designated bicycles as a symbol of the heroes who had helped her during her attack. In seeing this ink-filled image of a bike, I knew that I also needed to search for the people around me who would help me in the midst of my suffering.

When I got back to Toronto, the first place I wanted to visit was the yoga studio. For the first time in a year, I was able to attend a yoga class as a student, instead of as a teacher. It was in a hot yoga studio. I walked into the steamy, sweltering heat of the room and was shocked – I saw that men were practicing with their shirts off and women were in short shorts and sports bras. In Kuwait, it wouldn't be acceptable to be so exposed anywhere in public, and I'd grown used to seeing everyone cover their elbows and knees. Here, it was completely normal.

I didn't know the teacher. All I remember was that I got on the mat, in a room full of people, and then I started sobbing. A year's worth of tension was releasing from me like a tidal wave. I realized that I could only go back to Kuwait if I found yoga.

I made plans that first week back in Canada to meet up with my childhood girlfriends, including Olivia and Charlotte, at a patio downtown. There were about ten of us girls who had been close throughout high school and stayed in touch. A lot had changed in a year. Several of my friends had got into serious relationships, been accepted into graduate school, or started full-time jobs. I began to feel like I had been left behind. As the night went on, I thought about a conversation that I'd had with a relative a year before when I'd accepted the job in Kuwait. He said, "I don't understand why you young people want to travel abroad after finishing university nowadays. Don't you want to start your life?" Over the span of a year, I had expected Toronto to stay at a standstill while I traveled the world. I thought that the city would anxiously await my arrival, and I'd 'start my life' with everyone else. I believed that everything would be the same. But everyone around me had moved on, and their lives had changed a lot. Thinking back to my relative's comments, it felt like their lives had moved on and they were moving forward, while I hadn't progressed at all.

For some reason, these changes shocked and surprised me, but my amazement seems silly in retrospect. Of course the planet would keep turning in Toronto while I was in Kuwait. They hadn't moved forward without me; in reality, I had just moved forward onto a different path than them.

As the summer continued and the novelty of being back home wore off, I started to realize that I was physically home, but not really home, because my definition of 'home' had changed. The definition of how the world was through my eyes had changed. During the entire year that I was away, all I had dreamed of was the stability of Canada. Once I got to North America, however, I found that the stability of Canada left me bored.

I didn't have a car or a way to get around, and my mom and

all my friends were at work, so my days became vacant. Lost for things with which to fill my time, I'd move from the bed to the couch, to the patio, watch every series on Netflix, and make plans to get together for beers and wine with my friends. I was so used to being on an elevated plane of action – flying to Egypt, Bahrain, or Oman for the weekend. During that summer, nothing memorable happened. When I was in Kuwait, on the other hand, something memorable happened every day. I realized that even though it was extraordinarily challenging living in Kuwait, I was adapting to and enjoying the culture of the Middle East more and more.

While it was nice to have such a large amount of time together with my mom, we weren't really getting along. The smallest things would irritate the two of us. We were used to having our own space – and the space we shared, in the house where I grew up, felt too small. As much as I was enjoying being back in Canada, I was also eager to return to a 'normal' routine at home – and was sometimes shocked when I realized that 'home' and 'normal' now involved walking on a beach and listening to the nearby oil rigs in a small country between Saudi Arabia and Iraq. When did this foreign place start to feel like my home and my version of normal? I couldn't remember.

Lonely, and lost for ways to spend my time, I decided to spend as much time as I could going to the yoga studio. I felt so at home in that room, in that space, with those people – and I knew one thing: the Middle East was becoming my home, but once I went back there at the end of the summer, I had to find yoga.

PART THREE

Solar Plexus *Chakra* – I Am Empowered

The solar plexus *chakra* is located in the abdomen. Its Sanskrit term is *manipura*, which means 'lustrous gem'. It's the seat of our personal power and the sign of strength. When the solar plexus is in balance, we feel strong, competent and empowered. We're able to move through challenges with wisdom and strength (Judith 37).

SOLAR PLEXUS *CHAKRA* YOGA SERIES: EMPOWERED

So many of us struggle with self-doubt, imposter syndrome and are afraid of failures and falling – myself included. This is why I've created "Empowered" – an eight-class series that invites us to take healthy risks, build our inner strength and self-confidence, and challenge our limiting beliefs.

In this power yoga series, you'll build core strength, arm strength and build up to variations of crow, side crow and headstand. This practice will remind us how to face challenges both on our mats and in our lives as well.

https://bit.ly/TheMindfulLifePractice_Empowered

SOLAR PLEXUS *CHAKRA* PHOTO LIBRARY: MY KUWAIT EXPAT MEMORIES

In this photo album on my blog, I share some photographs from the time I spent in Kuwait in my second year there. You can look at the photo blog here:

https://bit.ly/TMLP_KuwaitMemories2

CHAPTER 25

FEELING MY SOUL AGAIN

After the summer, when I returned to Kuwait for my second year, I was determined to find yoga. The hardest part about my first year in the country was my lack of access to a yoga community. While I taught yoga at the hotel and to Atif, I hadn't taken a yoga class as a student since I'd moved from Canada, and teaching yoga is not the same as cultivating a personal practice. More than anything, I missed belonging to a spiritual community, or *sangha.*

Looking back, I find it bizarre how little I had considered this need for connection when I moved overseas. Yoga had saved me in undergrad in Canada, so why hadn't I put yoga at the top of my priorities when moving across the world and choosing a place to live? Upon reflection, I think that I didn't make yoga a priority because I considered myself to be 'healed' instead of understanding that healing is a continuous process. I couldn't just attend yoga for five years and think that I was fixed. Instead, I had to remain consistent in my yoga practice so that I could continue to experience all of the mental health benefits that yoga brings into my life.

I had seen on *Google Maps* that there was a studio in the city, but it was expensive. The classes were three times the price of classes in Canada. I knew I couldn't afford a class, but in my second year, once I was aware of how much stress I had been through and how badly I needed yoga, I decided that I was going to find a way to make it work. I figured out that I could afford a membership by taking on some extra tutoring gigs and I decided to commit to this solution, since I knew that yoga was essential for helping me to stay grounded.

The yoga studio was about a twenty-five-minute drive from the school – in the opposite direction of my apartment. The first class was at four in the afternoon. So, after school ended at two, I'd wait for two hours, take the first class of the day and then drive home to Mahboula. Returning home usually took another hour and a half due to the added distance and the rush hour traffic at this time of day. It meant I'd be out of the apartment for at least twelve or thirteen hours every day.

I quickly learned that the studio was run by someone who was the same age as me: a Kuwaiti man named Saad. I admired the fact that he'd achieved something I'd only dreamed about at such a young age.

Even though I had participated in a yoga teacher training in Mexico, taught yoga at a yoga studio in Canada, was employed as a yoga teacher at the hotel resort, and had been offering weekly, private yoga classes to Atif, I still didn't believe in myself as a yoga teacher. I didn't see myself as being on the same level as teachers at his studio; I saw myself as being beneath them. In my mind, I thought, *I'm not as good as these international instructors. He won't want to hire me*. But, to my surprise, he overheard that I was a yoga teacher one day in the lobby, and he approached me after class.

"Hey, Alex," he said. "Is it true that you're a yoga teacher? Do you want to teach for us?" I was in disbelief. He saw something in me that I didn't see in myself. We chatted for a minute or two and then arranged for me to teach him a private, one-on-one yoga session as a demo a week later. Even though he'd offered me this opportunity, I still doubted myself after the chat and went over every moment of the conversation between us in excruciating detail. *Did I embarrass myself? Did I say something dumb? Will he have changed his mind about wanting to hire me?*

I was so nervous about teaching a demo class. For the first

time ever, a yoga studio wanted me to lead a practice as part of the interview process. I met with Saad one day after work, and I guided him through a yoga class. By the end of the class, he'd verbally offered me a job on the schedule. I still didn't believe it was true, so I waited for the official email to come through from him about a week or two later. I was so happy when I was hired. I was given two classes a week – one was a hot yoga class on Thursday evenings, and one was a regular class on Saturday afternoons. Not long after, I was regularly down at the studio, subbing classes for other teachers and participating in classes as a student, just like I had at the studio in Canada. Words cannot truly describe what it felt like to be teaching and studying yoga with a *sangha* (community) of *sādhakas* (yoga practitioners) again. It didn't matter that it was a long drive away from my apartment. Finally, after a year, I was interacting with people who knew about the philosophy of yoga and were passionate about it, too. I was beginning to reconnect to myself. I was beginning to feel my soul again.

CHAPTER 26

IT EITHER EXISTS OR IT DOES NOT

In Kuwait, my relationships outside of school always started at either the hotel where I taught yoga or the yoga studio, and my relationship with my husband was no different. One Friday morning, I was at the gym running on the treadmill, and I bumped into a girl who had come to some of my yoga classes, Mariana. Mariana was from Spain, and she was super chatty. She was there with a co-worker, Santiago, to whom she introduced me. Santiago was from Mexico. He lived in the hotel and worked in the oil industry.

Whenever Santiago would later tell the story of our relationship, he often referenced the movie *Sliding Doors*. I'd not seen it at the time, but he told me the premise. The movie plays out two scenarios: in one scenario, a woman gets fired from her job, catches the train home and discovers her husband with another woman (*Sliding Doors*). She then goes on to meet the love of her life. In the second scenario, she misses the train and arrives home just after the woman has left (*Sliding Doors*).

Santiago was meant to fly to Oman for a holiday for the weekend, but his visa did not come through. He unexpectedly stayed at the hotel. In a terrible mood, he'd decided to spend the morning at the gym – and that's where he met me. If he had received his visa to Oman as he'd intended, we never would have met. Sliding doors. And it certainly changed the entire course of both of our lives, in significant ways.

Santiago liked me right away. I could sense that from the way he looked at me. "Hey, Mariana and I are going to a Kuwaiti party tonight," he said. "Do you want to come with us? We have some Kuwaiti co-workers around our age – one of them is having a birthday. It's gonna be super fun!" Santiago was handsome and had a bright smile, but there was something in his energy that didn't immediately feel right. What excited me was the idea of going to a party with locals my age. Since the Kuwaiti nightlife was so exclusive, I'd never actually been to parties with Kuwaiti people my age, and I was intrigued.

And that is how, a few hours later, I ended up in a house with gold-leaf tables, crystal chandeliers and strawberries dipped in chocolate. This was the type of party where I could mention I'd like an energy drink and, ten minutes later, a driver would return from the *Bakala* (convenience store) carrying every flavor imaginable for me to choose from.

I immediately loved the Kuwaiti couple that I met that night as a result of Santiago and Mariana's invitation. It turned out that they had graduated from the same international school where I worked, so they were extraordinarily wealthy. Even though they had a lot of money, you would never know that by just looking at the way they dressed and behaved. For example, Ahmed, having learned that I was from Toronto, answered the door in a T-shirt that said 'Toronto Vs. Everybody' – which was a very popular T-shirt at the time. The funny thing was, I had actually considered buying one when I moved to Kuwait, but I was concerned that people might find it offensive. Ahmed had traveled to Toronto the previous year. I loved that he made such an effort to connect with me and make me feel welcome. They were some of the kindest, most grounded Kuwaitis I had ever met, and they challenged every stereotype that I had in my head about what people from the Gulf were like.

I enjoyed Santiago's company, but I didn't feel the immediate butterflies that I'd hoped to feel around my future partner. But maybe butterflies weren't needed? Maybe butterflies were made up?

At this point in time, I wasn't sure if I could envision a relationship with Santiago, but I enjoyed building a friendship with him. He continued to invite me to dinner, games nights and gatherings with friends, and he also joined my friends and me on a trip to Beirut, Lebanon.

Teaching was just as difficult for me as it had been during the previous year. In my first year of teaching, I had complained about how hard it was, and a lot of my colleagues had reassured me by saying, "Don't worry, Alex. This group of students that you have is just hard. Next year you'll have a brand-new cohort of kids, and it will be easier." I did have a new group of students, but it wasn't any easier. The children as individuals were wonderful, and I cared about them a lot. But managing the classroom dynamics was as exasperating as it was the year before.

Not long into the school year, I was already worn out and sick of my job. The challenges did not seem to be worth the benefits. *Can I really do this repeatedly for the rest of my life? Can I really cope with the stress, the disrespect and the behavior?* I thought about quitting teaching often, and I also expressed this to everyone around me, Santiago included. More and more, I started to dream about leaving my job and teaching yoga full time.

One morning, I told Santiago about this internal conflict. I told him that I wanted to teach yoga full time, but I wouldn't make enough money doing so. Without even skipping a beat, he said, "I can financially support you." And I accepted this offer. I realize how absolutely wild this sounds with many years of hindsight.

Why would I accept an offer of financial support from a man that I'd known for less than a month? Why would I be willing to become dependent on a man who I hadn't even kissed?

But I was swept up in what I perceived to be a fairy tale. My dream was to teach yoga full time and someone was offering to support me. I felt like I had to give Santiago a chance and try dating him. This felt like the universe sending me a Prince Charming, and I couldn't say no.

It felt like every few weeks in Kuwait was a holiday or a vacation. It became normal to receive an email on Tuesday informing us that we would be having an unexpected long weekend the following week. The first weekend of December, we had a five-day weekend for the Prophet's birthday. We decided to travel to both Dubai and Abu Dhabi. I had traveled to Dubai many times to visit friends but had never been to Abu Dhabi. I had no idea that the two cities were driving distance from each other, but Santiago had made the trip many times. He suggested, therefore, that we fly to Dubai, spend a night there, and then drive to Abu Dhabi in the morning for the rest of the weekend.

We decided to go to Dubai for one night so that I could visit Claire, but instead of staying at Claire's villa, we upgraded. Santiago lived in the hotel full time in Kuwait, so he had plenty of hotel stay points, and we checked into a resort on the beach. Claire found this decision to be weird. When I'd come to Dubai in the past, I'd always stayed with her – and now she'd moved into a villa, so she even had a spare guest bedroom. But Santiago figured that if he had the points, then we might as well use them.

Because he was a diamond member of the hotel, we got to skip the line at check-in, and our room was also upgraded to a suite, which came with a tray of fruits and a tower of cakes, cookies and pastries. My jaw dropped. Claire came down to meet us in the hotel, and her jaw dropped, too. Every time we'd travel together or with our teacher friends, we'd try to find the most budget-friendly hotels and the cheapest restaurants. But with Santiago, everything was the best of the best. The glitziest and the most glamorous. I'd never experienced life like this.

When we entered the hotel room, what I was most in awe of was the bathroom. Inside, there was a shimmering, deep, beautiful bathtub, with a gigantic window beside it that overlooked the water. All my life, baths had been a crucial part of my daily routine – from as young as age six, I ended my day with a soak. What was special about baths for me was that, surrounded by warm water, I felt calm, quiet, relaxed and peaceful. At the time, I don't think that I was aware that taking baths was one of my resources in my mental health toolkit, but it was. It was my private space, away from others.

When I moved overseas, for some bizarre reason, I'd been nonchalant about the importance of this daily ritual: "Oh, there are no bathtubs in the apartments? No problem." (Nowadays, I never decide to live – or even vacation – in a place that doesn't have a bathtub – I've learned my lesson.) By February of my first year in Kuwait, I couldn't take it anymore, and I ordered a bathtub online. It was meant to be installed in a wall unit, but I obviously couldn't do bathroom renovations to my school-owned apartments, so I connected it in a very DIY manner. I removed a door off its hinges and squeezed the bathtub skeleton inside the bathroom. I found some bricks in Mahboula and propped up the tub, so that it was less rickety. "The bricks transformed my ordinary bathtub into a claw-foot bathtub," I'd joke. I then attached the showerhead to the side of the tub, so that it could be used to fill the tub with water. The homemade drainage system was leaky, but it worked. I was partially proud of my innovation, but I was also very embarrassed about the fact that I'd had to take on such an endeavor because my apartment didn't come with a tub. Needless to say, when Santiago and I stayed in hotels, the bathtubs were a huge deal.

The following morning, we booked a car to take us to Abu

Dhabi. We drove along Sheikh Zayed Road and, as we left Dubai, the road became quieter and calmer. We passed palm trees, deserts and camels. As we drove, I nodded off, exhausted from a night of partying in Dubai.

As we got closer to Abu Dhabi, Santiago gently woke me up. "Alex, I want to let you sleep, but you can't miss this. You have to see it." He pointed to the left and beside us was a gigantic, white, shimmering mosque with marble pillars, marble domes and shimmering gold. "That's the Grand Mosque."

I was in disbelief. I'd never seen something so beautiful. It was truly magical. It looked like something out of *Aladdin*. I'd heard about Abu Dhabi's world-famous Grand Mosque in books and had seen photos, but seeing it in real life it was on another level. We continued to drive, passing mangroves and admiring the crystal-clear waters that came into sight as we crossed a myriad of bridges. As we got closer to the city, we turned right off the road and pulled up to a hotel on Al Maryah Island. Every aspect of this moment made it feel like we were on a Hollywood movie set. I turned to Santiago. "We have to move here," I said.

"I knew you'd love it," he beamed.

I'd said that about almost every city that I'd visited in the Middle East over the past year – but this time, it was different. In Abu Dhabi, I felt an overwhelming sense of calm and peace. It felt like I had found my home.

Throughout the weekend, we went on a sunset desert safari, we visited the Emirates Palace and we explored the Yas Island Formula One Racetrack. We went back to the Grand Mosque to visit it at sunset, and it was just as breathtaking up close. The walls had intricate mosaic designs. I learned that mosques have mosaic tiles because the artists are creating geometric designs with the tiles to represent Allah. Since they do not believe in idolatry (depicting human figures), they are representing Allah using geometric shapes. They chose this mode of depiction because geometry is a perfect science, and they wanted to find a way to portray that perfection. There were also stunning crystal chandeliers that refracted the sunlight and projected dazzling rainbows on the walls of the mosque. There was also a carpet that Santiago told me was the largest hand-woven carpet in the world. After visiting the mosque, Santiago took me back for dinner at his favorite sushi restaurant in Abu Dhabi. This was the type of restaurant where you needed a reservation – you couldn't just walk in off the street.

When we booked the dinner at reception, the hotel receptionist made sure to inform us that the dress code was 'elegant smart'. I was hungover and wearing leggings and a wrinkly T-shirt. I said to Santiago, "We have to go back to the hotel room so I can change."

He looked at me and said, "Why do you need to change? You already look 'elegant smart'!"

I burst out laughing.

That's when I felt that this guy was something very, very special. No one had ever made me feel so beautiful when I looked and felt like such a disaster. In my mind at the time, all I could think was, *this guy is too good to let go.*

In the blink of an eye, my life had changed. I had one foot in Mahboula and one foot in five-star hotels every single week. Sunday to Thursday, I was dealing with my car breaking down, my stressful work environment, and all of the traffic, noise and chaos of my everyday life, and then on the weekends, I had fallen into a trap of escapism and getaways. I was running away from my problems and seeking refuge in an infinitely more extravagant lifestyle. Suddenly, for example, I found myself eating in first-rate restaurants that I'd only ever read about in magazines.

I grew up watching Disney movies. In the story of *Cinderella*, a beautiful woman escaped from her cruel stepsisters by running away to a ball and pretending to be a princess. She then met a handsome prince who saved her from her horrible life (*Cinderella*). Every time that I stepped outside of Mahboula and embraced this new lifestyle, it felt like I was becoming part of a real-life fairy tale.

The third *yama* of the *Pātañjalayogasūtra* is *Asteya*, or non-stealing. Non-stealing is most often literally translated into theft, but I believe it can go much broader: becoming aware of all the ways, large and small, in which we take what is not ours. This often has roots in a feeling of inadequacy or lack. A simple way to counter this feeling of lack is to cultivate gratitude for all of the abundance we already have. Because I was in a 'lack' mentality, I desired more. Instead of looking towards *puruṣa*, or my soul, to find contentment, I looked out to *prakṛti*, the material world, thinking that that was where I was going to find it.

I used the material world as an escape from everything: my work environment, my challenging students, my living environment. I had an escape from my pain. From my depression. From my sadness. I think a lot of women are socially conditioned to dream of having a man come into their lives and sweep them off their feet. At least, I know I was. I had this core belief that I couldn't create this type of fairy tale in my life without a man to create it for me, and he'd created it all right.

Because this was the first time that a man like this had come into my life, I didn't want to let him go. I couldn't let him go. I was determined to fall in love with him.

I just didn't understand that – no matter how determined I was – I couldn't force myself to fall in love. Falling in love is not something that you can create. It's a force between both of you which is either there or completely missing.

CHAPTER 27

IT CHANGED EVERYTHING

As soon as I met Santiago, my life changed instantly. In my first year in the Gulf, I had a full-time job at the school, part-time employment at the resort, and I was traveling around once a month on budget backpacking adventures. I had constant bouts of depression, I was crying all the time, and I just wanted to go home. But in my second year, when I met Santiago, a switch flipped. I was no longer the girl who was so overcome by crying spells and depressive episodes that she wanted to go home – I was happy.

I also became an extreme jet-setter. If I thought that I was traveling often during my first year in Kuwait, my excursions went up to a whole other level after I met Santiago. He had just arrived in the Middle East about a month before I met him and was much less settled than I was. While I was happy to spend a weekend teaching yoga and tutoring children, he was keen to leave the country every weekend and explore the region in the most luxurious way.

Prior to his time in Kuwait, when he was in Mexico, his company also housed him in a hotel since his projects were not in Mexico City, where he lived. As a result of his travels for work, he accumulated a ton of points for both hotels and North American airlines. So, when I was in Canada for New Year's Eve and his points were about to expire, Santiago spontaneously booked a flight from Mexico to Toronto. Like the Dubai trip, this hotel upgraded us to a suite with a huge sitting room and a bedroom attached, but because we'd gotten used to the life of luxury in Dubai, we were somewhat disappointed by it. In our eyes, this hotel had a dark, dingy lobby, the hotel room window only looked out onto a concrete wall, and the furniture was outdated.

We invited Zach and a few of my other high school and university friends over to get drunk with us one night in the suite. From their perspective, the hotel room that we were staying in was very impressive. "Woah, you have a sitting room and a bedroom! This is nuts! This hotel room is huge!" Santiago and I sheepishly looked at each other. It dawned on us how much living in the Middle East meant that we'd lost touch with reality.

When we got back to Kuwait that January, it was not long before we traveled to Doha, Qatar for Santiago's birthday. He arrived midweek and sent me a photo of a white, spotless, sparkly Jacuzzi tub from his hotel room. I couldn't wait until the weekend when it was my turn to join him. When I got there, we visited the Souq Waqif, the Museum of Islamic Art and the Katara – the Cultural Village Foundation. We went out for dinner and drinks with a few of Santiago's friends at Robert De Niro's five-course, gourmet restaurant, Nobu. Whenever I went on one of these trips, I was always mindful to post pictures of us engaging in casual activities, like standing on the street with a takeaway coffee in hand – I never bragged about the hotel bathtubs or the fancy restaurants. It felt too over the top, and I didn't want my friends and family to think that I was in the relationship with him for the wrong reasons.

Nonetheless, Charlotte, my friend from high school, commented on my *Instagram*, "You really are living the dream." That's what it felt like. Not only were we traveling often, but Santiago's points from work also allowed us to consistently stay in five-star hotels and dine in expensive restaurants. In other words, I was spending my time frequenting businesses I could never even dream to afford on my salaries as an educator and a yoga teacher. My life became a whirlwind – I felt like I'd come across the life and the boyfriend that every girl dreams of having.

One night, when we were still very early into our relationship, I shared with Santiago that my doctors suspected I had bipolar disorder, and they had prescribed me medication for it. "Did a doctor actually tell you that you have this?" he asked me.

"Well, he never saw me in a manic episode, so he couldn't confirm it. But he highly suspected it."

Looking back, I think that this statement very clearly reflected my lack of self-confidence in both myself and this diagnosis. To be honest, part of me wasn't even sure that I had bipolar. I clung to the doctor's use of the word 'suspect' and interpreted it as him having said 'I don't know'. I was never clearly told, "You have bipolar."

As a child, I was known to exaggerate. I didn't understand that this habit was a coping mechanism, and I didn't know that I was lying when I hyperbolized. When I realized that I had this habit as a young adult, I became obsessed with trying as hard as I could to always tell the truth. This strict adherence to the truth meant that because the doctor never categorically said to me, "You have bipolar," and instead said, "I suspect that you have bipolar," I never wanted to exaggerate by telling people that I had been given a diagnosis. In my mind, I hadn't been officially diagnosed yet.

My uncertainty and confusion were probably visible, and Santiago looked skeptical. "Alex, I really think that you're healthier than you believe." He shared with me that he had a friend who died by suicide at a young age, and he didn't think that I had the same problems as him. "Alex, trust me, you are perfectly normal. You are a very happy girl. There is nothing wrong with you that I've noticed."

I climbed back into my clam shell. Every time I'd opened up about mental health, the same thing happened – people questioned me and dismissed me, and so I shrank back, feeling small and doubting the validity of my own symptoms, experiences and diagnosis. Disclosing aspects of my mental health to others made me feel vulnerable. I didn't do it often because I didn't trust that I'd have support. I realize in retrospect that even though this was not his intention, Santiago fell into the category of not being able to support me.

Santiago is a genuine and loving person and always wanted the best for me. He truly wasn't trying to belittle me on purpose in this moment – he just had very little context for mental health. He did not acknowledge mental health as an issue and had a fixed mindset around what it was and wasn't. While I no longer identify with the diagnosis of bipolar disorder, I do believe that I had a highly dysregulated nervous system back in 2015. As a result of this dysregulation, the manic and depressive episodes that I experienced were very real.

Nowadays, I am entirely different when it comes to advocating for my mental health. I'm very self-aware of what I need, and I am quick and confident to express and explain these needs to the people around me. This self-advocacy has improved over time. Although I no longer identify with the diagnosis of bipolar, the diagnosis did help to make me more confident in articulating what I need. I explain to people that I experience big emotions. I also talk about the resources in my mental health toolkit, which allow me to regulate my mood. For example, I often share about my need for deep sleep, exercise and a spiritual practice, as well as the mindfulness that I have around what I am eating. I also emphasize how important it is that I surround myself with people who are able to hold space for my journey while exhibiting empathy and support.

While the diagnosis of bipolar and the use of medication are no longer a part of my personal journey, I believe that mental health is very real, I am an advocate for mental health, and I'm also someone who supports others as they learn about managing their own mental health. I listen, and I strive to foster a safe space where they can feel heard – because these are the supports that I was missing during my own mental health journey. And because I've created a safe space, more and more people are engaging with me and sharing their stories in a variety of formats. Whether it's people that I've met on *Zoom*, people that I have met in real life at my retreats and yoga teacher trainings, or even just people who have left comments on my *TikTok* videos or *Instagram* posts, I am able to see the direct impact that providing such supports can have on others. I now provide for others exactly what I didn't have.

But back then, I wasn't in that headspace yet. And I let Santiago's opinion impact me.

When it came down to the fundamental topic of mental health, the two of us did not agree. In hindsight, this difference of opinion should have been a sign for me to slow things down. In the many years since we were together, my beliefs, experiences and lifestyle have changed dramatically, and I am certain that Santiago has changed, too. I sometimes wonder about how things might differ if Santiago and I met nowadays instead of back in 2017. Would our conversations have led us in a completely alternative direction?

It was December, and I was six months away from my teaching contract ending in June. Recruitment in the international teaching world happens very early, sometimes a year in advance, as schools must begin to plan numbers and process visa paperwork for their new hires. I still had six months left to work, but I was ready to leave the school.

My colleagues were already signing contracts for teaching jobs elsewhere and turning in their resignations to the school for the following year. While everyone around me seemed to know what they were doing with their futures, I didn't have a plan. I was beginning to feel anxious whenever I compared myself to them and realized that I had no idea what was next. That daunting 'lack of plan' feeling that I was having made me consider applying to schools elsewhere.

I was still teaching part time at the yoga studio in Kuwait City. Saad, the owner of the studio, loved my classes. He texted me one night after joining my class: "You should work for the yoga studio full time!"

I was in disbelief. I was the girl who thought she wasn't even good enough to work part time at this yoga studio. Now I was being offered a full-time job there?

It was very affirming to hear that he wanted to hire me. This was my dream, but for so many years, I'd doubted myself. So now I had the dream boyfriend and potentially the dream job. I remember texting Saad back, "Are you serious about this?"

"Yes," he said, "come work for the studio after you finish your contract at the school."

I told Saad about looking for teaching jobs and being offered contracts for next year elsewhere. I explained that I needed to know if I'd have a job as soon as possible, or I might sign a contract somewhere else. "I need an offer sooner rather than later."

He prepared an official offer letter in less than a week. What I was making at the school was already tiny compared to the cost of living in Kuwait, but the salary that he was offering me was less than half of that. There was an opportunity to earn more money if I hosted additional workshops and events. I would be exclusively working for his studio, so I couldn't teach classes elsewhere in the city. He was also providing me with fewer days off (only one a week), thirty vacation days total per year instead of closer to four months, as I had at the school, and an apartment with a roommate. I continued a back-and-forth *WhatsApp* message chain with Saad until I was able to negotiate an apartment without a roommate and more classes a day for a larger salary.

I told Santiago about the offer. We were sitting in a taxi heading to the airport for another weekend getaway. He was ecstatic for me. Santiago knew that it was my lifelong dream to teach yoga full time and so he said, without even hesitating or skipping a beat, "Take this job. It's your dream. I'll financially support you through this." The wildest thing is, at this point in time, Santiago and I weren't even boyfriend and girlfriend yet.

And with that support and my full excitement, I signed the contract.

I started to get optimistic about our future in Kuwait. I would finish off the remainder of the winter at the school, travel to Bali for an advanced yoga teacher training, and then start teaching full-time yoga at the studio in September. Our plan as a couple was to stay in Kuwait one more year, while I taught yoga in the studio, and he worked in the oil industry. And then we'd move onwards together.

However, my life with Santiago got increasingly more tangled once I made this decision, and we suddenly went from being carefree, young, single expats to being tied together in more serious ways. We were leading independent lives that suddenly became entwined overnight. One of the many challenges that we faced occurred when Santiago's work fell through. I signed the yoga contract in December, right when Santiago was finishing a short-term project that he was working on in Kuwait. He had been offered a very stable, long-term job in the Middle East with the same company starting in the new year. He had intended to travel to Mexico for a month for Christmas and then return to the Middle East to begin his permanent job in January. He flew back to meet me in Kuwait in January, but right before he was meant to start work, the job suddenly wasn't available. It was a shock. He continued to use his points to live temporarily at the resort, buying time and insisting he'd find work soon, until finally I said to him, "Save your points. Move in with me."

He moved in with me in late January, for what was originally going to be a seven-to-fourteen-day period, maximum, until he found another job. But what started as a short-term solution gradually became a long-term one. And just like that, we went from being a newly happy couple, in an exploration phase of our relationship, to living together, in the span of a few months.

This is not the way that cohabitation typically occurs. Normally, things are planned, discussed, agreed upon and negotiated. With our new arrangement, however, we went from not living together one day to making grocery lists and sharing my car (which instantaneously became 'our car') the next. Part of this change was novel and exciting and fun. Our entire relationship, up until that point, was extraordinary. A typical weekend night involved camel rides into the sunset in the Abu Dhabi desert and dancing in a former bomb shelter turned underground nightclub in Lebanon. Now, our relationship had some ordinary moments, too – like making decisions around which brand of yogurt we wanted and determining which price we were willing to pay for a juicing appliance.

For as long as I could remember, I'd always dreamed of having a boyfriend with whom I could live and share my life. After all, this was how the fairy tale was supposed to end. Now, my life would enter the 'happily ever after' phase. I didn't question anything. It didn't even occur to me how rushed, unconventional and abnormal things between us were. Or maybe I was brushing any concerns aside, because I was swept up by what I perceived to be love.

While Santiago had lost his employment, he still wanted to carry on with the same jet-setting lifestyle that he'd been indulging in before. Traveling was the reason why he'd come to the Middle East, and he'd adapted to a luxurious way of living. Moreover, since he'd permanently lived in the resort for over six months, he had tons of points – points that were soon to expire. He had to use them up, or they'd go to waste. So, we put them towards our trips.

We continued to catch flights every other weekend as if our lives were just as charmed as they were before. That winter was a series of holidays – Doha, Abu Dhabi, Sri Lanka, Dubai, Beirut. As soon as the plane touched down in each location that we visited, Santiago and I would start drinking alcohol together. We almost never had the opportunity to experience the city nightlife because I'd pass out before eight in the evening – usually when I was lying across Santiago's lap in a taxi. On Saturday afternoon, I'd get on the plane hungover, return to Kuwait, barely awake, and then we'd do it all again ten days later. It felt like a whirlwind.

I was convinced that I was in love with him, but I think my giddy feelings were a mixture of a lot of things. Of course, our relationship was filled with excitement and joy – having so many adventures together created an adrenaline rush. Our relationship was also filled with euphoria, a special feeling of connection and romance. But it was also the first time in a long time that I wasn't in a constant state of depression, and I was often thinking, *Life's great! I've fallen in love, and I'm cured!*

The Kuwaiti law officially said that women and men were not allowed to cohabit prior to marriage, but within certain expat communities, exceptions were made. We never announced to security or my colleagues that Santiago had moved in – people just began seeing him more and more and made assumptions. This leniency wasn't the same at the resort. It seemed like the security guards there were specifically watching the cameras outside of his room, because just as soon as I crossed the threshold into his room and closed the door, the phone would ring. "Mr Santiago, please get the woman out of your room now."

Even though Santiago was able to move into my apartment, we started talking about marriage very quickly. By living together pre-marriage, it felt as though we were on the other side of the law, and I worried that Santiago could be caught at any time and be asked to move out. Plus, we thought that we'd need a marriage certificate once we moved into the apartment that was being given to me by the yoga studio since this new home wasn't part of a gated community.

Santiago said he was in love with me, and I thought I was in love with him too. We figured that if we were going to get married one day eventually anyway, then why not do it a little bit early?

Even though engaging in holy matrimony logically made sense, there was still a small, nagging feeling in the back of my mind that something wasn't quite right. I tried to talk myself into embracing this solution, but the persistent voice in my mind was coaxing me to stop, or at least slow down. Luckily, this was what I had booze for – for silencing these feelings.

Towards the end of April, one night, we sat on the rooftop of our building, watching the orange sunset over the mosque in Mahboula. We were discussing whether we'd go through with the marriage in the end. If we were going to do it, Santiago was going to have to organize some paperwork and make some calls the following week. I told him that I was excited about getting married, but part of me also felt as if I wasn't ready.

"It's just paper," he reassured me. "Our relationship won't change. Things will stay the same. We just won't have to deal with all of the headaches of being unmarried in Kuwait anymore." Swept up in the excitement of the moment, and despite the nagging feeling in my gut, I decided I'd do it.

We legally couldn't marry locally, as Santiago didn't have a work visa for Kuwait; he only had one for the UAE. We knew that the only place in the region where we could have a quick, spontaneous marriage was Cyprus. But because we couldn't fly directly to Cyprus and had to stop in Bahrain for a layover, it would take a full day of travel to get there from Kuwait. Due to this, we couldn't get married on a regular weekend. We'd be traveling through the air both days and wouldn't even have a full day grounded to tie the knot. We needed a long weekend, with an extra day of travel, to do the deed. At the time, there was only one long weekend until the school year ended in July: the Prophet's ascension. Since I was planning to travel to Canada and Bali in July, we decided on April.

"It won't change anything," he had said. "It's just paper. Our relationship will stay the same."

But it changed everything.

CHAPTER 28

ME AND YOU, ARMY OF TWO

What I remember of the day we married in Cyprus are moments. The moment when you and I walked to the town hall. You in your navy suit, and me in my white, vintage lace summer dress. You were so excited. I was excited too, but I also had nervous butterflies.

You told me that day, like every day, how in love with me you were. And I told you how in love I was with you.

I remember the moment when I was filling out the papers in the town hall, and I got to the part where I had to fill out your dad's name. I realized that I didn't even know your dad's name. And that was a moment when I thought, "I should not be doing this."

I remember the moment when we had to take out cash to pay for the marriage, and we walked together to the ATM. That was another moment when I thought, "I should not be doing this."

I remember the moment when you commented that everyone else in the room who was getting married that day looked like they were heading to a funeral. "It looks like it's the worst day of their life... it's the happiest day of mine!" My gut also felt like it was the worst day of my life. But I couldn't tell you. And that was a moment when I thought, "I should not be doing this."

By the time we got around to signing the papers and having our first kiss as newlyweds, I felt like it was too late to back out. And so, I kissed you back.

Anyone who sees pictures from that day comments on how happy I look. But the truth is I was pretending to be happy. Deep inside, I felt like my world had ended. But I thought if I pretended to be happy for long enough that maybe I could convince myself that I was.

We proceeded to go to a nearby restaurant to wait for the marriage certificates to be stamped and authenticated. We sat on the patio at nine in the morning smoking shisha and knocking back pints of the local Cypriot beer. Next, we picked up our marriage certificates and went to the beach where we drank long island iced teas and smoked more shisha. We came back to our hotel, while the sun was setting, and we had tequila shots.

We answered a phone call from your family in Mexico, who I had never met, and I tried as hard as I could to be thrilled about being called 'their new daughter'. On my end of things, I hadn't even told my own family that we'd gone through with the marriage. Both my parents and my sister had met you, and everyone loved you immediately – you were caring, respectful and lovable. They knew that we were talking about marriage and were in a very serious relationship, but I didn't tell any of them that we'd gone through with it. I knew that just by looking at me, my mom would know I was not on board.

We'd been married for eight hours, but he hadn't even proposed or given me a diamond ring yet. He later told me that he was just testing me to see if I'd go through with the marriage. I didn't realize how strange this was without hindsight. That night, we went down to the beach, where he set up tealight candles, got down on one knee, and offered me a diamond ring. In his proposal, he mentioned something along the lines of how marriage was an 'army of two'. What I remember specifically is that when he asked, my immediate thought was, *No.*

But how could I say no if I had already said yes?

I accepted the ring and tried to be thrilled about it – but I wasn't. I needed to get more drunk. So, we had shot after shot. We got so drunk that night that by the end of it, when we went to bed, we left our hotel door open. We woke up at 7am to a staff member poking her head into our room and asking, "Is everything okay in here?"

We got up and ordered breakfast. I barely ate, chalking it up to a hangover, when in reality it was probably much more than that. That afternoon, we got on the plane to Kuwait. Hangover anxiety and doomsday dread were already sinking in. What. Had. I. Done. But I tried to push my emotions aside. I tried to ignore it. Maybe these feelings were normal? Maybe people typically feel this way after getting married?

I didn't want to tell anyone that we were engaged, but Santiago, on the other hand, was thrilled. He wanted everyone to know. He said in his culture, the man proposed, and the woman shared the news. In modern day, that meant she posted on *Facebook* and *Instagram*. And so, reluctantly, late in the evening, I posted the photo on social media. And then I went to bed.

At 3:38am, I woke up feeling like I had been physically stabbed in the gut. It was a sharp, throbbing pain. My heart was beating out of my chest, and I was fully consumed with panic. I checked my phone and had nearly five hundred notifications of likes, comments and messages from friends who were congratulating us on our engagement. I barely hobbled my way out of the bed. I crawled into the bathroom in the hallway before shutting the door and collapsing on the floor. I had never, ever felt this way before or after about anything in my life. This was a drastic, physical reaction – my intuition was speaking loudly to me. The intuition that I had chosen to ignore.

In Brené Brown's book, *Atlas of the Heart*, Brown explores eighty-seven emotions and experiences, and even more powerfully, she gives us the vocabulary to define and describe what we feel. When I read Brené Brown's book years later and came across 'anguish', I knew that that was what I felt.

> *Anguish… not only takes away our ability to breathe, feel, and think – it comes for our bones. Anguish often causes us to physically crumple in on ourselves, literally bringing us to our knees or forcing us all the way to the ground. The element of powerlessness is what makes anguish traumatic. We are unable to change, reverse, or negotiate what has happened. And even in those situations where we can temporarily reroute anguish with to-do lists and tasks, it finds its way back to us* (Brown 101).

That night, in a moment of anguish, I pulled out my phone and started typing into my notes, while I laid curled in a fetal position on the tiled floor.

> *Alex's iPhone April 30, 2017, at 3:38am.*
>
> *"I woke up with this big feeling of anxiety and dread. What the hell did I do? This is crazy.*
>
> *I am scared he's not the one. But he is, now.*
>
> *I need to remind myself of all of the reasons I fell in love with him. He supports me, he listens, he lets me cry. He and I can talk about everything. We view the world the exact same way. We run* un apartmento chingón *[a Spanish slang word for awesome or very good]. He is brilliant. He showed up for me by flying across the world. He keeps showing up for me in ways that no boyfriends have ever shown up for me before. He loves me to the moon and back."*

Looking back, by writing these things, I see that I was trying to convince myself that I'd made the right choice, when it was so clear that I had not.

I got up off the bathroom floor. I hobbled back into bed and woke him up.

"Santiago?"

"Yes, my love?"

He rolled over and half woke up.

"I just wanted to tell you that I love you."

He kissed me. "I love you too."

For him, this was a loving moment.

For me, I was just testing how it felt to say it, to see if saying it would help me convince myself that I was okay.

But deep down, I knew that I was not.

CHAPTER 29

I CHANGED

When you ask people what went wrong in a marriage, often you hear them say that, after they got married, their husbands or wives changed. They were no longer the person they were before.

When asked about our marriage, I imagine that's what Santiago says about me. "After we married, she changed." Because the truth is, I did. In my mind, 'wanting' and 'wearing' a ring were two completely different things. And I was the one who changed.

But, I have no idea what he actually says about me because before contacting him about publishing this book, I hadn't heard from him since 2017. In 2020, I reconnected with someone who was in our circle of friends when we lived in Kuwait. It was the first time that I'd connected with someone linked to him in years. So much distance and space had been built between us. We'd grown so far apart. She told me what Santiago said happened between us. He simply stated, "One day, I woke up, and she was gone."

I only wish it was that simple: *One day, I woke up, and I was gone*. That's how I wanted it to go. I wanted to wake up and jump off the roof of The Oasis, and then I'd be dead, and the whole problem would be gone. But the truth was, it was not that simple. It was two months of absolute agony. Two months of me trying desperately hard to be happy. Two months of me trying as hard as I could to stay in the marriage. The last thing that I wanted to do was leave. I had nightmares, and I always cried – when I wasn't with him and when I was with him.

When we hear stories of heartbreak, we automatically villainize the heartbreaker. "How could she do that to him?" When often, leaving is the last thing that the heartbreaker wants to do. Usually, the heartbreaker tries everything that she or he can to stay. And when it ends, the heartbreaker is just as hurt as the broken-hearted. At least, that's what happened to me.

During those two months, my world had changed, and all of the joy, all of the love, all of the excitement, all of the passion, was gone. The realization that Santiago and I did not have a special connection and the knowledge that he was not my soulmate got stronger and firmer. I was no longer capable of eating food, falling asleep and staying asleep unless I had alcohol. I lost weight. The roots of my hair turned gray. I found it extremely difficult to be present in any conversation because my brain was being hijacked by overwhelming feelings of doom telling me to leave. Consuming alcohol was helpful because I could numb my overpowering feelings of despair, and it made it easier for me to sit in the company of others. So, as if I wasn't doing it often enough already, I got more and more drunk, more and more frequently. Whereas I had previously tried to downplay my drinking habits with Santiago, I no longer cared about what he thought. I was in survival mode.

I had to quit most of my tutoring jobs because the lovely Arab families that I worked for always wanted to feed me and couldn't stop asking me why I was no longer eating. Their favorite thing to say was, "You didn't eat anything! Why didn't you eat?"

I couldn't say anything other than, "I don't know," because if I said, "I'm not eating because I eloped in Cyprus last weekend, and I'm living in a twenty-four-seven state of anxiety and depression and panic with some suicidal thoughts mixed in," I'm sure that wouldn't have gone over well.

The hardest part about this time was that I'd posted on social media that we were engaged. And that meant that I could never, ever escape. Not even for a minute. When I woke up on my first morning back at school after the Cyprus weekend, I got into my hatchback and pulled out of the driveway. As I did this, my friend Emma appeared in the parking lot beside her car. She was jumping up and down as she waved and mouthed, 'CONGRATULATIONS'. I had to pretend to be excited and smile back, while deep down inside of me, no part of me was excited or happy.

And that was only the beginning. Every two feet, at work, in the compound and in the yoga studio, someone stopped me to congratulate me or examine my diamond ring. My friends from home wanted to have *Skype* calls to catch up. I found myself dreading answering questions about the plans for our wedding. The truth was I wanted to talk about anything but the wedding.

That first week of being married, Santiago knew that I was not doing well. My mental health had completely deteriorated. Overnight. The happy-go-lucky, confident girl he fell in love with was no longer there. Instead, it was a girl who could not stop crying and could not explain to him why.

He had to fly to Dubai for work the Sunday after our marriage weekend. I called him at midnight one night that week, amid a sleepless panic attack, and told him, "Santiago, I need to go to a doctor. I am very sick." He suggested that I take the week off work, fly to Dubai, and meet him on the beach. That would take my mind off things. Obviously, this advice wasn't really helpful, given that I had a full-time job.

I also knew that a trip to Dubai would not help me because my issues were deep, and they couldn't be fixed by simply changing my environment. To us, Dubai was always a whirlwind of beers and cocktails at sunset on the beach. But a drink and a walk on the beach were not going to be the answer this time. I didn't tell him that I was replaying my suicide repeatedly in my head because I didn't want to scare him. I couldn't identify my desire to jump off the building as a suicidal thought – I just knew that it was there, and it was strong. What I desperately needed was someone to hold my hand and get me to the doctor.

After hanging up the phone with Santiago, I finally texted

both of my parents and told them that I was married. I had been wondering if I had been experiencing so much anxiety because I hadn't told them about my wedding, and I thought that sharing this news might relieve my anxiety or help me feel better. But if telling them relieved any anxiety, it was not a significant amount compared to what I was feeling overall.

I don't remember what my dad texted me back about the fact that I was now married. But my mom texted me back saying that she found it "odd" and "interesting". By finally telling them, I felt slightly relieved. It helped settle me enough to fall into a somewhat restless sleep around two or three in the morning. When I woke up a few hours later for work, I was completely exhausted. I rushed around the apartment, frantically getting ready for school, and ran out the door and down to my hatchback. As I sat down behind the wheel, I finally had the chance to open my phone and quickly scan through the notifications I had received. That was when I saw that Santiago had sent me an email at two in the morning, with the subject line '*Chaparrita*'. His message listed all of the reasons why he'd fallen in love with me and wanted to marry me. In the email, he gave me the chance to opt out – to destroy the papers, give him back the ring and go back to being boyfriend and girlfriend. I wept over the steering wheel as I read his words of love.

At that moment, I knew. Santiago was an incredible man. And yet that didn't mean it was right for me to marry him. I had to give him back the ring. He'd given me the chance to opt out – and I knew it was what I needed to do – yet, for some reason, I couldn't.

Somehow, I could not find the courage to follow through with ending things. I could not find the courage to leave.

One night, he went out to play tennis at the hotel with one of his friends. I did my usual thing of scouring the internet and asking questions like: 'How to convince yourself to be happy in your marriage', 'How to get rid of marriage anxiety', and 'How to deal with engagement anxiety'. As luck would have it, I came across a course that was designed to help individuals reduce marriage and engagement anxiety. I was so desperate that I paid for the course, without a second thought. I started working through all of the exercises, which involved bubble maps expressing all the reasons you loved someone or all the reasons you were fearful of marriage. Looking back now, I can see it was a ridiculous idea for me to pay for this course. You cannot coach yourself into feeling love. Just like you cannot create it. You can't take a course on how to be in love. Elizabeth Gilbert wrote in *Eat, Pray, Love*, it is a magnet within both of your hearts that either is there or is not.

Santiago came home, and when I shared with him that I'd registered for this course, he was mostly in disbelief: "You paid for this?!"

Yes, I paid for this. That's how hard I was trying to stay.

The time came for us to finally move into our new apartment in the city, an employee perk that I was receiving from my new yoga studio job. Unfortunately, I was no longer excited about moving into the apartment. I wasn't even excited about the job. But none of my feelings had anything to do with the yoga studio. I was just so depressed that I wasn't excited for anything in my future… at all. My nervous system was so dysregulated that I found myself incapable of holding space for my yoga students. How could I create a healing, authentic space for a yoga class to occur, when I couldn't even create such a space for myself? A large part of teaching yoga is being very mentally present in the space – to mindfully sense the energy in the room. I was incapable of being present while I taught. My mind was always elsewhere.

We were moving into our apartment on the first weekend in June. Since the apartment was near my school, and home was a thirty-minute drive away, I asked Santiago to pack up some things and drive the car down to pick me up from school one afternoon. We could go straight from the school to the new apartment and unpack. Santiago was home all day while I worked full time – not only as a teacher, but also tutoring for various children around the city and teaching yoga. I rarely had a full day of free time. Santiago had much more time, and I was hoping that he could do some of the packing for us while I was at work.

For whatever reason, Santiago had only grabbed one bag of kitchen cutlery items and thrown them in the car, which immediately annoyed me. We started bickering. As we drove towards the new apartment, he told me he was annoyed that I hadn't filled the gas tank, and it was almost empty when he got in the car.

I had toured the apartment alone a few weeks earlier when Santiago had been out of town. By myself, the apartment seemed okay, and I was excited to move there. But that afternoon when the two of us arrived there, to me, everything felt wrong. Maybe it was just my depression talking. Maybe it was being with him. Maybe it was because it was all becoming real. We arrived at the new apartment building and rode up the elevator together. We opened the door. This apartment may have been in a nicer neighborhood in the city, but it was half the size of our apartment in Mahboula. The furniture was even worse than the school furniture. We lay on the bed, and the wooden slats cracked underneath our weight. I opened the oven, and the door fell off.

Santiago had to finish a document that he was sending over to a potential future employer, so he plugged in his computer at the table and got to work, leaving me to unpack everything. After I'd unpacked the kitchen utensils and dishes, which only took me a few minutes, I sat on the couch. There was nothing to keep me busy and nothing to keep my brain distracted. No wine or beer on hand to numb me. While I waited for Santiago to be finished with his document and for us to go home, I was forced to sit on the couch in the present moment. And the present moment was uncomfortable. The present moment was pain. I started to sob. I couldn't stop. I didn't want this apartment, this marriage, or this life, at all. The same one that I had willingly created with him.

Santiago looked up from his computer.

"Alex, what IS wrong?"

I didn't know.

"Alex… I really need to focus on my work. You have to stop crying."

I kept sobbing.

"Alex… I can't deal with this."

We got into the hatchback, and as we began to drive down the highway, the car engine failed. When it rains, it pours, right? (Although it rarely rains in the desert. It just gets dusty.) Santiago was behind the wheel when the car suddenly began to slow from its 140km/h speed to 20km/h. This deceleration might have been happening gradually as we drove, but we were both so involved in our intense argument that we didn't even notice that the car was slowing down. Santiago somehow miraculously managed to get the clunky, white, Desert Girl Cruiser to the shoulder of Highway 30 before it came to a complete halt. Even as he brought the hatchback to the side of the road, we continued arguing. I was convinced that he just wasn't pushing the gas pedal hard enough. Once we were safe on the shoulder of the road, I cried, and I cried.

"Alex, you have to tell me. What is wrong?"

But how could I tell him it was him? Why was it him? How had I become so narcissistic that I was willing to marry this guy one day and then wake up the next morning and realize that I had made an absolute mistake? I didn't even understand my actions myself.

I tried to come up with reasons for my crying that were not him because I wanted so badly to be in love with him. Above all else, I wished that my sadness could be caused by anything other than him. There was nothing that I wanted more than to keep the status quo between us. "It's the yoga studio job that's making me so upset," I told him, which was a complete and total lie. "I don't want to live in this crappy apartment. I don't want to go down to a smaller salary. I don't want to work for Saad."

We waited on the side of the road until my mechanic came to pick up the car. While stuck in the Desert Girl Cruiser, I asked Santiago if he wanted to play a word game where we'd shout out different words and try to say the same word at the same time. I think that I suggested this to have a distraction rather than sit in the present moment where it was slowly dawning on me that this present moment was not what I wanted anymore.

After the mechanic took the hatchback, we flagged a taxi, getting back to the apartment by 7pm. We'd been invited to a party in our building that night, starting in about an hour, but neither of us wanted to go. As I poured a glass of bootleg, homemade wine, he said, "Alex, I can't deal with this anymore. You need to figure it out tonight. Is it me? Or, is it the yoga studio job? And if it's the yoga studio job, you need to ask for your job back at the school." He said he'd leave me alone in the bedroom to decide, and I had one night to make the choice. And when I'd made my decision, I should come out and tell him.

I wasn't brave enough to accept and admit that it was him. So then, I decided, "It's the yoga studio job."

That night, I texted William and asked for my job back at the school. The place that I was so desperate to never return.

CHAPTER 30

I HAD TO BE BRAVE

I see now that I was in such an out-of-control mental health spiral due to everything that I was going through that all my decisions, in retrospect, don't make a lot of sense.

Everyone who's heard this story has asked me, "Why didn't you wait longer to decide whether it was the job or the relationship?"

The answer is, "I don't know."

"Why didn't you consult others?"

"I don't know."

"Why did you think that the only option you had was to return to the school?"

"I'm not sure."

"Why couldn't you decide to go home, or look for a job elsewhere?"

"I don't know."

I was in a spiral, but no one else around me seemed to be able to see the spiral. Not Santiago, not my parents, and not William. And, ultimately, I think that everyone in my life thought that by choosing to go back to the school, I was making the right decision. Santiago wanted me to be happier and thought this was the answer. My parents wanted me to have a secure job, with a salary and stability. And William was just glad to have someone to fill in for all of the runners from the school.

When I asked for my job back, William created a job for me called 'Rover'. In this role, I would basically do any of the jobs that he needed to be done. Essentially, I would fill in for all of the runners.

I didn't want to go back to this school at all, and I knew in my gut that it was the wrong decision. Yet, I still signed the contract. Like I'd signed the marriage certificate. It was like I no longer had control. I couldn't see the way out. And I was going through the motions. I was living on autopilot.

In having my old job back, I didn't feel happier at all. I knew that this was the wrong decision. It didn't change anything. I was still crying all the time. I still couldn't eat or sleep. I still felt awful. I started to have thoughts and dreams about killing myself. Death felt like the only way out.

After signing the contract, I kept it very under wraps that I was planning on returning to the school. I just didn't want to have any conversations with anyone about anything. I wanted to continue to fly under the radar as I sat in the mess of my life. I do recognize in hindsight that, despite everything, the fact that William offered me a job back at the school at this point was very kind of him. He didn't have to do that.

I had ten days remaining in Kuwait before I was due to fly to Canada for a short visit with my family. The last ten days were strange because our apartment had already been allocated to another teacher, who was moving out of the Addition. Consequently, we had to relocate again, this time to an apartment on the first floor, directly across from and at eye level with the mosque.

On the night that the school year ended, I left Santiago in Kuwait and boarded a flight to Toronto. The plan was as follows: I would spend ten days in Toronto, fly back to Kuwait, meet Santiago, and then together, we'd go onwards to our honeymoon in Bali.

As soon as I got to Toronto, I started to have the space for the reflection that I needed. Whilst Santiago whittled away at buying new furniture and renovating our apartment to surprise me when

I got home to Kuwait, it was slowly dawning on me – I had to end this. I had to be brave.

Moments. There was the moment when I went to a yoga class, and I decided to remove my diamond ring. I don't know why I decided to do that, but at that moment, I felt free. I realized that I couldn't put it on again. And so, I didn't.

There was the moment when I went to a meeting at the bank, and I discussed setting up a bank account for the small amount of savings that I'd acquired while in Kuwait and when asked the question, "Are you married?" I said no.

The final moment occurred when I was traveling up to a cottage in Muskoka, in Ontario, for a girls' weekend with high school friends. I had the intuitive sense that the girls had planned a surprise engagement party for me. When I arrived at Olivia's house, her mom, who'd known me since I was four years old, shrieked, "Alex! I heard you're engaged! Show me your ring!"

I sheepishly told her, "I'm not wearing it right now."

When we got into the car and started driving up north, midway through the drive, I told Olivia, "I'm not wearing the ring at all anymore."

She suggested that we stop at a fast-food restaurant along the way for dinner, and she told me later that while I was placing the order, she was frantically texting the girls in the other car: "Do not get the engagement decorations out of the trunk! Throw the cake away! I repeat! Party aborted!"

When we got back into the car, I told her, "I think I have to break up with Santiago."

As soon as I said the words out loud, I knew. I had to break up with him.

It was time for me to go back to Kuwait, and Mom and I were about to walk out the door of her tiny, three-bedroom, shoebox house in Toronto, Ontario, heading with my duffle bag to Pearson International Airport. She was checking to make sure that I had everything I needed before I returned.

"You've got your passport?"

"Yup."

"You've got your wallet?"

"Yup."

"You've got all your clothes, everything you need?"

"Yup."

"Hmmm, let's see… oh, I know… have you got your diamond ring?"

I burst into tears. Through weeps, I barely made out the words, "I think… I'm going… to give it back to him."

My mom's face fell. "Oh, honey, you should have told me that you were feeling this way… I had no idea." On the inside, I'd been falling apart – but my mom had no idea. I couldn't believe I'd hidden it so well.

The irony was that ten days before, when Santiago had asked me if it was him or the job, I'd told him it was the job. I had quit my yoga teaching job and signed back on at the school, all to avoid breaking his heart. And ten days later, I broke his heart. I could have just done it before and saved everyone else the trouble.

CHAPTER 31

THE ENDING

"Someone... please... get me water..." Overwhelmed by dizziness, fourty-five-degree Celsius heat and exhaustion, I could no longer stand. I collapsed, seated on the luggage conveyor belt at the check-in desk in Kuwait International Airport, holding my head in my hands. It was five in the morning, June 20th, 2017. After several back-and-forth calls with my mom and sister over the course of twenty-four hours, I'd found and booked a flight back to Canada. Every part of my body was in pain, and I was completely exhausted.

My memories from the night before are fuzzy. I wandered aimlessly around the apartment and randomly packed some things while arbitrarily leaving other things. I had no organizational system whatsoever. I ended up bringing about five or six bags worth of luggage to the airport. After balancing my tower of bags on a luggage cart, I slowly and arduously made my way to the check-in counter. I hadn't eaten in thirty hours. I hadn't drunk anything in thirty hours. I hadn't slept in thirty hours. I hadn't brushed my teeth in thirty hours. And, thirty hours ago, I had arrived in Kuwait on a plane from Toronto.

The check-in clerk representing British Airways looked apologetic as she leaned over the side of the counter and looked down at disheveled me, collapsed on the luggage scale at her check-in counter.

"Ma'am-Sir," she started. "Sorry, Ma'am-Sir, it's Ramadan. It is illegal to drink or eat in public. I cannot get you water."

A pang struck my gut. I was hungry, thirsty, incoherent and exhausted. And knew I wouldn't have anything more to eat or drink for a few more hours. But somehow, I mustered up the energy to stand up and move away from the airport check-in counter, towards airport security, and onto the plane.

And this moment is how I finally learned how to leave. Exhaustedly, unexpectedly, and with loose ends to be tied up everywhere; my bank account not closed, my work visa not canceled, my white 2004 clunky but cool hatchback (the Desert Girl Cruiser) not sold and still parked at my mechanic's garage, my apartment still furnished.

I felt awful – probably physically the worst that I have ever felt in my life – but a small part of me was relieved.

The night before, I'd had several back-and-forth calls with my mom and my sister. I truly don't recall the content of any of the conversations, as again, I was in a blackout state. From what I remember, when we first spoke, it was suggested that I should still go to Bali, but shortly after, they realized how unwell I was, and we all agreed on what I needed to do: I'd ditch Bali and go back to Toronto to see a doctor there. I found a flight leaving the next morning. At around 9pm that night, after the longest and most incoherent day of my life, my phone rang. It was Ife.

"Precious!" she said. "I am so glad you picked up. I have been trying to call Mr Santiago all day. I took some wicker baskets and fixed them, and I want to drop them off before you both leave on your trip."

"Ife," I started, "he left."

"I'll be right there."

She came that night and stayed with me, bless her heart. She didn't try to stop me from crying or make it better. She just sat in my sadness and cried along with me. All night.

At 5am the next morning, she helped me carry my things to Raghu's car. We drove to the airport in silence. As he pulled up to the airport, he looked at me in the rear-view mirror and asked,

"Alex, are you coming back to Kuwait?"

I said to him, "I don't know." My apartment was full of stuff, my car was at my mechanic's shop, and I had a contract with the school to return to. But instinctively, I had a feeling in my gut that I was never going to come back to this place. I had a feeling that everything was finally over.

The marriage.

The job.

Mahboula.

It was all. Finally. Over.

I got onto the plane, and luckily the seat beside me was empty. I lifted the armrest, lay across the two seats and, after thirty hours, I couldn't stay awake anymore. I finally fell asleep. I did not wake up again until the plane was landing in Heathrow Airport. Two Kuwaiti men were sitting on either side of me in their white dishdashas. As the plane landed, and I woke up, they both turned to me with love in their eyes and asked, "Is everything okay?"

Fighting back tears, I nodded. "Yes," I lied.

Everything was not okay, no.

But. It. Was. Finally. Over.

CHAPTER 32

MOMENTS

Moments of impact. The moment at Pearson International Airport, when you dropped me off at the security line in January, after spending New Year's Eve with my family and friends in Canada, and I cried all the way to the security check. The moment at the end of April, when I woke up in a panic, stomach wrought with knots, physically collapsing onto my knees, diamond ring on my hand, wondering what… had… I… done? The moment in June when you packed up all your things and walked out the door, finally losing patience with me. Moments of impact.

Extraordinary moments. The moment we rode a camel into the sunset in the Abu Dhabi desert. The moment we skated laps together around Nathan Phillips Square in Toronto. The moment we were dancing together in a former underground bomb shelter in Lebanon. The moment you proposed to me in Cyprus.

And then, just ordinary, plain old moments. The moments we lay in bed together in Kuwait, watching Netflix projected onto the wall. The moments we walked around the grocery store, shopping together. The moments we drove on the highway together, navigating the chaos with calm.

Moments of heartbreak. Mostly, one moment of heartbreak. When I arrived back to Kuwait from Toronto, en route to Bali with you, and told you I couldn't do it anymore. That I couldn't pretend to be excited for our wedding anymore because I wasn't excited, and I wasn't sure if I was in love with you.

These moments happened over the course of twelve months: twelve short and sweet months, when I became your girlfriend, your fiancée and your wife. Moments now are moments of anger. Punctuated by our formal communication about lawyers, money owed and locations for divorce. Moments of quiet sadness about the love that has disappeared from my life. Moments when I look back at places and memories, and I smile when things remind me of you. They always do.

PART FOUR

Heart *Chakra* – I Am Forgiving of Myself and Others

The heart *chakra* is called *anahata* in Sanskrit, which means unbeaten or unstruck. Its element is air, and its goal is self-acceptance. When this *chakra* is not in balance, we can experience grief and depression. It's physically connected to the chest, lungs and heart (Judith 36 – 37).

HEART *CHAKRA* YOGA SERIES:

We are all carrying trauma with us – childhood wounds, suffering, pain and sadness. How lucky are we to have access to yoga as a practice and a tool for us to heal?

"Heal" is an eight-class series working on back bends – lotus, camel pose, full wheel, and eventually king pigeon. We'll explore the themes of forgiveness, compassion, gratitude and having an open heart. Leave this practice feeling spacious, open and ready to heal.

https://bit.ly/TheMindfulLifePractice_HEAL

HEART *CHAKRA* PHOTO LIBRARY:

On the Mindful Life Practice blog, I created a post with photo memories from the summer of 2017 that show my healing journey in Canada and Bali:

https://bit.ly/TMLP_HealingFromDivorce

CHAPTER 33

I HAD TO HEAL MYSELF

I came out of the airport in Toronto thirty hours later, balancing a luggage cart with a tower of bags piled one on top of the other. I walked down the ramp to meet my mom, who had just said farewell to me and put me on a plane about three days earlier. I can't remember what she did or said because, at that point, nothing could make the pain go away. Nothing could make it better.

We pulled up to her house in Toronto. Like I was a four-year-old kid, I slept in her bed that night. My sister was there the following afternoon and spent time holding space for me and comforting me. But, a day or two later, she traveled up north to work on an indigenous reserve for the summer, and so again, we were apart.

By the next day, my doctor had opened the clinic after hours to see me at six in the evening because I was in a crisis. They put me on a heavy dose of mood stabilizers, which began to numb me. Numb me from the trauma. Numb me from the pain. Numb me from the divorce. Numbness wasn't what I wanted, but everyone around me seemed to think that was what I needed.

In this moment, the doctors diagnosed me with bipolar disorder. They said that I'd suffer with this condition and require medication for the rest of my life. At the time, I accepted this diagnosis, but I realize in hindsight that there was little acknowledgment of my current reality. I had a highly dysregulated nervous system. I had just been through the most traumatic two years of my life. I'd left a marriage, a challenging job, my apartment and my community;

traveled across the world and back three times in a week; had zero counseling or trauma therapy; was drinking alcohol; and had barely eaten due to all of the stress that I had experienced over the past few months. No wonder I was reacting the way that I was to my current scenario. The doctors said that there was a chemical imbalance in my brain that I was born with, and at the time, I accepted that these medical findings were true. Nearly a decade later, after having gained a lot of wisdom and life experience along the way, I no longer accept this as the truth. I believe there was no chemical imbalance in my brain. I believe that my mind, body and spirit were in crisis, and my mental health had completely deteriorated as a result. I had been diagnosed and pathologized by everyone around me – the doctors, my family, myself – instead of being nurtured, validated and loved.

There were so many details of my life that were a mess. I'd left an apartment full of stuff, which Santiago had spent a week purchasing and setting up. My hatchback was still with my mechanic, who'd repaired the engine a few weeks earlier. I was supposed to be on a plane on my way to my honeymoon in Bali, and since I'd planned every moment of our trip in detail, I had booking after booking to try to cancel and get refunded. After our honeymoon, I was meant to stay in Bali and do a 300-hour yoga teacher training, while Santiago was going to travel back to Kuwait. I had to figure out how to get that refunded too. Less than a month earlier, I'd signed a contract for the job I had so desperately wanted to leave. And let's not forget the tiny detail that I was legally married and needed to figure out how to get a divorce. My life was a disaster. But I couldn't even begin to think about all of these logistical details. I was just trying to stay on the planet.

The only time that I left the house was when I was going to appointments: social workers, psychiatrists and physicians. Once there, I spent hours in therapy. We went over every moment in detail: memories of us skating circles around Nathan Phillips

Square; memories of him curled up in a fetal position on the night that I told him I was not in love with him; memories of us going out for walks in Mahboula; memories of arriving at the Grand Mosque in Abu Dhabi just in time to see the sunset; memories of the way he put 'ito' and 'ita' on the end of every Arabic word, like Mahboulita; memories of how he cracked his bones as we were driving down Highway 30 in the Desert Girl Cruiser (and how it drove me crazy); memories of how he constantly stirred up his drinks by spinning them around; memories of waking up to his love letters and coming home to his hugs at night.

I missed him so deeply. When someone breaks someone's heart, there is often no empathy around it. "How could they do that?" But no one ever stops to think – what must have happened that led this person to this point of breaking someone else's heart? You have to be pushed to the wall to make such a difficult decision. But there was no space for me to say my piece because, from the minute that I said it, I'd already be judged.

"Oh, you didn't want him."

But it was much more complex than that. And I was just as messed up by breaking his heart, if not more. Even though I wasn't ready to be married to him, my decision to end the relationship didn't mean I didn't miss him. I felt lost without him. Uprooted. Unsure of my next step.

When I did hear from him to sort out details of the divorce, the text messages were brief, sharp and stinging. He made it clear that he wanted nothing to do with me whatsoever. I started personally taking all of the blame. But a breakup is never one person's fault – there are two people in every partnership. And I wouldn't have broken his heart if there was no reason. There is no smoke without fire. I took so much blame for this separation and had so much guilt.

I wondered, "How could he hate me so much?" But I also understood it – he felt like he didn't know me anymore. And so, he acted this way to protect himself. Who could blame him? I felt like I didn't even know myself anymore. And for many years, I carried the guilt and shame, and I took full responsibility for the way that things fell apart. I was the one who changed.

Because of this devastating sense of guilt, I was overwhelmed by grief. I was convinced that I was a bad person. I was unable to forgive myself. I was unable to move forward.

The whole world had become flat. I had no optimism or hope, for anything. I didn't want anyone to touch me. When my mom would try to hug me, I would physically pull away. At the beginning, I wasn't seeing anyone except my mom. I thought that the whole world would perceive me as a bad person. I didn't go to yoga. I didn't exercise. I didn't want to get out of bed. I didn't want to see anyone in the neighborhood, for fear that they'd ask me, "Why are you here and not in Bali? Where's your fiancé?" I moved from the couch to the bed, to the couch, to the bed, and back again.

My mom wanted so badly to be able to fix my low mood. She tried everything. By two weeks into my state of depression, she started arranging activities – walks in the park, visits to cottages and trips to the movies. As my mother, she wanted to heal me. What she didn't see was that this was not something that I could just turn off. And it was not something that she could fix with a walk. My mom was not responsible for, nor capable of, my healing. I was responsible for my own healing. I had to do that myself.

One afternoon, I went to lunch with one of my grandparents, who I love very much. Like every other time that I left the house, I couldn't stop crying.

My grandparent, clearly uncomfortable with the number of people staring at us in the restaurant, said to me, "Alex, you need to stop crying."

I stayed silent. On reflection, what I wished I had said was, "Of course, if I could control my crying, I would. The last thing that I want to be doing right now is sitting in a restaurant, crying, while everyone else stares. But I can't control it. I can't stop crying."

The grandparent continued, "Santiago must be very hurt right now." Again, I stayed silent.

What I wish I'd said was, "Thanks for mentioning that Santiago's hurt right now. I hadn't thought of that! For God's sake, of course I know that he's hurt right now. Of course, I know it's my fault. I don't need you to remind me. I want to jump off a building and kill myself – that's how terrible I feel about it. That's why I'm so messed up. I don't need anyone to remind me how hurt he is."

My parent told her that I was married, but that we should try to keep it a secret. "Well, now, what will I tell the rest of the family?"

But this time, I spoke up. "Tell them whatever you want. I literally don't care what you tell them. Tell them whatever you want."

For years, I've thought of this moment in time as a very sad moment where my grandparent was unable to emotionally support me in a time of suffering. Very recently, when I was a guest on a Recovery 2.0 Retreat in India, I was able to reframe the scenario. Instead of seeing it as a moment where my grandparent was unable to emotionally support me, I realized – what if I saw this moment as a window into my parent's childhood? What if I realized that this was the level of support that my grandparent was able to provide my parent in times of emotional turmoil as a child? Realizing that every moment of sadness expressed as a child and teenager was probably met with this lack of emotional intelligence makes my heart soften tremendously and feel a great amount of empathy for what my parents experienced. What I've said before is that, while my own childhood was challenging, I wouldn't trade it for either of my parents'. I also understand that I have a responsibility to show up in the world now as the most balanced, *sattvic*, that I can be each day, so that I don't react to such comments in a triggered way. Showing up in a *sattvic* state means eating well, sleeping well, and starting each day with my *sadhana*, or my yoga practice. The more *sattvic* I can show up in each moment, the more likely I am to be able to stay grounded in a moment like this, where I might otherwise be triggered. The more *sattvic* I am each day, the more likely I am going to be able to step outside of the situation and see it for what it is. I take full responsibility for the role I played in this moment.

I love all of my grandparents so very much, and I don't write this story to cause harm. I genuinely believe that all of my grandparents meant no harm to me by comments made during my childhood and young adulthood. But all my grandparents came from a generation of shame, secrets and sweeping everything under the rug. But at the time, this moment was painful to me. And what my grandparent told my family was the last of my concerns. My concern was trying to stay alive.

CHAPTER 34

YOU HAVE TO FORGIVE YOURSELF

My teacher Rolf Gates wrote in his third book, *Daily Reflections on Yoga, Addiction and Getting Well,* "Each of us has been given a portion of the world's pain. Yoga teaches us to take this darkness and turn it into light" (402).

This period of depression certainly felt like a pretty big portion of the world's pain. This period of depression was the worst state I'd ever been in. In comparison, the previous depressive episodes that I'd experienced as a young person were manageable. But this one did not feel manageable. I could no longer function. I didn't want to do anything. I was hiding in shame with my story and all of my secrets – my diagnosis, my divorce, the truth.

I don't have a lot of memories from this period of my life. I was gradually being put on more and more mood stabilizers, and I was being numbed to the world. When I look back at all of the notes, documents and messages from this time in my life, I see it was obsessive. I was writing and rewriting letters that I never sent. I could not forgive myself for all of the promises that I'd broken, and all of the times that I'd let people down.

I wrote apology after apology to Santiago. Some were steeped in storytelling of memories, some were steeped in lessons that I'd learned about my mental health, some were just apologies for what I'd done.

The second type of letter that I wrote included apologies to

Saad, for quitting my job at the studio and leaving him without a yoga teacher.

I wrote over twenty different letters to William, explaining that I wasn't coming back to work at the school (which I hadn't yet determined).

Of all the things I was hopeless about and dreading, the biggest was my return to Kuwait. I couldn't imagine going back and facing the mess that I had created.

The previous year, all that I could talk about was how I would be working full time at the yoga studio. Also, everyone thought that I was getting married. However, now I knew that I was going to be doing neither of these things when I returned in the fall. I was going to be single and working at the school. I was so embarrassed about how this looked on the outside. I was so worried about how people would judge me. I could not let it go.

All of my friends at home in Canada had been following my social media updates, and they all thought that I was engaged/married and living the dream on a honeymoon in Bali. I confided in some of my very close friends that I was back in Canada, but other than that, it was a very well-kept secret. I didn't want anyone to know. The shame was killing me.

At the time, I thought that more medication was what I needed. As that summer progressed, however, it was like I was slowly pulling back the curtains. I do believe the medication played a crucial role in intervening. I still cried a lot, but gradually, I started to see sunlight. While I was working on my well-being all summer, I still sometimes had suicidal thoughts from time to time. But each day, my desire to kill myself lessened.

Late July was my turning point. Tragedy shook the Canadian yoga community. A well-known Buddhist meditation and yoga teacher, Michael Stone, had passed away from an overdose. His wife, Carina, came out publicly and shared that he suffered from bipolar disorder. Influenced by beliefs in the yoga world that yoga and yoga alone can and should heal ailments, he'd spent a lot of his life trying to treat his mental health without medication, solely through yoga and mindfulness. When his pain became too unbearable for him to manage, later in life, he went on prescription medicine. But the meds weren't working as fast as he would have liked, and desperate to solve his agony, he sought out drugs. I had always heard this story and concluded that Michael overdosed on his first use, but there was no real clarity as to whether this was the case or whether he was addicted to drugs. What struck me, however, was the fact that Michael never once opened up to the public yoga community about his diagnosis, despite being well versed on mental health, knowledgeable about the issues, and an advocate for mental health himself. He feared the stigma that surrounds mental health would impact his career.

I remember hearing about his mental health diagnosis and feeling like the carpet was being pulled from under my feet. All this time, I'd been afraid to tell my yoga students that I struggled with my mental health, for the same reason. I didn't want to deal with the stigma. I thought that it would invalidate my credibility as a yoga teacher and an 'expert' on mindfulness if they knew how much I struggled. Yet one of the most famous yoga teachers in Canada had mental health issues too. Carina Stone's sharing about her late husband's diagnosis of bipolar disorder changed the way that I thought about yoga teachers and mood disorders. Maybe it was okay to be a yoga teacher and struggle with mental health?

As I'd built up my strength, by late July and upon encouragement from doctors, I'd begun attending yoga classes at a local studio near my mom's house. I remember one of the teachers using Michael Stone's incident as a talking and teaching point, and she opened up to us about her struggles with generalized anxiety disorder. Maybe, somewhere, the tides were turning, and the stigma around mental health was changing.

To memorialize Michael Stone, prints were made of the Night Chant, which was a favorite mantra of his:

Night Chant
Life and death are of supreme importance.
Time passes swiftly, and opportunity is lost.
Let us awaken.
Awaken!
(Do not squander your life.)

'Do not squander your life' started to become a mantra for me and a catalyst for change. I had to move forward. I could not squander my life.

My interactions with Santiago were hostile and aggressive, which I can understand. In my memories, on the night we broke up, he accused me of never loving him and being a narcissist, and he claimed that everything had been a lie. He said I had been pretending. I took this to my core and held it in my gut. I felt it in every moment of every day and believed it was true. The reality was, in retrospect, there are degrees of love. It's not black or white. Love is on a spectrum. It wasn't that I didn't love him at all. I dearly loved him, and we were the best of friends. But there was something that stopped me from being able to marry him. He somehow made me feel as if I'd faked love and fooled him or tricked him on purpose.

Recently, when listening to Kino MacGregor's podcast, she referenced an old tale about several men who are blind. Each man decides to touch an elephant to get a better idea of its appearance. However, because each of the men touches a different part of the animal, none of them reach the same conclusion about how the animal looks. The men then go on to describe the elephant differently based on which part of the elephant they are touching. One person perceives the elephant to be thin and floppy because he is touching the ear, while another person perceives the elephant to be a thick, strong, stable cylinder because he is touching the foot of the elephant, and so on and so forth. This tale speaks to the fact that all people have different perceptions and versions of every experience based on the lens through which they view life (MacGregor). This scenario, the breakup of Santiago and me, is no different. I am sure if you asked Santiago, he would tell the story about the exact same situation completely differently. The key is to be able to step out of our own personal lens of perception and realize that we all view things differently.

Santiago was set for us to have our divorce in Cyprus. But from my point of view, I had a hard time seeing how this location would be beneficial. If we got divorced in Cyprus, we would receive a Cypriot Greek divorce paper, which we'd have to translate into English, anyway. If we divorced in Cyprus, we'd also have to travel to Cyprus for the divorce hearing, and the cost was estimated at a price that was more than double the cost of a Canadian divorce.

I communicated to him via email all the reasons why I thought that this was a bad idea, and why it was so much more sensible for us to do this divorce in Canada, but he didn't reply to this suggestion. I offered to pay for the whole Canadian divorce and give him the divorce papers for free. Still, he insisted on going ahead with his divorce in Cyprus and refused to sign my divorce papers.

So now we couldn't even agree on where and how to get a divorce, and were concurrently doing two separate divorces in two different countries. After I filed for divorce in Canada, Santiago had a ninety-day window to sign the papers before the divorce would be taken to a hostile divorce court. I patiently waited for my papers to make it around the world to him, and for him to sign them and send them back.

Midway through the summer, I started reaching out to people. I had been extremely isolated up until that point, avoiding everyone and everything. I thought that all of my friends from my past would judge me and think that I was a bad person because of what I had done. But I decided to set an intention to reach out to one person each day. And each time that I connected with someone, I had such a positive experience. A lot of my old friends were happy to hear that I was in Toronto – they hadn't reached out because they'd all assumed that I was away, like usual. Getting together with them was comforting. They were less judgmental than I thought they'd be. They had a lot of empathy and a lot of support.

I also heard regularly from Ife in Kuwait. Ife could not read or write English, so all of her communications with me were over voice notes. She left them on *WhatsApp* often that summer, and I loved listening to them each time. I'm sure that she left voice notes for Santiago as well. During our conversations, I confided in Ife that I could not seem to let go of how angry Santiago was at me. "He's never going to forgive me for this."

Ife said, "Precious, it doesn't matter if he never forgives you. He'll hold that in his bones and body for his life if he wants to. You cannot make him forgive you. Let that go. You need to forgive yourself."

There is a word in yoga called *sushuma*, which refers to epiphanies, or moments of clarity, in which we have become or realized our most intuitive selves. It's the equivalent of having an 'aha' moment. When Ife uttered these words, something within me clicked, and I realized she was right. Santiago might never forgive me. But that was beyond my control. What was within my control was forgiving myself. And everyone in life suffers. Suffering is part of human life, and is referred to as *duḥkha* in the *Pātañjalayogasūtra* text. And I can either allow the gravity of my suffering to suck me in, or I can use the gravity to propel me forward. Suffering can be one of the greatest catalysts for a spiritual awakening. We all suffer. It's our job to transcend that and make life meaningful.

The doctors didn't want me on a flight or back in Kuwait at all. The idea of sending me somewhere where mental healthcare wasn't included as part of my health insurance was not a great idea, and the thought of moving back to the very building where I plotted my suicide was not so appealing, either. But I had signed a contract, and I felt it was my duty to return. I had broken enough promises and let enough people down in the past few months. I couldn't let anyone else down anymore.

The doctors said that I needed another few weeks of medication increases. I was given a physician's note to send to Kuwait, indicating that I medically could not return to work for the time being.

I was too afraid to tell my school administrators anything. I didn't want them to know that I was plotting my own suicide. I was deeply afraid of the stigma and terrified that word would get out in the international teaching world, and no one would want to hire me later in my life. My doctor and my mom both reminded me that in Canada, it was illegal for employers to ask their employees about their health. Full stop. So, I didn't give William any details and kept them closely guarded at my chest.

William emailed me a week later with the following request: "We will not pay you for your time off, and due to Kuwait labor laws, we need to receive photocopies of all your medical records."

My mom was shocked. "Alex, that is illegal. Do not send him those papers. I can't believe he asked you for that."

But I wasn't shocked in the least. "Mom, the laws are different in Canada than they are in Kuwait. It's not the same country. You don't understand."

"It is not right for an employer to ask their employee for

medical records. It is just not right." Slowly, my mom's words started to sink in, and I had a light-bulb moment. I suddenly realized just how unsupported I felt in my work environment. Whether it was legal or not in Kuwait didn't matter. It was the fact that I didn't feel safe and supported by my employers during my health recovery. I was never going to heal in the same place that made me so sick. She said, "Alex, you should quit your job. You can't go back there."

And I said, "Mom, this is just how they do things there."

But as I sat there staring at the computer, I realized she was right. The question should not be, "Do I have to go back there?" The question should be, "Do I want to go back there? Does this serve me?"

And I knew the answer instantly: this place did not serve me. I wasn't happy. I didn't feel supported. The environment was dysregulating for my nervous system, and wouldn't support me as I tried to recover and heal.

I did not need to return to my job just because I said I would. I was done believing that winners never quit, and quitters never win. I was done living in limbo and feeling scared to leave but desperate to go. And, in that moment, I realized that it would be okay if I decided to leave. My life would not be over. But *I* needed to decide to leave. No one was going to do that for me. I had to decide to move in the direction of my development, as opposed to my defeat.

For many years, I held an unconscious resentment of the whole leadership team at the school for how unsupported I felt in moments like this. But I don't think I was even aware of this resentment I held towards them until very recently.

I suddenly had a realization in 2024, that all the leaders at that school, who are collectively represented in one fictionalized character, William, probably didn't do a lot of the things they did during the two years that I was there because they were intentionally trying to hurt me. In this case, I doubt that I was asked for my medical records because the administrative team wanted to harm me. They probably asked me for my medical records because someone higher up in the school ownership structure asked them to do this, and they were just following their directions. All the leaders of the school were probably just doing the best they could do to run the school, in the circumstances they found themselves in. When I realized this, almost ten years later, I finally was able to begin to forgive them all.

Pātañjali tells us in Yoga Sūtra 2.33 that if we find ourselves feeling negative thoughts (*vitarka*) then we should immediately cultivate the opposite. This practice is known as *pratipaksha-bhavana*. So when I realized how resentful I was towards the leadership team, I started to cultivate loving kindness towards all of them. I realized that they too had been hired to be leaders at a school in Kuwait just like I had been hired to be a teacher there. They, too, were doing the best they could to navigate an environment where they might have felt unheard or unsupported. They too, were just humans, who wanted to be happy, healthy and free. And at that moment, in 2024, I was finally able to cut the energetic cord that tied me to that time in my life. I visualized it dropping to the ground and dissolving, and I was finally free.

CHAPTER 35

STEP BY STEP

Yoga's word for the cause of suffering is *avidyā* (Karambelkar 177). It means not seeing things as they are. The habits of the mind are what cause *avidyā*. The way to overcome *avidyā* is the practices that are outlined in the eight-limb path of yoga.

I once heard a metaphor by *prāṇāyāma* teacher Max Strom that I like to reference when teaching yoga teacher trainings. Strom compares life to driving in a dirty car with a windshield that is coated in mud. However, we don't even know that we're in the car because we can't see outside of it. Everything we know is in this car. Sitting in this muddy car is the way that human beings move through the world (Strom 48).

Then we start practicing postures and meditations, and the car windshield starts to clean (Strom 49). When the windshield cleans, we realize that there is a whole world outside of the car. There's a world outside of our bodies and minds. We realize that we are in the car, we're going somewhere, and there's a purpose for our body and our mind – it exists to bring us on our spiritual journey. Going on our spiritual journey is the practice of yoga (Strom 49).

When I sent my resignation email to the school, it felt like the mud covering the windshield was beginning to clear, and I started to see a future beyond my depression. After I decided not to return to the school, that meant I'd be in Toronto for longer into September. At this point, my sister was coming home from her summer working on the indigenous reserve, and she invited my mom, her now husband and me to fly to Winnipeg and meet her to drive her car back to Toronto. We were set to embark on a six-day camping trip that my sister had mapped out, stopping in national parks along the way. On the first night of the trip, I was still overcome by crying spells and was sobbing uncontrollably. But by day two or three, being out in the wilderness, I was starting to feel better again, bit by bit. At some point, I stopped crying so much. My sister had planned hikes almost every day. Hiking was the last thing I wanted to do. But I wasn't sure what else I would do, sitting on a bench, alone, with no phone signal, in the middle of nowhere. So, I forced myself to join. On the first hike that we took, we climbed to the top of a mountain, step by step. And with each step, I started to feel better again. I was breathing deeply, and the sunshine started peeking out of the clouds. When I got to the top, I genuinely smiled in a photo for the first time in a few months. Towards the end of the trip, I began to laugh. I didn't intentionally plan for this trip to be part of my treatment plan, but being in nature was a key turning point for my recovery. Sometimes what we want the least is what we need the most.

Somewhere along the way, I realized that it was a choice – to stop wallowing in my own pity and start to climb out of the depression just like I climbed up the mountain. What I'd been through had been hard, yes. It was shitty that I was struggling with my mental health. It was shitty that I was going through a divorce. My work situation was extremely hard. But a lot of people have had hard lives. And I had to climb out of my own depression. I had to forgive myself for all of it. No one was going to do that for me. I had to do it for myself.

I needed to go on a journey to forgive myself. And my intuition told me what to do next. For the first time in my life, I had zero plans: no apartment, no job, no car, no boyfriend. Half of my belongings were still in an apartment in Kuwait, half of my belongings were in my mom's house in Toronto. My car was with my mechanic in Kuwait. The school still owed me a few thousand dollars in my end of service bonus. My life was a back-and-forth *WhatsApp* thread with my ex-husband about documents, signatures, stuff. He was still refusing to sign my Canadian divorce papers and was concurrently proceeding with his own, separate, Cypriot divorce. I was a mess. And yet, none of that mattered. I just decided to walk away. And get on a plane to Bali.

CHAPTER 36

AWAKE IN BALI

The plane descended on the tiny island of Bali, and when I stepped out of the airport, my senses felt awake again for the first time in a long time. I was emerging from a period of deep, dark depression, and when I landed on that small island, I could feel the dirt between my toes, I could smell the rain, I could taste the fresh fruit, I could hear the hum of the jungle, I could see the orange sunrises and purple sunsets. I felt free. I stepped barefoot in slimy gecko poop. It was gross. I practiced yoga as the sun rose over the rice fields and meditated as the sun set in the jungle. I felt joy and grief and the full range of human emotions. After feeling nothing for so long, I felt it all.

As I got into a strange taxi at the airport, I couldn't help but feel nostalgic for Raghu. I missed the experience of riding through the streets with him in Kuwait a lot. Although it is extremely annoying and inconvenient to have to depend on a taxi driver twenty-four-seven, when all was said and done, we had developed a very close bond. Taxi services in every other country since Kuwait have felt impersonal.

My debit card wasn't working in any of the ATMs, so I didn't have access to any cash. Plus, my luggage was lost (again!), so I didn't have any of the things I needed. On top of all of that, a few days into the trip, I misplaced my passport. Every single thing that could go wrong, did go wrong. But instead of feeling like I was cursed and the victim of a series of terrible inconveniences, like I had in the past, I just accepted every moment as it came and trusted that it would work out as it was meant to.

After feeling numb to the world for so long, finally, the world was alive again, and I was seeing tropical flowers, treetops, rice paddies and volcanoes. It truly felt like life after death. I was waking up before sunrise, while the rest of the world was still asleep, and I could hear the Earth turning.

For the first week in Bali, before the advanced yoga teacher training began, I was on my own, and all I wanted to do was drink coffee, wander around Ubud, and practice yoga at one of the studios in town. So that's what I did.

It poured every day. As I practiced yoga, the rain pattered on the roof of the open-walled yoga *shala* and splattered onto our bodies and yoga mats. In Canada, when it rained, we would complain about its wetness and the inconvenience it caused us when we'd have to huddle underneath our umbrellas and try to keep dry as we ran between buildings. But after living in the dry desert heat for two years, I'd walk slowly through the Balinese rain, stepping barefoot in puddles, allowing myself to feel it all. "How can you complain about rain? It's the most beautiful thing that I've ever felt."

I was just grateful to be feeling everything. The rain, my breath, the movement, my body.

I rented a motorbike and learned to ride it, despite knowing that my parents would probably kill me if they knew. As I whipped around corners, under trees, up steep slopes and beside the rice paddies, every single breath and every single moment felt like the greatest blessing. I had never felt more alive.

There were several moments where I'd just park the bike, step back and stare: at the purple sunsets, at the Hindu temples and at the monkeys. Just one thought would cross my mind: *Thank God I didn't die.*

That one night in Kuwait, when I wanted to jump off the roof, I couldn't look forward to a time when I'd feel alive again. But here I was, breathing, heart beating, smiling.

Often, I'd become overwhelmed with tears, saying to no one in particular: "Thank God I didn't die."

Thank God I didn't die.

CHAPTER 37

I DID NOT

September 2, 2017
There were many days this summer
When I wanted to leave
Planet Earth
Today
I am glad
I did not

CHAPTER 38

IT'S ALL A STORY: AND THERE ARE NO VILLAINS IN THIS STORY

In his third book, *Daily Reflections on Yoga, Addiction and Getting Well*, my teacher Rolf Gates writes about how our yoga practice allows us to take a life skill and practice it in a manageable context (269). For example, the first *yama* is *ahiṃsā*, non-violence. Instead of learning how to practice *ahiṃsā* mid-argument with your parents at a holiday dinner, you practice *ahiṃsā* in a controlled setting, like on a yoga retreat, seated in meditation. You learn how to be kind towards yourself and kind towards others around you in the controlled moment of a morning on a yoga retreat. Then you keep practicing the skill each day on the yoga retreat. You practice kindness in a controlled environment so often that when you find yourself in heated moments outside of these controlled environments, your default reaction becomes kindness (Gates 269).

On the first day of the advanced yoga teacher training, I realized that I'd made a mistake in choosing it. When I chose my first yoga teacher training in Mexico in 2014, I'd spent months researching places, teachers and styles of yoga. I'd met some trainers, asking them about their style of teaching and their program. I'd asked all my favorite teachers where they'd done their training and researched these locations. I'd finally settled on attending an institute in Mexico, which had been recommended to me by my favorite yoga teacher at the time. She had completed her yoga teacher training at this center and had spoken very highly of it. The program did not disappoint. The training, the teachers and the space were magical.

For some reason, I hadn't researched my 300-hour yoga teacher training with such diligence. I hadn't thought about who my teacher would be and how that would shape my experience. I wanted to go to Bali, and I wanted to complete the whole thing in a one-month, intensive program; the timing worked perfectly for me since I had the summer off school, and the social media looked cool. I knew one girl who'd participated in the training who said it was great. So, I chose it.

But, unfortunately, the lineage of yoga and the style of the teacher leading the training did not resonate with me.

There are many different lineages of yoga. Iyengar yoga is alignment based and focuses on students perfecting the physical shape of every pose. Bikram (or sometimes now referred to as 26+2) yoga is rigorous, dictating that students must hold the poses a certain way or for a certain length of time in a certain temperature. *Ashtanga* yoga insists that students practice the same set sequence of poses, every single day, without variance.

Such rigid lineages of yoga never spoke to me – from as early as age thirteen, when I tried my first yoga class, they were not the right fit for me. My yoga teaching philosophy has always encompassed practices that are the exact opposite of what these lineages recommend. I teach with mindfulness, empathy and awareness towards the vast experiences that every individual student may be carrying with him or her into a yoga class. I never want to re-traumatize an individual in a yoga class, so when I teach, every pose is an invitation, with several modifications offered. I often say, "Yoga is not supposed to look good; it's supposed to feel good. So do a variation of the pose that feels good for you." I never insist that students bend their way into a shape that might cause injury or stay in a pose for longer than might be appropriate for their bodies. I often say, "You don't have to do this pose. The pose is not the goal. We're here to explore, not achieve poses."

In the early days of teaching yoga, I used to offer many hands-on assists without asking for consent because that's what other teachers did, and I thought that using touch would help me become a better yoga teacher. Now, I have a completely different perspective on hands-on assists. When teaching in the studio, I come into each class with hand-painted cards, which my students can use to indicate if they consent to being touched. The yang side, with a sun, says, "Yes, I'd like a hands-on assist." The yin side, with a moon, says, "No, please don't touch me today." I never want to do anything that may re-traumatize an individual, such as touching them unexpectedly, turning off the lights without their knowledge, or forcing them to close their eyes when they want to keep them open.

But the yoga teacher training that I'd ended up attending was not like this.

Ron was a walking man of wisdom – having several ancient yoga texts memorized by heart. He was in his late fifties or early sixties and could answer questions about the *Pātañjalayogasūtra* off the top of his head. He knew everything there was to know about the *Bhavagad Gītā*, the *Hatha Yoga Pradapika*, and other well-known yoga texts. The wisdom that he shared with us in lectures and classes was inspiring, moving and heartwarming. But I noticed quickly that he didn't seem to demonstrate the energy of yoga in practice. He just preached it. He talked the talk. He didn't walk the walk. He didn't embody loving kindness.

I felt this from the first morning that I practiced yoga with him. His class felt more like an army bootcamp than yoga teacher training. Our practice was ninety minutes in total each morning, and he would make us hold the poses for three minutes each. He said that if you couldn't hold a pose for at least three minutes, that you didn't know how to do the pose. There was no quitting.

There was no sitting out. There were no breaks.

My own approach to teaching yoga classes couldn't be more different. I encourage my students to take a break whenever it's needed. I never force my students to stay in a pose longer than they feel is appropriate for their bodies. I often say, "I am the second teacher here – and you are the first one. I don't know what it's like to live in your body – only you do. So do what feels good for your body today." When Ron taught, his teaching philosophy was the exact opposite of mine. On that first morning of our yoga teacher training, I remember thinking, "Why am I here? Why did I do this to myself?"

He said that he was providing us with resilience training. His idea of teaching yoga was to put our bodies into what he called "stressful situations" – AKA yoga poses. He wanted us to experience a stress response, and then separate our mental reaction from the actual pose itself. His belief was that if we could do this on the mat, then we could do it off the mat, with events in life.

While I agree with this teaching wholeheartedly, I also believe that it can be taught in a way to avoid injuring or traumatizing the student. This was not that.

There were rules for everything. We couldn't talk before ten in the morning. We couldn't comfort each other in the class when we were crying. We couldn't share an opinion that was different than his. We couldn't be late. We couldn't be early. (Seriously – we weren't allowed into the *shala* until 6am on the dot. Not a minute early and not a minute late.)

When it came time to practice teach, we had to lead only using his cues and following scripts that he had written. His way was the only way to teach yoga.

We couldn't be on our phones at any time in a public space.

He created so many rules, but then he wouldn't follow them. One day, a student in the class was ten minutes late to class, and when she arrived, in front of the whole class, he shouted, "We started at 3pm. Not 3:10." The day after this incident, he arrived late to class. Although our cell phones weren't allowed in the yoga *shala*, I had a digital watch on my wrist and watched the time ticking away. The other thirty students and I had arrived and were sitting silently because we weren't allowed to speak to each other until he arrived and rang a bell. We all sat there, waiting. Five minutes, ten minutes, fifteen minutes passed. When he finally arrived, coffee cup in hand, he sat down at the front of the class and said, "I've learned in life that if you're already a minute late, you might as well be fifteen minutes late – there's no difference."

It was not how strict he was that struck me, but the direct manner in which the rules seemed to only apply to the students – not him – and how he'd humiliate those who didn't follow them.

My teacher Rolf explains in *Daily Reflections on Yoga, Addiction and Getting Well*, that the book *A Course in Miracles* by Dr Helen Schucman and Dr Bill Thetford describes a miracle as a change of perspective (Gates 247). I see now that that's what had happened. An example of such change in perspective is a story of the Buddha. "The Buddha sat in meditation in an effort to understand himself," and he realized that certain actions create suffering, and others lead to freedom (Gates 50). He taught his students to observe the effects of their actions, and consider: when I do something, does it lead to freedom or suffering (Keeler)? I realized that by getting swept up in my emotions about disliking Ron, I was simply choosing thoughts that would lead to my suffering. Instead, I decided to choose thoughts that would lead to my freedom. I didn't allow Ron to impact or shape my experience of Bali. I didn't let *him* get in the way of *his message.*

I see in hindsight that I'd had a shift. I'd had a transition. I'd had a transformation. All throughout my life, I had allowed my emotions to be shaped by external factors. I'd allowed my emotions to be shaped by the individuals around me, and their actions and choices, rather than by me. But in Bali, I was going through another situation where I really, really didn't like a person that I'd met – I was experiencing *dveṣa*, aversion. It would have been easy to fall back into my old ways. I could have allowed Ron to shape my experience. But I'd changed. I was able to experience Bali on the whole and see the beauty and the benefit of the opportunity, without it being dominated by the person with whom I disagreed. And this growth was huge. I was working with Ron day in and day out and learning something from him that was so close to my heart – and yet I didn't agree with the ideology that was being presented. Despite this difference of opinion, I was able to reap many benefits from this training because I simply did not allow Ron to dominate the whole thing. For the first time in my life, I was letting it go.

I was choosing to not allow Ron to be the villain in my story. I was choosing to not allow Ron to shape my experience of Bali. For the first time, I realized that, ultimately, *everything* that happens to us in life is a story, and we tell ourselves the story in our own heads. We can choose to say that other people are villains, or we can choose to understand that they're humans. Ron was a human stuck in his own suffering, doing his best to navigate through life. And I wasn't going to let *him* get in the way of *his message.*

CHAPTER 39

HAPPILY EVER AFTER

There was a ninety-day limit for Santiago to sign my divorce papers before they'd be transferred out of my lawyer's hands and into the hands of a hostile divorce lawyer. This would be much more expensive, tedious and painful, and I was warned by my lawyer that we wanted to avoid this at all costs. What was taking Santiago so long to sign them? It was mid-October and close to day seventy-five at this point. I'd text him frequently, asking him to sign – and then simultaneously text my lawyer in Toronto, asking, "Have you received them yet?" Each time I was disappointed to hear that no, I was still waiting. One morning, a few days before the deadline, I walked down to the yoga *shala* for practice and, as I sat there, I burst into tears.

Ron's words during our yoga philosophy lecture that morning were exactly what I needed to hear.

"Nothing hurts more than a broken heart," he said. "I could break a bone, and it wouldn't hurt as much as a broken heart. Broken hearts hurt this much for a reason. They're saying, 'Pay attention. This is important. Love is important'."

Around the same time as this, I decided that I had to apply for another teaching job. I could not remain jobless for the rest of my life, riding my bike through Bali, discovering the meaning of life (although that's what I wanted to do). I was going to run out of money soon. I had to participate in the world instead of separating myself from it. So, I activated my profile on that same teaching recruitment website I had used to get my first teaching job two years before. To my surprise, the job offers started appearing one after another. Just like when I applied for my first job years ago, schools all over the world had contacted me. The same thing was happening now.

The senior leadership team of my former school always made us feel like if we broke a contract mid-year, we'd be blacklisted from international teaching jobs, and we'd never get a job again. There were rumored stories about people who had fallen victim to these hiring bans. When I quit, I expected my career to be over. Yet, when I finally got the courage to walk away, I discovered that apparently my life was not over. Despite knowing that I had broken a contract, schools still wanted to hire me. Lots of them.

I got email after email from schools in countries all over the world, just like I had two years before. There were lots of schools and lots of opportunities. None of them resonated with me, but I knew that one eventually would. My life was not over. I just needed to open my eyes. Something that I have heard commonly attributed to Lao Tzu (but since learned it is likely a misattribution, and the source is unknown), is, "New beginnings are often disguised as painful endings" (qtd. in Stenudd).

One day, I got an email from a woman named Emma at a school in Abu Dhabi. I recognized the logo on the bottom of her email signature – it was the same group of schools that Louise and Claire worked for in Dubai. As soon as I got the email, I knew that this was the right school for me.

I was so excited when I got on the call with Emma. My intuition was telling me that, this time, the information I was receiving about this school was real: this wasn't a catfish like my old school. She said to me, "Alex, you're the candidate I want." I asked her why, and she said, "Because I know where you're coming from. And if you can survive that experience, you can survive anything."

That's when I realized: employers wouldn't judge me for walking away from a place where I struggled so much; employers were impressed with me for staying. Employers were impressed with my resilience. It was a moment when I stepped back and realized that what I'd considered to be my biggest mistake, leaving that place, was not such a big mistake after all. And there was a world out there that considered me to be a vital resource. I mattered. I was better than how I saw myself.

And just like that, I was hired. I couldn't believe how casual I'd become about it all – no more planning and packing and fear and anxiety. Instead, I just casually threw some things in a suitcase and hopped on a plane. I'd had a transformation – I was now confident, brave and decisive. When I hit rock bottom, I became brave. And the minute that I became confident, opportunities came to me.

When I got off the *Skype* call with my new employers in Abu Dhabi, I opened my iPhone to text my parents the news.

But, when I opened my phone, I noticed right away that I had a text message from my lawyer. "Alex, Santiago has finally signed the papers."

Swept up in my job search, I hadn't noticed that it was literally day eighty-nine. He'd signed the papers at the last possible minute. My Canadian divorce was officially underway. We were no longer in limbo. It was over. I jumped up from the table and did a happy dance. I felt so free.

He texted me later that day to tell me that he'd signed as well. And until I contacted him in 2024 to get his permission about publishing this book, that was the last time that I ever heard from him.

For many years, from time to time, I would search for him on *Instagram*. He had me blocked for the longest time. I would try to find his profile and look at his account, hopeful that he had unblocked me.

What I wanted was to find out that he'd met someone, that he'd fallen in love, that he'd moved on. I knew that learning that he had moved forward, in some way, would help me find peace with it all.

One day, in July 2021, I happened to search for his account on *Instagram* and this time, for the first time, I wasn't blocked. I saw that he'd recently gotten engaged. I wrote a post on *Facebook* about it:

July 22, 2021
He has found his happily ever after.

I have found mine.

Proof that our happily ever after was never ours. It was actually two separate stories.

From two different books.

We were just characters in each other's stories. Passing through for a chapter.

Neither one of us villains. (I'm possibly the villain… but I have learned to let that go too.)

I have a lightness and lift. I once struggled to forgive myself for this terrible, horrible mistake. But I'm here and I'm happy. Proof that the effort that we put into our healing journey can heal all wounds.

With a peace that sits so deeply… that part of my story comes to its close.

CHAPTER 40

REFLECTIONS FROM BALI

Live soulfully. Meaningfully. Presently. Authentically. Inhale and exhale, fully and consciously. Participate in the world in the way that it is, as opposed to separating from it. Know that the darkest part of the night is right before the dawn.

Refuse to let loss define your relationships. Learn how to sit with loneliness. Invest in good peanut butter, and eat it on banana every damn day.

It's okay to get swept under waves of grief. But come up for air when you can. Cling to the buoy as you watch waves of grief wash around you. Resist being carried by them through the rest of your life.

We don't choose the moment we live or die. All we can do is choose what happens between our first and last breath. Live fearlessly. Live beautifully. Realize that each breath you have left is precious. Surrender to the process of life and death.

There is no guru. You are the guru.

Sometimes all you need is the science of yoga. Sometimes what you need is the science of modern medicine. For instance, a compressed nerve from a motorbike accident is not a kundalini awakening. Go to an actual doctor for a second opinion! Know yourself well enough to know the difference. Do not allow anyone else to tell you how to heal.

Follow your soul. Always, always. In doing this, from time to time, you will let other people down. Release yourself from the guilt that you harbor from this. "If you want to leave and you're following your soul, you have my support. Because your soul is more important than my selfishness."

And don't preach. Let people believe what they want. Be the living embodiment. That's how you share what you've learned.

PART FIVE

Throat *Chakra* – I Am Authentic

The throat *chakra* is the fifth *chakra*. Its Sanskrit name is *Vishudda*, or purification. The fifth *chakra* is physically connected to the shoulders, neck and jaw. It's all about living your truth and finding peace with your truth (Judith 36).

THROAT *CHAKRA* YOGA SERIES: AUTHENTIC

What does it mean to be authentically and unapologetically you? The throat *chakra* is all about speaking our truth, which is why I've created this Mindful Sweat five-class series intentionally designed to build strength and have fun.

The "Authentic" series is unique because it's Mindful Sweat – a yoga-barre fusion very authentic to me, because I created it.

I became certified to teach Barre classes in 2019, shortly after becoming sober. I loved teaching Barre, but I also felt like an imposter teaching it: it just did not come naturally to me. I was not a ballerina; I was a student of yoga. That's why I ended up gradually fusing more and more of my yoga training into my Barre classes, until they became what was authentically me: and thus, Mindful Sweat was born.

During these classes, after a yoga-inspired warm-up, we will move into power mode – toning and strengthening the body with functional movement exercises set to upbeat music. Depending on the theme, there may be a focus on core, arms, legs, or cardio (with low-impact options offered). We'll seamlessly transition into a mindful stretch at the end, followed by *savasana*. You'll leave having strengthened and stretched your body and centered your mind.

https://bit.ly/TheMindfulLifePractice_MindfulSweat

THROAT *CHAKRA* PHOTO LIBRARY:

In the Throat *Chakra* section of the book, I share photos from my time when I moved to Abu Dhabi in 2017:

https://bit.ly/TMLP_ExpatLifeInAbuDhabi

CHAPTER 41

SANSKĀRA(S)

According to the *Pātañjalayogasūtra* text, *sanskāra(s)* are not the memories that we hold, but the conditions around the memories. They are an imprint on our minds, or a tendency that we might have, due to our past actions. *Sanskāra(s)* are the emotional content around the memories. They create a story within us that we might carry with us through the rest of our lives.

Michael Stone wrote in his book *The Inner Tradition of Yoga* that it can be helpful to think of *sanskāra(s)* as seeds. Whatever seeds we have planted in the past will affect what we do, and how we feel about the present in positive and negative ways (Stone 97).

My teacher Ron on my advanced yoga teacher training further explained that, at some point, all of us have been sold a story of who we are: 'I am unloved', 'I am smart', 'I am ugly' and so on. These stories originate from relationships and life experiences. We spend a great deal of our lives playing out these characters, sometimes all our lives, until we run into a wall that makes us go in the other direction.

Once we begin our healing journeys, we must continue peeling back layers of ourselves, to discover where these *sanskāra(s)* are and how to break free from them.

Before I knew it and within a week of interviewing and accepting the job, I found myself at Jakarta airport, waiting for a plane to Abu Dhabi. It happened within a week of being interviewed and accepting the job. As I sat there, my phone lit up with a message. Out of the blue, I was asked to be featured in my high school's alumni newsletter as a 'success story' from the class of 2010. When I got the message, I thought, *Me? You think I'm a success story? I'm a twenty-five-year-old divorcee who almost killed herself and is constantly running away. My life is a mess.*

It began to dawn on me how warped my self-perception was. Clearly, I was my own harshest critic. I had told myself a story that I was the worst person on planet Earth. In reality, I was actually doing okay at life. For the better half of 2017, I'd thought of myself as a complete and total mess and wanted to end my life. Meanwhile, others saw me and my international teaching career as an inspiration worthy of being featured in an alumni newsletter.

Receiving the message made me realize the following things: first, mistakes sometimes make it feel as if the world is ending. But it's not. Everyone in life makes mistakes. Second, our mistakes don't negate who we are or our past/present/future contributions to our community. We have all done things that we wish we hadn't, and we all sometimes fall from grace. It's not those mistakes that matter; it's how we move forward that matters. And third, we have all achieved so much more in our lives than we give ourselves credit for. And what's the fourth lesson? Everything is a story, and it is up to us to rewrite the narratives. I had to rewrite my own narrative from Kuwait. Santiago wasn't going to do it for me. I had to do it for myself. No one else.

When I boarded the plane, I heard the call to prayer come over the loudspeaker, just like it did the first time that I traveled to Kuwait all those years ago, and I felt an overwhelming sense of coming home.

As soon as I got to Abu Dhabi, it was as if the curtains opened, and the sun started shining in. When Emma picked me up at the airport, I tried as hard as possible to not be the person who bad-mouthed their former school. But I couldn't hide my reactions. I was elated about everything: the air conditioning in the apartment worked; the facilities were just as Emma had described them; my new home had proper bedding and a brand new bed; and the keys to my apartment had not been given to anyone else, which meant that no one had free access to my living quarters. And I hadn't even seen the school yet! I didn't say anything negative about my former school. However, Emma was able to conclude that my experience wasn't great when she saw how overwhelmingly excited I became when we toured this very ordinary apartment. We walked out onto the apartment balcony, which had a view of a gorgeous, blue, lit-up swimming pool. The pool had small concrete islands within it, connected by bridges and covered with palm trees. You could see the shore of the ocean and hear the waves crashing. There was a quiet road below. I was in awe. I remember her asking me, "Alex, what was the housing at your old school like?!"

I don't remember specifically what I told her, but I said something about how challenging my living situation had been, and how I didn't feel I could quit. Feeling forced to stay until the end. Feeling afraid that I couldn't leave.

She said to me, "Alex, what you've been through sounds horrible. No principal would ever judge you for breaking a contract early at a workplace where you were so unhappy."

And I finally understood. I should never have allowed an employer to convince me that my life would have been over if I quit or broke my contract. It is always okay to quit a job, leave a partner, or end a friendship, if I am unhappy. Contrary to my lifelong belief, quitters can win, and winners can quit. Quitting did not mean that my life was over.

After my arrival in Abu Dhabi, I took a photo of the sunrise one morning before work and wrote underneath the photo on *Instagram*: "Every day is a miracle," and, "Everything is magic," and both of these observations were true. My current existence felt like life after death. I felt the difference. Immediately.

When I was in a state of depression, I was convinced that I could not get out of it, and I couldn't see a future in front of me. It felt like there was no escape and no ending. But because I had traveled to the abyss and managed to make it out alive, afterwards, every goddamn day was a miracle.

We all experience darkness from time to time. There is light and dark within us all. *Ida* and *Pingala*, the solar and lunar energy channels in the body. *Sukha* and *Duḥkha*, sweetness and suffering. *Sattva* and *Tamas*, energy and lethargy. Happiness and sadness. It's just the ebb and flow of life. We must be brave enough to make our way through the darkness. Come up for air and grab hold of a buoy as the waves of grief wash around us. We must. It's the only way to make our way towards the light.

During my time in Kuwait, I was oscillating between high and low, but by the time I'd arrived in Abu Dhabi, I'd learned how to ride the waves of my life. I no longer feared the ups and downs of my mood – I'd learned to work with them. I knew that if I didn't learn to work with them, I couldn't survive. I'd seen the deep end, and I didn't want to go back there.

For the first time in my life, I didn't have an opportunity to teach yoga, and I focused on attending classes myself. What I remember about this time was colleagues saying things to me like, "You're the chillest person that I've ever met," or, "Your presence is so calm."

I'd burst out laughing, remembering when I'd be wandering around the hallways of the school in Kuwait, sobbing.

"Me? Chill? Me? Calm?" They knew a different version of me. I wasn't high, and I wasn't low. I was just in the middle. I was in a place mentally and physically where I was finally flourishing.

CHAPTER 42

WHAT'S IN A YEAR?

April 29, 2018, 8:28pm.

Alex's iPhone

What's in a year? There is the month that I broke four promises and let down approximately one billion people in the process. There are the three jobs that I quit. There's the day that I had several of the hardest conversations I've ever had in my life. There are the four different apartments that I moved in and out of in Kuwait and Abu Dhabi. There's the week that I flew back and forth from Toronto to the Middle East not once, not twice, but three times (around seventy-two hours of flying in ten days).

There's the day that I decided to shed what wasn't sitting well with my soul. There's the three months that I felt lost in my life. Six seasons of Sex and the City. *Three months of recovery. One camping trip. One obsession with watching every documentary that I could find about Princess Diana. Five 1000-piece puzzles that I put together while eating Chicago mix popcorn at my mom's dining room table.*

There's my incredible family and friends who packed for me, organized for me, moved my stuff for me, lunched with me, dined with me, yoga'd with me, Skyped *with me, puzzled with me, walked with me, sang with me, messaged me, simply showed up for me and supported me through it all. Even friends that I hadn't seen in years. Thank you is not enough. You know who you are.*

There's the day that I decided to move in the direction of my development as opposed to my defeat. Five weeks that I spent sitting in silence for over eight hours a day. My Eat, Pray, Love *month in Bali. Three hundred more hours of yoga teacher training. The month that I learned to meditate. Posing and smiling and laughing by the pool in the jungle. The incomparable lessons that I learned from many teachers.*

There's the time that I wept in the airport in Guangzhou, China, because my luggage was lost, and I thought that my stuff mattered. There's the day that I fainted on a luggage scale in the Kuwait International Airport, and they wouldn't let me drink water because it was Ramadan and illegal to eat and drink in public. There's the day that I fell off a motorbike in Indonesia and learned how to make friends out of strangers. There are the times that I made 'strangers out of friends'.

There are the ten new countries that I crossed off the map. Twenty-eight flights around planet Earth. There's the week that my life fell apart and then the week (four months later) that my life fell together. There's the day that I randomly interviewed for a job in Abu Dhabi. There's the day that I moved here and everything, every moment, every mistake, all of a sudden made sense.

There's the day that I realized that mistakes don't negate our past and present contributions to our community – that we have all done things that we wish we hadn't, and we all sometimes fall from grace. It's our ability to rise from the ashes that defines us.

If there's one thing that I learned from being twenty-five, it's that following your soul isn't selfish. When you're happy and free, it serves and benefits everyone around you.

When I look back, it's hard to believe twenty-five was only a year and not a lifetime. It sometimes feels that way. I don't remember or recognize the person that I was twelve months ago.

Twenty-five killed me. And yet from it I was reborn.

And it's who we are now that matters.

CHAPTER 43

A NEW LIGHT

About six months after my time in Kuwait, I ended up going back. When I departed in July 2017, I'd left everything in a state of disarray, having thrown in a little of this and a little of that into all of my suitcases and got on a plane. Ife and Rebecca had packed and gone through all my remaining things, and I had left a ton of stuff that needed to be picked up. I had packed in a moment of incoherence; I couldn't even remember what was there and what wasn't.

I'd also left the Desert Girl Cruiser with my mechanic, parked on the side of the road, and I needed to pick it up and transfer it to a new owner.

Atif, my family in Kuwait, invited me to stay in his villa with him for the weekend. He sent his driver to pick me up, and I rode in a white, air-conditioned car. The driver handed me chilled bottled water for the drive that came out of a cooler. Instead of The Oasis in Mahboula, we pulled up to the hotel.

This was the resort where I had met my husband. Where I used to teach yoga. And when I first met my husband, he was living in this resort. Santiago had once said to me, "Kuwait is really quiet." I asked, "Kuwait? Quiet? Are we talking about the same country?" I was thinking of the water trucks backing up. The 4am mosque calls. I was thinking of Mahboula. That was my Kuwait.

Earlier that year, I'd had a conversation with a friend who was raised in Kuwait, and she said to me, "Kuwait is easy to love." At the time, I didn't understand it – but I understood it now. There is not one lived experience of any country, any city, or any one place on Earth. We all experience a city or country differently, based on who we are and our context. My Kuwait was not her Kuwait. And Santiago also had a different perspective of Kuwait – the kind of perspective that one acquires when living in a quiet resort. Staying at the same resort for the weekend was like seeing a different Kuwait through different eyes. That's when I realized that Kuwait was never the problem. It was never the country itself that was the issue for me – it was my experience within it.

I set my alarm early every day that I was there and got up and watched the sunrise on the beach. This time, I experienced Kuwait joyfully. Anais Nin wrote, "We don't see things as they are, we see them as we are" (qtd. in Gomez). I was happy, so I saw Kuwait differently than I did when I was sad. I wrote on *Instagram*, "It's a funny feeling, coming back to a place that was once your home, and seeing it in a different light. When I left Kuwait in June, I left it during a period in my life that was filled with the worst, worst memories. And now my last memories here will be really, really nice."

Even though this visit was less than a year from when I'd left this country, it felt like a decade had passed since I'd been there. I felt so much older and wiser. I felt like a completely new person. I experienced a myriad of emotions that weekend. Joy and nostalgia, mixed in with pride. As I rode in a car to The Oasis and walked in the door, I remember getting tears in my eyes. Here I was, returning to the very building I'd once planned to jump from. But I didn't. Not then and not now. And I will always be so grateful for that.

PART SIX

Third Eye – I Am Intuitive

The sixth *chakra* is the third eye *chakra*, or the *ajna chakra*. It is at the center of the forehead, in between the two eyebrows. The third eye is associated with intuition and wisdom. It's all about the cultivation of self-reflection (Judith 35 – 36).

THIRD EYE *CHAKRA* YOGA SERIES: INTUITIVE

The "Intuitive" series is a yin-style series, inspired by the *yama(s)* and *niyama(s)* of yoga. We'll hold deep stretches for three-to-five minutes at a time, designed to help release tension from the tissues and ligaments of the body. Whilst doing this, Alex will introduce to you and you'll explore some foundational concepts from yoga philosophy. The *yama(s)* are moral commitments and the *niyama(s)* are ethical commitments. Each practice also teaches you a unique *mudra* and offers a special meditation and *asana* sequence that are relevant to the *yama* or *niyama* we are discussing. Expect to leave this practice completely grounded and having released what is no longer serving you.

https://bit.ly/TheMindfulLifePractice_YinYoga

THIRD EYE *CHAKRA* PHOTO LIBRARY:

On the Mindful Life Practice Blog, I created a photo album of photos from my first year sober, which you can see at this link:

https://bit.ly/TMLP_FirstYearSoberBlog

CHAPTER 44

DECIDING IT'S DAY ONE

"Forever making up for two years in a dry country!" That was one caption I wrote on a photo that I posted on *Instagram* while opening a beer at 11am on a Friday. In the picture that I posted, I was wearing a white crop top and a striped mini skirt, nude wedge heels on my feet, blasting Taylor Swift, and doing my hair and makeup. I had a Heineken in my hand. I was getting ready for a brunch.

Abu Dhabi and Dubai are the lands of brunches. Bottomless, all-you-can-drink brunches. At the time that I was living there, the weekend was Friday and Saturday (it has since changed to be Saturday and Sunday). When I was there, expats from all around the world would get together on Fridays, begin drinking at noon and carry on until 8pm. Sometimes an 'after brunch' party continued into the early morning. It's also the land of the ladies' nights. Every night of the week in this city, you can find a venue where women drink unlimited rosé, red and white wine, and sugary, frozen, pink mocktails for free. Such events are designed to draw in crowds on what would otherwise be quiet nights for the bars and restaurants.

Growing up in Canada, I was surrounded by a culture that encouraged alcohol at barbeques, weddings, funerals and birthday parties – but there were never events every night of the week where women could drink for free. In Abu Dhabi, alcohol was free flowing and abundant at every expat event. When I look back on my life, I see how I've found myself in the most extreme environments. Abu Dhabi was a contrast to not only Canada, but also Kuwait, where alcohol was completely illegal.

One theme that I teach in classes often is 'clarity in contrast'. I think that I heard this concept once in a Rolf Gates class or meditation. We have this experience when we, as yoga students, transition from balancing in *vrkhsāsana*, tree pose, with only one foot anchored on the mat, to a pose with both feet firmly planted and rooted into the Earth, such as *tadāsana*. 'Clarity in contrast' happens when we, as practitioners, go from movement, pose after pose, linked with breath after breath, to the absolute stillness of *tadāsana* pose – or mountain. 'Clarity in contrast' is what occurs when the music accompanying our practice suddenly fades into the distance, and we transition to the silence of *savāsana*. My move from Kuwait to Abu Dhabi was like this too. I'm not suggesting that *all* expats party in Abu Dhabi the way that I did. I am simply explaining that the environment made it possible. And when moving from a country where alcohol was completely illegal to a country where it was more normalized to party every day of the week, I experienced 'clarity in contrast' big time.

In Abu Dhabi, it became acceptable and excusable to drink every night of the week. In my mind, I had a constant reason for my drinking: I'd spent my early twenties living in a country where alcohol was illegal. I would chalk it up to the extremes of these two places. Making up for lost time.

What I see now was that I completely lacked understanding of why I drank so much. My overindulgence of alcohol wasn't about the laws around alcohol whatsoever. No matter how far I traveled, my problems would follow me there. I would be the exact same person, having the same issues with alcohol, whether I was working and living in Abu Dhabi, spending time on a family all-inclusive vacation in Jamaica, or partying for a weekend in Lebanon. I hadn't processed my past and made peace with it. I hadn't yet created a life that I didn't want to escape.

I lacked the skills to process my trauma, and to cope with it, so I turned to alcohol. And rather than processing this trauma, I ended up keeping it all within me. We all carry that trauma somewhere. Somewhere within us. It doesn't just go away.

I'd already been casually drinking every night of the week before moving to Abu Dhabi, but once I moved there, the environment made it acceptable for me to start drinking to excess as early as noon on Fridays and Saturdays, as well as multiple nights a week at ladies' nights. I even started going for beers a few times a week after yoga. In hindsight, it became abundantly clear that I was pushing the 'drinking problems' scale further and faster than I wanted to.

One of the biggest struggles that I had when I moved to Abu Dhabi was making friends. I had friends in the UAE, Claire and Louise, but they lived in Dubai, not Abu Dhabi, which is around an hour's drive away. Within Abu Dhabi, when I'd just arrived, life felt isolated and lonely for me. It was difficult and different from Kuwait.

At my old school, the teacher turnover happened quickly, and there was a camaraderie amongst everyone – a 'we're all in this together' type of energy. It had a turnover rate of over 50%, so plenty of new teachers came into the country at the same time each August and were keen to befriend and support each other quickly. People like Ife, Raghu and Atif saw my isolation and took me in as family. But in Abu Dhabi, I made no such connections. I arrived in November, when the school year was already in full swing, and the small number of new teachers had already been through the orientation process and formed bonds with one another. Everyone on my teacher team in Abu Dhabi had lived there long term and were content with their lives. Many of my colleagues had worked at the school for five or ten years, and they had spouses and families and fully-furnished homes around the city. It was a much healthier work environment in many ways for this reason, but it was also a much more isolating living environment. Because my colleagues were so settled, it wasn't top of their mind to embrace the newcomers, like it was for teachers in Kuwait. I loved Abu Dhabi, but I also felt very lonely.

When I did go out and party with my colleagues, part of me found it hard to connect with others because I wasn't being authentically me. I was so afraid of the stigma when it came to mental health that I kept my secrets close to my chest. No one at my work knew that I was married, processing a divorce, or struggling with what had been diagnosed as bipolar disorder. No one knew I had run away from Kuwait and got on a plane to Bali. I was ashamed of it all. At the core of it, I held a belief that I had really made a mess of my life, and people would judge me for it.

When I drank, I found it easier to open up and share these stories with people. Part of me felt that if I shared my stories, it would help me connect and bond with others, and I could pass it off as a drunken disclosure in the morning. But the connection that sharing secrets built wasn't authentic – it was fabricated and lubricated by booze. It was also a trauma response. My reaction of blurting out my stories to anyone who would listen was coming from a wounded part in me. The wounded part in me wanted my relationships to be strong, safe and intimate quickly, but it did not possess the patience to put in the time and trust necessary to build a solid relationship. And in the morning, I never knew what the other person remembered or forgot. The 'you're my best friend!' bonds that were shouted over shots, loud music and dancing between strangers at 2am often evaporated and disintegrated the next day, and I would be left with hang-xiety, feeling anxious that they were either sharing my secrets with everyone or had completely forgotten them.

During that time in which I was drinking so frequently, my dependence on alcohol never interfered with my work. I like to point out this fact because my story defies our stereotype of what a 'problem drinker' is. I was very high functioning. My work was often praised by my management team. I never once showed signs that I was struggling. Like the yin and yang of yoga, my work environment seemed to fit into the yin part of my life, whereas my partying corresponded with the yang. I gave the appearance to others that I knew how to balance it all.

But I knew the truth. The casual glass of red wine with dinner was happening every single night, the binge drinking of frozen margaritas at ladies' nights were occurring multiple times a week, and the all-you-can-drink beer was taking place at brunches every weekend. The first year that my mom visited me in Abu Dhabi, she asked me, "You're only drinking this much because I'm here, right? You don't drink this much normally, do you?"

"No, definitely not," I reassured her, glass of red wine in hand. I don't even think that I was aware that I was lying because I'd convinced myself otherwise.

As my first year in Abu Dhabi went on, the calm, cool and collected girl that had arrived was once again deteriorating and falling into depression. All this time, I'd thought that living in a country where alcohol was legal would solve all of my problems, but it created more. In Kuwait, money was never a problem because there was nowhere for me to blow through hundreds of dollars every weekend on partying, but in Abu Dhabi, I was madly in debt and had maxed out two credit cards with charges from booze and brunches at the bars.

It started to dawn on me. I was doing everything right in my life. I had a good job and a nice apartment. I was eating healthily, exercising and doing yoga. I should have been happy, right? But I was still so unhappy. By process of elimination, part of me knew that it was alcohol. I began spending a lot of time on Google at night with a glass of red wine in my hand, searching 'how do I quit drinking?'

New Year's Eve, 2019, I was in the beautiful, peaceful, isolated and landlocked South-East Asian country of Laos, upset that my night was 'ruined'. Why was it ruined? Because I couldn't drink.

In 2018, for the first time since I had moved overseas, I decided not to travel and meet my family in Jamaica for the Christmas holidays. Instead, I would travel on my own, backpacking around South-East Asia. It was an opportunity to party. I had planned to spend two weeks in Vietnam, one week in Laos, and one week in Thailand. I was on one of those group tours, with a bunch of people aged between eighteen and thirty. Every single day and night involved drinking buckets of mixed drinks, shots after shots and beers upon beers. The evenings would end with me stumbling down the cobblestone streets and arriving in hostel beds that were not my own.

New Year's Eve happened to be the one night that we were scheduled to ride a slow boat up the isolated, swampy, rocky Mekong River and stay in a homestay in a rural, riverside Laotian village. We'd have a campfire, eat traditional Laotian food, and play with the local children. This was how I would ring in 2019. The next day, we'd continue riding the slow boat up the Mekong River to cross the border into Thailand. This voyage should have been an extraordinary experience. A once-in-a-lifetime opportunity. And yet, I was angry. I was angry because it was New Year's Eve, and I wouldn't be wearing a silver sparkly crown that said '2019' while dancing on tables and knocking back tequila shots in the city. I wouldn't be kissing some stranger at midnight – I'd be in bed before the clock even struck twelve. I tried to skip the whole boat ride and schedule a plane ride instead from Laos to Thailand, just so that I could be in Bangkok and have a proper party to celebrate the new year. But it was going to cost me thousands of dollars that I didn't have. So, I sucked it up, filled my bag up with beer, and got on the boat to Thailand. I remember people laughing at me. "Why do you have so many bags of beer? Are you packing for a week away?"

A boy that I'd met, who had been spending the majority of the trip around me, also brought beer, and together, we managed to drink everything before 4pm that day. As the whole boat ran out of alcohol, the rest of the group regretted not bringing more with them, too. We arrived at the village. There were villagers everywhere, with whom we could connect, and I ended up playing with a little girl for most of the time. I was able to engage with them, but in the back of my mind, I was also fixated on where I could have the next beer, and I was annoyed that I couldn't have one. I was so happy when a case of beer arrived in the room with dinner as a surprise because it was a special occasion.

I see now how my ideas and opinions about alcohol being necessary to have fun shaped my entire narrative of this experience. My New Year's was 'ruined' by being forced to be sober, but was it, actually? That was all in my head. At that point in time, I thought that a fun New Year's needed alcohol, and without alcohol, it wouldn't be fun.

But on reflection, my New Year's Eves with alcohol were never all that fun. Alcohol just made every New Year's Eve more chaotic, dramatic and expensive. Most people that I speak to who are now sober have similar New Year's Eve stories. Year after year, we spent a fortune on tickets to events that weren't great. We got hypothermia as we waited in long lines to try to get into bars. We got into arguments with our friends and partners. We lost our wallets. We had accidents. We got trapped for hours waiting for a taxi ride home.

Being in an isolated village in Laos away from all of those stressful situations should have been ideal. Why couldn't I see that?

Social Media can sometimes be used as a force for good. And that's what happened to me. Over the course of January and February 2019, I was spending a lot of time googling 'how to quit alcohol'. I started seeing targeted ads on *Instagram* and *Facebook* for a program for quitting drinking. These advertisements were either thanks to the algorithms or the universe. The people featured in the targeted ads seemed just like me. None of them called themselves alcoholics or had joined AA – they were just drinking too much, too often, and wanted to cut back, so they joined a twenty-eight-day, ninety-day, or full-year challenge to quit. I was looking at their testimonials, and I was so impressed with them – all of them focused on the positives of going alcohol free. All of them said, 'I'm so much healthier', or 'I'm so much happier', or 'I have so much more money'. These testimonials were inspirational for me. I couldn't see myself going to AA or calling myself an alcoholic, but I could see myself joining an alternative organization such as this one. The people whose stories were told in these ads seemed like me.

The more that I read, and the more that I learned about this program, the more inspired I was. I considered quitting alcohol right then, but the timing didn't feel right. I had too many special occasions coming up, and not being able to drink would 'ruin' these holidays for me. I had begun to become integrated into the social scene at my school in Abu Dhabi, and I was excited to finally be invited to join one vacation with a group of friends that I was so desperate to fit in and be included with. We were going to Norway. It was going to be a long weekend of tobogganing, hot chocolate and winter fun. In March, I was planning to get together with one of my childhood friends and her father, whilst they were in Abu Dhabi to cheer on a relative who was competing as a powerlifter in the Special Olympics. In April, I had the annual trip with my mom in the Middle East, where we'd backpack around Morocco, eating tagine, riding camels into the Sahara Desert, exploring the passageways in Fez and discovering the souks of Marrakech. I considered quitting alcohol after these occasions and started to get curious about the idea, but I was also scared. Whenever I woke up with a pounding hangover, or sometimes even late at night, glass of wine in hand, the thought of quitting drinking would cross my mind, and I'd check out this program's website or *Facebook* page. But I didn't think that I could go more than a day or two without alcohol. I had a sense of resistance towards giving up drinking. I thought that being sober wasn't for me and that I couldn't do it. I'd put this idea of going alcohol free on the backburner.

Bright patterns and colors on rugs hanging in local souk shops, the winding maze-like passages through Fez, and the stunning, strong and steady High Atlas Mountains greeted my mom and me in Morocco for our annual trip together. Again, it would be a once-in-a-lifetime trip. We'd travel around the country with a tour group, similar to my visit of South-East Asia, meeting local people along the way and experiencing their hospitality by sampling tagine, Arabic coffee and sweets.

"You cannot get alcohol in the following regions..." our tour leader Osama went over on the first night, "so if you want to drink, make sure that you purchase some alcohol ahead of time. I will bring you to the alcohol store tomorrow."

He was well versed in outlining these alcohol restrictions for his guests on the first night on the trip, as clearly, due to how rampant drinking culture is, this topic had come up with previous tours. After having lived in the Middle East for several years and touring many Middle Eastern countries, this was old news to me. I knew that there would always be a way to find alcohol. As my teacher Rolf wrote in his book, *Meditations from the Mat*, "If drinking is your priority, you will find a way to do it whether there is a roof over your head or not" (31).

Every time that we passed through a town with a liquor store, all of the guests – not just me – were filling their backpacks with bottles of wine and cans of beer. On one of the first days, a bag was dropped and a bottle of red wine spilled all over the sticky, brown mats of the bus floor. I learned my lesson and began wrapping my bottles up in all of my clothing to protect the glass in case a bag fell. Each day, I'd hoist my heavy red backpack onto the bus to make sure that I could always have a drink – behavior that didn't seem problematic to me at the time.

On April 7th, 2019 – my twenty-seventh birthday – we were scheduled to take a long, winding hike up the High Atlas Mountains as part of our tour. Once at the top, we would arrive at an isolated homestay with a rooftop garden and a stunning view of the steeply sloped, snow-tipped mountains. Since it was such a strenuous hike, we left the majority of our bags and belongings locked on our tour bus, taking with us only one small carry-on bag each up the mountain.

I had to leave the majority of our alcohol stash behind, but I carried one bottle of red wine on my back while we scaled the mountainside, with the intention of drinking it once we reached the top. I wasn't sure if anyone else in the group had brought wine with them, but I said to my mom, "Mom – do not share this wine with anyone. I want to drink as much as I can because it's my birthday."

"Happy birthday too youuuu, happy birthday too youuuuu, happy birthday dear Alex, happy birthday to you!" The group gathered in song, singing around the table, as a large, sprinkled vanilla cake with the words 'Happy Birthday', written in many colors, got rolled out by the homestay staff. A fireplace in the sitting room was prepared and lit, and the flames began to crackle and blaze, to keep us warm while we ate dinner in the below-zero weather.

"That cake was carried up to the top of this mountain on

the back of a donkey!" my mom told the group, while everyone laughed.

By this point in the night, our one bottle of wine was already finished, and I wished that the donkey had brought up an extra bottle of wine instead. Because my tolerance was so high, an entire bottle of wine wasn't enough to get me drunk. I lay in bed that night and thought about it. I just didn't want to live like this anymore. I knew what I needed to do.

Life was slipping away from me. I couldn't keep track of what day it was or even distinguish one day from the next. I was constantly away from the present moment. I was constantly focused on where and when I'd get my next drink. And the moments when I didn't have access to alcohol were controlling and shaping my experience of everything. As I got unhappier and unhappier, I realized that if I quit drinking now, I could wade up from whatever trenches I was in, before I ended up stuck in them.

In my teacher Rolf's third book, *Daily Reflections on Yoga, Addiction and Getting Well*, he writes about how the Buddha identified three steps on the route to freedom (Gates 20). The first is the quest for gratification, and that was the experience that I had when I was in active addiction to alcohol. In the second stage, we look at the price we pay for gratification. That was the stage in which I started to question my alcohol consumption. And in the third stage, we seek freedom (Gates 20). And that is when I made the decision to become sober.

And so, I decided, enough was enough. We had a few nights left of the trip, and I went out with a bang – the typical ringleader, I gathered everyone up and pressured them to come out drinking, dancing and laughing. At 2am, I finally made it back to my hotel room, stumbling home down the cobblestone streets with the rest of the group.

I flopped down into my coach seat of the plane on the final day of the trip, heading back from Casablanca, Morocco, to Abu Dhabi, UAE. And I decided that was it. I was exhausted and depressed. Despite the fact that I always ordered a beer whenever I was on the plane, I had made the decision. Today, April 13th, 2019, this was day one. I was going to quit alcohol for twenty-eight days. And just like I had to dig myself out of my own depression in 2017, I had to dig myself out of my dependence on alcohol, too. I had to decide to stop drinking. No one else was going to decide it for me.

At the time that I was on that flight from Morocco to the UAE, I wasn't aware that I would never drink again. Initially, I only committed to being alcohol free for twenty-eight days. Then I extended it to ninety days. Then I extended it to one year. Somewhere along the way, I knew that I didn't want to drink any longer at all.

Since I've quit drinking, people have often asked me how I did it. What made it different from other times that I'd tried to quit? And I often tell them: it was a mindset shift. It was a decision. I had to choose to be sober. I could no longer say, 'I'm trying to stop…' or 'I wish I could cut back…' I had to make a decision. "I no longer drink." That's what changed. Making that decision was extremely difficult, but it also felt freeing and liberating. And although the cravings were excruciatingly hard, and the depression felt intense, I just had to trust that, like the people in the targeted ads that I saw, the longer I stayed sober, the happier I'd become.

What was the motivation behind the change? There wasn't one epic night or big failure or giant mistake. I didn't hit rock bottom like you see in the movies. Over time, I had just realized that I couldn't live in the abyss anymore. I was done with it.

CHAPTER 45

IT WILL GET EASIER

It is often said that the darkest part of the night is right before the dawn. The same thing is true about sobriety. It gets worse before it gets better.

Isolation, loneliness, sadness, exhaustion – these were all the feelings that I was submerged in during the first week of sobriety. That week of my life was equally as painful as the depression that I experienced in 2017. When I quit alcohol, my body immediately went into withdrawal. I was physically craving it. I wanted it every day. Every day was a fight against cravings. Again, I started planning my suicide, and I was overcome with thoughts of jumping off the balcony of my apartment building to my death. I wondered if jumping from the tenth floor, where I was living, to the fifth floor, where the pool was located, was enough distance to be successful, or if I would just badly injure myself and end up regretting my actions.

Even though I was experiencing suicidal thoughts again, this time was different from 2017 because I no longer feared these thoughts. I knew that I was ultimately in control of my actions and could ignore these ideations. I knew that I wasn't going to jump. Because my suicidal thoughts had passed in 2017, I understood that they would pass in 2019 too. In 2017, it felt like I truly might jump. In 2019, it didn't feel that way. I had hope.

On my fifth day alcohol free, the withdrawals began to feel excruciating. Everyone's experience of early sobriety is different – mine was tough. If you drink once in a while, you may not have withdrawal at all. But if you drink as heavily as I did (almost every night of the week, increasing with frequency, over a decade), then you may have symptoms of withdrawal.

"Are you going to the pub on Thursday?" my colleagues asked me repeatedly at work that week. There was a bar across the highway from the school. Once a term, the administration team at the school paid for the first round of drinks for everyone on the team. This event lined up with day five of my sobriety.

When the subject came up, I told a few friends that I wasn't sure if I'd come because I was trying to cut back on my drinking. A friend said, "Can't you just come and have one? It's free!"

That's when I realized that it would be best if I avoided the bar altogether. How do you rationalize and justify not drinking that free drink? It's free! There's no reason to turn it down. So, instead, I spent the night at the gym. I think I went to three exercise classes in one night, which was excessive but also necessary to keep me busy.

The early days were the hardest ones. I learned that I had to be selfish. I couldn't go to the bar. I couldn't go to the party. When I was four days alcohol free, it was tempting to have just one. So, I got away from anyone and anything that might trigger me. I didn't worry about telling anyone – I just focused on me.

I also had a birthday party planned for myself on the Friday evening of my first weekend of sober living. My birthday had occurred a week earlier, in Morocco, but I'd planned a party with my friends a week later. Before I quit alcohol, I loved throwing parties and was typically the host that had a fridge full of beers, a cupboard full of wine, and was constantly encouraging people to just stay and have one more drink. I canceled my birthday party because I wasn't up for entertaining, and I didn't want people to show up with the expectation that I would be providing drinks, in my usual party-hosting style. I felt like, as a host, there was a pressure on me to provide drinks, get drunk, and make the party fun for everyone.

Before I became sober, it was important to me to be the friend that never canceled plans or backed out of something that I said I was going to do, so making this decision was hard. It felt awful to cancel a party and be *that* friend who backed out. But it would have been worse to have a drink. I wanted to avoid any situation where I might have been tempted. I am so glad I did.

I had invited about twenty friends to the party. When I canceled it, I told everyone that I was feeling sick. I decided to text my best group of three girlfriends and tell them the truth. I told them that I was canceling the party because I was taking a break from alcohol. I wasn't up for hosting a party.

One friend suggested instead, "Why don't we just get together and host a board game night?"

This sounded like a great idea.

Another friend texted the group back and asked, "Would I be the worst friend if I went out for drinks with Sophie instead?"

"No," I said, "go ahead." What I wish I'd said was, "Yes. You would be the worst friend ever." I assumed she'd know how hurt I'd be by this. But she didn't, and she went anyway.

The other two friends still wanted to get together, so I went up to one of their apartments on Saturday night for board games. They invited both of their husbands to join us, and the four of them sat around pouring their own glasses of red wine while I chose not to take part. They were all understanding that I didn't want to drink, and no one passed me the bottle or asked me if I wanted a glass – but they just didn't know how to support me in this transition. They didn't know what to say or do. They didn't know how to be present with my newfound sobriety. They said nothing, while they drank their wine, and I drank my water. In retrospect, I suppose saying nothing was better than if they had tried to pressure me to partake in drinking with them.

The first game that we played was a silly game where we had to come up with lists of synonyms for a variety of different words. I was feeling so low mentally that I had great difficulty generating synonyms for any of the words on the list. It was like a fog was hanging over my mind, and my thoughts weren't processing at regular speed. When my friends laughed at me for making mistakes, I couldn't laugh at myself with them. Instead, I felt like I was going to cry. I spent the night trying to blink back tears. What was hardest for me about that night was that I'm sure it was obvious to everyone around the table that I was in a fragile state, but no one said anything. No one asked, "Alex, are you okay?" No one said anything about the fact that it was supposed to be my birthday party, or that I was sober, or that I was clearly in a depressive state.

At the time, I took their silence very personally. In retrospect, I truly don't fault them at all for their lack of reaction to my sorrow. They meant no harm. They were raised in the same culture as me – the kind where you don't talk about your mental health problems. You don't talk about your pain. And if we as a culture aren't taught how to talk about mental health, and we aren't taught how to support someone in a mental health crisis, then we simply don't know how to do so.

When I was quitting alcohol, I didn't have anyone in my life who understood what I was going through. It was so hard for me to go through it by myself. The first time that I started meeting other sober and sober curious people on *Zoom* didn't even occur until almost a year later. There is this feeling of comfort that is generated when you're in a space with other individuals who understand what you're going through that I didn't have in my initial sobriety. It was out of that need for connection that the idea for Sober Girls Yoga blossomed.

But that night, I didn't have access to any of these supports. I went home and cried, and I thought more about jumping off the building. How was it possible that I had friends such as this?

What I've learned about alcohol withdrawal, through reading books, listening to podcasts and engaging with sober influencers online, is that alcohol has a depressive impact on your system. It slows down brain function and changes the way that nerves send messages back and forth. Over time, your central nervous system adapts to having alcohol in it all the time. Your body works hard to keep your brain awake. When you quit alcohol, your brain stays in this keyed-up state. And this altered state is what causes the withdrawal. Symptoms can show up as soon as six hours after you put down the glass. Symptoms can include anxiety, trembling hands, headache, insomnia, sweating and nausea. For me, my most serious withdrawal happened about a week later. I had a lot of anxiety and an inability to stop crying.

During the first week of sobriety, my withdrawals were awful. But I was strong willed. For some reason, despite all the challenges of the withdrawal, I was set on being sober. Each day, I gained more and more momentum, and I was proud of the days as they added up. My worst fear was having to restart at day zero. I was determined to keep powering through. And I did it alone – which amazes me in retrospect – for the first seven days; I used sheer willpower to stay sober.

By day seven, I was feeling isolated. I needed to reach out to people. One of the things that had jumpstarted my sobriety was seeing inspirational advertisements for a program that had helped others to quit. I realized that sobriety was not something that I could do alone. While I was in the process of learning how to be sober, I needed to rally a community around me and learn how to succeed. I'd originally set the goal of making it to twenty-eight days, but while this withdrawal was occurring, I realized that twenty-eight days was not going to be enough – I needed to readjust my goal and stay sober for ninety days. I bought the ninety-day challenge.

At this point, I had joined the program itself, but I was so ashamed of it that I didn't even want to join the *Facebook* group. It was a closed group, so no one outside of it would ever see what I posted, liked, or commented on within it, but joining the group nonetheless was still something that might be visible on my friends' timelines. In my paranoid mind, I thought that everyone else would be looking at my *Facebook* content and become aware that I had a drinking problem by seeing that I'd joined this sober group.

The people who were running the program sent daily emails, and in each email, they spoke about the strength of the community, and the value in joining the *Facebook* group and connecting with others. I waited a few days before the pain was excruciating. Despite my fears of being found out by others, I had to join it.

I will never forget the first time that I logged onto the *Facebook* group. The first post that I saw was a woman on day 511 who was proud of herself for completing a whole airplane journey without drinking alcohol in the airport bar or on the plane. For a long time, I didn't remember her name, but that post resonated with me. At that point, I'd been an expat for four years living in the Middle East, and so I'd spent a lot of time on planes, and my flight ritual included: getting a beer/wine at the airport bar and drinking as much as I could on the flight. I couldn't even imagine going to an airport without having a drink. And I remember reading her post and thinking, *How on Earth did she make it to day five hundred and eleven? I can barely make it to day eleven!*

But I made it to day eight. And nine. And ten. And eleven. Once I hit the double digits, I felt good about myself. There was something about that milestone that mattered to me.

By the time I was becoming sober, I had started teaching yoga again in the United Arab Emirates. I was teaching yoga at a gym in Jebel Ali, just outside of Dubai, which was a thirty-minute drive from where I worked in Abu Dhabi. On my eleventh day sober, I sat outside the gym in my tiny blue Honda Jazz car sobbing, like I had been doing most of the week. I had driven there right after work, even though I didn't teach yoga until 6:30pm. I planned to take the shape class and the spin class and then teach yoga – basically anything to keep me busy. I walked into the gym, and the operations manager, Lucas, was on his way out. I guess I was still teary eyed, as I was during his class the day before.

"Alex, is everything okay with you?" he looked directly into my eyes and asked.

When I'd met this guy a year earlier, I instantly noticed that we had a connection that was undeniable. It was as if we were drawn together by a magnetic force. For a million different reasons, I tried so hard to ignore this magnetic pull that existed between us. To start, Lucas was much older than me, and everyone knew that he had no long-term plans to stay in Abu Dhabi, due to family reasons.

I had put up a shield between myself and everyone else and had been hiding what was going on with me, but with him, for some reason, the shield was gone. "No," I said, candidly. "I'm in the middle of quitting drinking. It's day eleven."

"Come join me while I eat my lunch – let's talk."

I had told my close friends via text message when I was canceling my party that I was quitting drinking, but because they avoided the subject, we didn't have any conversations around sobriety. Lucas, on the other hand, was the first person to look me in the eyes when I shared that I was going sober – to acknowledge my suffering – and hold space for it. And that immediately formed a special bond between us. This bond already existed, as we were friends already, but by me confiding in him, it grew stronger. That day was the moment in which something in our relationship changed. He said one thing to me that day that I'll never forget: "I have to tell you something, Alex. When I first met you, and I added you on *Instagram*, and I saw your *Instagram* stories, I turned to Lynda, and I said to her, 'I think Alex has a problem with alcohol.' But I never felt as though I could speak to you about it before today."

I burst into tears. I felt so ashamed. Here I was, sitting with someone that I'd never even socialized with, who'd never even seen me out drinking, and he was aware that I had a problem with alcohol. Even from afar, he was able to see me with absolute clarity. He hadn't even spoken to me, and yet, he was able to look at my *Instagram* and understand that I had a problem.

From the outside looking in, he was able to see my issues with alcohol when I couldn't see them within myself. The fact that he knew that I had a problem, by merely glancing at my *Instagram* stories, provided me with tremendous insight. I was in a deeper situation than I realized. He was able to infer all of this about me, whilst I had thought I was hiding it well. I'm sure that there were plenty of other people who had been looking at my life on social media over the course of ten years and thinking the same thing, too.

When I committed to quitting alcohol ten days before, I had only committed to a twenty-eight-day challenge. I thought I was a normal person with ordinary drinking habits who needed to take a break from alcohol. I hadn't classified myself as 'having a problem' because the group that I had joined wasn't marketed towards people who had a problem. I was taking a breather, and it was a break – it wasn't a lifestyle decision. It was only once I'd had this conversation with Lucas that I started to identify myself as having an unhealthy relationship with alcohol. I didn't have the necessary level of self-awareness to discern that my interactions with alcohol were problematic.

I reached this conclusion on my own. And every time that I've come to a conclusion on my own, I've moved into action mode. Because of my personal experiences with needing to reach my own conclusions and decide what works best for me in my life, I'm aware that everyone has to come to decisions on their own about all lifestyle choices – about quitting drinking, about hiring a coach, about practicing yoga. No one can make that decision except us.

I built the Sober Girls Yoga community at The Mindful Life Practice to be very open-minded and non-judgmental, and this is intentional. I don't want people to come into our community and have to label themselves as an alcoholic or feel forced to declare, "I'm never drinking again!" like they would in Alcoholics Anonymous (AA). I don't mean to put down AA; I've actually since attended AA meetings and absolutely loved them once I was several years into my sober journey. But at this point, I am no longer in a fragile state, and I take what inspires me from the meetings and leave the rest. In the world of sobriety, I have met people who love AA and credit it with saving their lives. But it didn't resonate with me in my early days of recovery. I don't see anything wrong with this recovery program; I just don't think that it's for everyone, and I think that there are many different methods of becoming and staying sober.

Because of my experience, I think that it's important for my 30- and 60-Day Sober Girls Yoga Challenge participants to reach their own conclusions about their relationships with alcohol, and where they want to take this insight afterwards. I encourage my participants to choose their own words to describe their sobriety, whether it is 'sober', 'sober curious', 'teetotal', 'dry', 'alcoholic' or any other term that best defines their journeys. For some people, their sobriety journey may encompass taking a thirty-day challenge and then drinking again in moderation afterwards. For others, their path to sobriety may involve joining several short challenges before sobriety finally sticks. For some people, they may enter into our Sober Girls Yoga program with the awareness that they have a problem, and they never want to drink again. We have the wisdom within us – and sometimes we just need to be seen, heard and supported to find it.

CHAPTER 46

THE FIRST SOBER DATE

By the time that I was three weeks alcohol free, I was feeling brave enough to re-enter the Abu Dhabi social scene. My mood had rebalanced, and the fog over my brain, that came from constantly being hungover, had lifted. My eyes were clear, my face was no longer puffy and, for the first time in a long time, I was really, truly happy. I felt stable and balanced. I was no longer uncomfortable with the idea of being around alcohol. I felt somewhat ready for it.

On the Thursday night of my third week alcohol free, the same friends from the birthday party a few weeks earlier were going to an all-you-can-drink wine event, in typical Abu Dhabi fashion. '30 on Thursday' was the name of the event, and the goal was to try thirty types of wine for around $30. I was so nervous about showing up sober, but I didn't want to skip it just because I didn't drink. I wanted to show my friends that I could still show up and have fun even without alcohol.

I didn't want to be put under pressure to drink, and I was scared that if they didn't know I was still sober, they might try to convince me to join them in tasting the wine. Since the night of my birthday party a few weeks before, no one had asked me any questions about how it was going, or if I was still abstaining from alcohol. I hadn't said anything.

I decided that the best thing to do would be to message my friends in our *WhatsApp* group: "Is there an alcohol-free package?"

I had already scoured the website and seen that there wasn't one, but the point of asking the question was not to get an alcohol-free package: it was so that everyone was aware that I was still sober, and I would not be drinking with them that night. The fact that I had to announce my sobriety seems ridiculous in retrospect – no one ever announces that they drink alcohol. But for some reason, because it is assumed that the average white woman from Canada drinks, we alcohol-free folks must announce our sobriety in our communities. There is a pressure from our culture to consume alcohol and a social conditioning that drinking is the norm.

When I arrived there that night, all of my friends were extremely curious. "You're not drinking? Why not?" I told my friends enthusiastically that I hadn't drunk for twenty days. I was proud of it – it was a huge accomplishment for me. It was the longest that I'd stayed sober since I could remember. I told them that I never wanted to drink again. Instead of celebrating this achievement with me, as I'd hoped, one friend said, "Woah, woah, woah, let's not get too crazy, Alex!"

Another told me, "Can't you just cut back? Why do you need to quit altogether?"

But I didn't care – this night was one of my proudest moments. It was day twenty, and I had paid for a package that included unlimited alcohol. I could, technically, drink as much as I wanted to – but I no longer had that desire. At all. A switch within me had flipped. At one point in the night, a friend stuck his glass of wine underneath my nostrils. "Doesn't it smell so good?" he asked. My stomach churned, flipped over, and I wanted to throw up. Wine no longer smelled good to me. It smelled gross. I realized in that moment that something within me had truly shifted.

After the wine event, my friends were heading down to a pub to continue to drink beers. I had no interest in going, so I became the designated driver instead, and I took people home if they wanted to leave early. I started to believe that I really could make it to ninety days.

"Let's meet up for a drink," suggested my first sober date, who I had met through a parent at my school. I panicked. How would I deal with this? Would I tell him beforehand? Would I say nothing and just wait to see what happened? What if I told him that I wasn't drinking, and he no longer wanted to go out with me?

We made plans for Friday night. I was so nervous that I booked an appointment to get my hair done at a hair salon that afternoon – it was as if I thought that I could overcompensate for being sober by making my hair look beautiful. Maybe if I looked beautiful on the date, he'd overlook the fact that I didn't drink?

It was mid-Friday, and he still hadn't texted me to confirm our plans. I was in the middle of getting my hair done when he sent me a text. "I'm just waking up. I am so hungover from last night... I partied until sunrise." It was 4pm. Oh God.

I nervously messaged him. "Just so you know, I'm doing a dry month right now," I wrote.

"What do you mean?" he asked.

"I'm not drinking right now. It's kind of like 'Dry January'. But in May. But it's fine. I'll get a mocktail!"

Unlike the night before, when I confidently told my friends that I never wanted to drink again, I wanted to downplay this fact to my date. I was afraid that he wouldn't want to go out with me if he knew I'd never drink again. I made light of my decision to become alcohol free by rebranding it as a month off booze.

On the way to the bar, he spent the walk down through the hotel and onto Saadiyat Beach trying everything he could to convince me to drink with him. "Come on – you can just have one," he said.

"I'm not drinking for a month."

"But what's the big deal with just one? It's nothing!"

"It is a big deal," I said.

"It's just one, come on."

"I'm twenty-one days alcohol free," I said to him. "Tomorrow can't be day one."

Once he knew that I was three weeks into it, he changed his stance. "You're twenty-one days alcohol free?" he said. "Wow. I could never do that."

We sat down, and I took my time examining the menu. I finally chose to order a mocktail, and a shisha, because I thought that smoking shisha would make me seem more fun and compensate for the fact that I was sober. When I ordered the mocktail, the server said, "You know that that drink you chose has no alcohol in it, right?"

"Yes, I know."

"You're no fun!" said the server.

My date laughed. "Right? That's what I said. Boring!"

I laughed along, but part of me died. I said nothing.

I ended up spending most of the night trying to convince him why it was so important that I stay sober. I went into detail about how much I drank, and how much it impacted my mental health, and what an achievement it was for me to make it to twenty days without alcohol. After being vulnerable and honest, he finally agreed that yes, it was probably a good thing that I was taking a break from booze. But also, at the end of the night on the way home, he said that he was worried it was a 'red flag' that I didn't drink alcohol.

A red flag? It should have been a red flag to me that he was partying until sunrise. But why couldn't I see it that way? I was so anxious and upset that he wouldn't like me for being sober. I should have been thinking, *This guy has a problem with me being sober. Do I like him?*

I had been so submerged in my heavy drinking and alcohol-saturated world, that at this point I truly didn't think that sober people existed. I didn't think that I would find them. Our perspective creates our reality. I thought the world was the way the people around me were. I didn't have any sober friends, and I'd never dated any sober guys. I lacked perspective on the fact that I could find sober people out there if I looked hard enough.

I wrote a post about this first date in the sober *Facebook* group that I had joined.

> *"Last night, I had my first sober first date. He was extremely hungover from his evening of partying the night before, but he still wanted a couple of beers and tried to convince me at the beginning to join him. 'What's the big deal with having one drink?!' I ordered a mocktail, and the server called me boring. But I stayed strong despite these reactions. Later on, as I got comfortable, I told him all my reasons for being alcohol free and why I am where I am today, and once he understood, he was extremely supportive. I think our lifestyles won't match, and one of us has to change (and it certainly won't be me!). But I will give him a shot. And at the end of the night on our way home, he said, 'Hmm… I hate being hungover, maybe I'll try an alcohol-free challenge too,' so who knows?! Here I am, smiling and shining on Saturday morning. Another day sober to check off in the books."*

My posts in the *Facebook* group were beginning to get a ton of momentum, comments and likes. I remember noticing that on this particular post, everyone who replied seemed to share the same fears as me. Would anyone ever love them, now that they were alcohol free? What I realize now is the fact that we thought we'd never find a sober person to date is somewhat ridiculous, considering there were twenty thousand people in the *Facebook* group alone.

But somehow, I thought that I'd never find a sober person to date, and so I was clinging onto this guy, even though he put me down, belittled and questioned my choice. There was a part of me that was so desperate for love and so desperate for a partner that even though he had spent a whole night criticizing me, I still went out with him on a second date, and a third. I was devastated when he finally ghosted me a few weeks later. If I were dating him now, two years later, I'd never go on a second date with him, or a third. If my date had a problem with me being sober, I'd get up from the table on night one.

Even though I didn't possess enough confidence in myself to get up from the table in that moment, little by little I was changing. I was developing strength. I was also coming to a few realizations: first, if I could sit through a date with a guy, one-on-one, while he tried to pressure me to drink, I could pretty much do anything. Second, I was no longer obsessed with disappointing the people around me. Now, the priority was that I did not disappoint myself.

CHAPTER 47

I WAS THE ONE HOLDING MYSELF BACK THIS WHOLE TIME

Alex's iPhone
May 13, 2019
Today.
Is day thirty.
Alcohol free.
May 13, 2019.
I woke up at 3:45am to walk into the sunrise. Because. It has been.
A month of sunrises.
A month of tears.
Peanut butter truffles.
Hugs. And tears. And tears. Within hugs.
Yoga. Yoga. Yoga.
Loving kindness meditations. Offering love. In all the ways I can.
Shape. Pump. Spin. Choir. Guitar.
Making the bed in the morning. Washing the dishes each day. Pausing to eat breakfast.
One small habit change has had a ripple effect through my life.
Nachos without beer.
Pasta without wine.
Workouts without hangovers.
Brunch exactly as it should be. With coffee. (WHO KNEW?!)
Here I am. Grateful.
After twenty-seven trips around the sun. And twelve of those with

a drink in my hand. And four of those in the Middle East. Which brought me face to face. With this…

I feel free. And I now realize that I was the one holding myself back. This whole time.

Thank you. Thank you. Thank you. To everyone who walked beside me this month.

You know who you are.

Near and far.

I did this myself. But I couldn't have done it without you.

Here I go. Stronger and wiser. Into month two.

CHAPTER 48

PINK CLOUDS AND THE COMEDOWN

Once people get through the initial alcohol withdrawal, they often enter a mental state that is referred to as the 'pink clouds'. 'Pink clouds' is a phrase that is used to describe the elation and euphoria that is often felt in the early stages of sobriety (Raypole). It's when the curtains are pulled back, and you see the sunlight. It's the light at the end of the tunnel. It's the life after death.

My pink clouds were like everyone else's. I was getting up at 5am and doing yoga on my balcony at sunrise. Posting things like 'Live/Laugh/Love' on *Instagram*. I'd wake up and be moved to happy tears as I sat behind the steering wheel, gazed at the Abu Dhabi Grand Mosque as it glinted golden in the sunrise, and reflected on how lucky I was to not be hungover.

Every day was a gift, and everything was brilliant, and I found myself constantly wondering, *How has no one else figured this out? Being sober is actually awesome!* It felt like I had a secret superpower.

People say that pink clouds in sobriety can be dangerous. Pink clouds can create a false perception of what it's like to be sober. People start seeing rainbows and butterflies and think that life without alcohol is amazing. But once the pink clouds fade, they're confronted with actual, plain old life. Having to face the reality of their everyday lives can feel overwhelming, and it is one of the reasons people eventually go back to alcohol. Pink clouds can enable you to ignore life's problems, form unrealistic expectations of life in sobriety, create a false sense of security and confidence, and cause disappointment when these feelings of euphoria fade. And that is what happened to me.

By day thirty, real life was coming back to me. I didn't love my job. I was never meant to be a teacher. I was not courageous enough to focus on yoga, so I was trying to figure out alternative ways to stay in my career but find a way out of the classroom. Maybe I could do a master's in counseling and become a school counselor? Maybe I could become a Physical Education teacher and draw on my love of yoga? Maybe I could become a reading specialist?

I talked about these various options often with one of my colleagues, Chen. Every day, when the students were gone from the classroom, we'd discuss how unhappy I was in my job, as well as how unsure I was of what I would do next. Ever since I'd met her two years before, she had talked about this fortune teller that she'd met in Dubai – she swore that he had helped her to find direction at a time when she was lost. I listened to her without paying much attention – it all went in one ear and out the next. Astrology, psychics, *reiki* and tarot card reading had all been a part of my first two-hundred-hour yoga teacher training, years ago, but I didn't believe that any of these services actually worked. I was raised by parents who believed in science and found it difficult to connect with anything spiritual.

But this time, something had shifted within me. Perhaps it was sobriety that was allowing me to foster a deeper connection to my soul. My spirituality. My inner guidance. My intuition. One day, when Chen said, "Alex, you should really see my fortune teller in Dubai," I thought, *What do I have to lose?* I was desperate and in pain, so I went. If it was a waste of money, then I'd never go back again – but at least I'd tried.

Dan was in a suburban home on the outskirts of Dubai, so I drove an hour and a half one way to get there. I parked my car in the driveway and texted him, waiting for his response. I don't know what I was expecting, but he did not fit the preconceived notions that I had about what a psychic or fortune teller would look like. Dan was a young, hip and stylish guy from India who looked to be in his thirties. He led me through the living room of the house, past two large pug dogs who were snoring on the couch, and up the stairs towards a spare bedroom. Upon entering the bedroom, I was greeted by the smell of incense burning, and I took notice of a table that was not only covered in a beautiful indigo sarong but also displayed a deck of cards, which had been spread face up. I sat down across from Dan. He told me to close my eyes and count backwards from twenty-one to one. And when I opened them, he told me, "You were never meant to be a classroom schoolteacher. You were meant to be a healer."

As soon as he said this, tears leaked from the corners of my eyes and started streaming down my face. He didn't tell me to stop crying, or ask what was wrong, or anything. He just kept talking.

What astounded me was that he knew so much about me – he knew that I had lived in the Middle East before, in a country that sounded to him like it started with a "Q."

"Was it Qatar?" he asked.

"No, Kuwait," I said, as tears streamed down my face.

He knew that I was drawn to Spanish-speaking men and had been in a serious relationship with a someone from a Spanish-speaking country, Santiago. He knew that I was from Toronto. And he knew that I was a teacher of what he thought was tai chi (of course, it was yoga).

He told me what I was going to do with my life, and it was actually something that I'd dreamed of all along.

"You're gonna open up a retreat center that's very different. A fusion of everything. Tai chi. Yoga. Meditation. Dance."

I cried for the entire hour as he looked at me and pretty much told me everything that I already knew about myself but didn't trust. It was like he was seeing me when I couldn't see myself. He was seeing everything I'd always dreamed of but never believed e a choice. I had to save my own life. And I ove in the direction of my development, rather

tuitive healing sessions online in collaboration Mindful Life Practice.

a natural born psychic, with over fifteen years' experience in the field of psychic readings, holistic healing and providing spiritual guidance to people across the world.

Completely free of any particular religious beliefs, his readings are a reflection of your current situation, identification of the cause of certain situations or patterns in your life and a practical guide to action – steps you need to take to realise your desired outcomes.

Born and raised in Toronto, Dan is currently based between Mumbai and Dubai. He travels across the globe for in-person readings and is available for The Mindful Life Practice community members to do sessions over the phone or video calls.

In order to book a call with him, you can do so here:

https://bit.ly/IntuitiveHealingWithDan

CHAPTER 49

YOU ARE NOT UNLOVABLE

A narrative I convinced myself of, when I was going alcohol free, was that I was unlovable. I thought that no one would ever love me again because of how messed up I was. I was recovering from symptoms of a mood disorder, a drinking problem and trauma. I'd thought about killing myself a lot. I was divorced. All of these difficulties happened before I was twenty-six years old. There were so many things that were unlovable about me at this point, and I couldn't imagine sharing about my past obstacles with a new potential partner, and him not running for the hills. It felt like confirmation when the guy that I went out with for a few dates ghosted me and cited my being sober as a 'red flag'. I was convinced that no one would ever love me again.

One of the things Dan told me during our session was that, contrary to my beliefs, someone would fall in love with me again. He said that I was going to meet a Spanish-speaking man, who also worked in the wellness industry, and we were going to be partners: both in business and romance.

Although I continued to keep my eyes peeled for the Spanish-speaking gentleman who was destined to win my heart, my relationship with Lucas, one of the managers at the gym where I worked in Jebel Ali, just outside of Dubai, was also growing. Lucas and I shared a special connection ever since I confided in him about my sobriety a few months before. He wasn't a Spanish-speaker – he was from Greece. He was almost twenty years older than me. He wasn't like anyone else I'd dated in the past ten years. We were spending a lot of time together, going for long walks on the island where I lived and sharing deep and meaningful conversations.

Initially, I assumed that he was only interested in a friendship, since he was so much older than me. When I began to wonder if he was interested in something more than friendship, I also had trouble picturing the two of us together. We were just so different.

This was the first time in my entire life that I was dating as a sober person. When alcohol is involved, it's easy to feel confident enough to make a move, and then if you get rejected, you can blame it on the booze. "Man… what a crazy night… I don't remember anything." Alcohol is an easy escape. But when I was sober, there was no other choice but to own all of my actions. Sharing my feelings with someone took a lot more courage. Being intimate came with vulnerability.

From what I remember, one night, after dinner at my apartment, he finally said to me, "At every point in a female/male friendship, I think the thought crosses both individuals' minds."

"What do you mean? What thought?" I asked him.

"I mean… have you ever thought about dating me?"

It was so quiet, and the energy was so powerful in the room that it felt like I could hear both of our hearts beating. This is sober dating. Vulnerable, scary, quiet, honest and intimate.

We were stripped of alcohol as our armor, and it was the first time in my adult life that I felt fully present as we leaned in for our first kiss. It was terrifying because I was present for every single moment. There wasn't a part of the kiss that could be blacked out, or numbed, or forgotten, or regretted. Neither of us, the next day, could act like we didn't mean it. It was raw.

My previous relationships were meaningful and special, yes, but all of my dating experiences up until this point revolved around alcohol. This sober moment was unlike anything else. We were conscious. Present. There.

We snuggled into each other – his belly pressed upon my back – and, for the first time, love didn't feel influenced or created by the buzz of being tipsy or drunk. Instead, the feelings were just automatically there. Authentically, and soulfully. Soberly. When it comes to matters of love, there is a magnet that either exists or doesn't exist. And when it came to how I felt about Lucas, it existed all right.

Prior to this point, I had a genuine fear that no one would ever love me again after becoming sober. I was damaged. Badly. I was divorced. I was recovering from a drinking problem. There were a lot of things that felt unlovable about me.

But Lucas? He was drawn to me. Despite all of my imperfections. And that was exactly what I needed.

CHAPTER 50

BELIEF IN OUR POTENTIAL

Yoga Sūtra 1.20 says that the path to yoga consists of four practices: faith, vigor, memory, and the intellectual understanding of *samādhi*. *Śraddhā-vīrya-smṛti samādhi-prajñā-pūrvaka itareṣām* (Karambelkar 59). In *Sūtra* 1.19, we learn that there are some people that seem to be born into the world enlightened (Karambelkar 54). I learned recently from my teacher Anvita in Mumbai that these people who seem to be born into the world enlightened have actually worked towards this state in a previous lifetime. So, when they are born, they are starting closer to consciousness than the rest of us. Most of us have to work for it, and we must follow a very rigorous path, which includes:

1. Faith (*śraddhā*): we have to trust that there is something bigger, something better, something beyond us as individuals.
2. Vigor (*vīrya)*: we must be committed and make wholehearted effort.
3. Memory (*smṛiti)*: we must continue to practice dedicated focus and mindfulness.
4. Wisdom (*samādhi-prajñā*): intellectually, we have to understand what the goal of *samādhi* is, consciousness, and why we are working towards it. This is why we continue to study yoga texts. I offer advanced yoga philosophy classes online like the *Yoga Sūtra* Study, and also beginner yoga philosophy classes online to support students coming closer to that goal.

The sober summer of 2019 was slightly daunting to me. Ever since I'd moved abroad, the summers that I'd spent in Canada revolved around going to patios in the late afternoon and having beers with friends from high school and university. It also involved sipping wine at barbeques with my family. Many of my friends and family still didn't know that I was sober. At that point in time, I really hadn't shared about my sobriety with many people. Would going back to Canada this year be different? Would it be hard? I sent a message ahead of time to tell my best friends from high school that I was no longer drinking. They were the same friends who'd planned the engagement party for me a few years before. Thoughtfully and kindly, they planned a surprise gathering again, with alcohol-free mimosas, for my sober journey to be celebrated. Talk about meaningful moments.

I decided that, instead of focusing on partying, like I had in the past, I would use my time in Canada to begin working towards the future that Dan and I had discussed. This was my practice of dedication, or *vīrya.* This vision of my future wasn't something that Dan had pushed upon me. Instead, Dan had helped me to see the future that had existed within me all along. It was the future that I had dreamed about long before I had moved to Kuwait but had chosen to ignore. Dan had lit the match and illuminated my path, but it was up to me to carry the torch and embark on my journey.

Prior to my summer in Toronto, the sober organization to which I belonged decided to reach out to me when I was around sixty days alcohol free. They asked me if I would be willing to write one of those same testimonials for an alcohol-free life that I had once found so inspiring. I was selected to write the testimonial because I had been heavily engaged and involved in their private *Facebook* group, and a large number of community members were continuously expressing that my posts resonated with them. But while I'd posted a lot on their private page, I hadn't yet posted anything publicly about my journey. I had an internal battle waging inside of my mind. Was I ready to share my story? Would people judge me? Would speaking my truth affect my job? Would people no longer respect me? While I wanted my story to inspire others, the way that others' stories had inspired me, there was also part of me that was scared of the stigma around those who misuse alcohol, just like I'd been scared of the stigma around bipolar. After a month's debate, I finally decided that I would write my testimonial on day ninety.

I'd been in Toronto for a week or so at the point when I finally pulled the trigger and submitted the post. When I submitted it, it meant my story would be out in the world. So, I decided to post it on my own *Facebook* page first. I wanted to get ahead of the story and tell it myself before people found my testimonial on their targeted ads and started gossiping about it. If I told the story, it wouldn't be gossip – it would just be my truth.

When I posted the story on *Facebook*, I was terrified. Lucas immediately called me from Abu Dhabi on *Facetime*. "Alex, aren't you worried about losing your job by posting this? What if a parent in your school community sees it?" A small wave of anxiety rushed through me. I sat still and breathed into my fear. While a wave of worry was there, a deep sensation of peace simultaneously washed over me. Intuitively, I knew that posting my story was the right decision. If I lost my job, then I'd lose my job.

I didn't. In fact, my post garnered sweeping support. I got hundreds of likes and comments from people in my life who shared how inspired they were by the risk that I took by being vulnerable and sharing my story with alcohol. People privately messaged me to say that they, too, had issues with alcohol. It felt freeing and liberating to tell my truth. I began to become an advocate for living alcohol free, and I gradually started posting more and more about my sobriety on my page.

could be possible. That session changed my life.

One of the things that he said to me was, "Don't go b[illegible] school and get a master's in counseling. You should become a li[illegible] coach."

What stunned me about this suggestion was that I didn't even tell him that a master's in counseling was something that I was considering at the time, but he knew.

A life coach? At the time, I didn't even know what that was. But I went home, did some research, and found a course.

I took several psychology courses during my time in undergrad and had personal experience with counseling, so I knew what counseling was all about. It's about trauma and mental health. As I learned more, life coaching attracted me because it has a different objective. Life coaching is about helping individuals achieve their goals and get to where they want to be, faster than they would on their own. If you were to imagine where you are, and where you want to be, as two points with a tense elastic band between them, the coach helps release some of the tension of the elastic band before it breaks, and she then brings the two points to meet.

I left my session with Dan with renewed purpose and hope. I was going to create a yoga business and become a life coach. And I knew, finally, after years, I was choosing to step into my purpose. I was choosing to step into my *dharma*. I was beginning to ask myself, "What am I here to do? What am I here to share with the world? What do I offer?" All these years, I had been a schoolteacher simply because I had specialized in education during my undergraduate degree program. But when I was a young kid practicing yoga for the first time, I knew that yoga was my purpose. I knew it was my *dharma*. And by ignoring my *dharma*, I became depressed.

Dan was telling me what I already knew – I was put on this Earth to be a healer. And I could continue to waste the rest of my life ignoring my destiny, staying safe and maintaining the status quo as a schoolteacher, or I could take the risk and step into my potential.

"You need to get another barre instructor!" I jokingly said to Lucas and Lynda, the managers of the gym in Jebel Ali, one night on my way out. I'd heard their only barre instructor was leaving at the end of the month, and I was sad to see her go.

About a year before the summer of 2019, I had tried my first barre class. Barre is a fitness fusion of yoga, Pilates and dance. Spontaneously signing up for a class that wasn't yoga was totally out of character for me, but I happened to join this class simply because there was no yoga on Thursday afternoons, and this sounded like the closest thing to it. After one session, I'd fallen in love with this style of fitness. Barre is a functional movement exercise class, set to upbeat music. It was completely different than any of the exercise programs that I had joined previously.

"You know who would make a great barre instructor?" Lucas asked me.

I wracked my brain, trying to figure out who he was speaking about. I genuinely had no idea. "Who?"

"You," he said.

Although I heard his suggestion, I had never properly considered it – that is, until I told Lucas my dreams of working full time in yoga, and he offered to help me bring them into fruition. He recommended that I work on more related qualifications, which would allow me to progress towards a management role at the gym.

"Alex... you'd be an amazing full-time general manager of the gym. The gym needs a barre instructor – would you ever consider that? Have you ever thought about becoming a spinning instructor?"

Me, a barre and spinning instructor? It seemed so out of character for me. But Lucas believed in me so much that I began to believe in myself. I signed up for both certifications. I worked on the spinning instructor qualification during the months of May and June by completing a program that Lucas and Lynda ran in Jebel Ali, Dubai. In July, while I was in Toronto, I was able to earn my barre instructor certification. These experiences defied my views about myself. I was never strong or active as a kid, so when I became a barre and spinning instructor, I far exceeded my own expectations about my fitness capabilities. It was hard – I didn't have a six pack or a background in fitness like the rest of my classmates – but it was such an achievement when I completed both.

Back in the UAE in May and June, when I first decided to quit drinking, one of the things that I decided to do was reread a favorite book of mine from so many years ago, *Meditations from the Mat.* I read this book when I started on my yoga journey nearly ten years before, and it had changed my life. I remembered that Rolf Gates identified as a recovering alcoholic, and many of his stories in the book revolved around his personal relationship with drinking and his struggles to get sober. I circled back to his book about a decade later, rereading everything and taking new meaning out of it. I felt that I had to meet him. I went on to his website and saw that he was leading an advanced yoga teacher training in the middle of July, and it coincided with my hundred days alcohol free. I booked it. I was so excited for this moment – for me, seeing Rolf Gates was like meeting a guru or a mentor. Reading his book changed my life all those years ago.

I borrowed my sister's car and drove fourteen hours through the forested trees and rural roads of Ontario, New York State and Massachusetts to get there. The training was at an old *ashram*-turned-retreat-center set on a lake in the middle of the Berkshires. The idea of meeting this man, who had changed my life so many years ago and who I admired so deeply, was terrifying, exciting and nerve-racking. Would he live up to his reputation? Would he be as amazing and inspiring in real life as he was in his book?

Unlike some of my previous yoga teacher training leaders, I had this feeling that Rolf truly walked the walk. As soon as he sat down and started talking, I knew that I had nothing to worry about. Right away, I sensed a humble, generous and loving energy emanating from him. This was the kind of yoga teacher that I wanted as a mentor. This was the kind of yoga teacher that I wanted to embody. A course is only as good as its teacher. We were truly fortunate on that training. Despite how famous Rolf is, there were only eleven people who had signed up for the program, which allowed each of the participants to form close connections and benefit from an intimate classroom experience.

When it came time for me to introduce myself, I didn't want to admit to a room full of strangers that 'I'm here because I had a drinking problem, and I'm obsessed with Rolf'. So, instead, I bumbled, "I'm from Abu Dhabi, and I really like yoga workshops."

Later on in the week, when I confided in Rolf about the true reason why I was there, he said: "Yeah, I was wondering about that. I mean, I was thinking, she came all the way from Abu Dhabi to Massachusetts to learn about yoga workshops? That's weird. I guess she must really like yoga workshops." The truth was, I had just gotten sober, and I wanted to meet Rolf – he'd changed my life. That was why I was there. But, on the first night, I wouldn't tell anyone that.

Rolf gave us a task that week – to choose an ordinary moment from our lives from the past ninety days, connect it to the philosophy of yoga, find some *āsana* cues to embody it and write a *dharma* talk. We would then teach a yoga class that incorporated all of these required elements. By the last night of the training, I still had no idea what to write about. For one, none of the moments in my life had been ordinary during the past ninety days – every single moment of every single day had been extraordinary. I'd gotten sober. I'd met Dan. I'd changed the entire course of my life path and journey. There were no ordinary moments. Second, nothing that I wrote felt new or original. So much of my meaning, so much of how I came to understand the world, was from

Meditations from the Mat. Anything that I came up with felt like I was plagiarizing a page from a Rolf Gates' book.

The night before the presentations, Rolf volunteered to sit in the room and be available for anyone who had questions for him. I went up to him and burst into tears.

"I can't do the project!"

"Why not?" he asked.

"Well, none of the moments in my life have been ordinary during the last ninety days because I am 100 days sober. And every time that I write, it feels as if I'm plagiarizing a Rolf Gates' book!" He laughed. I explained to him that I was actually a huge fan of his books and had read them hundreds of times. I had memorized many essays and read several passages out loud at the end of many of my yoga classes over the years.

"Alex… first of all… congratulations on being 100 days sober. That is a huge accomplishment. And if you feel like you can't do the task, then it's okay… you don't have to do it."

I exhaled a sigh of relief.

"But on the note of plagiarism… do you think that I invented kindness? Do you think that I invented telling the truth? Do you think I invented Warrior 1 and Warrior 2? Anything that you teach won't be plagiarizing my book because yoga doesn't belong to me. It's been passed from heart to heart, through thousands of years. I'm just passing on what my teachers have taught me. And one day you'll pass on what I taught you."

His response gave me shivers.

After my conversation with Rolf, I realized that my limiting beliefs were preventing me from doing the task. I put together the presentation and taught it to my class the next day. Rolf and I shared a moment where he told me that he thought it was my *dharma* to teach yoga – something that I'd told my mom so many years before. It was one of the deepest compliments that I'd ever received from a mentor.

You travel the whole world, only to return home. I'd been all over the world, and I'd ended up back where I'd started – with Rolf Gates, author of the book that started it all ten years before: *Meditations from the Mat*. This moment was me finally coming home to myself.

The final training of that summer, in early August 2019, was my life coach certification. I had researched a few life coach certifications and chosen a training through a school that would certify me as a 'life purpose coach'. I wanted to do a training in person, as I wasn't comfortable with participating in an online program, but I hadn't been able to find one that worked for me timing-wise, so I joined a weeklong training on *Zoom*.

At this point, I was still fresh in my alcohol-free journey. I was just over one hundred days into it, and I didn't even use the word 'sober' to describe myself. I didn't see myself becoming a sober coach – I didn't even know that they existed. I didn't investigate certifications for sober coaches – I just looked into general life coach certifications. This training called to me.

The summer days continued to fly by, and soon, it was almost time for the training to start. Even though Lucas and I had been texting and calling each other every single day at this point, I still hadn't told him about signing up for this certification. He knew about all of the other courses and trainings that I had done that summer, but I didn't tell him about this one.

He was a life coach himself, and he'd gone on and on to me about how a bunch of trainings out there were not high quality. I had chosen this school purely on gut instinct without asking him or telling him – gut instinct seemed to be how I was making all of my decisions nowadays. If it felt right, then it felt right. I hadn't done a lot of research. And I was worried that he would tell me that the course that I'd selected was not the right choice or the best class to pick. In spite of all the reasons why I didn't want to share this information with Lucas, I felt guilty about keeping a secret from him.

I couldn't continue to hide this information from him when I would be unreachable by phone for the next week, so I finally told him about the training the day before it started. In retrospect, my discomfort with letting Lucas know about my decision shows me that there was a power imbalance in our relationship. I looked up to him as a mentor, and I valued his opinion, so much so that I didn't even want to tell him about my enrollment in a course. I also felt like I couldn't keep any secrets from him – which, in retrospect, seems ridiculous, as I would later learn he was keeping many large secrets from me.

It was mid-August, and I was around 120 days alcohol free when I joined the life coach certification course. At the beginning of the training, just like the other trainings that I'd participated in that summer, we had to introduce ourselves and share what had led us to this point, and why we wanted to become coaches. On the barre training, the spin training, and even the yoga training, when it came time to introduce myself to the group, I didn't mention anything about my sober journey. While I might have brought it up during the trainings later, or one-on-one with classmates individually, it was not an aspect of my journey that I included in the way I introduced myself. I was ashamed. I was too afraid to talk about my sobriety amongst strangers.

But this time, I confidently told my story from day one. The course was online, and it was my first time ever logging on and using the software *Zoom* (which, nowadays, doesn't even need an introduction). We logged on, and all of the little squares appeared on the screen. I was asked to introduce myself. I took a deep breath, remembering what I learned on my first yoga teacher training, all those years ago. "Hello, my name is Alex. I decided to become a life coach because I recently got sober." When I said this, my voice cracked, and I started to tear up. "When I got sober, I met a psychic, and he told me that I was meant to become a life coach. So here I am."

That week was exceptionally healing for me. As we took turns coaching each other over the course of six days, I started to confidently step into my *dharma*. I knew that Dan was right by sending me on this training.

At the end of the course, we had to define our niches as coaches. If we didn't have niches, we might not resonate with our potential clients. My teacher explained to us that simply being a "life coach" was too vague and broad in a world saturated with coaches. My classmates were niching down in areas such as business, relationships and health. I contemplated what specialty might be best for me, and I settled on "life purpose" coaching.

I bought a domain name that consisted of my social media handle "alexmcrobs", and I spent time designing the website, which included my uploading photos from a couple of photoshoots that had taken place earlier that summer. I worked on an intake form and client contract. I made a logo and titled my business, 'Wellness with Alex McRobs'. And then, I announced on social media that since I was newly trained as a life coach, I would give away four sessions with four lucky clients. I hadn't realized what a big community I'd developed since going public about my sobriety, but I already had over two thousand followers, and many were interested in the free coaching sessions. I had over twenty-five people respond to that initial post. Once those free sessions got underway, and I began to receive my clients' testimonials, I started to get the ball rolling.

After the coaching course ended, the final stop of the summer of 2019 was Paris. It was the end of August by this point. Like in 2016, when I stopped in Spain on the way back to Canada, in 2019, I had planned a stop in Paris on the way back to Abu Dhabi. Paris was a city that I'd always dreamed of visiting. But I'd booked this trip before I'd gotten sober, back in April. I'd had visions of sitting on a terrace surrounded by green hedges and plants, gazing at the tall, towering, metallic Eiffel Tower with a glass of red wine in hand. I had fantasized about having a glass of wine in the café at the Louvre after wandering through aisles and rooms of ancient paintings and archaic statues. I had imagined sipping a glass of wine while watching slow, steady boats, as they leisurely snaked up and down the green and narrow Seine River.

As the trip was approaching, I seriously thought about canceling my plans because I just didn't know how I'd spend my time in Paris if I wasn't getting drunk. But eventually I realized that this would be the ultimate test. If I could survive spending a week in a city that I'd only associated with wine, I could survive anything. So, despite my urge to cancel, I went anyway. I spent my days doing things that I never would have scheduled if I had been spending my time drinking – I rode motorized scooters through the city, visited the Eiffel Tower and drove up to Versailles.

I posted in the sober *Facebook* group after a few days of adventures:

> *"Day 129, and I'm in Paris! I booked this trip about a month before I quit drinking, and I honestly almost canceled it after I quit because my vision for this trip involved me drinking a glass of red wine while looking at the Eiffel Tower… and I couldn't imagine Europe without alcohol. I'm so glad that I didn't cancel it… it turns out the Eiffel Tower looks exactly the same whether you've had a drink or not, and vacations sober are 100x better because you're not hungover every day at museums and tourist sights. Traveling is so much cheaper when you're not spending all your money on expensive wine. And also, you get to truly experience the culture*

and remember it all. How on Earth did this take me so long
figure out?? I guess we learn about life by living it!"

Out of this holiday came a brand-new resolve: sobriety might be something that I managed to do not just for a few months, but for the long term.

CHAPTER 51

THE MINDFUL LIFE PRACTICE

Lucas and I had become super close. We were calling and texting every single day. He knew everything about what I was doing, the people with whom I was spending my time and even how I was managing navigating sobriety and my relationships with my parents. But things were extremely complicated with this guy, which is how he convinced me to keep our relationship a secret from everyone around us. He couldn't just elope with me and start a yoga retreat center on the other side of the world. He was twenty years older than me and had a family business on an island in Greece. His father was sick, and he was planning on returning to Greece in the next year to restart his life there. "We can't tell anyone we're dating because they wouldn't understand our love with the age difference between us," he said.

In both of our eyes, our relationship became a romanticized modern-day *Romeo and Juliet* story. He wanted to move back home, and I wanted to move to Bali. He wasn't in the same life stage of exploring and traveling as I was – he was in a life stage of wanting to return to his roots. And there was absolutely no way either of these dreams would mix. And no way either of us would compromise each other's dreams. But we were both in love, and we were willing to ignore all of our incompatibilities for a while, so we could enjoy our secret romance. For me, this felt like the first time that I'd ever genuinely fallen in love. Soberly. Authentically.

I booked another session with my psychic, Dan – not to talk

about my business or my future, but to discuss my relationship with Lucas.

I walked in, counted backwards from twenty-one to one, opened my eyes, and told him: "Dan, I've fallen in love with someone, but he's not from a Spanish-speaking country. He's Greek… and he's not a student of yoga. But he is a fitness trainer, which is kind of close to what you said. He has a family business, a coffee shop, in Greece. I think he's the one."

"Show me a picture," he said, and I did as I was told.

Dan looked at the picture for half a second and said to me, "Nope, not the one. He's a womanizer. He's going to hurt you. He's cheating on you. You're going to meet your soulmate in November."

And then he wanted to talk about the business. "Do you have a name for it yet?"

I was annoyed with him. I was here only to talk about Lucas, not about the business. My career in wellness was going well. I was teaching more yoga classes at the gym in Jebel Ali and had started teaching spinning and barre. After I'd done my free one-on-one life coaching sessions with my first clients, they'd done some testimonials on *Instagram* for me, and now I had my first few paid life coaching clients. I was there because I wanted Dan to tell me that Lucas was the one. That was my focus. Instead, Dan was telling me to get away from Lucas. To stay as far away from Lucas as possible.

He told me to put some money into marketing, stop focusing so much on the gym where Lucas and I worked, and instead concentrate on my own business. "So, have you come up with any ideas for what you'd like to name it?" Dan asked.

"Well… I haven't thought about it."

"What about 'Mindful Practice'?"

I googled it as we were talking. "It's taken," I said.

"What's your favorite number?" he asked me.

"117," I told him.

He laughed. "Okay… that's not going to work. How about we take one number from that? How about 'Mindful Practice Seven'?"

The number seven didn't quite resonate, but the 'Mindful Practice' did. I went home, typed billions of variations of this phrase into Google and came up with nothing. However, later on in meditation, the perfect name came to me: 'The Mindful Life Practice'. I bought the domain name, claimed the *Instagram* handle and designed a simple logo. But after that, I pretty much set my business plans aside. I wanted to focus on being in love.

After spending only one short week in August in Abu Dhabi, it was time for me to fly back to Canada for my sister's wedding in early September. During that week in Abu Dhabi, I had spent all of my days at school, getting my classroom set up for my next group of students, and all my nights with Lucas. He and I had been separated for six weeks, and we were dying to have time together. We were both worried that our connection wouldn't be as strong after a summer apart, but we were able to pick up right where we left off.

This period of my life truly felt like a whirlwind – after a summer in Toronto, I spent a week in Paris, a week in Abu Dhabi and another week in Toronto. I was so excited about this wedding, but I was also nervous – aside from the wedding I'd gone to sober in the first few weeks of living in Kuwait, this was going to be my first sober wedding where others were drinking. I wanted Lucas to come with me, as my date, but he'd made me promise that we wouldn't tell our family and friends about our relationship.

"We shouldn't tell them until we are sure that we want to be together forever, or it will just cause too much drama," he'd said. I initially agreed to this plan. So, he stayed in Abu Dhabi, and instead, I invited my friend from university, Zach, as my date to the wedding. He had been Nick's roommate back when we were in university, and even though Nick was no longer a part of my life, Zach and I had remained very close friends.

The hardest part of the first year alcohol free is all of the firsts: the first time that you tell someone else about your decision to become sober, the first party that you attend when you are alcohol free, and the first trip abroad without an alcoholic drink in hand at all times, for example. Yet another first was whenever I had to attend a special occasion that had been infused with drinks in the past. My sister's upcoming wedding was one such event. What would it be like now? Would it be ruined? When you're so used to drinking alcohol, the idea of being sober can be really scary.

My sister and her husband were getting married at a summer camp in Algonquin Park, Ontario. This occasion was daunting because it was a full weekend event and – knowing our childhood friends – it would be rowdy and wild. I'd bought a case of twenty-four alcohol-free beers and sharply said to my mom, "Make sure that this case of beer isn't behind the bar. I'm afraid that people will drink it by mistake, and then it will run out." This request seems ironic given that I'd said nearly the same thing to my mom in Morocco about the bottle of wine (that had alcohol in it!) in April 2019 right before I got sober. It turned out no one at the wedding even touched the alcohol-free beers I'd chosen. People who drink alcohol would never make the mistake of accidentally drinking an alcohol-free beer. (Duh!)

My sister's husband is Jewish, and their wedding was a beautiful opportunity for me to learn about and honor the ceremonies of his religion. For example, at the wedding, my sister asked my uncle and I if we could hold the *chuppah*. I soon learned that *chuppah* means 'covering', and it's a traditional wedding canopy. My sister's husband is very handy and constructed the *chuppah* himself. My sister explained to me that the *chuppah* represented the new home that she and her husband would share. She also described how four people are responsible for holding the *chuppah* above the couple during the wedding ceremony. These individuals

CHAPTER 52

YOU MUST CARRY THE TORCH

"Lucas… I really want to come back to Greece with you for Christmas. To get to know where you live, meet people, and see if I could actually envision myself living there. What do you think?" I was lying in bed beside him, in his tiny studio apartment in the outskirts of Dubai, near the gym where we worked in Jebel Ali. This part of the UAE kind of reminded me of Mahboula in Kuwait. It had lots of old villas that had been renovated into several studio apartments. Lucas lived on the first floor, in a tiny studio apartment that might have once been the living room of an Emirati mansion. The door handle pretty much always fell off when you tried to open or close the door. The toilet seat was broken. In the kitchen area, there was no oven. Instead, there was only a fridge and a countertop. Lucas always kept the countertop piled high with stacks of branded water bottles from the gym, cups and bowls that needed washing. The room was full of all the belongings he'd accumulated from years of living in the Middle East; books, clothing, gym equipment and a TV. To the right of the bed, there was a big desk where Lucas would work, sometimes until three in the morning, while I would snooze beside him.

Despite Dan's insistence that I stay away from Lucas (since I would be meeting my soulmate in November), stop focusing on my boyfriend, and start concentrating on my business, I did the exact opposite. I continued spending all of my free time with Lucas, and each and every day, I was falling more deeply in love with him. When I wasn't with him, my days were filled with teaching children at school, and my evenings were filled with leading adult spin classes. In addition to teaching spinning, I was still teaching yoga and barre. I was scrambling to complete all of my life coaching assignments to finish my course. I was also working with a few life coaching clients. By the time I'd get home or arrive at Lucas' apartment at night, I was completely exhausted. Balancing so many responsibilities at once was draining. At the same time, I also continued to wonder why my own business was growing so slowly. Why, after putting in so much effort, did I barely have any coaching clients?

I was truly happy with Lucas. However, there was one nagging thought that kept repeating in the back of my mind: I had asked Lucas if I could visit him in Greece at Christmastime, and he had told me no. "Oh, Alex. I would love for you to come to Greece... but it really wouldn't look good. We have to keep it a secret, or it would cause a lot of drama at the gym. Lynda would probably want to fire you."

Lynda was another one of the managers at the gym, and Lucas had repeatedly told me that she had issues with older men dating younger women. Her discomfort with age gaps in relationships had been one of Lucas' main reasons why we should keep our relationship a secret.

Looking back, I am now able to see that there were some warning signs about Lucas that I wasn't able to detect through my love goggles. For example, he constantly spoke about his exes in a negative way. 'She's a psycho', or 'She's stalking me' were some of the things that he said. I felt like I'd heard this script before – it reminded me a lot of Nick. There are two sides of every story, and it worried me that he didn't seem to be able to take even a slight bit of the blame in any scenario. But when you're in love, it's very hard to see red flags – even when they are waving right in front of you.

I was so, so happy. And I saw a huge difference in my overall outlook on life. In Kuwait, with Santiago, no matter what apartment we lived in, it didn't look nice. But with Lucas, I could be in the dumpiest place in the world and still be happy. He was over fifty years old and his life was a constant juggling act, which required him to strike a balance between helping with his family business in Greece and maintaining his career in Abu Dhabi. However, none of these traits or obligations mattered. All that mattered was that I was with him. At that time, I felt that that was what love is. When you are in love, it doesn't matter where you are in the world or how little money you have. As long as you are able to gaze into that person's eyes, none of the external challenges matter.

In the meantime, even though I was barely making enough money to scrape by through my job teaching yoga part time at the gym, I wanted to quit my job as a teacher. So, in December 2019, I submitted a letter to the school stating that I was quitting in July 2020.

I parked my tiny, dusty blue Honda Jazz outside of the Abu Dhabi golf club one night in December 2019 and paused, tears in my eyes. It was pitch black outside, and I was wearing the same white, glittery, sparkly dress that I'd worn to the staff Christmas party the year before. I stopped for a moment to look at myself in the rear-view mirror before getting out of the car. I had a flashback to my former self – the Alex who attended this very same party just one year ago – and I couldn't help but get emotional when I thought about how much I had changed. This would be yet another first for me: my first time being sober at a work Christmas party.

I posted in the sober *Facebook* group:

"I'm having a moment outside, with tears welling in my eyes, before I enter the work holiday party tonight, and I'm thinking about how far I've come in a year. At this same party last year, I was the girl

serving the glittery red and green vodka and gin 'welcome drinks': 'One for you, one for me!' I was blackout before the meal was even served. I can't remember what I did or said, though I'm sure it was embarrassing. I woke up with anxiety like a ton of bricks weighing me down, and it was one of the weekends where I said, 'I need to quit drinking,' yet I carried on for three more months. Today, I'm 235 days alcohol free, and I might be wearing the same dress that I wore last year, but: same dress, different girl. All I have to say is 'thank you' to this community. I am SO glad that we found each other."

Prior to the Christmas party in 2019, I'd asked him, "Please, Lucas… come with me to the party." I was so desperate to show him off and to have him show up for me and support me at all of these important events – like the staff Christmas party, my choir performances, and more.

Like always, he said that he couldn't. "Oh, Alex… think about how much drama that would cause. You can just come over to my house afterwards."

I was so sad when I was clicking the checkbox on the Google form to indicate that I was not bringing my spouse or a significant other to the party. We agreed that I'd go without him, and then I'd drive to his apartment afterwards in Jebel Ali to sleep over. I decided to get my hair straightened that evening, and I went to the party late to avoid that nervous buzz that people have before they drink their first drink. I was so apprehensive about being sober that I decided to show up about an hour into the event.

By the time I walked up the stairs, I'd missed the welcome drinks, and everyone was happy. Someone had taken over my role as the person mumbling into the microphone. I was happy to pass him the baton and extremely entertained by the antics of everyone else. I felt proud as I flung my hair around dancing to 'Good as Hell'. No one could stop me from having fun. I'd have fun even though I was sober.

I will never forget waking up the next morning with the

brightest beaming smile on my face. Lucas had already gotten up and gone to work at the gym while I slept in. Later that morning, when I was sitting in my parked car outside of Lucas' apartment, I took a selfie of myself smiling and posted it in the sober *Facebook* group.

> *"Here she is, folks – the girl who is NOT hungover the morning after her work Christmas party!"*

"So good to see you, niece!" Uncle Rick wrapped me in a big bear hug as he greeted me at Pearson International Airport in Canada in December 2019. He brought me my Canada Goose knee-length winter jacket, but even with that, as soon as I stepped out of the airport, I felt a chill through my bones. I hadn't been home in the winter in Canada in years. It was colder than I remembered.

I was sad that Lucas didn't want to spend Christmas with me in Greece but excited to be reunited with my family. On the drive home, I told my uncle about my idea for The Mindful Life Practice and an online thirty-day yoga challenge at home. At that point, I was familiar with *Zoom* – I'd used it for my life coaching training – but it was blocked in the UAE, so I imagined I'd do it on YouTube. I asked him for business advice as he had a career in sales and marketing. He wasn't very receptive to the conversation. I think he was being cautious – he didn't want to give me advice that could go wrong – but, at the time, I interpreted it as a lack of support.

At home, things were hard for me. It was my first winter in Canada in six years. I still had my warm winter jacket, but I felt perpetually cold – no fireplace could warm me up. The darkness began to depress me, and the cold wind stung my skin. On top of all that, I could feel Lucas slipping away from me. In the summer when I was in Canada, he messaged me and called me daily. But this time, it felt like I was persistently the one reaching out, always the one vying for his attention. He said that his dying father was the reason why he had been out of touch – he was constantly in the hospital with him. I began to apologize for reaching out and bothering him so much when he was clearly so busy.

On Christmas Eve, my family showed up with the most thoughtful gifts for me – my uncle purchased gift cards for me, my sister framed pictures from the wedding, and my mom bought me nice clothes. My grandmother paid for our Christmas holiday together. I was in tears when I saw how much effort they had put into selecting the perfect presents – I hadn't even thought to bring them anything. I felt like the most awful niece, sister, daughter and granddaughter. Who shows up to Christmas with nothing? I was so focused on my business and my future that the thought hadn't even crossed my mind. My family insisted that they didn't mind, and that my presence was the present, but I couldn't help but feel awful – obsessive thoughts about all of the ways that I was a failure, including my unsuccessful business, began to play in an incessant loop in my mind. Suicidal thoughts crossed my mind that day.

I flew back to Abu Dhabi in January 2020. I was so low. Per Lucas' encouragement, I had resigned from my job at the school. He said he'd find me full-time work at the gym, and I could grow my business on the side. But nothing was happening with my business. It wasn't growing. I had no new life coaching clients. And I was starting to get a gut feeling that things were not good with Lucas, either. He'd promised me so many roles at the gym during the year we were together that hadn't manifested: from managing the gym, to being their main barre instructor, to full-time instructing. Every time a job didn't come through, according to Lucas, it was always Lynda's fault. Lucas was the gatekeeper between all of my communications with both Lynda and the rest of the staff at the gym.

I was so annoyed. I began to think that following Dan's advice had been a waste of my time and money, and it might just be wiser to stay a teacher. I arranged an appointment with him to talk about my frustration. I drove down to Dubai, walked in the door, closed my eyes, counted backwards from twenty-one to one, and then opened them. "DAN!" I immediately said. "I did everything you said! And nothing's happening! My life coaching credentials were a waste of so much money. I am not financially secure enough to quit teaching. And I never met my soulmate in November like you said I would!"

Dan asked me, "Are you still dating that guy?"

"Yes," I told him, sheepishly.

Dan said, "Ya, your soulmate hasn't shown up because you're still dating him. There's no room for your soulmate to show up if you're dating someone else. You haven't done anything I said. You need to plan some programs for The Mindful Life Practice. You need to put some money into marketing. You need to focus on that."

But I didn't listen. I'd done trainings, started planning retreats for the gym, and worked my butt off. I was so mad at him. I left in the car, and as I drove back to Abu Dhabi, I thought about how Dan was a waste of money and a waste of time. Couldn't he see? I'd done so much and yet nothing was happening. Defeated, I thought that I was going to be a teacher forever. *What am I doing with my life? All of this time that I've spent on my business has been completely pointless.*

At the time, I couldn't see my faults, but I see them now. Dan was right. I had taken a coaching course, a barre course, and a yoga teacher training, yes, but that was it. I'd set up a website, yes, but that was it. I hadn't put in the necessary time, effort and energy to grow a flourishing business. I was putting all of my effort into my represent the community of family and friends that will support the couple throughout their marriage. I was honored to play a small but meaningful part in the ceremony.

At one point in the night, my mom led the champagne toast. I was so envious of everyone around me who was drinking a glass, and I wanted one too. I picked up the glass of champagne in front of me and had a sip. Then I put it down and stopped. I realized that if I started, and if I drank that glass, I wouldn't be able to stop, and I'd be all the way back at the beginning. So, I didn't drink it.

Being sober that night ended up being incredible. Once I got over the nervous energy of the cocktails before dinner, everyone forgot that I was sober. I laughed, I danced and I cried, all without a drink. While I was terrified, I ended up being so proud of myself. I was super in control and had no regrets. I was able to show up for my sister and my family in the best way possible.

relationship and my life with Lucas. I was spending all of my time, effort and energy on my love life, instead of on myself. Of course nothing was happening. He was completely right.

The thing is – it was Dan's job to lay down the breadcrumbs. It was my job to follow the path and pick the breadcrumbs up. No one will change your life for you. No recovery program will make you get sober. No life coach will help you find a new career. No counselor will heal your wounds from trauma and abuse. No psychic will make your business blossom. No one is going to save your life. They can light the match, but you must carry the torch.

CHAPTER 53

BACK TO THE BEGINNING

I was driving my tiny, dusty blue Honda Jazz down Sheikh Zayed Road when the phone rang.

"Alex, one of your headlights is burnt out," Louise said. She'd driven up in the car beside me and thought she'd call me to let me know. One year before, Louise had moved from Dubai to Abu Dhabi, and she had transferred to my school. Now, our classrooms were right next door to each other.

I had been on the verge of crying the whole drive home, but when I heard her voice on the other end of the line, that's when I burst into tears.

"Alex... what's wrong?"

That was when I told Louise, who was one of my best friends, that Lucas was my partner. I thought that I was crying because I was sad that we'd eventually break up and part ways since our paths had begun to diverge. I realize now that I was actually feeling low because our relationship felt like a never-ending emotional roller-coaster ride. I just didn't understand what my emotions were trying to tell me at the time.

It felt like Lucas was quietly tiptoeing out of my life, and I was grasping at straws in an attempt to get him to come back. However, the tighter I held on, the faster he let go. Part of me felt like he wanted to end things with me, but he was too afraid to go through with it – especially since he had been the one who was speaking about our relationship as if we were soulmates.

In a light, joking tone, my boss John walked into my classroom one day in January 2020, asking, "Alex, what are you doing? Are you coming back to the school, or are you leaving?"

Despite the resignation letter that I'd submitted to the school a month earlier, he had a new contract in his hands for me to sign for the 2020–2021 school year, starting in August 2020. I think it was clear to him how little confidence I had in my future. I was working part time at the gym teaching yoga but that only accounted for about half my salary. I was also coaching on the side but had only made a total of two hundred US dollars coaching.

"I want to do yoga full time!"

"Alex, how are you going to afford to do that?"

"I dunno… move into my boyfriend's studio apartment and work at his gym?"

He laughed. "Alex… don't do that. I quit teaching for a few years and ran a business in my twenties, and it was hard. I support you following your dreams, but I don't want you to quit your job here until you're financially secure enough to survive on your own. Stay here. You have my full permission to build your business on the side while you stay."

"Really?" I asked him.

"Yes. When you're making more money in your business than you are making at the school, that's when you should quit. And you have my full permission to do so."

A few years ago, he'd given me permission to teach yoga outside of school part time, but we never talked about me starting my own business. Being on a studio schedule for some classes a few times a week felt like one thing – launching my own brand, running an effective marketing campaign and overseeing sales online felt like another. In my mind, it was okay to be a follower, but it wasn't okay to be a leader. I think that this fear of leadership was one of the reasons why I'd subconsciously self-sabotaged – I was scared that in the process of launching a business, I might create problems or get into trouble. But now, after having received John's blessing to work on building my business while receiving a steady income from the school, I felt a huge sense of relief. At that moment, I signed the contract to return to the school. And with my financial security in place, I felt this urgent calling… to go back to Bali. I couldn't explain why. I couldn't explain what I needed to do. I just needed to be there.

I bought the ticket on Tuesday and got on the plane on Thursday. It was midterm break in Abu Dhabi that week. I landed in Bali on Friday afternoon, and just like when I had first arrived years earlier, it was pouring rain when I arrived. I embraced the rain in the same way that I had embraced it so many years ago. As the water gently cascaded from the sky, it nourished me. It replenished me. It washed away all of my anxieties and worries.

I took a taxi up to Ubud, parked myself in a cheap hotel on Monkey Forest Road, and got a yoga pass to one of the studios that I'd discovered when I was there in 2017, prior to my yoga teacher training. Once again, on this island, I was fully present. The hum of the jungle, the geckos on the walls, the smell of incense, the flowers marking my path. I was home again.

A friend from Abu Dhabi ended up being there at the same time as me, and we hiked up Mount Batur. It was my 300th day sober. The sky was pitch black as we began our ascent, but as we got to the top, the golden-orange sun rose over the mountain and peeked at us beyond the cloud-dusted horizon. I felt an overwhelming sense of clarity and peace. For the next chapter of my life, this was where I was meant to be. Not the desert. The jungle.

Climbing Mount Batur was a powerful experience for me, so much so that I like to include it as part of my Sober Girls Yoga retreats in Bali. In January 2023, I wrote on *Facebook*:

On day three of my Sober Girls Yoga retreats in Bali, I always take my group for a sunrise hike up Mount Batur. This is stunning and not to be missed when you visit Bali! We leave at 3am from the retreat center and then hike through the darkness in order to be at the top, the volcano crater – for sunrise.

It's a challenging hike, and each person gets there in their own time and in their own way. Some people race to the top. Others move slowly and steadily. Some stumble along the way. Some need a holding hand reaching out for stability and support. Some become that holding hand for others. Some decide to hire a motorbike for part of the way. Accompanied by two tour guides, plus me – we make sure that no one gets left behind. And at the end, we all congregate at the top and have a hot chocolate or hot coffee to celebrate. As we have our beverage, we watch the orange sunrise peek through the clouds over the mountain top.

When we got to the top today, I reflected on how this hike is much like sobriety. Every single person's journey along the way looks different. Some people use the twelve steps. Others find support in a rehabilitation program. Some people choose sobriety on their own. Some people become sober in one attempt, others have blips, setbacks and resets. Some people choose modern online sobriety programs – like Sober Girls Yoga is today.

Much like today's hike, sobriety is not a competition. There's no prize for who gets to the top first. There are no awards. No one wins at the hike. Just like sobriety is not a race. There's no prize for who is the most sober or who has the most days sober.

There are several paths to get up the mountain – just like there are several ways to become sober. And the only thing that matters is that you have the courage to start the climb.

I set off walking down the winding, humid, bustling streets of Ubud and followed the GPS map for the home of Ketut Liyer. Dodging motorbikes piled high with dogs, stacks of wheat, boxes of tools and families of five all wedged onto the seat of the bike, I walked past vegan cafes (stopping in one for coconut ice cream!), crystal shops and market stalls piled high with fresh fruits and vegetables. I was rereading *Eat, Pray, Love*, and I'd decided to try and find him: the infamous medicine man whom Elizabeth Gilbert met when she was in Bali, almost twenty years ago.

At this point, I was annoyed with Dan, my psychic, and I didn't believe in psychics anymore – but I also had an idea. What if I went to see this Ketut Liyer, and I didn't tell him anything about myself, about Dan, or about my dreams? If he said the same things as Dan, then I'd know Dan had spoken the truth. Or maybe, he'd say something completely different. Maybe he'd say that Lucas was the one, and I should just stay in teaching. Either way, I was curious. It wouldn't hurt to meet him.

I found the pale green sign at the end of the road. 'House of Ketut Liyer, Medicine Man and Healing'. When I arrived, I poked my head in the gateway and was met by a woman who was balancing a basket full of Balinese offerings on top of her head. The basket was piled high with incense, colorful flowers and crackers.

"I'm looking for Ketut Liyer," I told her.

"He died," she said.

"He's dead?"

"Died."

The old Alex would have been disappointed to have walked all this way, only to find out that this respected healer was no longer living. But I was at the stage in my journey where every single thing happened for a reason. Every moment. The universe had my back, and there were no mistakes.

"But you can meet his son, who does healings too. Nyomang."

My face lit up. "Oh! That is great! Yes!"

Lucas texted me back a few hours later that his father had died at the same time that I'd sent him that message. It was a sad ending. I was learning how to love and let go. That's what I'd been learning to do the entire time that I'd been inhabiting planet Earth. How to love and how to gracefully let go of the things that were not meant for me.

Going to Bali ended up being the best decision that I made in early 2020. Not long afterwards, the world would go into full lockdown, and travel wouldn't be an option until 2021.

PART SEVEN

Crown *Chakra* – I Honor the Divine Teacher Within Me

The seventh *chakra* is the crown *chakra*, or the *sahasrara chakra*. In English, it translates to 'thousand-fold'. Its purpose is awakening, understanding and consciousness. When it's out of balance, we may experience attachment or ignorance. When it is in balance, we will experience awareness and intelligence (Judith 34 – 35).

CROWN *CHAKRA* MEDITATION SERIES: MEDITATIONS FOR DIFFICULT EMOTIONS

I have been living with a mood disorder, anxiety and chronic stress since I was a child and teenager. These mental health issues went undiagnosed, leading me regulate and manage my mental health struggles with the two things that helped: alcohol and yoga. I began teaching yoga at age twenty-one, and although I knew it was my life purpose, my self-doubt and my drinking problems held me back.

Once I got sober, I no longer had booze to help me regulate my nervous system, leading me to get more and more passionate and serious about mindfulness, yoga and meditation to manage my moods. And this is why I've created this ten-part series for you: "Meditations for Difficult Emotions". There are three yoga practices and seven meditation practices that are your go-to if you're experiencing extreme mind-body states and need to anchor, reconnect and regulate yourself. Note: I do not encourage stopping taking your medication during this program.

https://bit.ly/TMLP_MeditationsForDifficultEmotions

CROWN *CHAKRA* PHOTO LIBRARY: BUILDING THE MINDFUL LIFE PRACTICE

In this photo album, I share some images from the creation of the Mindful Life Practice:

https://bit.ly/TMLP_BuildingTheMindfulLifePractice

CHAPTER 54

"YOU DO WHAT YOU THINK IS RIGHT"

Everyone has a different story about how they lived and experienced 2020. Whether they were stuck abroad away from home, lost their jobs, or were confined in isolation with a young baby, everyone has a different version of the same period. While we all experienced the same storm, we completed the voyage on different boats.

My version of the story is as follows: a week after I returned from Bali in 2020, towards the end of February, Lucas and I went out for coffee. The goal of this meetup was to gain closure on our relationship. He had just gotten back from Italy, where an outbreak of the Coronavirus disease (Covid-19) had overwhelmed the country. As we were sitting in the restaurant, our phones lit up, and we got the news that two hotels on Yas Island, about ten minutes away from where we were, had been suddenly locked down after Covid cases were found there too.

Just a few short months prior to this coffee meetup, Lucas, Lynda and I had begun planning the gym's very first yoga retreat, and ten participants had registered. This trip was slated to run in Nepal in March 2020. Discussions grew every day amongst us in a *WhatsApp* group. Should we run the retreat, or should we cancel it? At some point in late February, we made the decision to cancel the event. Not long after, at the very beginning of March, the world began shutting down. The schools in Abu Dhabi were already closed. Gyms in Canada were closed. Kuwait was in lockdown.

Lucas and I spoke every day via text about options for the gym. At this point, even though I was no longer his partner, Lucas made it clear that I still had a place and a role at the gym as a future manager. I researched platform options for when the inevitable happened – and we would have to pivot to an online model. When I found the platform for the company that I thought would be best – what was once called *Namastream* and is now *Marvelous* – he texted back, "We can do this – together."

It felt like the world was slowly ending. Despite Lucas' and my preparations and our texts back and forth in reference to the foreseeable shutdown, day by day, the time continued to fly by, and the United Arab Emirates government still hadn't declared any shutdowns. I taught full classes of yoga, spin and barre. Because the government hadn't mandated any closures, Lucas didn't want to make the decision.

Looking back, now that I am a business owner myself, I understand. Bricks and mortar business owners were put in unbelievably heart-wrenching positions, including gym managers. The gym had been Lucas' dream. And so many employees' livelihoods depended on them. Until the government told them that they had no choice, they did not want to shut the gym down.

On Tuesday night of the first week of March, the school had already been shut down – put on early spring break – and I drove over to the gym to teach my candlelit yin yoga class. The same group of people attended the class every week. All throughout the class, one of my regular students, James, had a dry, harsh cough.

I walked around the room, providing hands-on adjustments in *savāsana*, as I always did. At the end of the practice, I caught James on the way out of class.

"Are you okay?" I asked him.

He said he had seen his doctor, and he had a dry cough. "Don't worry, I do not have coronavirus," he reassured me, with a chuckle.

But at that point, we knew nothing about Covid – how it would hit our systems, who would be okay and who would not be.

My fear was never that I would die of Covid – my fear was that by unknowingly carrying the virus and passing it onto someone else, I would be the cause of their death. Trying to prevent the spread of coronavirus was my act of *ahiṃsā*, or loving kindness. The role and responsibility that I had in this moment as a student of yoga was to put everything that I had learned into practice.

I bought a thermometer and started regularly monitoring myself. I had no cough and no sore throat, but a slightly elevated temperature of thirty-eight degrees Celsius was enough to convince me.

"Lucas, I think I have coronavirus."

I was panicking and spiraling, and I sent him screenshots of Covid statistics around the world and photos of my thermometer giving me a slightly above average temperature result. All of the world leaders were telling us to stay home because we could unknowingly pass on the virus. This advice was being given long before people were regularly being tested for Covid.

"Lucas, we need to close the gym. I am not okay with teaching yoga in person. This is not safe anymore."

He refused to close the gym, but I didn't want to teach in person anymore. I offered to livestream my classes. I suggested that my classes could test out the new platform, for when they decided to go online. He said no.

At a time when the world was shutting down, and there was an impending disaster, teaching yoga was extremely important to everyone's mental health and well-being – myself included – so I didn't want to cancel my classes. But teaching in person, at a time when the rest of the world was social distancing, did not feel

I wandered into the house. An assistant helped me to get dressed in a yellow patterned sarong with a fluorescent pink sash, which I wore around my waist, in traditional Balinese style. When it was my turn to speak to Nyomang, I was invited to sit on the porch, legs crossed, just like Elizabeth Gilbert did in *Eat, Pray, Love*. I outstretched my hand.

Nyomang smiled and asked me, "What is your name?"

I told him, "Alexandra."

He cupped his hands around the back of my right hand and lifted my palm closer to his eye level. He carefully and slowly examined the lines on my palm, following the wrinkles with his fingers. "Are you a yoga teacher?" he asked. My eyes widened. Then he said, "Alexandra, soon you will become a very successful yoga teacher. People will be saying your name. 'Alexandra. Alexandra. Alexandra.' You will come back next year to Bali, with your boyfriend. You will be very happy."

I felt excited about the idea of returning to Bali, but I doubted that Lucas was going to come with me. Maybe that meant that there was someone else out there for me, and Lucas was not the one. Maybe that meant that Dan was right. And I certainly didn't know how I was supposed to go about becoming this successful yoga teacher – I barely had a following on social media and I'd signed the contract to return to the school.

In spite of all of these uncertainties that were running through my mind, Bali gave me the energetic space to do what I so desperately needed to do – to end my relationship with Lucas. There is something about this island, Bali, and the energy inside of it – I can't describe it. I loved him, but he was not the one. He was tiptoeing out of my life, waiting for me to cut the cord. I finally texted him, saying, "We need to end this. This isn't working for either of us." Before he could respond, I put the phone in airplane mode and back in my bag. While resting in child's pose and listening to 'The Scientist' by Coldplay, I cried. The lyrics, which described how difficult it is to lose someone, felt poignant.

right either. His solution was to get substitute yoga teachers for my classes. I said no. I wanted to continue to teach. Yoga is my purpose and my passion. I needed it as much as my yoga students did.

But my moral compass was screaming at me to 'STAY. HOME'.

I called my mom in a panic. "I don't know what to do. The gym wants me to carry on teaching in person. But if I do that, I'm so worried that I'll pass on the coronavirus. What if I am an asymptomatic carrier, and someone dies from my yoga class? But I don't want to stop teaching."

I will never forget what she said in that moment because it was probably the best advice that I've ever been given. She said, "Alex, this is a global pandemic. You will remember the decisions that you made during this time for the rest of your life. So, make a decision that will make you proud when you look back on it." And she was right.

It turns out that I didn't even have to make the decision. I'd been checking the schedule every day to see if the gym was closed. A few days later, in early March, I woke up one day and checked the schedule and saw that my name was no longer on it. They had found other yoga teachers to substitute for my yoga classes. I had put my heart and soul into this gym, and it was like I didn't work there anymore. They didn't even contact me to let me know. Just. Like. That.

There seemed to be a ton of misinformation and confusion, for some reason, between me and all of the team members at the gym. Lucas was my primary point of contact, yet for some reason, everything seemed to get miscommunicated between all of us. So, I sent a mass email, cc-ing everyone on management, articulating that I was sad to see myself removed from the schedule, asking if I had their permission to teach my own yoga classes on *Zoom* and inquiring as to whether it would impact my future career with the gym.

Lucas called me. And in summary, he said the words, "Alex, you do what you think is right."

"Lucas, what does that mean?! Are you okay with it, or are you not?"

He made me feel like I was asking for too much. Like I was overreacting. "Alex, I don't have time to have these conversations with you repeatedly. You just need to do what you think is right."

So that was it. I needed to do what I thought was right. I thought about it for a few hours.

What I thought was right was offering yoga classes on *Zoom*.

So, I did what I thought was right.

I put out a survey, asking on *Instagram* if anyone wanted to do yoga with me. Sixty-one people responded yes and provided their email addresses. All these years, I was convinced that I wasn't good enough. I was convinced that if I started my own thing, no one would join me. I was convinced that I wouldn't have a community. But I did. And that group grew. Quickly.

After I made the decision to offer yoga classes on *Zoom*, I never heard from Lucas again. He and the other managers of the gym promised that they'd contact me when they were ready for me to teach online from home, but they never did. I saw on his *Instagram* story that, not long after we last spoke, he'd returned home to Greece. He had finally left the gym and the United Arab Emirates behind, to be where he'd always wanted to be. He didn't even tell me. It seemed like 'You do what you think is right' was code for 'You start your own thing, and it's over'. It was heartbreaking to lose my partner, my yoga students and my gym community overnight. But I had no regrets. I'd done what he'd told me to do. I did what I thought was right. I poured my heartbreak into growing my own community online.

I see it clearly now, looking back. When I finally stopped pouring all of my time and energy into Lucas' dream, and I funneled all of that effort and passion into my own business, everything finally came together. What had started as sixty-one people, who had expressed interest in my online yoga classes, was quickly growing into many more. All along, I had been terrified of starting my own business because I didn't think that I was good enough or capable enough to do this on my own. But all of a sudden, I was starting to find my confidence. I believed in myself – because I had no other option. It is said that when one door closes, another door opens. When the gym fired me, I was able to open up another door – as well as all of the windows – and all of my dreams, plans and ideas came rushing in like a breath of fresh air.

Months prior to this, I'd bought the domain name for The Mindful Life Practice, taken the *Instagram* handle, had a friend produce a jingle and had a brainstorming session about a thirty-day challenge. I even paid for a logo design and had started a *Facebook* group for Sober Girls Yoga. In spite of all of the progress that I had made with my business, I'd abandoned my momentum to focus on the gym that Lucas managed. However, two weeks into the lockdown, everything just naturally fell into place, and I finally created that thirty-day challenge with The Mindful Life Practice that I'd thought of months before. When I first started practicing yoga, back in 2010, I had joined a thirty-day yoga challenge at my studio, and it had been an integral component of my healing journey. I wanted to provide that same experience for others, at a time when they so desperately needed it.

I didn't know if I'd have any takers. But I had forty people sign up for that first challenge in April. The program was a mixture of live and on-demand classes. I had also recorded every class that I'd taught since the beginning of March, and I wasn't sure what I'd do with them, and suddenly it became clear. I'd create a database of classes, and then if people couldn't attend the live classes, they could replay the on-demand ones. And just like that, The Mindful Life Practice had begun.

On my birthday, April 7th, I had seventy friends come on a *Zoom* call with me to take a yoga class. The year prior, I felt like I had no friends on my birthday. And this year, I had seventy. I realized that no one was going to create my loving community for me. I had to create this space for myself. I had to do what I thought was right.

CHAPTER 55

STEPPING INTO MY PURPOSE

In June 2020, after The Mindful Life Practice took off, I was still working on life coaching, but it hadn't gained momentum. I didn't know why. Because I had been searching for my own path in life only a year before, I had decided to niche down and become a 'life purpose coach' to help others, like me, in their quests to discover their life goals. I'd coached ten different people over the course of a year. Many of these people had come to me through *Instagram* or friends of friends. What I found was that nine out of ten of them had the same issue: although finding their life purpose interested them, they really wanted help with giving up alcohol. I'd coached them under the guise of helping them to find their life purpose, but in reality, I ended up assisting them with their desire to become sober, maintain an alcohol-free lifestyle, and learn how to navigate the world without the use of drinking.

After teaching online from home since March 2020, in June, I had to drop back into my classroom at school to clear it out for the summer. The Mindful Life Practice hadn't built up enough that I could quit my job, unfortunately, so I would be returning for another school year. I walked into the classroom, and there was a letter sitting on my desk from one of my former coaching clients, who was also a colleague at my school. She'd made ninety days sober, which she credited to my support. At the end of the letter, she wrote, "Thank you for saving my life."

And that's when I knew that during that chapter of my life, I was meant to become a sober coach. For the next few years, I

The idea for Sober Girls Yoga came to me in January 2020. The original logos that I designed were neon pink. They've since subdued a lot. I also already had a *Facebook* group for the community. But I just hadn't started developing the program. I had the ideas but none of the follow through.

After I became a sober coach, my business gradually and naturally started coming together. Today, Sober Girls Yoga includes an online thirty-day challenge (https://bit.ly/TMLP_30-daySoberChallenge) to help women quit drinking for a period of time and start practicing yoga. There is also an option for participants to extend to a sixty-day challenge. Additionally, I offer other in-depth programs, which occur over a longer period of time and help members deepen their spirituality. I am always the core facilitator of these groups. There are usually two or three other assistant facilitators with each group, who have graduated from one of the yoga teacher training programs themselves.

The thirty and sixty-day programs are a deep dive into the *chakras* and use the *chakra* model as a method to bring about holistic healing. This model allows participants to reflect on and set goals for a variety of areas of their lives, such as their mental and physical health, their relationships with family and friends, their management of finances, and their ability to express themselves authentically … to name a few.

The Sober Girls Yoga programs also encourage participants to begin incorporating yoga into their daily routines. What's the benefit of daily yoga in the Sober Girls Yoga programs? What's the benefit of practicing yoga in sobriety? There are five key scientific reasons as to why a daily yoga practice is instrumental in helping our challenge participants to heal. The first relates to the nervous system. Yoga is beneficial because it has been proven to positively impact the nervous system and reduce stress (Forbes 79). Scientific studies have also established that yoga is able to alter brain chemistry more efficiently than regular exercise, as it stimulates the relaxation response (87). Third, yoga helps practitioners bring attention to the present moment, and present moment awareness is a key element in relieving symptoms of anxiety (90–93). Another advantage of yoga is its ability to help us to cultivate self-awareness without judgment. This increased introspection enables us to observe our patterns, habits and tendencies and consider how we can make positive changes to our lives off our yoga mats (97–98). And lastly, yoga can help us to have an embodied experience. The insights that we gain from feeling connected to our bodies in the present moment can often have a long-lasting and advantageous impact on our mental health (Forbes 102).

Habit changing specialists have often advocated that when you have a bad habit, you should replace it with a good one. And that is why I have found that committing to a daily yoga practice can be tremendously valuable. Program participants are replacing their daily habit of drinking alcohol with the daily habit of getting onto their yoga mats. My members are also able to draw on the Sober Yoga Girls community – whether they're regularly attending the live *Zoom* calls or just engaging with the *Facebook* group (https://www.facebook.com/groups/sobergirlsyoga – free for all sober-curious women) and our other private community channels.

Personally, I have found the experience of running this program to be extremely rewarding – it feels like I am providing others with the support that I once wished that I had. This community became a shelter for me as much as it was a shelter for my members. Sober Girls Yoga allows me to integrate all of my individual skill sets – both my background in coaching and my experience as a yoga teacher – into one program, which is offered virtually over *Zoom*. Through the creation of these challenges, I have been able to provide my clients with an experience that is unique – just as Dan had predicted.

Many of those who complete the thirty and sixty-day challenges and other programs that I offer, go on to become students in my yoga teacher training programs (YTTs). These YTTs are beneficial not only for those who want to teach yoga one day, but also for those who want to become students of yoga and learn more. In 2021, I graduated the very first group of YTT students from The Mindful Life Practice.

As of 2024, at the time of publishing this book, I've graduated hundreds of students from my programs. Currently, I offer the 200-hour yoga teacher training program in several formats: there is an online option on *Zoom*, which takes place over seven months (https://www.themindfullifepractice.com/online-200-hour-yoga-teacher-training); a twenty-one day program that meets in person in Bali (https://www.themindfullifepractice.com/bali-200-hour); and a hybrid version that is comprised of four months online and ten days in Bali. It's my long-term goal to offer these yoga teacher trainings at other retreat centers, elsewhere in the world.

Additionally, I lead a 300-hour advanced yoga teacher training (https://www.themindfullifepractice.com/online-300-hour-ytt) with a focus on mental health. 100 hours of this program is a *Yoga Sūtra* study, or in-depth study into the *Pātañjalayogasūtra* text, a key guiding philosophy for me on my journey. You can enroll in this program as a stand-alone course or as part of the complete 300-hour advanced program. There are also modules in other subjects, including: *prāṇāyāma* for mental wellness, meditation for mental wellness, *āsana* adjustments and assists, and yoga entrepreneurship. (You can learn about this here: https://www.themindfullifepractice.com/online-300-hour-ytt).

We also offer a membership to The Mindful Life Practice where members can access yoga classes and sober girls club meetings live on *Zoom* with me (https://themindfullifepractice.uscreen.io/catalog). Additionally, there are several years' worth of on-demand classes, which were recorded in the past, that are available for members to use on our app, *Mindful Life*, at any time.

After having run my business for several years now, I realize that I am ever-evolving, and the community is ever-evolving. As a result of these ever-changing dynamics, I am constantly generating new programs, offerings and ideas. In 2024, at the time of publishing this book, I've organized my own yoga retreats around the world. I have hosted retreats in Mexico, Bali, the United Arab Emirates, India and Canada. Additionally, I've been invited to teach yoga on retreats for several big sobriety influencers around the world. For seven months, I was the Lead Vinyasa Teacher on faculty at a Yoga Teacher Training School in Bali. So not only do I offer several online programs, but I have several in-person offerings now, too. The Mindful Life Practice will always be growing, changing and evolving, like me – as I grow, change and evolve, too.

CHAPTER 56

TWO ARROWS FLY

The Buddhists say that when misfortune strikes, two arrows fly – one being the event itself, and the other being our reaction to it (Nathan). This reaction, or story, has a word in yoga too: *sanskāra*. A *sanskāra* refers to a subtle karmic impression. According to expert Pandit Rajmani Tiguṇait:

> Whatever actions we perform through this mortal part of ourselves – physical, verbal, or mental – create impressions in the unconscious mind. They are stored there in the form of *sanskāra(s)* and motivate our mind, senses, and body to undertake more actions. This vicious cycle never ends unless we apply the techniques of spiritual discipline... Once you attain freedom from the *sanskāra(s)* stored in the unconscious, semi-mortal part of your being, however, you realize that you are pure Atman, the eternal Self, which is not subject to either birth or death. Such a realized person is 'immortal' (Rajmani Tiguṇait).

One of my most formative relationship experiences was the love pentagon between Nick, Claire, Tori, Chelsea and I. He was dating many of us at the same time, pitting us against each other, gaslighting us and playing us as fools. This experience, at such a young age, shook me to my core. It was a realization that not all people are intrinsically good. It was a realization that the true relationship was not how I perceived it to be at the time. I was committed to Nick, but he was not committed to me. I was furious with him and disturbed by the situation. My paranoia had me convinced that, everywhere I went, I was the laughingstock of the university campus. I couldn't get over the fact that our relationship wasn't 'real', that my version of events wasn't 'true', and that I didn't know the 'real' Nick. How could he do this to so many women?

At that time, I remember promising myself that I'd never fall for it again. I'd never let a guy force me to keep a relationship secret. I'd never ignore red flags when they appeared, such as a man villainizing his exes. I'd never ignore my gut.

About a year after I ended things with Lucas, and months after I wrote this book, it came to light that my adult relationship hadn't been as different from my relationship with Nick as I had thought. What I had perceived at the time as love and a connection between 'soulmates' ended up only being one side of the story. In reality and unbeknownst to me, he had been dating multiple other women all along, and as if that wasn't enough, he also had a wife and a family back in Greece.

I was truly shocked when I learned about this betrayal, but I also think there was a part of me that was aware of it all along and in denial. Once the evidence was visible, reality sank in, and I was able to let go of my denial and accept it for what it was. Dan, my psychic, had told me about Lucas' unfaithfulness since the beginning. And once I came to terms with what had happened, I realized that there were so many similarities between Lucas and Nick. Both had love-bombed me and befriended me over a long period of time before suddenly telling me that they thought we were soulmates. Both had forced me to keep our relationship a secret, citing various individuals who would be upset by it. Both vilified their exes, called them 'psychos' and told stories about how unstable they were. Both had claimed to have various women in their lives who were 'stalking them'. And both had the ability to lie and would do it right in front of me – lying about their would work with women and help them to change the entire trajectory of their lives by going alcohol free. I also strove to infuse spirituality and community into their journeys.

As soon as I changed my name to 'Sober Yoga Girl' and identified myself as a sober coach, I was flooded by direct messages on *Instagram*. Almost immediately, I began working one-on-one with several individuals around the world. What I've learned is that the secret I so deeply tried to conceal for so long is a problem that a lot of people in our society have. In fact, according to recent research conducted by Veylinx, "More than 75% of Americans surveyed said they've temporarily given up alcohol for at least a month, [a]lmost half (46%) of drinkers said they are trying to reduce their alcohol consumption right now" and 52% indicated that they are substituting "alcohol with non-alcoholic beverages" ("Tips and tricks for drinking less"). If you are having trouble with your relationship with alcohol, don't worry. You're not alone. And it's not your fault. Because alcohol is addictive.

Every individual should have the power to define his or her own sober journey. Whether you call yourself 'teetotal', 'sober', 'alcohol free', 'a recovered alcoholic', or something else is completely up to you. Personally, I have never liked the word 'alcoholic'. That's because I think it places all of the blame on the individual, and no blame on the alcohol.

Alcohol is an addictive drug. Like nicotine, like opioids, like caffeine. But we don't call people who are addicted to cigarettes, cigarette-a-holics, do we? We don't shame them into carrying this label for the rest of their lives. We don't call them 'dry smokers' if they have given up smoking but not participated in a program. So why do we refer to drinkers in these ways?

My mission, in my work as a sober coach and the owner of The Mindful Life Practice, is to show individuals that you don't need substances to be your best self. You don't need to be an alcoholic to give up alcohol. And you don't need to hit rock bottom before deciding that it's day one.

whereabouts when the phone would ring. Both times, I thought that this dishonesty was a romantic secret.

Learning the truth about Lucas shook me and devastated me. With Nick, it took me a few months to fully accept the truth of what had happened – with Lucas it took over a year. How could I not see that I was in an unhealthy relationship again – and only make the connection a year later? But hindsight is 20/20. I couldn't beat myself up for what I didn't know. When this information came to light, I debated about what to do with the memoir. I wrote this book as if Lucas was the greatest love of my life.

The old Alex would feel the need to rewrite the story now that she knew the truth. But something had changed within me. The memoir is not about these two men – the memoir is about me. These men are not the main characters of this story – I am. There are many sides of every story, and this book is my side of my story. Not theirs. Rewriting the part of the story in which Lucas appeared didn't feel important because at the time that we were together, I perceived us as being in love.

Even the way that I was reacting to this new version of reality was different. When I learned that Nick had been deceiving me all those years ago, I allowed the revelation of his cheating to rock my whole world and change my definition and understanding of the relationship. This experience was heartbreaking. This time, with Lucas, I didn't react in the same ways. I didn't beat myself up for falling for his lies. I didn't worry that I looked like a fool to anyone else who knew me at the time. I was able to realize that, even if he cheated on me, hurt me and was dishonest with me the entire time, these actions don't change the role that he played in my life as I perceived it to be at the time. He helped me to feel lovable again after so long, move past my divorce, and move forward towards my dreams. He believed in me before I even believed in myself. In the early days, our relationship was one of the happiest times of my life. I don't have to rewrite my version of the story and the part of the memoir in which he appears just because I now know the truth to be different.

The universe sends us the same lessons repeatedly, until it teaches us what we need to learn. It sends us the same lessons over and over again, only to test how far we have grown. How far we have come. And in the words of Gabby Bernstein, "We will continue to meet the same person in different bodies until we show up for the universal lesson." I began to have deep epiphanies about my own childhood, and why I was attracted to certain people.

When Nick hurt me in my early twenties, I was stuck in the mindset of 'Why has this happened *to* me?' In this second relationship, I was able to see the beauty that Lucas brought to my life – not just the pain. I was able to see that this had happened not *to* me but *for* me. It's because of Lucas that I am a barre instructor and a spinning instructor. And it's due to Lucas' actions that I left the gym and finally started to put into motion all of the ideas that I had around The Mindful Life Practice, Sober Girls Yoga, and my yoga teacher trainings and retreats. It's because of Nick that I formed such a beautiful friendship and bond with Claire, which carried me through my early years in the Middle East. Likewise, through Lucas, I have forged lifelong female friendships with his other victims. The purpose of my listing all of the blessings that stemmed from these relationships is not to forgive Lucas or Nick or to say that what they did is okay – instead, it is to assert that, through them, I have learned so much. Had these things not happened to me, I wouldn't be who I am today.

I also knew that Lucas and Nick weren't hurting me on purpose. Don Miguel Ruiz wrote *The Four Agreements*, and one of them is "Don't take anything personally" (47). Neither of them cheated, manipulated, or lied to me because of me. They did it because of them. Lucas clearly was acting out of his own unresolved trauma and pain. Unfortunately, I just happened to be on his path. He never singled me out to hurt me. Me being his victim had nothing to do with me and everything to do with him. This ability for me to accept the reality of what had taken place during Lucas' and my relationship, but not attach any baggage to it, and not allow it to change or destroy my story with him, that was the real marker of growth. It was in this moment that I was able to clearly see how much I had transformed during my journey.

CHAPTER 57

THE REST IS HISTORY

In May, June and July of 2021, everything started to come together. I happened to be in the right place at the right time when someone suggested that I run a Sober Girls Yoga brunch at their venue. It was fully booked. I met an Emirati who owned a yacht that, for most of the time, was docked in the Yas Island Marina, and with his encouragement, I launched a monthly yacht cruise featuring yoga, alcohol-free wine and beer and a women's circle. I then happened to meet and befriend the owner of a five-star hotel in the UAE, who invited me to host a yoga retreat at his property. And, in June 2021, I hosted my first yoga retreat. Even more proof that once you step into your *dharma*, everything falls into place. It was a few weeks later when I officially resigned from my teaching job – for the final time. This is what I wrote on *Facebook* about my decision:

June 30, 2021
Tomorrow is my last day in the classroom, and I can't help but look back on my teaching career with nostalgia. I moved to Kuwait at twenty-three to become a teacher. That first year was the best and most challenging year of my life. With mental health challenges, culture shock and a particularly tough group of kids, I spent most of that year crying. I'll never forget my colleague coming into my room one day in October and genuinely asking, "Alex, do you think you'll survive until the end of the year?" Between sobs, I said to

him that I'd have to stay until March because my mom had already booked her flight to visit me.

Six years later, I'm still in the Middle East, and I have launched a business here, so I guess my time in the Gulf got better! But seriously, teaching is one of the hardest jobs in the world. It got easier when I moved to the paradise of a school I've been at in Abu Dhabi for the past four years. I ended up here by a stroke of luck. I left an apartment full of stuff in Kuwait while I was out on a mystery sick leave due to my mental health falling apart (which I was afraid to tell anyone about at the time because of the stigma around mental health conditions). After I'd recovered, I needed a fresh start – by chance, I received a recruitment email for a job that had opened up in the late fall in Abu Dhabi. I got so lucky. It's one of the best schools in Abu Dhabi. While this past year with the Covid pandemic has been particularly tough, I'm immensely grateful for the way that I've been supported, loved and cared for by my community while I lost and found myself over the past four years and started the side hustle that eventually became my current full-time job.

Beginning my business has been so scary and so hard, and I've worked my butt off for three years to get to this point – with very few days off (if any). When not at school, I have worked every evening and every weekend, and I have missed countless events and special occasions because I had to work. I have set my social life aside. It's been so, so hard. But when you love what you do, and you want to build a business doing what you love, I've learned that so many sacrifices must be made.

The next chapter is daunting, but I've been working hard to get here, so I can't turn back now. Time to dive off into the deep end. Let's hope that I float!

The Sober Girls Yoga challenges, weekend retreats in the UAE, events, workshops, classes and online yoga teacher trainings were in full swing and growing. I had been featured on national news, radio shows and podcasts in the Middle East. I was making my mark on that region of the world as 'Sober Yoga Girl'. I had full intentions of remaining in Abu Dhabi full time, getting a new apartment, outfitting it with furniture, and setting up Wi-Fi at my new place.

But, for some reason, at this point in my journey, every single logistical thing kept going wrong. For example, my residence visa wasn't properly canceled by the school, but my healthcare was – and without being able to create a new proper residence visa, I couldn't get new healthcare. On the day that I was meant to move into my new apartment, it wasn't ready. I signed the wrong lease by mistake. I couldn't seem to get in touch with the building management to book the elevator on my apartment move-out day. Whatever could go wrong, did go wrong.

After this run of bad luck, I finally got settled into a new apartment in Abu Dhabi, which I loved. Even so, something about my fresh start didn't feel right. And I couldn't explain what it was.

I decided to drive down to Dubai to meet with Dan, for the first time since January of 2020, to receive some guidance from him.

"I see you on an island..." he said. "Maybe it's Greece."

I knew immediately when he said it. "Dan, it's not Greece. It's Bali."

"So go to Bali," he said.

"But how will I move to Bali? What about my cat? What about my car? What about all of my stuff?"

"Find somewhere to park your car. Find someone to look after your cat. Put your stuff in storage." Dan said all of this matter-of-factly, as if it were easy.

"But what about the new lease for the apartment that I just signed?"

"Can you get out of it?"

"What about getting a visa to enter Bali? There are no tourist visas."

"Are you sure there's no way?"

"And what about having to quarantine for a week in Jakarta?"

"Just quarantine for a week in Jakarta."

The whole thing seemed crazy to me. To just pack up and leave this life that I'd spent years creating. But I slept on it, and by the next day, I started selling my furniture and belongings online. A few weeks after that session with Dan, I moved to Bali. I packed up all of my things, put them in storage, and arranged for one of the managers of The Mindful Life Practice to take care of my cat, Princess. I parked my car with my mover in a suburb outside of Abu Dhabi. And then I got on the plane to Bali. And the rest is history.

CHAPTER 58

UBUD MEANS MEDICINE

The word *ubud* means 'medicine'. "As far back as the eighth century, royal families, from across the island of Bali, sent their" sick family members to be cured in Ubud (Beck). Now, Ubud has become a magical place for people all around the world to come for healing. Ubud has a sacred water temple called Tirta Empul, where you can bathe in its holy water and be cleansed from bad spirits. It is also common for Balinese people to consult Balinese healers, called Balians, instead of or in addition to receiving treatment from a medical professional who specializes in western medicine. Whether it is a malady that affects an individual's physical health or mental health, Balian healers are able to make use of natural remedies to heal many illnesses (Beck). Raw foods, essential oils, and detox practices are found everywhere. There are plenty of yoga studios that offer every style of yoga and an ample amount of retreat centers. An energy of healing, health and wellness radiates from Ubud.

When I arrived in Ubud in 2017, returned in 2020, and moved here in 2021, I had a firm belief about my body and my health. I thought that western medicine was the answer. Doctors told me that I would be on bipolar mood stabilizers for the rest of my life, and I thought that anyone who told me otherwise – in other words, the people that I met in Ubud – had something wrong with them. I thought that acne was part of my genetic makeup because my grandfather had it. I assumed that psoriasis was part of my genetic makeup because my nana had it. I concluded that migraines were something that I would have to live with for the rest of my life.

But somewhere inside of me, there was a little voice telling me that there was another way. There *must* be another way. I just had to find this alternative pathway. And this is why Ubud, in particular, was calling me.

Our environment shapes who we are. I'm the prime example of this: in each place where I lived – whether in my parents' house in Canada, or in my apartments in Kuwait, Abu Dhabi and Bali, I became a very different person. And that's because everything, from our beliefs to our values to our perceptions of the world, are taught to us. We learn them from the world around us. I came into Bali with one philosophy of life, yet after living in Ubud for around four or five months, I began to wonder how all of these people who were avoiding western medicine seemed so healthy and free – so much healthier and happier than the majority of people that I had met living in Kuwait, Abu Dhabi and Toronto.

In January of 2022, I began leading an online 300-hour advanced yoga teacher training that specialized in yoga and mental health. One of my yoga teacher training students recommended a book to me entitled *Own Your Self* written by Dr Kelly Brogan, a psychiatrist who takes an alternative approach to mental health, involving holistic recovery. As a result of reading this book, I began to contemplate the root causes of mental illness in our current society. I started to wonder, with the massive number of people around the world who are now being diagnosed with 'incurable' mental health conditions – myself included – and the huge increase in mental health medication – with one in four women taking a mental health drug daily (Bekiempis) – is it possible that our modern-day environment is having a massive impact on our overall sense of well-being? Perhaps more so than genetics? After all, if medication for mental health was only invented thirty or forty years ago, how did cultures historically manage mood? Is it possible that our modern diets are causing these mood swings or worsening them?

Then, unrelated (or so I thought...), in August of 2022, I went to see a naturopathic doctor about my acne. I had tried everything that western medicine recommended, from salicylic acid peels, to medications, to removing my IUD, to face masks. I decided to google 'acne doctors in Bali'. A naturopathic doctor was recommended. When I went to meet her and told her about my struggles with acne, she asked me, "What else is wrong with you?"

"Nothing," I said.

"Nothing?" she asked.

As she continued to ask questions, I realized that there was a lot wrong with me other than acne: psoriasis, childhood migraines and bipolar disorder.

What I discovered and have been learning is that my 'hereditary illnesses', which I have been dealing with throughout my life, were not just random. According to the healers in Bali, my persistent ailments were signs from my body. "The best doctor is the doctor within," they explained. My body was inflamed, and it was sending me signals. Psoriasis outbreaks from the age of one, splitting migraines from the age of six, mood episodes from the age of fifteen, acne from my mid-twenties. Exhaustion. Dizziness. Fatigue. Inability to get up in the morning. All of these things were not just randomly happening to me or happening because my family members had these illnesses, too. They were all signs. My brain and body were saying, "Alex, this way that you're living, it's not working."

Throughout my twenties, I didn't understand the connection between my lifestyle and my overall sense of health and well-being. Consequently, I followed western doctors' recommendations. I kept taking more and different medications – birth control pills, topical creams, mood stabilizers and salicylic acid peels, to name a few. One of the problems with our medical model in the west, however, is that although doctors, parents, teachers and friends are extolling the virtues of a healthy diet and telling one another to 'eat healthy', there is an overall lack of clarity surrounding this advice. What does it even mean to eat healthy? That is so vague.

The naturopathic doctor that I saw in Ubud encouraged me to stop taking my mood stabilizing drugs and seek alternative therapy. She recommended that I both reduce my medication over a period of time and try a fast for seven days, and then I could start reintegrating foods and see what triggered both my moods and my skin. I want to mention, as well, that fasting and/or weaning off psychiatric medication should not be done without the recommendation, support and supervision of a doctor. If you have curiosity about either of these processes, consult a doctor. It is dangerous to withdraw from prescription medication or fast for any period of time without medical supervision.

Within eight days of fasting and coming off my medication, my acne had largely cleared. Please remember that I have incorporated many daily practices into my routine, which help me to remain steady off medication. Each day, I follow a consistent morning routine, I practice yoga, I meditate, I exercise in nature, and more. I did not decide to stop taking psychiatric medication randomly – the choice was made with the guidance and the supervision of a naturopathic doctor.

Since this time, I have discovered that it is extremely common for those who have been diagnosed with bipolar disorder to also have irritable bowel syndrome, celiac disease or gluten intolerance (Adams 2). These conditions, which provoke gastrointestinal distress and a myriad of other symptoms, do not appear in individuals who have been diagnosed with bipolar disorder by coincidence. It is now my opinion that my mood and my mental health were heavily impacted by what I was eating. I believe my body was not able to digest something that I was eating, and as a result, I was not getting the nutrients that I needed to live healthily. Most of the meals I ate as a child came out of a box:

boxed pasta, boxed pizza and boxed macaroni and cheese. I simply was not getting the nutrients that I needed to maintain balanced mental health as a child and teen. As an adult, I was not equipped with the knowledge that I needed to nourish myself properly. I also had unprocessed and unhealed trauma. These issues in my lifestyle and history were leading me to experience depressive and manic episodes. In my case, I also wasn't sleeping enough, I was exhausted all of the time, drinking more than two venti americano coffees per day and snacking on croissants and chocolates to try to give myself more energy. This manufactured energy boost would then trigger even more mania. From there, my gut health only continued to worsen.

Learning about how the foods we eat can impact our mood and our gut health has transformed my journey and my perception of reality, but it's an ongoing process. I am still learning.

Another choice that I recently made, after years of being vegan, was to start eating meat again. This decision also had a dramatic impact on my gut health and digestive system. Many people have different belief systems when it comes to veganism. For instance, I know many individuals who have become vegan and have never felt healthier. For me, eating some meat products has reduced the inflammation in my body, and it has provided me with the nutrients that I need to feel well. In addition to studying the work of Dr Kelly Brogan, two other books in the field that have influenced my thinking are *The Glucose Revolution* by Jesse Inchauspé and *Eat to Beat Anxiety and Depression* by Dr Drew Ramsey. When reading Inchauspé's book, I came to understand how the order in which I was consuming my food was likely leading to glucose spikes, which were causing a lot of my mental and physical health issues. Learning to regulate my glucose has been essential in helping me to manage my overall physical and mental health. In Ramsey's book, I came to understand the seven main categories that he encourages us to integrate into our diets in order to reduce symptoms of anxiety and depression.

Earlier in this book, I introduced the concepts of the *guṇa*. According to the *Pātañjalayogasūtra* text, all material things move through change. These three material states are *rajas*, excitement or energy, *tamas*, lethargy or sadness, and *sattva*, which is a balance of the two (Karambelkar 199 – 200). I now believe that the experience of most mental health conditions are just extreme experiences of normal human emotions: the emotion of sadness and the emotion of anxiety. All humans, diagnosis or not, are constantly in a practice of coming back to the middle.

The best teacher is the teacher within, and everyone's journey looks different. I just want to provide you with an alternative ending to the story and invite you to get curious about your own journey. Western medicine can be a helpful support, but it's not the only method to recovery. Get curious about alternative supports like nutritional psychiatry, naturopathy, *aryuveda*, holistic healing and more. When I was in my twenties, I never would have dreamed that I might one day be able to live in a balanced and joyful state without medication. I also know that if I ever had to, I would choose medication again. Both are valid paths to recovery. But I'm grateful to have found a way that works for me.

CHAPTER 59

THE SITUATION/ DISPOSITION BIAS

By November of 2023, after two years living in Bali, I'd been faculty on several yoga teacher trainings in Bali and online, graduating a few hundred yoga teachers, and both hosted and taught on several yoga retreats, not just in Bali, but around the world. Through these retreats and trainings I'd had so many different experiences navigating different group dynamics and interpersonal situations. Each time, there would be key teachings, lessons, takeaways and insights.

Yoga Teacher Trainings, in particular, are intensive experiences. Students are living in a confined retreat center for a long period of time, usually between 3–4 weeks. The students are in class for thirteen hours each day. Often, all the students in the courses are working through and navigating their own emotions, drama, stories and situations that are arising – just like I was navigating my own emotional circumstances on every training when I was a student, too.

There have been trainings and retreats that I've led where I haven't been proud of how I've navigated situations. There have been trainings where my ego has gotten in the way. There was one particular training where I just couldn't handle the drama of my students. I was exhausted. With one student who challenged me, I watched myself turning into a version of someone I remembered from my past: Ron, my advanced yoga teacher trainer, who in 2017 I disliked so much. I heard myself snapping at students, losing my temper with them, and threatening to take away a student's phone if he was on it during silent breakfast. This wasn't the kind of teacher I wanted to be.

One of the biggest things I learned in hosting these groups was the absolute crucial importance of me being committed to my own well-being practice. I had to start each day with my own *āsana*, meditation and *prāṇāyāma* practice. It meant getting up at five in the morning: but I have to start each day with a personal practice in order to tap into the energy of love and compassion as a foundation to stand on as I move through my day. As a teacher, I had to be the living embodiment: and the only way to do so was to honor my practice. As *Yoga Sūtra* 1.14 reads: *Sa tu dirghakala nairantarya satkara adara asevito drdhabhumih.* The practice, performed for a long time, without pause, and with sincere devotion will become the rock you stand on.

As I got deeper into my practice, I started to become who I wanted to be as a teacher and approach these trainings less like Ron, from my 300-hour yoga teacher training, and more like Rolf, who in my opinion, really walked the walk of yoga.

In late 2023, I had a regular position at a yoga teacher training school that, coincidentally enough, ran monthly programs out of the same retreat center where I trained with Ron over seven years before. One day, on the way home from work, I was riding my motorbike in Ubud when it ran out of gas. I pulled over at a gas station I don't normally use, and drove up behind an older man. As I watched him wait to fill his motorbike tank with gas, I realized: I think that's Ron.

Ron – my advanced yoga teacher trainer who, in 2017, I disliked so much. He was wearing sunglasses and his motorbike helmet, so I wasn't entirely sure it was him. In the two years since I'd lived in Bali, I'd never run into him. I knew he was still running trainings just outside of Ubud, but we'd never crossed paths.

I watched him for a moment, debating whether to reintroduce myself and say hi. I wondered if he'd even remember me, or the impact he'd had on my life.

Finally, I decided to just introduce myself.

"Are you Ron?" I asked him.

He turned around and smiled a fluorescent white smile. "I am Ron."

I took off my sunglasses and my helmet so he could see my face.

"I'm Alex," I said to him. "I did your yoga teacher training course seven years ago."

His face suddenly dropped, and he removed his sunglasses too.

"Wow," he said. "It is so nice to see you." He pulled me into a hug. "What are you doing now?"

I told him that, just like him, I was now running yoga teacher trainings and retreats, largely in Bali but also around the world. "Wow," he said, "that is amazing. Congratulations."

He paused for a moment, and then looked down at the ground. "Alex, you must have done your yoga teacher training with me in, what, 2016? 2017?"

"2017," I told him.

"Alex," he started. He cleared his throat and then looked me in the eyes. "I am so sorry for how I was as a teacher back then. I've learned a lot since. I was going through a really, really hard time in my life." His voice began to crack and tears came to his eyes. "But I'm glad you had a good time."

This conversation wasn't what I was expecting at all. And I thought about how, for all these years, I'd thought that the way he'd behaved as a teacher in 2017 was because of *who he was.* Maybe it wasn't about *who he was* but more about *what he was going through?*

This conversation reminded me of something I learned in first year psychology at university, called the "Situation/Disposition Bias."

According to a 1977 study conducted by Ross, Amabile & Steinmetz, human beings have a tendency to attribute the things that *we* personally do as impacted by our own situation (485). We have a tendency to attribute the things that *others* do as influenced by their disposition, or their personality (Ross et al. 485).

An example of this would be if I were to see someone driving illegally on a motorbike the wrong way up a one-way street, I would have a tendency to think that this person is a reckless driver. When I am a reckless driver myself, I have a tendency to attribute my behavior to the situation that has caused me to drive recklessly, such as being late, or being in an emergency.

A few days before meeting Ron, I actually had an incident where I was driving in a way that could be seen by others as reckless. I was driving my motorbike the opposite way down a one-way street. I wasn't doing this on purpose, however – I truly thought that driving your motorbike in the opposite direction of traffic was legal in Bali on all one-way streets because I'd seen many motorbikes do this over the two years I'd lived there. It turns out that it's only legal on some parts of some one-way streets, and you have to look closely at the signs to see where it's legal and where it's not.

I got pulled over by a police officer and got a traffic ticket.

Of course, I knew that there was a situational circumstance for my driving like this: I truly didn't know it was illegal. But others might have looked at me in that moment and thought I was a reckless driver because they didn't understand the situation I was in.

The same thing could be true for me and my teacher, Ron. Ron might have been having a really tough month at the time he was my teacher. As a human being, I have a natural tendency to blame this on his disposition: I might assume that he is an angry person, or he doesn't embody yoga.

Meanwhile, I had a month like that as a teacher, and I blamed it on my situation: I was exhausted, I was struggling, and I was triggered by the students.

This is the situation/disposition bias. We are more likely to attribute individuals' behavior to their dispositions instead of their situations (Ross et al. 485). This moment of meeting Ron was a beautiful opportunity to remember this.

Ron and I went on to sit down and have a coffee together about a month later. In that time, we had an opportunity to speak about the experience from both perspectives, teacher and student, and I learned many lessons from him.

I told him that even though I had resentments towards him for what happened in 2017, I also could see things from his side now. Having been a teacher on intensive yoga teacher trainings, I'd had moments where I'd behaved like him. I realized that often it is our situation that impacts our behavior, not just our disposition.

I walked away from this get-together with an opportunity to heal and move past my resentment of Ron.

What reconnecting with Ron reminded me is that there are many sides to every story, and there are no villains in any story. How we behave in one circumstance is not who we are as people. And we all have the power and ability to change.

CHAPTER 60

THIS IS WHERE I LEAVE YOU

In January 2023, out of the blue, I got a *WhatsApp* message from Dave. Dave was the Australian guy that I'd dated for a short period of time in 2015, when I first moved to Kuwait. He was in Bali and wanted to know if I wanted to meet up with him for dinner.

I was only twenty-three years old at the time of our relationship, and Dave and I were living in a dry country, which posed a significant challenge to our party lifestyle. I have many memories of the two of us during this time together. For example, I remember how we used to sneak bootleg alcohol into our bags at the resort, and how we went on dates on embassy properties, where alcohol was legal. Back then, sneaking around and drinking alcohol felt fun and rebellious. However, our relationship was short-lived and drew to a close after a month or so because his project ended, and he had to go back to Dubai, where his company was based. I remember crying as he dropped me off at my apartment, and I thought that I'd never see him again. I love this past version of Alex. She was so naïve and didn't realize how small the world is.

I've found that the longer I work as an expat abroad and move around the world, certain people keep being put on my path again and again in different countries and continents, and he's one of them. About two and a half years after we broke up in 2016, I heard from Dave again. It was 2018. Since he and I had last spoken, I'd been married and divorced, had a suicidal breakdown, walked away from my life in Kuwait and started anew in Abu Dhabi. Dave had reached out to me because he had a project in Abu Dhabi. And just like that, we were in each other's orbits again.

I am only able to remember one of the nights that we spent together in Abu Dhabi when we reunited. Dave and I were drinking on a Sunday night at the rooftop bar of the hotel where he was staying. We ended up staying up all night, and I had to call into work sick the next day because I was so exhausted and hungover. Eventually, I stumbled into my own apartment at 9am the next day while my housekeeper was cleaning my home. I was still wearing my dress and high heels from the previous night, and my makeup was stuck to my face. That's the only time that I remember seeing him in Abu Dhabi in 2018.

After chatting with Dave in 2023, he reminded me of a few more occasions when we'd spent time together in Abu Dhabi, so I think that we might have dated for a few months in 2018, too. In all honesty, I don't remember that time period of my life very well. Everything was a blur, as my journey with alcohol was well underway, and I am certain that I was drunk every time that the two of us got together. However, I'm sure that our relationship concluded the same way that it did the first time – his project ended, and he moved away.

When I compare how drastically different my memories and experiences with Dave were in 2015 versus 2018, I am able to see how issues with alcohol can stealthily creep up on you. No one starts out drinking as a young person with the intention of one day having a problem with it. What had started off as me networking with people to gain admission into embassies in Kuwait where booze is legal, ended up with me calling in sick to work because I was too hungover and exhausted after a night of partying. And it ended up with me barely able to remember an entire period of my life when my drinking was at its worst. Comparing and contrasting these two periods of time has resulted in some very meaningful self-reflection.

The night that we got together for dinner was the first time that he'd seen me in five years – since 2018 – and the first time that he'd seen me as a sober person. Given that Dave doesn't have social media, I am relatively certain that he was unaware that my being sober had essentially become my entire identity. He had two beers and a glass of wine while I sipped water. I had to leave dinner by 8pm to get home for a one-on-one call with a sober coaching client. At the end of the night, he said that he thought he might try a sober challenge. I felt so proud of myself because I know (based on history) that if I were drinking alcohol with him, I'd probably have woken up in his bed the next day.

Joan Didion wrote:

> *I think we are well advised to keep on nodding terms with the people we used to be, whether we find them attractive company or not. Otherwise, they turn up unannounced and surprise us, come hammering on the mind's door at 4am of a bad night and demand to know who deserted them, who betrayed them, who is going to make amends. We forget all too soon the things we thought we could never forget. We forget the loves and the betrayals alike, forget what we whispered and what we screamed, forget who we were* (qtd. in Akram).

Dave and I ended up spending the week together in Bali. It was such a magical, special time together. As an expat, people come in and out of your life, and it is rare when someone has the opportunity to interact with you in every environment and every state, as Dave has. He'd seen me pre-addiction, during addiction and post-addiction. Over the years, he's also grown and changed, too. When we met face to face, it felt as if we were holding up a mirror to each other, which allowed us to see the reflection of our past and present selves. The insight that was gained from this process enabled us to dream about our futures selves, and the people that we could one day become, as we continued to grow and to transform our lives.

Towards the end of the week, we got together one last time. This is what I posted on *Facebook* afterwards:

January 6, 2023
He said, "There must be some reason why we keep ending up in the same place all around the world at different times." Kuwait, 2016. Abu Dhabi, 2018. Bali, 2023.

So, we got together one last time before he left Bali.

The weird thing about catching up with an ex so many times in one week is that the conversation changes pretty quickly each time. Dinner one is shallow: small talk and catching up on the last five years. Dinner two becomes medium: happy nostalgia and laughable memories. And by dinner three, you're deep. He reminds you of the little moments, like that one time he made fun of your Birkenstock shoes in 2016, and you completely flipped your lid and started crying and called him sexist.

But then you tell him what you have come to realize with age and wisdom and sobriety: that there were many small moments that led to up to this outburst of emotions. The earrings. The outfit. The bandage. The cancelled plans. The no-shows. And because you didn't know how to advocate for your feelings back then, they all bubbled up inside of you and exploded over a pair of shoes. You know now that you have to tell people how you feel, or they never know.

And then he tells you what he sees with his own age and wisdom: that he wasn't happy at the time. And his sarcasm and small jabs were a reflection of that unhappiness. Since then, he has gone to therapy and done inner work. He's happier now.

We wondered how life would play out if we got back together, eventually deciding that it would never happen. I know what my life purpose is, and my plan is to follow it. There is absolutely zero chance that I'll drop my career leading yoga retreats and yoga teacher trainings and move to a small town in Australia with him. (And he said life with me would be too much social media.)

Knowing that I won't drop my career for anyone is an amazing feeling, I realized – because this was not who I was eight years ago when I dated him. Eight years ago, I was the girl who would agree to follow a boyfriend wherever he wanted to go. Greece? Sure! The USA? Okay! 2023 Alex is like, "I know where I'm going, and you're either coming with me or not."

After talking about how we used to live – late nights and early mornings, coffee cup in hand, call to prayer and sunrise over the desert – and how it is for both of us now – slow, easy, simple – I said, "Our lives are a lot different now."

We both run businesses and are self-employed. We no longer work 24/7 (or when we do, we enjoy it!). We no longer live in the Middle East. We're both a lot happier.

"Yeah," he said, "our lives have changed… for the better."

I agreed.

"So, maybe that's the reason," he said. "Maybe we just keep crossing paths all around the world so that we can see that our lives are changing for the better."

So, this is where I leave you.

See you in two to five years.

CHAPTER 61

A LOVE LETTER TO THE MIDDLE EAST

MAY 30, 2023

I'm visiting the United Arab Emirates right now. I lived in the Middle East as a teacher for seven years between the ages of twenty-three and thirty. During the pandemic, I started an online yoga business, moved to Bali, began hosting retreats around the world… and the rest is history!

Even though I love my life so much – truly the life of my dreams – I have this bittersweet nostalgia for the Middle East.

Last month, this couple I met at an event in Bali asked me if I missed the UAE… and my eyes started glowing. I gazed off into the distance, and I started talking about this place like it was an ex-boyfriend with whom I was still in love. They asked me what I missed, and I started talking about the sunrises. UAE has the most beautiful sunrises and sunsets you'll ever see in your life. Burnt orange and glowing red. I told them about the hummus, tabouleh and shisha. I told them about the moment when the Friday call to prayer echoed through Mahboula, and the whole neighborhood entered the energy of respect, let go of movement and received stillness. Let go of chaos and received calm.

I told them about the camels, the palm trees, the dates, the

Arabic coffee. The dust storms. I told them about how Thursdays will always be special.

I told them about halloumi cheese and the word *Inshallah*, and how walking outside in the summer is like walking through a hairdryer.

Sometimes when I get into these states of nostalgia, I just want to move back to the Middle East full time. I am super fortunate I get to travel here every few months and run yoga retreats for my former clients.

Today, I was thinking about it as I sat in the car driving down the highway. "What do I love about this place so much?" I realized that I think what I love the most about this place is that I feel like I see former versions of myself everywhere.

I arrived in The Walk at Jumeirah Beach Residence today, and I saw the version of myself who would fly to Dubai from Kuwait with her fiancé/husband and get blackout drunk by 11am on the beach. I visit Al Maryah Island, and I see the girl who moved here for the ladies' nights and brunches and got so deep in her addiction that she knew she had to get sober in a year. I drive to Jebel Ali, and I see the gym I worked at during 2019, and I see the version of myself getting sober. I visit Al Reem Island, and I see the girl who became obsessed with building a career in yoga – working 24/7 while being a full-time teacher – to create the version of reality in which I now live today.

All those former versions of Alex would be amazed to know that I'm here today – popping over to the UAE for a week to host a yoga retreat.

So, maybe that's what the UAE is for me. Maybe I don't need to move back here full time. Maybe the UAE is an ex-boyfriend I'm still in love with, a person from my past. And maybe I just keep coming back here every once in a while, to meet former versions of myself and see how far I've come.

CHAPTER 62

MILLIONS OF MOMENTS

I was home in Canada for Christmas in 2019, just before Covid. On Boxing Day, I woke up to an *Instagram* message from someone who I hadn't heard from in years – one of my best friends from middle school, Olivia. She told me, "Alex, I have to tell you some sad news. Yesterday, Charlotte died by suicide."

In middle school, there were three of us that were very best friends: Olivia, Charlotte and me. We all struggled with our own mental health issues: disordered eating, drug and alcohol addictions, anxiety. I was shocked to receive this message. I hadn't heard Charlotte's name in years. I always wondered what had happened to her.

Olivia and I got together for coffee. We recounted the memories that we had with Charlotte. She was creative, silly and funny. I told Olivia about my journey with mental health over the past few years, and how grateful I was to have learned how to overcome my mental health struggles and to have become sober.

Olivia said to me at one point: "Did you ever hear the story about that one night in high school?"

I said, "What story? I have a story to tell you about another night... but you go first."

Olivia proceeded to tell me a story. Olivia and Charlotte had gotten drunk at a park party when they were thirteen or fourteen years old. At some point, she lost Charlotte, and when she found her, Charlotte was passed out with an older guy. The police broke up the party, and Olivia carried Charlotte out of the park. She got as far as a few houses down the road, when a woman came out of her house and called an ambulance.

The most bizarre thing was that this was the same story I was thinking of telling Olivia, too. I had been there that night. It was one of the formative memories of my adolescence, which shaped my life significantly. But I didn't remember Olivia being there. In my version of the story, I remembered carrying Charlotte out of this party, on my shoulders, alone. In Olivia's version, she had carried Charlotte alone. In reality, it had been the two of us together. We were both there when the police and the ambulance had shown up. How is it possible that our brains had tricked us in this way and enabled us to forget each other's presence on this night that impacted us both so deeply?

We were both the only people who had stayed: everyone else at the party had left us behind. They fled the park because they didn't want to get into trouble: other friends, our classmates from school, and even the older boy who was with Charlotte. Everyone.

When I recounted this story to Em and her partner, Noa, my sister made sense of the situation by explaining that she believed that the memory had been so deeply isolating, scary and traumatic for both Olivia and me, at such a young age, that both of us weren't able to recall the other person being there. We both remembered ourselves as being alone because we'd felt so alone at the time. The human brain is a fascinating thing. Our minds are able to rewrite memories for us. Both of us had a different version of the truth – and neither version was completely true. The reality was somewhere in the middle.

Olivia may not have remembered me being there, but I am one-hundred percent certain that I was there that night. That distressing experience has stayed with me forever. I will never, ever forget that night. As I mentioned earlier in this book, the police made us call our parents. My parents asked me to get a taxi and come home immediately. The conversation with my parents is the last moment that I am able to remember from my version of the story. In Olivia's version of the story, she also remembered calling home. She had tears streaming down her face when she spoke with her mom on the telephone, and her mom responded by saying, "Honey, don't move. I'm coming." However, Olivia's memory of that night continued far past the phone call. She remembered that the police took Charlotte, who was unconscious, in an ambulance to the hospital, and Olivia's mom trailed behind with Olivia in their minivan. Although Charlotte was still largely incoherent at that time, Olivia's mom hugged and comforted both girls while the three of them waited for Charlotte's parents to show up.

In contrast to Olivia's mother, Charlotte's parents and my parents were furious with us. My parents were so mad at me that they grounded me for two months (which they don't remember, years later, but I do). I wasn't allowed to attend a sleepover at a friend's house for the rest of high school (which they don't remember either, but all of my friends and I do). We never talked about that night. I never had a chance to process or discuss what was an enormously traumatic event at such a young age. And what stands out to me the most is the fact that they were so mad that I had lied and gone to a party. They never acknowledged that I had also demonstrated many positive qualities that night by acting selflessly to help my friend.

Yes, it was wrong to lie about going to a party. Yes, it was wrong to drink at age fourteen. But aside from that, what I had done that night was stay with a friend when she was unconscious. When everyone else went home, I made sure that she was safe. And I called my parents and told them the truth. Despite knowing that I'd get in trouble. From my perspective, when I look back on this incident, I can't help but think that the decisions that I made that night should have been celebrated.

A year later, I went to a house party, and when I showed up, Charlotte was there. I can't remember if we'd planned to meet each other at the party, or if we'd just happened to run into each other at the event. When I arrived at the party, she was drunk and throwing up on the front steps. I knew that my parents might find out if decided to stay and help her, or even if I called someone for help. So, I walked past her. I pretended that I didn't know her so that I wouldn't get grounded again.

I'll never know how she got home that night. I will always regret my choice to walk away from a friend. As an adult, I am able to understand that my parents were just doing the best that they could. No one knows how to raise their kids the 'right' way because there is no right way. All parents make mistakes. But I know that those early, traumatic experiences with alcohol shaped Olivia's, Charlotte's and my life and set each of us on paths of self-destruction. I just wish that my parents had realized that this event was traumatic for me, so that they could have provided me with the support that I needed. But again, they were doing the best they could at the time. And I am providing myself with the support I needed at that time, now.

I asked Olivia towards the end of the coffee date, "Olivia, do you know how Charlotte died?"

"She jumped off a building."

When Olivia told me about the details of Charlotte's death, shivers ran up my spine. I confided in Olivia that I had repeatedly planned to end my own life in the same way. Over the span of several years, I had wanted to jump off a building. Olivia was the first person with whom I had ever shared this information about myself.

Olivia sat, hands wrapped around a cup of coffee, eyes wide. She had shivers too.

Hearing this truth hit me very hard. And I realized that, when Charlotte was feeling so depressed, I probably didn't even cross her mind. Why would she think of Alex McRobert, someone who had been her friend in middle and high school? She hadn't seen or heard from me in ten years. Yet here I was, sitting with Olivia over coffee, grieving her.

This realization started to help me to see the bigger picture when it comes to our existence on Earth. Our lives form large, intricate webs. People whose lives we've touched. Millions of moments. Moments of impact. Moments when we have helped others and shared love with them or inspired them. We have all been a part of so many people's stories. And in the moments of my deepest depression, my deepest despair, I wasn't able to see all of the ways that I had positively influenced others. I could only see Santiago, the person whom I had hurt.

I'm sure that there were hundreds of people who didn't even cross Charlotte's mind before she died, and many of them gathered to grieve for her after she passed away. I was one of them. And I realize now that if I'd died – if my life had ended, as I'd planned – hundreds of people would have probably gathered and grieved my passing, too. Hundreds of people who wouldn't have entered my mind: Atif, Ife, Rebecca, Raghu, all of the children that I have ever taught, and all of my yoga students. And even though he hated my guts, I bet that Santiago would have grieved my loss, as well, if I had followed through with my plan to jump off our apartment building on that heartbreaking morning in 2017. I was part of a million people's stories in a way that I didn't even know. Just like Charlotte was a part of my story, in a way that she didn't know.

In that moment when I wanted to jump off the building, I couldn't see beyond that one tiny moment in which I'd hurt Santiago deeply. I couldn't comprehend that, in reality, my life was made up of millions of moments. And one tiny moment did not define me. It did not make me a bad person.

CHAPTER 63

WALKING ON THE EDGE

I find it ironic that in Mahboula, Kuwait, in July 2017, I was constantly planning my death by jumping off a building, considering that I have had such a ginormous fear of heights throughout my life. When I was nineteen years old, I was taken on a mystery road trip for frosh leaders. As frosh leaders, the other students on the trip and I were all serving as peer mentors to incoming freshmen at university. When I discovered that part of the trip included a surprise zip line, I cried and refused to go up on it. As a kid, I also used to refuse to climb the wall at camp, go sailing and dive off the diving towers. I didn't want to participate in any of these activities because I was too scared. I still have never been off the summer camp diving towers, even though I taught diving classes there for three summers.

In the summer of 2019, after becoming sober, one of the things that I decided to do was face this fear. My Uncle Rick suggested that we do the CN Tower Edge walk.

At that point in my life, I'd told no one about my past suicide plans, so Uncle Rick didn't know the significance of this day to me at all. He just thought that this walk, which takes place 116 stories high above the city of Toronto, would be a fun 'uncle and niece event' ("Edge Walk at the CN Tower").

I nervously stepped towards the edge of the tallest building in Toronto, and I leaned off it.

I was standing on the edge of one of the tallest skyscrapers in the world. The safety precautions would make this impossible, but in my imagination, I could have unhooked myself and ended my life right there. But I didn't want to anymore. I didn't want to jump off a building anymore. I no longer wanted to kill myself. I wanted to be alive.

I never told my uncle the meaning of that moment for me, but it was huge.

There was a time when I didn't want to exist on planet Earth anymore. There was a time when all I'd wanted to do was to jump off a building and end it all.

But I'm here. I'm sober. I've learned how to turn my trauma into a triumph. While I still go through the yin and yang and the ebb and flow of life, overcoming my bipolar disorder diagnosis and discovering a life of joy and balance has been the greatest achievement of my life. At the time when I was experiencing depression, I thought the depths of my darkness would never end. It's been a journey of learning and unlearning. I've finally reached the point where I'm grateful to have walked down the complicated path that has been my mental health journey. I never would have imagined that, one day, I'd get to live the life that I am living now. I started my own business, and I'm finally doing what I love. I'm finally teaching yoga. Most importantly, I am alive. I am so happy to be alive.

I am so happy that I didn't jump off The Oasis tower in Kuwait in 2017.

And every day, when I wake up, I am so, so thankful that I am here to see another sunrise.

CHAPTER 64

WE CLOSE WITH AN INTENTION

When I participated in the advanced yoga teacher training with Rolf Gates in Massachusetts at Kripalu Yoga Center, he finished every yoga class with a variation of the following words. I have carried on this tradition by repeating these same words at the end of every single yoga class that I have taught since that time. It feels fitting to close the main text of this book with those words, as well:

> *"We close with an intention, an ancient intention. But perhaps the original intention. That has been passed from heart to heart, for thousands of years. That our yoga practice remains steady, and that our efforts remain continuous, and that our yoga helps and heals, and serves and benefits all beings, everywhere.*
>
> Lokah Samastah Sukhino Bhavantu.
>
> *May all beings be safe, be happy, be healthy and free – and may the thoughts and actions of each of our lives contribute to this."*

CHAPTER 65

HE WAS MY SOULMATE, AFTER ALL

When it came time to publish this book in 2024, there were a few people that I needed to reach out to. Even though everyone in the book's identity has been changed, and no one's character is identifiable, it felt like out of respect for some individuals, I had to let them know about this piece of work's soon-to-be existence in the world. One of the most important people I had to tell this to was Santiago.

I hadn't heard from or spoken to him in seven years when I sent him an email to let him know that I wrote a book, and he was in it. The goal of the book was to help other women struggling with mental health and addiction, I told him. If he wanted to, I was inviting him to read it.

He emailed me back two days later.

"Hi Alex,
You're never going to believe this. But I'm also five years sober, and I also wrote a book, and you're in it. You also are unidentifiable, and I have no plans on publishing mine. But I'd be happy to share mine with you, and I'd also be happy to read yours."

This email shocked me.

Talk about full-circle moments.

It was almost as if Santiago and I came into each others' lives for the very purpose of leading each other to hit rock bottom, experience so much suffering and sadness that we had to change our lives, and become sober, healing through narrative medicine. It's exactly what Elizabeth Gilbert defined a soulmate as in *Eat, Pray, Love.* It was almost as if we existed in each others' lives to help each other find this freedom.

Santiago read the book and gave me his feedback as well as his permission to go ahead with the publication. And this was the moment that I knew the book was ready to be shared with the world.

Yoga Sūtra 2.21 is *tadartha eva dṛśyasya-ātmā.* Every single thing that happens to us in the material world exists for us to learn (Karambelkar 217 – 218). The goal is to begin to move through the material world, learn from the experiences, and then rise above them and into the state of *samādhi*, or consciousness.

The thing about life is sometimes, when you are enduring suffering and moving through these experiences in the material world that the *Pātañjalayogasūtra* text explains, you can't see the purpose for this pain. But many years later, I see the purpose for the pain Santiago and I both went through, together and apart. It was to lead us to where we are now.

As far as I can tell from social media, I think Santiago is remarried with children. I am so happy that he is happy.

As for me, I am still single, living in Bali, Indonesia. My dream one day soon is to have invested in the first yoga retreat center for The Mindful Life Practice to have as our community hub. My long-term vision is to have multiple centers around the world. For the first time ever, it feels attainable and not too far off in the distance. This retreat center will be the home base for *āsana*, *prāṇāyāma*, meditation and more training programs. We will also continue to do destination retreats around the world for our community to gather, connect and heal.

Brené Brown wrote, "One day, you'll tell the story of what you overcame, and it will be someone else's survival guide" (Halpert 1).

If this book served that purpose in even one individual's life, then I have accomplished what I set out to do.

When Taylor Swift released her album *The Tortured Poets Department* in 2024, she wrote on *Instagram* about it:

> *This period of the author's life is now over, the chapter closed and boarded up. There is nothing to avenge, no scores to settle once wounds have healed. And upon further reflection, a good number of them turned out to be self-inflicted. This writer is of the firm belief that our tears become holy in the form of ink on a page. Once we have spoken our saddest story, we can be free of it* (Swift).

CHAPTER 66

EPILOGUE

During my 300-hour advanced yoga teacher training with Ron in Bali, I learned about the Four Aims of Life (The *Puruṣarthas*). The *Puruṣarthas* are referred to in Vedic texts as our 'goals of existence'. They are:

1. *Dharma*. Purpose. This is the desire to fulfill your purpose and potential. To become all that you are capable of being.
2. *Artha*. This is the means necessary to accomplish your *dharma*: Food, physical well-being, a roof over your head. Without these things, fulfilling your *dharma* would be impossible.
3. *Kama*. This is joy and pleasure. How and in what ways have your actions, thoughts and words brought you joy?
4. *Moksha*. This is freedom. In what ways have you achieved freedom from fear, anger, grief, anxiety and anything that weighs you down? It's the full awakening to our true nature and liberation from our suffering.

These four aims of life are fulfilled by the choices we make when we live our yoga off our mats each day. The poses that we do in yoga – that's just preparation.

I originally wrote this book in 2020, during the Covid pandemic. At that point, I was living in Abu Dhabi and finishing my last years as an elementary school teacher. As I built my global yoga community, The Mindful Life Practice, I began to fulfill the first aim of life. I began to step into my *dharma*, or my purpose.

During the year of 2021, the second year of running The Mindful Life Practice, I built it up enough to quit my job. This was my *artha*, the second aim of life. This was establishing the means necessary to accomplish my *dharma*. How could I run The Mindful Life Practice if I wasn't able to feed myself or have a roof over my head? By building my business financially, I was able to sustain myself in doing what I love.

During years one and two, I worked so hard that I didn't have much joy in my life. So, during the year of 2022, my third year of running this company, it was all about joy. Joy is the third aim of life, *kama*. I moved to Bali and started to enjoy my life. I practiced *Kirtan*, practiced yoga and spent time in nature. This was my development of *kama*.

Finally, in my fifth year of running this business – in 2024 – I began to set the last piece in place and accomplish the fourth aim of life, *moksha*. I prepared to find freedom by publishing this story and sharing my truth with the world.

PART EIGHT

Soul Star *Chakra* Glossary – I Can Live Yoga

The soul star *chakra* is known as the 'seat of the soul'. It's the *chakra* that connects you to your higher self. This *chakra* also holds all of the information about your past lives. It's a vault where your soul's true purpose resides. And with practice, we can tap into this energy center. This *chakra* connects to divine love, compassion and selflessness.

YOGA SŪTRA STUDY

If you are interested in learning more about the philosophy of yoga, I offer a Yoga Sūtra Study class, which you can sign up for here:

https://bit.ly/TheMindfulLifePractic_YogaSutra_Study

I also have various Yoga Teacher Trainings online and in person all throughout the year on different subjects. You can learn more about this here:

https://www.themindfullifepractice.com/

CHAPTER 67

SOBER YOGA GIRL PHILOSOPHY

The *chakras* are spinning energy wheels throughout the body that collect and channel our *prana*. Our *prana* is our life force or our energy. There are several different *chakra* models out there – however, the most commonly and widely accepted model contains seven *chakras*. These seven *chakras* are:

1. **The root chakra** – the foundation of safety and security within the body. This is the color red. Balancing this *chakra* is about making sure our basic needs are met. We have food, safety and water – all the essential needs.
2. **The sacral chakra** – this is the basis of emotions, letting go, and going with the flow. This is the color orange. It's about processing our emotions, feeling our emotions, and drawing boundaries around others.
3. **The solar plexus chakra** – this is about empowerment, strength and believing in ourselves. It's the color yellow. I think about this *chakra* as embodying the way we move through the world – taking up space, speaking our truth and recognizing the power we hold.
4. **The heart chakra** – this is the color green. It is about healing, forgiveness, love and compassion. The heart *chakra* is the bridge between the lower *chakras*, which are more about the outer world, and the upper *chakras*, which are more about the inner world. This is about healing any grief or unresolved trauma that impacts how we move through the world.

5. **The throat chakra** – this is the color blue. It is about speaking our truth and being authentic. If we have any secrets we're holding close to our chests or stories we feel like we need to tell, then this will create a throat *chakra* blockage. Those who overtalk and over dominate a conversation may also have an imbalance in their throat *chakra*.
6. **The third eye chakra** – this is the color indigo. The third eye is about trusting our guts and going inwards. As we go higher up the *chakras* and start to balance our higher *chakras*, we can begin to really tap into our intuition or gut feelings. Having a strong intuition can help us to make important decisions about our lives that protect us from harm.
7. **The crown chakra** – this is the color violet. The crown *chakra* is about spiritual connection, connection to others and connection to yourself. When you've reached a state of consciousness, then your crown *chakra* is in balance.

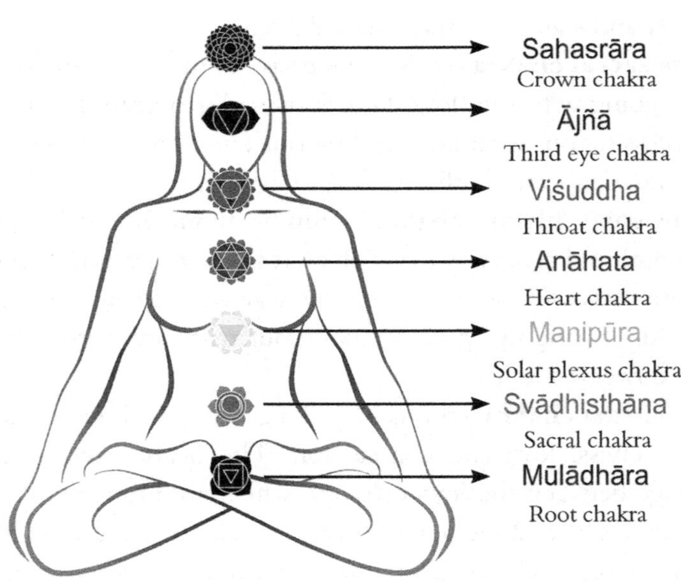

I teach my yoga classes based on the seven-*chakra* model, which is something I learned in both my *reiki* training and also my Rolf Gates trainings. When students come to learn how to teach classes from me, this is the model I present to them to structure all *vinyasa* classes during my 200-hour yoga teacher trainings. The seven-*chakra* model is also how I've designed many of my courses, including the 200-hour yoga teacher trainings and 30-hour sober curious yoga training, and it was the original structure of this book.

In every single yoga teacher training that I lead, I learn more and more. In October of 2023, I was teaching for a group, and one of my students told me that there were actually eight *chakras*, and I was wrong. Initially, I felt annoyed that she was disagreeing with me as a teacher. I think that most of my annoyance was related to how much of my work at that point was based on there being seven *chakras*, not eight, and also my own ego. I said to her, "Thank you for sharing that with me…" and carried on. But the truth is,

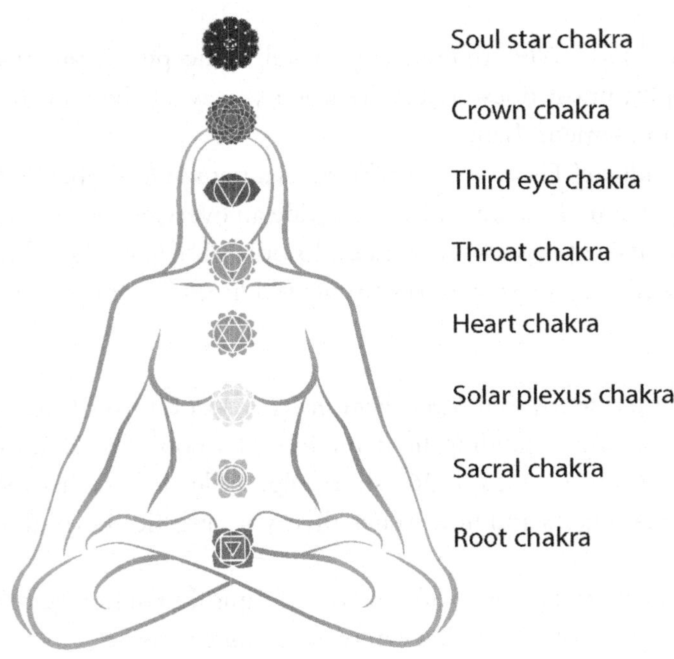

by not being open to her point of view, I was being rigid in my perspective.

Then, as time went on, I started to open up to the idea. As I learned from my student, the soul star *chakra* is known as the 'seat of the soul'. It's the *chakra* that connects you to your higher self. This *chakra* also holds all of the information about your past lives. It's a vault where your soul's true purpose resides. And with practice, we can tap into this energy center. This *chakra* connects to divine love, compassion and selflessness.

The reality is that every single person you speak to about most philosophical concepts from yoga will have many different perspectives, ideas and beliefs. The longer you stay in the yoga world, the more you have to open your heart to the idea that there is not one single truth.

As I sat with this idea, I realized that it had been directed to me for a reason. An eighth section of the book: "The Soul Star *Chakra*."

Sober Yoga Girl references several concepts from yoga philosophy, but it doesn't actually teach you what they mean or how to implement them.

So, I added "The Soul Star *Chakra*" chapter in December 2023. In this portion of the book, I will provide an overview of the most fundamental concepts from yoga philosophy that have altered my life, as well as some stories to help the teachings become relevant to you.

When I first discovered *Meditations from the Mat* by Rolf Gates in 2010, it became a guiding light for me. His book breaks down the eight limbs of yoga in 365 short, digestible stories, that help the readers understand how to live their yoga practice beyond the postures.

The *āsana(s)* (postures) of yoga are one thing, but understanding the philosophy of yoga – that can really change your life.

We study the teachings of yoga to change the way that our brain thinks. Then, we embody the teachings of yoga by doing our *āsana* (physical practice). Finally, the philosophy and practice have an impact on the way we live our lives by altering everything we do outside of our practice. That's the whole point of yoga – to change the way we think and act.

THE EIGHT-LIMB PATH OF YOGA

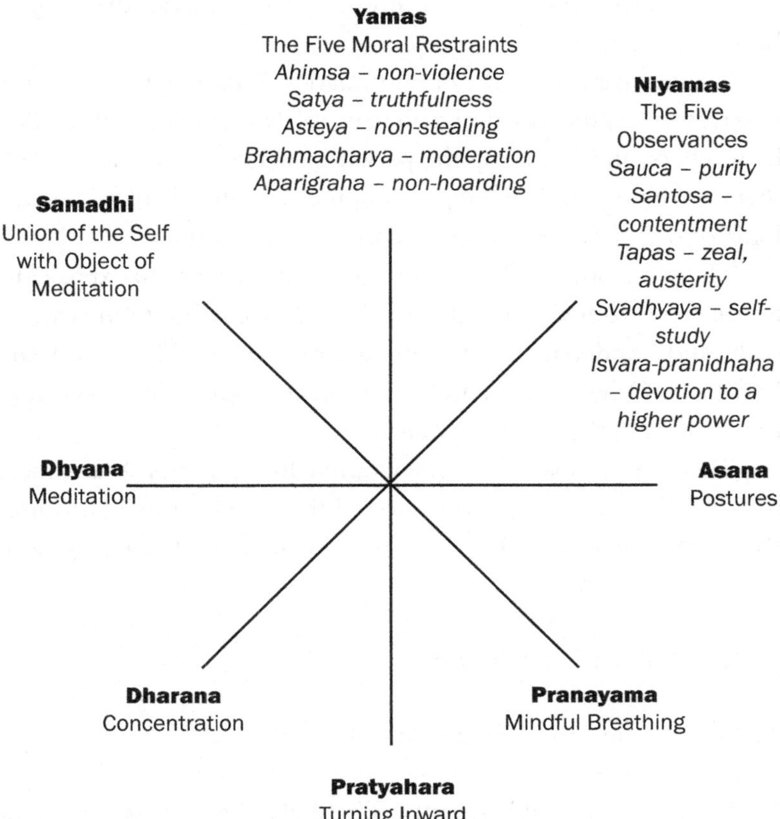

PĀTAÑJALAYOGASŪTRA

The eight-limb path of yoga originates from *Pātañjalayogasūtra.* The reason why I refer to this text as *Pātañjalayogasūtra* and not "Pātañjali's *Yoga Sūtras*", as commonly referred to in English, is because as part of my studies with my teacher Anvita in Mumbai, I have learned that this is the correct way to refer to this text. In the Sanskrit language, the *Sūtra* are referred to as singular. Additionally, Pātañjali is written as Pātañjala. Pātañjali was a revered yogi and scholar of many subjects. The *Pātañjalayogasūtra* text is thought to be written 200 years BCE, or over 2,000 years ago.

The word '*Sūtra*' refers to thread – as in a thread that strings beads together.

Each *Sūtra* is short – they're summaries. This brevity is really for two reasons, 1) they are designed to be easily expanded and recalled by teachers, and 2) during the period in which they were created, there were no photocopiers or computers, so they couldn't be too long, or they'd take too long to reprint, copy and share.

There are other ancient yoga texts that I have been exposed to but haven't studied in depth yet – as I've taken about ten years to truly study, understand, integrate, practice and be able to teach the *Yoga Sūtra*. Other texts include *The Bhavagad Gītā, The Hatha Yoga Pradapika*, and the *Gheranda Samita.*

There are 196 *Yoga Sūtra(s)*, divided into four chapters. What's most widely known and understood around the world is the Eight-Limb Path of Yoga, which originates in chapter two of the *Pātañjalayogasūtra*.

THE EIGHT-LIMB PATH

There are eight limbs on the path to yoga. They are:

1. **Yama(s)** – moral restraints. These are things I like to think of as more external practices that impact how we interact

with the external world (however, they can involve internal practices too).
2. **Niyama(s)** – observances. These are things I like to think of as more internal practices that impact how we interact with the inside world (however, they can involve external practices too).
3. **Āsana** – the postures.
4. **Prāṇāyāma** – controlled breathing.
5. **Pratyahara** – turning inwards.
6. **Dharana** – concentration.
7. **Dhyana** – meditation.
8. **Samādhi** – union of the Self with the object of meditation, or a state of meditative consciousness.

If you are interested in learning more about the *Pātañjalayogasūtra* text and how to apply the philosophy to your life, I lead a 100-hour *Yoga Sūtra* study course online. I also integrate these teachings as part of my 200-hour yoga teacher training courses and my retreats.

I do want to introduce you to *Yoga Sūtra* 1.2, so you can understand the purpose of yoga driving the entire practice.

THE PURPOSE OF YOGA (*YOGA SŪTRA* 1.2)

Yoga Citta Vṛtti Nirodhah
Citta – thoughts/whirlpools
Vṛtti – a fluctuation of the mind
Nirodhah – to control, to let be

Yoga Sūtra 1.2: Yoga Chitta Vṛtti Nirodhah. Yoga is stilling the fluctuations of the mind. This *Sūtra* is the heart of why we practice yoga (Karambelkar 5 – 8).

It took me many years to realize that essentially, what Pātañjali is saying is, we do yoga for our mental health. The fluctuations of the mind are the tendency to worry, get sad, or engage in any thoughts that draw us away from this moment right now. The aim of yoga is to still the fluctuations of the mind. The aim of yoga is to bring us into focus, so we can understand that this moment, right now, is all that there is.

Yoga for me began as a healing tool for my mental health many years ago. Although I practiced yoga on and off from age ten and throughout my teens, yoga had the most impact when I was in crisis around age eighteen, and I didn't have any mental health resources. During crisis, yoga was the only thing that helped. I didn't understand how it worked: I just knew it worked.

All my life, up until that point, I was living with anxiety and depression all around me. After trying my first hot yoga class at age eighteen, however, I felt clear for the first time ever. For the first time ever, I felt still.

When teachers guided us to be in the moment, I used to worry that I was a fraud and that everyone else knew how to do this 'present moment thing' except me. I now understand: no one knows how to do it. That's why we're all here: to learn.

LIMB ONE AND TWO: THE *YAMA(S)* AND *NIYAMA(S)*

The *yama(s)* and *niyama(s)* are limbs one and two of the eight-limb path of yoga, or *raja* yoga (Karambelkar 231 – 239). They are basically a guideline for our thoughts, words and actions.

The reason why I have written *yama(s)* and *niyama(s)* with the (s) in brackets is because in traditional Sanskrit, *yama* and *niyama* are actually not pluralized with an 's'. This pluralized 's' was added onto the words when we brought yoga from India to the Western world and translated it from Sanskrit to English. During my yoga philosophy studies with my teacher Anvita in Mumbai, I learned the correct way to pronounce them, even in plural form, is simply the yam and niyam. However, Anvita recommended I write *yama(s)* and *niyama(s)* the way that I did, with the (s) in brackets, to acknowledge the two different spellings and pronunciations of the same concept in the West and the East.

When I was first exposed to the concept of the *yama(s)* and *niyama(s)*, I became obsessive about them. I would use them to judge myself and ultimately tell myself that I wasn't a real *sādhaka* (practitioner of yoga) if I was dishonest, if I took something that wasn't mine, or if I couldn't let go. Ultimately, many years later, I now understand that they are simply a framework that we can use to help guide our behavior towards the goal of stilling the fluctuations of the mind (*Sūtra* 1.2).

When we find ourselves moving in the wrong direction with the *yama(s)* and *niyama(s)*, the goal is to just practice presence, and gently and lovingly call ourselves back. When we catch ourselves gossiping, for example, we can remind ourselves, "This is not helpful to be judgmental" and then start again. We don't need to be perfect to be students of yoga – we just need to practice.

LIVING IT: *YAMA & NIYAMA*

What do we do when we find we're moving in the wrong direction with our thoughts, words or actions? Being a student of yoga doesn't mean you're perfect – it means you're in practice.

The goal is to practice presence and gently and lovingly call ourselves back, saying to ourselves: "This is not helpful... let's start again."

LIMB ONE OF THE EIGHT-LIMB PATH OF YOGA: *YAMA(S)*

The first limb of the eight-limbed path is the *yama(s)*. These are ethical commitments – they pertain to the way we interact with the world around us. However, I believe they can also relate to the way we interact with ourselves. They are:

Ahiṃsā – non-violence
Satya – truth
Asteya – non-stealing
Brahmacharya – moderation
Aparigraha – letting go

(Karambelkar 239 – 248).

Ahiṃsā:

The first *yama* is *ahiṃsā*, or non-violence.

I grew up in a culture of gossip. What I didn't realize about my gossiping was that it didn't just affect the person I was gossiping about. It also affected me. It made me feel more shame. It made me perceive the world as more judgmental. It made me perceive the world as less safe.

I avoid gossiping now because it makes me feel bad about myself. I know I'm causing harm to the person that I am speaking about. The practice of *ahiṃsā* is commonly translated as the practice of non-violence. I sometimes prefer the word 'non-harming' because the term 'non-violence' is something that we often associate only with physical violence such as punching, hitting, kicking, etc. But the practice of violence can go well beyond physical violence, as it can affect how we think, speak, etc. Some of the ways that I have striven to practice *ahiṃsā* over the past ten years as a student of yoga are:

- **Avoiding gossiping if possible.** Gossip is done from a place of harm – for the purpose of gaining attention, we share someone else's private stories and/or information that they shared with us in confidence. I used to gossip often as a young child and teenager. This behavior came from a few places: 1) I was raised in a culture where gossiping was normalized and 2) I was seeking attention, and I got attention from gossip. What I've realized is that I don't feel good if I gossip. I try to step out of and away from conversations where I have found myself engaging in gossip and always return to love.

  A question that almost always comes up when I'm discussing this with my students is: how can we clarify when it's gossip and when it's venting? Sometimes, you have to vent about a problem that you've experienced to your friends or family or coach or therapist to help you process it. When you're processing your own trauma, the situation, or your feelings about it, then I define that as an okay story to tell. As soon as the story moves out of my own personal story and moves into a story I shouldn't tell, or if I am name calling the person involved, that's when I know that I have stepped into the field of gossip, and I gently and lovingly call myself back.
- **Thinking loving thoughts about myself.** One of my tendencies at a young age was to get into negative thought patterns about my capabilities, whether or not I am loved, the future, the past, etc. When I catch myself in a negative thought pattern, I try to choose again and shift the thought from the negative into the positive. For example, a common thought I used to have was, "I am a terrible person." Now, I actively shift that to, "I am a good person."
- **Avoiding the situation/disposition bias.** When I was in first year psychology, I learned about a tendency called 'The Situation/Disposition Bias'. This bias discusses the human tendency to perceive our own behaviors as caused by situations, while viewing others' actions as caused by their

dispositions (Ross et al. 485). For example, if I am rushing in traffic, I have a tendency to attribute this acceleration to my situation. It might be that I am late for an appointment. On the flip side, if someone else is rushing in traffic, we have a tendency to attribute their acceleration to their disposition, e.g. that they are impatient. They are reckless drivers. The goal is to constantly notice when I am attributing behavior to someone's disposition and wonder if I could actually attribute it to their situation.

- **Practicing on the mat.** Part of non-violence includes refraining from causing ourselves harm during our yoga practices. Instead, we should strive to take care of our bodies and not push ourselves too hard during our *āsana* practice.
- **Intervening when confronting violence.** One of the most common issues I find in the yoga world is thinking of *ahiṃsā* as a passive act. For example, a person could be passively kind by ignoring a racist comment or joke made by a friend. But *ahiṃsā* actually isn't passive… *ahiṃsā* is active. *Ahiṃsā* is an intervention. It is standing up and speaking up. If you're practicing *ahiṃsā*, you are intervening when you see violence or harm occurring.
- **Practicing veganism?** Should you be vegan or vegetarian to embody *ahiṃsā*? When I talk about this subject, the question of dietary practices almost always comes up in groups. Many yoga teachers preach this way of eating. There is a great podcast called '*Yoga is Dead*' in which they have one episode about the role of veganism in the practice of yoga. I highly recommend listening to this recording. My personal belief is that you have to feed yourself the food that is going to make you feel well – with the guidance of a doctor. If it makes you feel well to be vegan or vegetarian, then do it. But I wouldn't prioritize being vegan over speaking up against genocide, for example. Being vegan or vegetarian is one way to practice *ahiṃsā*, but there are many ways to embody it. Judging other

yoga students and teachers for not being vegan is actually not practicing *ahiṃsā* because you're being judgmental towards others.

- **Perceiving love or a call for love.** Marianne Williamson suggests seeing all human behavior as one of two things: 1) love or 2) a call for love. When I begin to look at others through this lens, I can start to recognize that even if someone is hurting me with their actions, they may be just calling out for love – or coming from a place of love. Usually when I do this, it helps me approach the situation with compassion.

Satya

The second *yama* is *satya*, or truth.

Agreement two of *The Four Agreements* by Don Miguel Ruiz is, "Don't take anything personally." Something that I struggle with is directly articulating to the people around me how things make me feel. I will interpret others' behavior very personally, and instead of communicating this to them, I'll keep it bottled up inside. (Generally, when I have been engaging in a consistent *āsana*/meditation/*prāṇāymā* practice, I struggle with communicating my feelings much less than I do when these practices are not as routine. Similarly, when I am sober, eating well and sleeping well, I also do better at this.)

This difficulty with communication has been one of my biggest struggles with *satya*, or telling the truth. I dated someone for a short time in 2023 with whom I noticed I had a tendency to express the emotion of being annoyed much more frequently than he did. After contemplating the difference between the two of us, I realized that I was consistently bottling my emotions up inside of me as they arose rather than sharing my truth or *satya* all throughout the day. Then, I would let it explode when speaking with a safe person, my partner.

In spite of my tendency to avoid expressing my emotions, I have started to learn more and more that when I tell my truth, it usually helps the other person understand where I'm coming from and brings us to a good conclusion.

For example, I recently had two friends visiting me who came on a yoga retreat. I loved having them, but they stayed with me for about ten days before the retreat, and they lived with me during the retreat, too. What I discovered is that it was just too much time with other people. I need to have downtime to process, digest and rest.

They had asked me if they could stay with me after the retreat too, and I said "yes" – but I realized mid-retreat that I really needed them to leave my house so that I could have more space. I was so afraid of confronting them and letting them know that their staying at my house wasn't working well for me anymore. I was so afraid of upsetting them.

My most common way to deal with something like this is to send the communication via text. But the two were doing a digital detox, so they didn't have the ability to receive a text.

Finally, I faced my fears, and had the conversation with them face to face. They were completely understanding and actually thanked me for telling them.

What I realized from this experience is that conversations where you share your truth are actually really positive. When you communicate something that's bothering you – before it explodes up out of you like a shaken up can of soda ready to explode – often you can avoid worsened conflict.

The practice of *satya* is to tell the truth, or to not lie. This concept has been an interesting one for me over the years, because when I first started deeply reflecting on *satya*, I realized that while I may not be directly lying, I have also had a tendency to embellish or overexaggerate stories. I believe this habit came from my desire to seek attention. I didn't feel like I was validated or acknowledged enough as a child, and as a result, the story always had to be bigger, more significant, more impactful and more dramatic in order to get attention. An example of this exaggerative storytelling would be, for example, telling others that my partner had gone to the hospital when having an allergic reaction when he actually had recovered from the allergic reaction at home. I was trying to make the story more dramatic to get sympathy and attention from others, or to entertain others, when really, I could have just told the truth.

Some of the ways that I have striven to practice *satya* over the years have been:

- **Speaking my truth:** Speak my authentic truth. This means that I should tell people how I feel and be honest and open.
- **Understanding subjectivity:** Understand that the truth is subjective. What I perceive to be the truth might be different than how someone else perceived the truth. It doesn't mean that the other person is lying: it just means that he or she has a different perception of what happened.
- **Applying of *ahiṃsā*:** Remember that *ahiṃsā* must always be applied to determine whether a truth must be spoken. When I taught my grade one and grade three students at school, I'd teach them to always ask themselves the following before they spoke: "Is it true? Is it necessary? Is it kind?" If something is true, but it's not necessary to voice it, then perhaps restrain from saying it.
- **Avoiding exaggerating/embellishing:** Avoid lying. I try to catch myself when I'm overexaggerating or embellishing a story and always return to truth.
- **Practicing on the mat:** Being honest with myself about my limitations in my *āsana* practice.
- **Writing:** Write to express my truth. Even the process of writing this book was a practice of *satya* for me, as I made peace with my truth and peace with my past. I highly recommend writing to heal your past trauma.

Asteya

The third *yama* is *asteya*, or non-stealing.

When I was in my early twenties, I worked at a summer park's program. We were allocated a small budget for craft supplies, games and sporting equipment. We were allowed to do fundraising events to raise money for other things, such as popsicles or pizza parties.

My colleague at the park was a woman who had worked for this summer park's program the year before. She was also at least five years older than me. Back then, I thought of people older than me as more authoritative, and because she had experience, she almost framed it as if she was my mentor, and I was the new staff working with her.

She worked three part-time jobs: at a bar, a grocery store and here at the park. She was paying her own way through college. We came from wildly different life experiences. I was very fortunate to have the opportunity to have my university education paid for by my parents, as well as my housing. All the money I earned went to other things, like food, festivals and partying.

My work partner suggested that we have a fundraiser to organize an end-of-summer pizza party for the campers. I believe it was a car wash fundraiser. I actually wasn't even there on the day of the fundraiser: I'd called in sick to work. On the day of the fundraiser, someone pulled up who worked for a pizza place and said he'd just donate the pizza for the day.

My partner suggested to me that we keep the money since we spent so much of our own money on the children anyway.

Anyone that's ever worked in education or at summer camps will know that this assertion is true. I spent a lot of my own money on buying the kids toys, art supplies, treats, etc. I spent a lot of my own time creating scavenger hunts and activities for them. The money that we kept from the pizza fundraiser ended up being less than $20 total. But I kept it. I stole something that wasn't mine.

I was also off work and absent on the day that the pizza party occurred. However, I soon learned that my boss had become aware of the fact that the pizza had been donated, and my partner had lied by saying that we had paid for it. She then completed paperwork requesting to get reimbursed for the pizza – the same pizza that we had gotten for free and pocketed the money that we'd fundraised for it. So, she would pocket the money twice.

My boss quickly figured all of this out and called me to tell the truth.

I was stuck between staying loyal to my partner or telling the truth. So I told the truth. I told my boss we'd fundraised the money and after the pizza got donated, my partner suggested we steal the money, and I went along with it.

They called me in for a meeting at the end of the summer and told me that because I told the truth they wouldn't hold it against me, that no note would be left on my file and that they wanted me back the following summer.

I will always remember this experience because it was the first time in my life I was acknowledged, recognized and honored for telling the truth. My boss told me that we will all make mistakes in our lives – but it's how we redeem ourselves that matters.

I also looked at my partner with compassion, as I understood that she was in a tough situation and probably needed the money more than me.

Undoubtedly, my boss at that summer park's program was one of the best bosses I ever had because she taught me such a valuable lesson. First of all, the practice of non-stealing is important – but also, we all make mistakes, and it's how we redeem ourselves that matters.

Asteya is the practice of non-stealing. Most literally, this can be interpreted as not stealing something like money, expensive items, etc. But *asteya* pertains to much smaller things too, such as not returning someone's pants that you borrowed, for example, or not taking up other people's time.

Some Practical Actions for Asteya:

- **Gratitude practices:** Engage in such practices as gratitude meditations, daily journaling for gratitude, or reflecting on what you're grateful for with a friend or partner. Most of the time, we are experiencing a sense of lack when we take things that aren't ours. If we feel a sense of abundance, we are less likely to steal.
- **Punctuality:** Try to be on time for appointments and other commitments. Respect others' time. If, for example, you're leading a yoga class as a teacher, try to end the class on time or inform the students if it will go overtime, while giving them the option to leave class early if they have a prior commitment.
- **Returning what you've borrowed:** Be mindful of things you've borrowed from others that you haven't returned. During my early days of sobriety, I made it a practice to return everything that wasn't mine. I moved around my house and discovered things that seemed small, that might have been big to others: books, kitchenware, clothing. I had held onto these out of a feeling of lack. When I returned all of these items, I felt lighter.
- **Giving credit where credit is due:** If you repost something on a social media site such as *Instagram*, make sure to tag the person who created the content originally. At one point in the early days in my online yoga career, I took someone else's words and put them on a sweater and sold them without giving her credit. To me it didn't seem like a big deal, as I thought the phrasing was pretty universally used. But this action hurt her, and it destroyed our friendship. I felt sad about that for many years. I learned that I should always give credit when I get inspired by others, and I am very mindful to do so. I tried my best when working on this book to give proper credits to everyone that inspired me.

Brahmacharya: Moderation

The practice of *brahmacharya* is moderating all energy that enters your life. The most traditional schools of thought in yoga would translate this as complete abstinence or celibacy. However, celibacy is not always realistic or relevant to modern practitioners of yoga. I believe it can be applicable to everything we engage with, not just sex. Whether it's food, alcohol, sex, sugar, caffeine, money… you don't want to engage with anything that comes into your life in excess.

Moderation can apply to so many energies in our lives, and most people who are on some kind of sobriety journey know that it's not easy to moderate! For me, I've struggled with moderating alcohol, coffee, sugar, social media… all of these things at some point in my life!

Practices for moderation:

- **Alcohol:** For me, full abstinence from alcohol was more helpful than having it in my life in moderation. If alcohol is an energy you struggle with, consider the Sober Girls Yoga 30-Day Challenge or another program to remove it from your life.
- **Money:** Develop a healthy relationship with money. Set money dates with yourself to chart your finances and note where you've spent money and what you may be overspending on. Be mindful of your relationship with money. This is a practice I'm still working on.
- **Self-soothing:** Notice when you use different substances in your life to self-soothe: for example alcohol, drugs, cigarettes, caffeine, sugar.
- **Sex:** Allow yourself to have a healthy relationship with your sexuality. It doesn't mean that you have to practice abstinence or only have sex in a healthy closed relationship. It means that you are happy with the choices you're making around sex,

and you aren't judging others for the choices that they make around sex (or judging yourself).

Aparigraha: Letting Go

In the house I grew up in, my dad had hoarding tendencies. What this meant is that he collected many items and had trouble letting go. The problem this created for me is that my house was consistently full of belongings, and our home was very chaotic.

I learned these behaviors from him and started behaving in the same way. Everything was important, and I couldn't let anything go. I collected photos, books, memories, CDs, clothing. I would grieve when something went missing or disappeared. I felt it was important.

I moved through life this way. When I went to university, I collected objects and carried them with me from house to house. My space was always messy.

When I moved to Kuwait as an expat at age twenty-three, it was the first time I ever had to embrace and live with lightness. I had to let go. I could only bring two suitcases with me. I had to sift through my belongings and find out what was really necessary. And what I experienced from this letting go was lightness.

As I moved from Kuwait to Abu Dhabi to Bali, over and over I had this opportunity to release. To empty. To get rid of things that I didn't need. At first, this process was hard, and I grieved these losses. Then I realized that some of these things were truly unimportant, and I didn't even miss their presence. In fact, I began to realize that getting rid of these items not only gave me more physical space, but they also gave me more mental and energetic space.This lightness in letting go transformed me.

This is *aparigraha*: the practice of letting go. The practice of *aparigraha* might involve letting go of our physical belongings or even letting go of our relationships. Anything we're holding on to that we don't need anymore can be released to make space for something new.

Practical Applications of Aparigraha:

- **Decluttering:** Spend time decluttering your physical space. Donate, throw away, or give things to people who need them.
- **Rituals**: Make peace with letting go of relationships that no longer serve you. I find it helpful to journal, receive therapy and also reframe my thinking.
- ***Āsana***: See if you can release any harmful thoughts that are swirling around in your mind while you are on your mat practicing *āsana.*
- **Letting go meditation:** Practice daily meditations. There are a lot of excellent meditation practices available around the theme of letting go.
- **Alternative therapies:** Consider seeking out alternative therapies. I've personally engaged in several alternative therapies to aid in this process, including hypnotherapy and craniosacral therapy. The key thing is to find a therapy that works for you.

LIMB TWO OF THE EIGHT-LIMB PATH OF YOGA: *NIYAMA(S)*

The *niyama(s)* are most commonly translated as internal practices or personal practices. My teacher Rolf translates them as observances. Although these are internal commitments to yourself, they can also have external applications, as we will discuss. The *niyama(s)* are:

Śaucha – Cleanliness
Tapas – Commitment
Santoṣa – Contentment

Svādhyāya – Self-reflection
Iśhvara Praṇidhāna – Spiritual devotion

Śaucha – Cleanliness

Śaucha has been one of my longest struggles. Whilst my mom is a very tidy and clean person, my dad is a bit messier. Something I didn't learn was how to take care of and organize my belongings. *Śaucha* doesn't come naturally to me. I am constantly working on this.

One thing I've always been dedicated to is my nightly bubble bath ritual, and I learned as I got older that many cultures have ritualistic bathing practices, such as the ablution process before going to the mosque to pray in Islam.

Ways we can embody and practice *śaucha*:

- Keep our yoga props clean and tidy in our yoga studio (if we are owners, students or even teachers of a studio).
- Avoid walking on other people's yoga mats.
- Keep internal cleanliness with our thoughts.
- Keep our organs clean and healthy with the foods we put into them.

Saṃtoṣa

Saṃtoṣa is the practice of contentment. I see *saṃtoṣa* as having the ability to find joy in every moment. When we are practicing *saṃtoṣa*, we are able to find joy even amidst our struggles and suffering.

Saṃtoṣa, or contentment, was a struggle for me for a long time. I was constantly thinking that I would find happiness in the next place. It would be in the next place where I could get access to alcohol, quit my job, become a yoga teacher, live in Bali, etc. It was only when I reached the peak of what I was striving for

– quitting my job and becoming a yoga teacher in Bali – that I realized that happiness wasn't in another place – it was within me all along. For me nowadays, I realize that my daily practices build up my contentment or *saṃtoṣa*. What an ideal day would look like includes:

- An *āsana* practice/meditation that gets me into a space of loving awareness.
- A stronger form of exercise like a HIIT workout, personal training, barre, or cycling, which gets my heart moving and my body sweating.
- An opportunity to write, journal and process.
- Some time reading and learning in other ways like listening to a podcast or watching a webinar.
- Time withdrawn from social media.
- The consumption of good food that helps me stay well.

Saṃtoṣa, to me, is the cultivation of daily habits that bring me into a place of joy. I can make any place a place of joy – even if it's somewhere I don't particularly want to be.

Ways to practice saṃtoṣa:

- A gratitude practice.
- Practicing mindfulness when you have unexpected time (waiting in lines, etc.).
- Noticing when you're allowing your thoughts to spiral you into a negative state of mind and gently calling yourself back.

Tapas – Commitment

When I think of the practice of *tapas*, or commitment, I like to imagine the visual of a fire. I am not sure if I came up with this idea on my own or if someone inspired me with it years ago. *Tapas* is your commitment to keep showing up, day after day.

Most students of yoga excel in group yoga class settings. But put them inside their apartments, trapped during Covid… and the practice disintegrates.

I myself am included in this. For years and years, I've required the energy of a group to stay committed to my practice.

Very recently, I realized that if I depend on a group to stay committed, it will mean that when the group is not available to me, my practice will fall apart. For example, when I was living in Kuwait, and the nearest yoga studio was an hour away by car, I was unable to consistently practice.

Now, it's more important to me that I do an online practice at home than it is that I get to a physical class in a studio. Classes are excellent sources of community building and inspiration, but I'm trying to build the muscle within me of *tapas* – of discipline – of commitment. I make sure I do a practice every single morning on my own first thing when I wake up at 5am. Then, if I can make it to an additional class, that is great, but that's in addition to my personal practice, which is a non-negotiable.

Ways to practice tapas:

- Anything that you're practicing discipline with in your life is a practice of *tapas*. For example, the discipline of:
  - ⋆ Sobriety
  - ⋆ A regular bedtime
  - ⋆ Abstaining from foods that don't make you feel good
  - ⋆ Abstaining from social media and constant scrolling
- Learning about habit formation from yoga philosophy by studying such concepts as *sanskāra* and *vāsanā* and examining how they relate to patterns of behavior.
- Committing to a daily yoga practice. If you commit to a daily yoga practice, can you do it in an attainable way? For example, only ten minutes a day might be more realistic than one hour.

Svādhyāya

Svādhyāya is the practice of self-reflection. Pretty much anything that involves turning inward is *svadhyaya*. This includes coaching, journaling, reading self-help books, taking part in sharing circles/ sober circles, etc. Having regular *svādhyāya* practices are crucial for us to make sense of our lives and go inward.

Ways that we can practice svādhyāya:

- Journaling
- Therapy
- Studying philosophy texts
- Yoga teacher training courses
- Anything that helps us obtain wisdom

Iśhvara Praṇidhāna

Something that I avoided talking about for years when it came to speaking about yoga was *Iśhvara Praṇidhāna*. This is spiritual devotion. For people that do not practice religion, this can be alienating as they feel they need some kind of religious belief to be a true *sādhaka* (yoga practitioner).

My viewpoint is that whatever your beliefs are, whether they involve believing in God, Allah, Buddha, or some other religious figure, just having some kind of faith or trust or hope is essential for when times get tough. Since I began believing in the universe and the power of the universe, I have a lot more faith when things go wrong that everything will be okay.

My practice of devotion doesn't take place inside a formal church: however, I love taking part in religious practices with my friends and family of all faiths, whether it's lighting the candle with my family at Hannukah, saying grace with my family at Christmas, or joining to break the Iftar Fast during Ramadan.

Something I wrote with regards to the spirituality of my yoga practice that I want to share here is:

November 11, 2023
My morning āsana *practice isn't really a workout, it's a work in. Later in the day, I will lift weights or box or walk my 10,000 steps. This isn't my workout… it's more like a prayer. It's a moving meditation. It's a moment of pause where I appreciate the fact that I have been gifted another day living on this earth. I have been gifted food to eat. I have been gifted water to drink. I have been gifted freedom and peace and safety. I let the energy of gratitude weave its way through my life.*

I call to mind all beings in suffering and think loving thoughts.

I consider yesterday's resentments and try to reconcile them in my mind and heart.

I send healing and compassion to those who have caused me pain.

I look back at yesterday and forgive everyone. I look forward to today and trust everything.

I wish that all beings everywhere are happy, healthy and free. And I pray that the thoughts and actions of my day today contribute to this. Not just today, but each and every day.

This is yoga.

Iśhvara Praṇidhāna is a devotion to a higher self, and when we cultivate this, it is evident in all of our relationships. Some things that we can devote ourselves to are:

- God
- Buddha
- Allah
- Spirit
- Source
- Higher Power
- Higher Self

- Truth and Love
- Nature
- The Universe

LIMB THREE OF THE EIGHT-LIMB PATH OF YOGA: ĀSANA

The *āsana* practice of yoga has somehow taken over in the Western world. We believe that an *āsana* class is yoga in and of itself. In actuality, the *āsana* are really just a vehicle for us to start to embody the teachings of yoga.

The goal of yoga is threefold (as taught to me in a yoga class by my teacher, Rolf):

1. **Educate:** we educate ourselves with yoga philosophy. We read books, we learn, we study.
2. **Embody:** we then embody the teachings through the execution of our yoga postures.
3. **Express:** lastly, we express the teachings in the way we live our lives.

In the example of *ahiṃsā*, or non-violence, this three-part goal might look like this:

1. **Educate**: we learn that *ahiṃsā* means non-violence.
2. **Embody**: we embody *ahiṃsā* in our *āsana* (posture) practice by approaching our practice with this goal of loving kindness.
3. **Express**: we then practice loving kindness in the way we interact with our family, our friends, our pets and our community.

Educating ourselves is really important because, otherwise, we're just making shapes with the body. We need to be exposed to the philosophy, the texts, and the teachings of yoga to have an impact. But also, if none of this changes our behavior – if none of this changes how we move through the world off our mats – then there isn't really a point.

We do the *āsana* to practice embodying the philosophy that we are learning.

I love to attend yoga classes whenever I can, but I also choose to start each day with an *āsana* practice. It's difficult to summarize all of the different postures and shapes that one can do in order to start the day, but there are many available on my YouTube channel: @themindfullifepractice. Additionally, I have an app available called *Mindful Life*, which features many *āsana* practices.

LIMB FOUR OF THE EIGHT-LIMB PATH OF YOGA: PRĀṆĀYĀMA

Prāṇāyāma practices are practices of controlling the breath in order to quiet the mind and open the heart. My daily *prāṇāyāma* practice each morning is something that I do before my *āsana* practice.

Again, I have offerings on my YouTube channel, @themindfullifepractice, and also on my app, *Mindful Life*, which both feature many *prāṇāyāma* practices.

LIMBS FIVE, SIX, SEVEN AND EIGHT OF THE EIGHT-LIMB PATH OF YOGA: PRATYAHARA, DHARANA, DHYANA AND SAMĀDHI

When I first encountered the eight-limb path of yoga, I struggled to differentiate between *pratyahara*, *dharana*, *dhyana* and *samādhi*. They all sounded similar to me. Whilst the first four limbs are very clear practices, the last four limbs are a bit more abstract. The short differentiation is as follows:

Pratyahara – Turning inwards.
Dharana – Short periods of concentration.
Dhyana – Long-term meditation.
Samādhi – The state of consciousness.

These limbs are mostly done in succession. First you go inwards, (*pratyahara*), then you practice concentration (*dharana*) and then you practice sustained concentration (*dhyana*). These steps will lead towards consciousness (*samādhi*). Over time, you get better and better at engaging with these practices, so much so that they seemingly happen simultaneously. This practice is called *samyama* when you are going inward, practicing concentration and sustaining meditation all at once. In reality, they aren't happening simultaneously, but they happen so quickly that it feels as if they are simultaneous.

To elaborate:

LIMB FIVE OF THE EIGHT-LIMB PATH OF YOGA: PRATYAHARA (TURNING INWARDS)

Pratyahara is the practice of turning inwards. Most often on a yoga teacher training program, we will practice what is called silent breakfast in the morning or *vipassana*. The idea is to restrain from talking, using devices, etc. The goal is to go inwards and notice what's happening inside. I like to imagine a turtle putting its head inside his shell and looking inwards. That's *pratyahara*.

If you want to go deep into yoga, you have to have a regular practice of *pratyahara*. This is the gateway towards meditation and eventually consciousness. The best time to practice *pratyahara* is in the morning. When you wake up, make the choice to disengage with the outside world by staying off *Instagram*, *Facebook* or other things on your phone and refrain from speaking to others. Practice your rituals, whether they are *āsana, prāṇāyāma*, meditation, journaling or reading. Devote time to go inwards at the start of the day.

If this isn't possible in your life, another way that you can practice *pratyahara* is to simply show up early to the yoga studio before your class and sit in silence in the studio, or find a quiet spot during the day. When I was a school teacher and the children went out in the morning, I would sit inside a closet and do a twenty-one-minute *reiki* practice every day. This practice was supportive to me.

LIMB SIX: DHARANA (CONCENTRATION)

Dharana is concentration.

When I think of *dharana*, I like to think of the metaphor of a ticket taker at the movies.

There's a whole lineup of people who are waiting to give their tickets to the ticket taker.

If the ticket taker stopped and got distracted by any of the tickets, then the whole line would be held up, and no one would get in to see the movie.

The tickets are our thoughts (*vṛtti*), and the ticket taker is our mind (*citta*). We have to accept that thoughts will enter or come near our minds. However, we only need to allow these thoughts to enter – we don't need to engage with them. As soon as we start to get swept up in these thoughts or brought into a spiral, that's when they can cause harm. For example, if I start getting into a negative thought pattern about how I am not good at yoga in a class because I can't do a certain pose, that line of thinking can bring me into a really negative spiral that takes me out of the moment. Instead, I can practice skillful awareness and notice that the thought has occurred, but just witness it, and gently call myself back to the present.

That's *dharana*. After we practice *pratyahara* and go inwards, we have an opportunity to start to concentrate.

LIMB SEVEN: DHYANA (MEDITATION)

One question that I ask my students during every yoga teacher training is, "Is meditation a process or a state?"

We often think of it as a process. For example, we are doing meditation. We are going to a meditation class. We are doing our meditation before our morning *āsana* practice.

In actuality, meditation is a state that we are striving towards. We are striving to enter meditation in every moment of our lives: when we are out to lunch with a friend, when we are in deep conversation with our partner, when we are writing an essay, or when we are reading a newspaper. Meditation is sustained concentration for a long period of time. It's like getting into a flow state.

My teacher Rolf Gates introduced me to a metaphor that compares the 'sky holding the weather' to *dhyana*. My understanding of this metaphor was that our brain is like the sky holding the weather when it holds our thoughts. The weather rolls in and out without our control. It's sunny, then it's rainy, then it storms, then it's snowy. The sky just holds the space for these transformations to take place. This is the same way our brain holds space for positive thoughts, negative thoughts and balanced thoughts. These thoughts roll in and out.

There are many ways to meditate. I do a daily seated meditation. I like *japa* meditations and also self-healing *reiki* practices. I also attend a weekly *Kirtan* practice in Bali where I chant. *Kirtan* is part of *bhakti* yoga, or the yoga of devotion. It is a call and response musical meditation.

For some people, seated meditations just don't work. They would consider activities like playing an instrument, walking, or scuba diving their meditation. Just find an activity that brings you into a flow state – and that's your meditation.

LIMB EIGHT: SAMĀDHI (UNION OF THE SELF WITH THE OBJECT OF MEDITATION)

The final goal of our yoga practice is to reach a state of *samādhi*, or the path of consciousness. In *samādhi*, the separation of ourselves and the universe dissolves. It's the experience of ecstatic oneness.

GLOSSARY OF SANSKRIT TERMS

Abhyasa – practice

Anahata – the heart *chakra*, meaning 'unstruck'

Ahiṃsā – non-violence

Ajna – the third eye *chakra*, meaning 'command center'.

Anada-Samādhi – causeless Bliss. This is referenced in the book when speaking about the four phases towards *samādhi*. *Anada* is the third phase

Aparigraha – letting Go (The fifth of the *yama(s)*)

Asmita – ego, and the second of the five *kleśa(s)* (note that *asmita* when referring to the *kleśa(s)* is not the same as *asmita* when referring to *samādhi*)

Asmita-Samādhi – absorption with the sense of I-ness, and the fourth stage of *samprajnata samādhi* (note that *asmita* when referring to *samādhi* is not the same as *asmita* when referring to the *kleśa(s)*)

Asteya – non-stealing (the third of the *yama(s)*)

Avidyā – lack of spiritual practice, and the first of the five *kleśa(s)*

Āsana – posture

Bhakti – the yoga of devotion. This can include chanting

Brahmacharya – moderation

Citta – the mind

Dharana – concentration

Dhyana – meditation

Dharma – it can have many meanings. In this case, it means an individual's life purpose

Dukha – pain
Dvesa – aversion
Ishvara – faith
Ishvara Pranidhana – devotion to faith, and the fifth of the *niyama(s)*
Karuna – compassion
Kleśa(s) – the five causes of human suffering
Manipura – the solar plexus *chakra*, meaning lustrous gem
Maitri – friendliness
Mudito – goodwill
Muladhara – the root *chakra*, meaning root support
Nirvichara-Samādhi – the second phase of four phases towards consciousness. Referenced in *Sūtra* 1.17, this refers to our emotional response.
Niyama(s) – the five ethical commitments and the second of the eight-limb path of yoga
Om – the most sacred mantra in Hinduism, which is at the beginning and end of most Sanskrit mantras. It stands as a representative of the divine
Purusa – the innermost self
Prakṛti – the material world
Prajna – intuition (in context of the five practices to yoga in *Sūtra* 1.20)
Prāṇāyāma – breathwork practices
Rtambhara Prajna – flashes of intuitive wisdom
Rajas – one of three *guṇa*. The powerful energy of heat, to create and manifest. When in excess, *rajas* show up as anger, stress, or mania in individuals
Sādhaka – yoga practitioner (according to my teacher, Anvita, who grew up in an *ashram* in India, this is more appropriate than calling someone a yogi)
Sahasrara – the seventh *chakra*, meaning thousand-fold. Connected to awakening
Samādhi – consciousness or integration

Sanskāra(s) – impressions on our mind

Samyama – the cumulative experience of *dharana*, *dhyana* and *samādhi*

Santosa – contentment

Sangha – community

Sattva – one of three *guṇa*. When *sattva* is dominant in someone, they are embodying equilibrium, wisdom and happiness

Satya – truth, and the second of the *yama(s)*

Saucha – cleanliness, and the first of the *niyama(s)*

Savāsana – corpse pose (practiced at the end of every *āsana* class)

Shala – home (most commonly used to describe the yoga *shala* in yoga retreat centers, and most commonly misspelled as a 'chalet')

Smriti – mindfulness (in context of the five practices to yoga in *Sūtra* 1.20)

Svadhisthana – the sacral *chakra*, or 'one's own place'

Svadhyaya – self-reflection, and the fourth of the *niyama(s)*

Sushumna – moments of epiphanies

Sraddha – faith (in context of the five practices to yoga in *Sūtra* 1.20)

Tadāsana – mountain pose

Tamas – one of three *guṇa*. The energy of sadness, slowness and lethargy

Tapas – discipline, and the third of the *niyama(s)*

Upeksha – neutrality, in reference to how we should behave towards our enemies

Vitarka-Samādhi – the first phase of four phases towards consciousness. As referenced in *Sūtra* 1.17, this is thought and reasoning

Vikalpa – imagination, and one of five *vṛtti*, or thought whirlpools

Vishuddi – the throat *chakra*, meaning 'purification'

Viyadhi – animosity

Vāsanās – larger personality traits shaped by our *sanskāra(s)*

Vīrya – dedication (in context of the five practices to yoga in *Sūtra* 1.20)

Vrksasna – tree pose
Vṛtti – thought spirals
Yama(s) – the five moral commitments and the first of the eight-limb path of yoga
Yogi – a yogi is the most revered title, given to those who are incredibly dedicated to their paths. According to my teacher in Mumbai, Anvita, it actually shouldn't be used as informally as we use it today. I now try to refer to my students as *Sādhaka*, someone who completes their *Sadhana*, which is a spiritual practice

WORKS CITED

Adams, Jefferson. "Can a Gluten-Free Diet Help People with Bipolar Disorder?" *Celiac*, 14 Aug. 2019, https://www.celiac.com/celiac-disease/can-a-gluten-free-diet-help-people-with-bipolar-disorder-r4887/. Accessed 29 Feb. 2024.

Akram, Rabia. "To keep on nodding terms with the people we used to be (What does that mean?)." *Medium*, 3 Sept. 2023, https://medium.com/illumination/what-does-this-statement-to-keep-on-nodding-terms-with-the-people-we-used-to-be-mean-65ecd2213992. Accessed 25 Feb. 2024.

Alderman, Lesley. "Breathe. Exhale. Repeat: The Benefits of Controlled Breathing." *The New York Times*. 9 Nov. 2016. https://www.nytimes.com/2016/11/09/well/mind/breathe-exhale-repeat-the-benefits-of-controlled-breathing.html. Accessed 25 Feb. 2024.

Beck, Katie. "Changing lives and perceptions in Ubud." *BBC*, 31 Jan. 2013, https://www.bbc.com/travel/article/20130125-changing-lives-and-perceptions-in-ubud. Accessed 25 Feb. 2024.

Bernstein, Gabrielle [@gabbybernstein]. "Show up for what's up or it will keep showing up…" *Instagram*, 28 Jul. 2021, https://www.instagram.com/p/CR1qnjAr_I0/?igsh=eTNtcDFjNWxlc29t. Accessed 25 Feb. 2024.

Bodhi, Bhikkhu. "Spiritual Friendship." *Bodhi Monastery*, 4 Aug. 2008, https://bodimonastery.org/spiritual-friendship.html. Accessed 25 Feb. 2024.

"Break the Cycle: How Yoga and Meditation Can Help Heal Addiction." *Kripalu Yoga Center*, 2024. https://kripalu.org/resources/break-cycle-how-yoga-and-meditation-can-help-heal-addiction#:~:text=In%20the%20Eastern%20approach%20to,and%20aversion%20to%20the%20unpleasant.%E2%80%9D. Accessed 25 Feb. 2024.

Barua, Bacchus and David Jacques. "Waiting Your Turn: Wait Times for Health Care in Canada, 2018 Report." *Fraser Institute*, 4 Dec. 2018, https://www.fraserinstitute.org/sites/default//files/waiting-your-turn-2018.pdf. Accessed 22 Feb. 2024.

Beckiempis, Victoria. "Why one in four women is on psych meds." *The Guardian*, 21 Nov 2011. https://www.theguardian.com/commentisfree/cifamerica/2011/nov/21/one-in-four-women-psych-meds . Accessed 20 May. 2024.

"Bipolar Disorder." *Cleveland Clinic*, 12 Apr. 2022, https://my.clevelandclinic.org/health/diseases/9294-bipolar-disorder. Accessed 23 Feb. 2024.

Brogan, Kelly. *Own Your Self.* Google Books ed., Hay House Inc., 2019.

Brown, Brené. *Atlas of the Heart: Mapping Meaningful Connection and the Language of Human Experience.* iBook ed., Random House, 2021.

Bryant, Edwin F. *The Yoga Sutras of Pantanjali: A New Edition, Translation, Commentary.* iBook ed., New York, North Point Press, 2009.

Cinderella. Directed by Clyde Geronimi, Wilfred Jackson, and Hamilton Luske, Disney, 1950.

"Countries Where Alcohol Is Illegal in 2024." *World Population Review*, 2024, https://worldpopulationreview.com/country-rankings/countries-where-alcohol-is-illegal. Accessed 24 Feb. 2024.

"Culture shock part 1: the four stages." *Murdoch University*, 10 Jan 2023, https://www.murdoch.edu.au/news/series/series-articles/making-the-move-to-murdoch-and-perth/culture-shock-part-1-the-four-stages. Accessed 23 Feb. 2024.

"Edge Walk at the CN Tower." *La Tour CN Tower, A Division of Canada Lands Company*, https://www.cntower.ca/brave-the-edgewalk . Accessed 21 Feb. 2024.

"Eid al-Fitr." *Brandeis University*, 2024, https://www.brandeis.edu/spiritual-life/resources/guide-to-observances/eid-al-fitr.html. Accessed 24 Feb. 2024.

Elsayed, Mohamed, et al. "The potential association between psychiatric symptoms and the use of levonorgestrel intrauterine devices (LNG-IUDs): A systematic review." *Taylor and Francis Group*, vol. 24, no. 6, 2023, pp. 457-475, https://doi.org/10.1080/15622975.2022.2145354. Accessed 21 Feb. 2024.

Farah Therapy and Coaching Center. "Narcissism and the Trauma of Narcissistic Abuse." Farah Therapy and Coaching Center, 19 February, 2020, https://www.farahtherapycentre.co.uk/blog/narcissism-and-the-trauma-of-narcissistic-abuse#:~:text=The%20experience%20of%20childhood%20trauma,they%20were%20not%20good%20enough. Accessed 13 Aug 2024.

Felsenthal, Julia. "Augusten Burroughs on Writing Memoir and Falling in Love with His Agent." *Vogue*. Condé Nast, 30 Apr. 2016, www.vogue.com. Accessed 20 Feb. 2024.

Forbes, Bo. *Yoga for Emotional Balance: Simple Practices to Help Relieve Anxiety and Depression*. Colorado, Shambhala Publications, Inc., 2011.

Garrett, Leslie. "Why We're a Culture of Addicts." *Uplift*, 2021. https://uplift.love/why-were-a-culture-of-addicts/. Accessed 25 Feb 2024.

Gates, Rolf. *Daily Reflections on Addiction, Yoga, and Getting Well*. iBook ed., Hayhouse, 2018.

Gates, Rolf and Karina Kenison. *Meditations from the Mat*. iBook ed., New York, Anchor Books, 2002.

Gilbert, Elizabeth. *Eat, Pray, Love: One Woman's Search for Everything Across Italy, India and Indonesia*. iBook ed., New York, Riverhead Books, 2016.

Gomez, Skyler. "Quotes by Anaïs Nin on Writing, Life and Love." *Literary Ladies Guide*, 2 Sept. 2022, https://www.literaryladiesguide.com/author-quotes-writing-life-love/. Accessed 25 Feb. 2024.

Harris, Gabrielle. *The Language of Yin: Yoga Themes, Sequences and Inspiration to Bring Your Class to Life and Life to Your Class.* iBook ed., Luminary Press, 2019.

Hassan, Fayyad. "Opinion: The Muslim holiday Eid al-Adha is for 'eating, drinking and remembrance of God.'" *The San Diego Union Tribune*, 27 Jun. 2023, https://www.sandiegouniontribune.com/opinion/commentary/story/2023-06-27/opinion-muslim-holiday-eid-al-adha-san-diego-festival-sacrafice. Accessed 24 Feb. 2024.

Haupert, Tina. "One-Day." *Carrots'n'Cake*, 30 Mar. 2021, https://carrotsncake.com/one-day/. Accessed 25 Feb. 2024.

Holcombe, Kate. "Life Happens: The Yoga Sutra's Take on Suffering." *Yoga Journal*, 2 Nov. 2021, https://www.yogajournal.com/yoga-101/philosophy/yoga-sutras/life-happens/. Accessed 6 Mar. 2024

Holleis, Jennifer. "What is the Palestinian Nakba and why does it matter?" *Deutsche Well*, 15 May 2023, https://www.dw.com/en/what-is-the-palestinian-nakba-and-why-does-it-matter/a-65539735. Accessed 23 Feb. 2024.

Jack, Claire. "The Day You Discover You're a Victim of Narcissistic Abuse." *Psychology Today*, 20 March, 2020, https://www.psychologytoday.com/gb/blog/women-autism-spectrum-disorder/202003/the-day-you-discover-youre-victim-narcissistic-abuse. Accessed 13 Aug. 2024.

Jack, Claire. "5 Reasons You're Attracted to Narcissists." *Psychology Today*, 3 June, 2020, https://www.psychologytoday.com/gb/blog/women-autism-spectrum-disorder/202006/5-reasons-youre-attracted-narcissists . Accessed 13 Aug. 2024.

Judith, Anodea. *Chakras Made Easy: Seven Keys to Awakening and Healing the Energy Body*. London, Hay House, 2016.

Inchaupsé, Jesse. *Glucose Revolution: The life-changing power of balancing your blood sugar.* New York, Simon & Schuster, 2022.

Keeler, Alexandra. "What if you could rewire your brain to conquer suffering? Buddhism says you can." *Big Think*, 8 Feb. 2023, https://bigthink.com/thinking/buddhism-rewire-brain/. Accessed 25 Feb. 2024.

King, Lucy. "Who Said Change Is The Only Constant in Life?" *Medium*, 1 Apr. 2019, https://medium.com/mindset-matters/who-said-the-only-constant-in-life-is-change-233fd9e27b87 Accessed 25 Feb. 2024.

La Pera, Nichole [@Theholisticpsyc]. "We're subconsciously attracted to partners who have the same traits as a parent we had a conflicted relationship with." *Instagram*, 20 Feb. 2023, https://twitter.com/ Theholisticpsyc/status/1627744721463554048?lang =en. Accessed 21 Feb. 2024.

Macgregor, Kino. *Yoga Inspiration Podcast*. Accessed 25 Feb. 2024.

Marschall, Amy. "Should you say 'Person with Autism' or 'Autistic Person'?" *Verywell Mind*, 12 Jan. 2023, https://www.verywellmind.com/should-you-say-person-with-autism-or-Autistic-person-5235429. Accessed 24 Feb. 2024.

McKenzie, Jean-Philippe. "20 Quotes from Wild's Cheryl Strayed That Will Lift You Up." *Oprah Daily*, 11 Apr. 2019, https://www.oprahdaily.com/life/g27100424/cheryl-strayed-quotes/. Accessed 25 Feb. 2024.

"Mental Health Disorder Statistics." *Johns Hopkins Medicine*, 2024, https://www.hopkinsmedicine.org/health/wellness-and-prevention/mental-health-disorder-statistics. Accessed 21 Feb. 2024.

Miller, Chanel. "Chanel Miller reads her entire victim impact statement." *60 Minutes Overtime*, 9 Aug. 2020, https://www.cbsnews.com/news/chanel-miller-reads-her-entire-victim-impact-statement-she-wrote-to-address-brock-turner-60-minutes-2020-08-09/. Accessed 23 Feb. 2024.

Nathan, Andy. "The Two Arrows: Pain & Suffering." *Wanderlust*,

2019, https://wanderlust.com/es/journal/the-two-arrows-pain-suffering/. Accessed 25 Feb. 2024.

Ni, Preston. "Difference Between a Narcissist vs. Narcissistic Behaviour." *Psychology Today*, 11 August, 2019, https://www.psychologytoday.com/gb/blog/communication-success/201908/difference-between-a-narcissist-vs-narcissistic-behavior. Accessed 13 Aug. 2024.

"Night Chant." *Michael Stone, Inc.*, 19 Jul. 2017, https://michaelstoneteaching.com/heart-sutra-bodhisattva-vows/?highlight=night%20chant. Accessed 23 Feb. 2024.

Patel, Tajal and Jesal Parikh. "Vegans Killed Yoga." *Yoga is Dead*, episode 5, 12 Nov. 2019, https://www.yogaisdeadpodcast.com/episodes/2019/11/11/veganskilledyoga. Accessed 25 Feb. 2024.

Rajmani Tigunait, Pandit. "Purpose of Life: Swami Rama's View." *New Age Islam*, 10 Jul. 2013, https://www.newageislam.com/spiritual-meditations/pandit-rajmani-tigunait-phd/purpose-life-swami-rama-s-view/d/12550. Accessed 25 Feb. 2024.

Ramsey, Drew. *Eat to Beat Depression and Anxiety: Nourish Your Way to Better Mental Health in Six Weeks*. New York, Harper Wave, 2021.

Raypole, Crystal. "Navigating the 'Pink Cloud' Phase of Recovery." *Healthline*, 11 Feb. 2020, https://www.healthline.com/health/pink-cloud. Accessed 23 Feb. 2024.

Robinson, Bryan E. "The 90-Second Rule That Builds Self-Control." *Psychology Today*, 26 Apr. 2020, https://www.psychologytoday.com/ca/blog/the-right-mindset/202004/the-90-second-rule-builds-self-control. Accessed 25 Feb. 2024.

Ross, Lee D., et al. "Social Roles, Social Control, and Biases in Social-Perception Processes." *Journal of Personality and Social Psychology*, vol. 35, no. 7, 1977, https://doi.org/10.1037/0022-3514.35.7.485. Accessed 21 Feb. 2024.

Ruiz, Don Miguel. *The Four Agreements.* Amazon Kindle ed., San Rafael, Amber-Allen Publishing, 1997.

Sandstedt, Nicolina, "Four Keys to Peace from Pantanjali's Yoga Sutra 1.33." *Yandara Yoga Institute*, 11 Nov. 2022, https://yandara.com/blog/

four-keys-to-peace-from-patanjalis-yoga-sutra-1-33. Accessed 24 Feb. 2024.

Santos-Longhurst. "Everything You Need to Know About Intrauterine Devices (IUDs)." *Healthline*, 13 Nov. 2023. https://www.healthline.com/health/birth-control-iud. Accessed 24 Feb. 2024.

Sliding Doors. Directed by Peter Howitt, Intermedia Mirage Enterprises, 1998.

Sparrowe, Linda. "Understanding the Gunas Can Help You Find Balance and Insight." *Yoga Journal*, 2 Sept. 2021, https://www.yogajournal.com/lifestyle/health/yoga-philosophy-101-3-gunas. Accessed 6 Mar. 2024.

Stenudd, Stefan. "Fake Lao Tzu Quotes." *Tao Te Ching: The Taoism of Lao Tzu*, https://www.taoistic.com/fake-laotzu-quotes/. Accessed 25 Feb. 2024.

Stone, Michael. *The Inner Tradition of Yoga.* iBook ed., Colorado, Shambhala Publications, 2008.

Strom, Max. A *Life Worth Breathing: A Yoga Master's Handbook of Strength, Grace, and Healing*. Google Play Books ed., Skyhorse Publishing, 2012.

"Suicide and Self-Harm Statistics." *Centers for Disease Control and Prevention*, 2023, https://www.cdc.gov/nchs/fastats/suicide.htm. Accessed 21 Feb. 2024.

Swift, Taylor. [@taylorswift]. *Instagram*, 19 Apr. 2024. https://www.instagram.com/p/C57c1DWMkf_/?img_index=1. Accessed 20 May 2024.

Taylor Counselling Group. "Narcissistic Manipulation Tactics and How to Deal With Them." Taylor Counselling Group, 2 April, 2024, https://taylorcounselinggroup.com/blog/narcissistic-manipulation/. Accessed 13 Aug. 2024.

Thompson, Jennifer. "Whet you appetite with Anthony Bourdain." *Medium*, 27 Apr. 2022, https://medium.com/illumination/whet-you-appetite-with-anthony-bourdain-5d4f8e2d96f8. Accessed 22 Feb. 2024.

"Tips and tricks for drinking less." *United Health Care*, 2024, https://www.uhc.com/news-articles/healthy-living/tips-and-tricks-for-drinking-less. Accessed 24 Feb. 2024.

Williamson, Marianne [@marwilliamson]. "We always have a choice on how we interpret events." *Twitter*, 20 Aug. 2012, https://twitter.com/marwilliamson/status/237580962219839489. Accessed 23 Feb. 2023.

Made in the USA
Middletown, DE
13 October 2024